MARS
ADAPTING

Titles in the Series

Transforming War

Paul J. Springer, editor

T o ensure success, the conduct of war requires rapid and effective adaptation to changing circumstances. While every conflict involves a degree of flexibility and innovation, there are certain changes that have occurred throughout history that stand out because they fundamentally altered the conduct of warfare. The most prominent of these changes have been labeled "Revolutions in Military Affairs" (RMAs). These so-called revolutions include technological innovations as well as entirely new approaches to strategy. Revolutionary ideas in military theory, doctrine, and operations have also permanently changed the methods, means, and objectives of warfare.

This series examines fundamental transformations that have occurred in warfare. It places particular emphasis upon RMAs to examine how the development of a new idea or device can alter not only the conduct of wars but their effect upon participants, supporters, and uninvolved parties. The unifying concept of the series is not geographical or temporal; rather, it is the notion of change in conflict and its subsequent impact. This has allowed the incorporation of a wide variety of scholars, approaches, disciplines, and conclusions to be brought under the umbrella of the series. The works include biographies, examinations of transformative events, and analyses of key technological innovations that provide a greater understanding of how and why modern conflict is carried out, and how it may change the battlefields of the future.

M A R S
ADAPTING

MILITARY CHANGE
DURING WAR

FRANK G. HOFFMAN

NAVAL INSTITUTE PRESS
ANNAPOLIS, MARYLAND

Naval Institute Press
291 Wood Road
Annapolis, MD 21402

Library of Congress Cataloging-in-Publication Data

Names: Hoffman, Frank G., author.

Title: Mars adapting : military change during war / Frank G. Hoffman.

Other titles: Military change during war

Description: Annapolis, MD : Naval Institute Press, [2021] | Series:
  Transforming war | Includes bibliographical references and index. |
  Identifiers: LCCN 2020050495 (print) | LCCN 2020050496 (ebook) | ISBN
  9781682475898 (hardback) | ISBN 9781682475904 (ebook) | ISBN
  9781682475904 (pdf)

Subjects: LCSH: Military art and science—Case studies. | Military
  doctrine—United States—Case studies. | Operational art (Military
  science)—Case studies. | Tactics—Case studies. | Adaptability
  (Psychology) | Organizational learning—United States—Case studies. |
  Organizational change—United States—Case studies.

Classification: LCC U104 .H57 2021 (print) | LCC U104 (ebook) | DDC
  355.02—dc23

LC record available at https://lccn.loc.gov/2020050495

LC ebook record available at https://lccn.loc.gov/2020050496

♾ Print editions meet the requirements of ANSI/NISO z39.48-1992 (Permanence of Paper).
Printed in the United States of America.

29 28 27 26 25 24 23 22 21   9 8 7 6 5 4 3 2 1
First printing

Contents

Illustrations

Acknowledgments

M ajor projects, like writing a book, accumulate many debts. Words cannot begin to recognize properly the many individuals and institutions that have supported my work. Nor is my prose adequate to the task of expressing my appreciation to so many people. But a public acknowledgment is a start.

Foremost among my intellectual creditors is Prof. Theo Farrell, former head of the War Studies Department at King's College, London. A long-standing scholar of military change and an extraordinarily supportive teacher, Dr. Farrell has consistently steered me with probing Socratic questions and the discipline of Occam's razor. Theo brings to mind the famous line attributed to Pericles that "what you leave behind is not engraved in stone monuments, but is woven into the lives of others." His books are wonderful, but his greatest achievement is woven into the minds and output of many students.

Dr. David Betz, also from KCL, routinely provided further counsel. Dr. Sergio Catignani of Exeter University and the noted historian Dr. Robert Foley, at the Defence Academy of the United Kingdom in Shrivenham, offered numerous improvements. I am also grateful to Dr. John Stone of King's College and Dr. Thomas Rid, now at Johns Hopkins University's School of Advanced International Studies in Washington, as well as the insights and assistance of KCL graduates James Russell and Raphael Marcus.

Likewise, many academics, including Mike Noonan, Adam Grissom, David Ucko, Terry Terriff, Josh Jones, John Kuehn, and Randy Papadopoulos, have been active guides. Prof. Williamson Murray, a lifelong mentor, has been extraordinarily instructive (and patient), and his friendship and editorial guidance have meant much to me. Navy commander Joel Holwitt chipped in at a critical time, with both comments and sources. Trent Hone, author of *Learning War*, an outstanding study of the Navy's surface fleet in the interwar era, was an extremely incisive commentator on the entire draft. A great deal of encouragement was rendered by my colleague-in-arms, Col. George "Pat" Garrett, USMC (Ret.).

As anyone doing primary research realizes, archivists too often are underappreciated. The professionals at the Library of Congress and the National Archives and Records Administration (NARA) were invaluable to my World War II work, especially Nathaniel Patch at the latter, who is extraordinarily knowledgeable. Likewise, Theresa Clements at the Naval War College archives went beyond the call of duty. Tim Francis at the Navy Heritage and Museum Command rendered assistance. The Army's Education and Heritage Center in Carlisle was very useful and flexible. Finally, Dr. Charles Neimeyer of the U.S. Marine Corps History and Museum Division in Quantico supported my research. The archivists there, particularly Dr. Fred Allison, were uniformly helpful. The National Defense University library at Fort McNair was an invaluable resource.

I am extremely fortunate to work at the Institute for National Strategic Studies (INSS), which has sustained a high standard of serious and collaborative scholarship for many years. Its scholars are great teammates. I am especially thankful to Dr. Richard D. Hooker Jr., the director of the INSS, for his material support when I was researching this book. My office mates, Phil Saunders, Chris Yung, and T. X. Hammes, offered valuable feedback. Finally, Ted Pikulsky helped in editing and Michael Davies was a candid sounding board.

I would be remiss if I did not thank the leadership at the U.S. Naval Institute (Vice Adm. Pete Daly and now retired Fred Rainbow) and the numerous guiding hands at the Naval Institute Press, especially Glenn Griffith. I am especially proud to be part of the series edited by Dr. Paul Springer, whose encouragement and guidance made this a far better book.

Most scholars conclude by recognizing the sacrifices that their spouses made while the author was burrowed in research. This is not a pro forma exercise in this case. Through research trips and over countless weekends in what she refers to as "the cave" at home, my wife, Kay, enabled me to pursue a long-standing dream. She shouldered my responsibilities on top of her own and kept track of our four adventurous daughters. For her being the rock-solid foundation of our family and a daily source of inspiration, this work is appropriately dedicated to her.

Frank G. Hoffman
Fairfax Station, Virginia

CHAPTER 1

Introduction

This is an aspect of military science which needs to be studied above
all others in the Armed Forces; the capacity to adapt oneself to
the utterly unpredictable, the entirely unknown.

—BRITISH MILITARY HISTORIAN MICHAEL HOWARD[1]

A merican military historian Victor Davis Hanson once observed in *The Father of Us All: War and History*, "As a rule military leaders usually begin wars confident in their existing weapons and technology. But if they are to finish them successfully, it is often only by radically changing designs or finding entirely new ones."[2] Contemporary conflict confirms this historical conclusion. In 2004, when former U.S. secretary of defense Donald H. Rumsfeld was challenged by a U.S. soldier about why his comrades did not have the kit they needed to succeed in combat in Iraq, he noted, "You go to war with the army you have."[3] Although his comment produced derisive criticism, it was historically accurate. In reality, Rumsfeld stated the obvious, you *do* go to war with the army you built and trained in peacetime.

War is an arbiter of how military institutions and states perceive the context of future conflict, how they prepare for war, and how well their intelligence and force-generation processes succeed in capturing emerging technologies and foreign military innovations. But the ultimate test of military preparation and effectiveness does not end once a war begins. On the contrary, history strongly reflects the enduring phenomena of learning and implementing change during war as well. You may go to war with the army you have, but you do not necessarily win with the same army. It has to adapt itself. The late British military historian Michael Howard long ago recommended that this aspect of military science receive greater study, and his advice is finally being heeded.

Why Wartime Change Is Important

The requirement that a force must adapt while it is in combat is built into the inherent nature of war. The great Prussian general and military theorist Carl von Clausewitz observed that war is filled with friction and chance and that "in war more than anywhere else, things do not turn out as we expect."[4] The essence of war is a competitive reciprocal relationship with an adversary who has unique capabilities and the capacity to make choices in battle. It is impossible to anticipate and predict all those choices and the contours of all future conflicts with any precision. Reacting to the unforeseen character of war—whether it involves the geography or environment or unanticipated aspects of the enemy's approach—is usually necessary. Accordingly, during the violent clash of weapons both commanders and institutional leaders must recognize shortfalls in the middle of the fog of war and against a thinking opponent. Recognizing the need to adapt and implement the requisite changes is therefore inherent to the nature of war. The clash of arms is also a competition in cycles of learning, reaction, or counteraction. The side that reacts best (and perhaps faster) increases the chances of prevailing. Recognizing and responding to these environmental stimuli is necessary but not necessarily easy.

Military forces face a great paradox. They are tasked to maintain highly efficient bureaucratic structures designed to carry out complex and dangerous tasks in a routine manner, mandating almost autonomous responses or reflexes. Military institutions that are built around these routines and core competencies are hard to alter, even under pressure. Nonetheless, they must assess what they and the enemy are doing, recognize the actual conditions that they face, and alter their responses under fire to obtain success. Their ability to adjust, adapt, and innovate determines how that paradox is resolved.

That reality is now belatedly recognized in U.S. military circles with calls for innovation and adaptation.[5] Drawing on a decade of conflict against asymmetric adversaries, scholars have placed the need to adapt in the forefront of research about military organization. Reinforced by hard-learned lessons from combat over the past decade, the role of learning and innovation on the battlefield is becoming more salient. In the United States over the past decade the Joint Chiefs of Staff has identified adaptation as a critical lesson.[6] Certainly the experience of the North Atlantic Treaty Organization (NATO) forces in Afghanistan would confirm that.[7] Given the uncertainty of our future security environment, the ability to change rapidly may be a strategic necessity, not just a source of relative tactical advantage. The tragedy of 9/11—the terrorist downing of four civilian airliners in New York, Washington, and rural Pennsylvania on September 11, 2001— began a chain reaction of decisions that resulted in the United States undertaking two major protracted wars (in Iraq and Afghanistan) over the next ten years. The merits of the policy decisions and the limits of the military planning deficiencies in those conflicts will be debated for many years. What was patently evident, however, was the lack of intellectual preparation by the U.S. military for sustained stability operations in the face of irregular opposition. Instead of facing disruptive means or the transformation of war defined on its own terms, the U.S. military found itself struggling to master a mode of warfare that would have been familiar to Rome's legions or Alexander's troops fighting on the same terrain. Eventually, U.S. forces and their allies found themselves adapting their current repertoires of doctrine, kit, and predeployment training to meet the unexpected demands of this decade-long struggle. What eventually emerged—what one scholar called a "Revolution in Military Adaptation"—was really a slow incremental evolution.[8] The halting change that characterized American and British alterations to operations Iraqi Freedom and Enduring Freedom suggests that we still have much to learn about military adaptation under wartime conditions.

The U.S. armed services have recognized the need to think about adaptation for some time. "In the volatile, uncertain, complex, and ambiguous environment we face for the foreseeable future," one pair of Army officers wrote in 2004, "if we were to choose merely one advantage over our adversaries it would certainly be this: to be superior in the art of learning and adaptation."[9] The Army's capstone concept was titled Operational Adaptability, which it defined as "a mindset based on flexibility of thought calling for leaders comfortable with collaborative planning and decentralized execution, a tolerance for ambiguity, and a willingness to make rapid adjustments according to the situation."[10] This definition suggests that adaptability is linked to decision-making by commanders under conditions of ambiguity. This identifies a potential focus, but only at the individual level.

Institutional factors that abet adaptation have also been studied by the historical community. One historian posits a direct correlation between the willingness and ability of military institutions to emphasize empirical evidence in peacetime innovation and their ability to assess actual conditions in war and adapt to them.[11] Military historian Williamson Murray has argued, "Those military organizations that display imagination and a willingness to think through the changes in peacetime have in nearly every case been those that have shown a willingness and ability to adapt and alter their prewar assumptions and preparation to reality."[12] There is a strong element of truth to this conclusion, given the role of visionary leadership and cultures that favor empirical and rigorously analyzed solutions to critical operational challenges. However, using Murray's own case studies, the conclusion may be overdrawn. The Germans were very creative in peacetime innovation in the interwar era, as Murray has demonstrated, and they learned from their early campaign troubles in Poland in 1939, where they stepped back, evaluated their performance, and then improved their communications, logistics, infantry-and-armor coordination and enhanced their ground-and-air coordination. But one is hard-pressed to see how adaptive the Germans were in their eastern front campaigns or in their air attacks against Great Britain at any level of war.[13]

The converse is also true: the U.S. Army's prewar intellectual preparation and acquisitions of modern armor warfare before World War II left much to be desired. However, its learning and adaptation rate from 1942 to 1944 was quite impressive and was even noted by the Germans.[14] Innovation and adaptation rates appear to vary by institution and in context between war and peacetime.

Another example of limited prewar preparation is that of the Israeli Defense Force (IDF) in the Yom Kippur War of 1973. The IDF clearly had failed to detect Egyptian president Anwar Sadat's preparations for crossing the Suez Canal or for girding for Egypt's use of guided antiarmor weapons and sophisticated air defenses. But it was more than just an intelligence failure. By focusing on tank-on-tank warfare and by arrogantly dismissing Arab fighting spirit, the IDF also had failed to anticipate the strengthening of Egypt's military capabilities and thus had to improvise in extremis.[15] It did so with stunning speed.[16]

Good innovators have been less-than-stellar adapters, and, conversely, institutions that have seemed complacent in peacetime sometimes have proven to be extraordinarily adaptive when pressed. Are different institutional characteristics or attributes at play? Do different drivers and shaping factors influence forms of military change, in peace and war? Does history suggest that external shapers stimulate innovation or adaptation under fire, or do the most pertinent facilitators derive from within a military institution? This book strives to answer these critical questions.

Military Change: Adjustments, Adaptation, and Innovation

The military change literature is currently fragmented. The majority of research and the most often-cited theories focus on the sources and drivers of paradigm shifts in military practice. Such theories are almost entirely focused on these major innovative leaps, which virtually always occur during peacetime, when states and their military institutions have the time and resources to explore new technologies and innovative concepts. Innovation studies have focused on rare but significant shifts requiring both a new "theory of victory" and the creation or change of a primary combat arm.[17] This focus has produced an orientation in the field that emphasizes externally driven change based on alterations in a nation's security situation, either by new threats or by the introduction of new military-related technologies. The new technologies may generate greater threat levels or new opportunities.

Until recently, what had long been missing was an appreciation of the innovation that occurs during wartime. Yet, over the past decade, the gap in the literature has closed rapidly. The unique circumstances that help spark changes in the underlying institutional structures, weapons, doctrine, and tactics of a large bureaucratic entity under extreme pressures are now recognized. Several scholars have emerged with detailed studies of how military organizations have learned from their intense operational experiences. This rich body of literature has generated a greater appreciation for wartime change and for the incorporation of inputs from real operational experience generated at the tactical level.

At the same time, the need for organizational capabilities to evolve in response to emerging or unanticipated challenges often produces a sense of urgency that

should promote rapid changes—in order to secure better performance and to preclude strategic or operational defeat. Yet, history is littered with examples of sta-
sis or defeat in the face of severe pressure. It is not easy for military leaders to alter
their operational praxes and generate new skills or competencies in the midst of
battle, but it does occur. Examining the conditions that are needed to accelerate
learning appears to be a worthy task.

Another aspect of the fragmented nature of the literature deals with definitions of innovation versus adaptation. Some theorists have drawn a line separat-
ing peacetime innovation as new and very significant, while treating wartime
adaptation as much less important. More productively, political scientists Theo
Farrell and Terry Terriff define military adaptation as the alteration of existing military means and methods.[18] Farrell later adopted a slightly different definition of
adaptation as a "change to strategy, force generation, and (or) military plans and
operations that is undertaken in response to operational challenges and campaign
pressures."[19] This definition emphasizes adjustments to current strategy, doctrine,
or plans. Farrell captures the actual manner and conduct of military operations as
well, but his identification of changes to force generation includes weapons and
new equipment and the supporting doctrine for employing them—a definition
that captures the reaction and response that is associated with an adaptation but
does not address how much it has enhanced operational performance levels.

Farrell has argued that efforts to draw too fine a line between adaptation and
innovation are counterproductive and has offered a sliding scale as an analytical
framework. After an extensive and quixotic effort, I agree that definitional purity
is not very fruitful and only serves to continue fragmenting an appreciation for
organizational processes that support learning and improved organizational performance. As a result, this book employs Farrell's framework of a sliding scale, with
a slightly modified definition in table 1.1.

Military change covers a continuum that ranges from mere adjustments or
switching of extant organizational capabilities to wartime innovation that occurs
in direct response to interaction with an adversary. Initially, operational units employ
and adjust current capabilities, exploiting existing frames, routines, and weapons.
If gaps persist, the institution and its operational forces may explore adaptation to
reduce performance gaps and increase their chances of success.

Military adaptation incorporates inputs from direct field experience into new doctrinal, organizational, and technological solutions to enhance current organizational capabilities beyond what a military organization had before war began. At the highest range—innovation—the force develops entirely new skills and shares them to support new missions, new values, and entirely new organizational competencies. For this study we have defined adaptation as "the alteration of existing competencies at either the institutional or operational level, to enhance performance based on perceived gaps or deficiencies generated by combat experience during wartime." A number of adjustments and adaptations may be aggregated into a new organizational competency that constitutes an innovation for that organization. The organization may acquire the knowledge from its experiences or may emulate what another source has found. Adaptation requires a dynamic process that involves the acquisition of knowledge, the utilization of that knowledge to create altered capacity, and the sharing of that learning with other units to integrate and institutionalize the new operational practice to improve performance.[20] As Farrell suggests, operational units can then share that information across the institution to enhance the armed service as a whole through its force-generation activities.

Like those of Farrell and professor James A. Russell, my definition captures its temporal dimension during conflict, and its source—a wartime response to the enemy's own (unexpected) actions or novel campaign circumstances. But the definition also builds on the Organizational Learning literature with respect to existing competencies and organizational repertoires. More significantly, our definition requires that the changes not reflect existing organizational capacity by simply switching from an extant skill set or competency. For this study, there is an element of discovery and

Table 1.1. Wartime Military Change Continuum

Adjustments ➡	Adaptation ➡	Innovation
Switching between current competencies (corrective reforms)	Learned changes to existing competencies and capability	New organizational competencies, doctrine, and tasks

growth inherent to adaptation, both in degree and impact. It may not be a significant alteration, but it does require learning and some form of knowledge creation
and change beyond a mere application of existing skills.

"Switching" implies extant organizational knowledge and behavioral capacity. By not simply "switching" its mode of operating—but by learning and applying altered tactics and operational methods that have to be tested, absorbed,
and encoded into revised standard operating procedure or doctrine—this effort
becomes an adaptation. Adjusting existing military means and methods "under
fire" or changing from one extant organizational competency to another is properly defined as more of a switch that demonstrates the breadth of an institution's
competencies. Switching with agility between existing skills and modes demonstrates agility and versatility, but not adaptation. An organization or individual
with multiple competencies is versatile. But versatility is not adaptability, which
requires the capacity to identify, assess, design, and implement modified operational or tactical capabilities.

Additionally, this definition, in line with previous scholarship by RAND Corporation analyst Adam Grissom, incorporates "enhanced organizational performance." This is to reflect the better fit between the organization's outputs and the
environmental and campaign pressures faced by that organization.[21] The change
continuum comports with a recent but well-supported element in the contemporary literature that holds that a bundle of adaptations can lead to the evolution of
new means and methods that constitute an innovation.[22] The cases studied in this
book reflect that to some degree.

State of the Literature

The complexities of military change have been recognized by security studies students and historians for some time. The ability to challenge norms, assumptions,
methods, and structures in the face of severe stress is often a fundamental part of
success in combat. Learning, adapting, and innovating do not stop when conflict
begins. Professors Eliot A. Cohen and John Gooch created a very useful framework for analyzing military failures across the temporal dimensions of before, during, and after conflict. They identified the inability to adapt during war as a key
contributing cause of military failure. "Where learning failures have their roots in
the past," Cohen and Gooch stress, "adaptive failures suggest an inability to handle

the changing present."[23] They fault institutions over individuals in their analysis. "The requirements to adapt to unexpected circumstances test both organization and system," they observe, "revealing weaknesses that are partly structural and partly functional, whose full potential for disaster may not previously have been noticed."[24]

Although this framework suggests institutional or systemic elements of learning failures, it does not attempt to identify the best practices and institutional processes that are needed to abet effective adaptation in wartime. Given the wide set of missions that contemporary military institutions must be prepared to conduct, under increasing budgetary constrictions, the ability to adapt is fast becoming an institutional attribute highly prized by policymakers and military leaders.[25]

Despite these historically grounded observations, scholarly interest in how military organizations change during war has emerged only recently. A significant component of the research to date has focused on successful peacetime or interwar innovation. Besides the interwar study of Allan Millett and Williamson Murray, others, such as David Johnson's *Fast Bombers and Heavy Tanks* and William O. Odom's assessment of U.S. Army armor developments, also mined the innovative era between the world wars.[26] Political scientist Stephen P. Rosen's *Winning the Next War* was the exception; it devoted one chapter to innovation during war.

In the 1990s and up to September 11, 2001, defense reform focused on rare, transformational breakthroughs based on revolutionary and disruptive technologies that created entirely new ways of fighting and winning wars. Reformers passionately embraced large-scale shifts in investments to take advantage of the purportedly substantial competitive advantage inherent to the Information Age. Advocates of the so-called American "Revolution in Military Affairs" (RMA) that followed the 1991 Persian Gulf War argued for radical changes to seize a paradigm shift in how military power was applied and later was used to "lock out" future competitors.[27] Many of the proposed changes would have required investments in computers, precision-strike systems, and surveillance and reconnaissance assets at the expense of more traditional weapons, such as tanks and airplanes. Over time the defense reformers found further support from academic research on large organizational changes that resulted from disruptive technologies that displaced dominant companies in the business literature.[28] There were countervailing arguments from traditionalists and from historians.[29] Criticisms about the Department of Defense's initiative focused on its excessive reliance on technology and lack of analytical rigor, as well as on its failure to take account of the actual nature of opponents when it considered the character of warfare.[30]

This intense debate was short-lived. Senior U.S. policymakers officially embraced the need for reform under the so-called transformation initiative.[31] Indeed, in the late summer of 2001 the Department of Defense's was preparing to release its congressionally mandated Quadrennial Defense Review, embracing a technology-centric approach applicable to conventional warfare between major powers. Just as that was about to take place, however, a group of al-Qaeda agents launched the September 11 attacks: two hijacked passenger jets slammed into the World Trade Center in New York, a third hit the Pentagon itself, and a fourth crashed in rural Pennsylvania. War had come to the United States in a manner that few had conceived, and terrorism had returned to the fore, making the Defense Department's transformation plan suddenly seem largely irrelevant.[32] Thus, the reform initiative was even shorter-lived than the RMA debate.

More recently, after years of protracted counterinsurgency and stability operations in Iraq and Afghanistan, academics have generated numerous studies on the complexity of military change during war that have significantly increased both interest and insights into how institutions respond to what Howard called the "utterly unpredictable." Together they reflect a recognition of a gap in our understanding of military innovation as well as the leadership challenge inherent to preparing military forces for the ever-evolving character of contemporary conflict.

Even so, until recently the security studies community had rarely examined how wartime innovation and adaptation might be achieved under battlefield conditions. Historians have generally focused on large-scale innovation in peacetime. The literature was sparse with respect to formal theories on how military organizations change or evolve during war. The conspicuous exception was the study of German tactical experimentation in World War I.[33] A few historians have broadened the research base with studies of American adaptation during the closing European campaign of World War II. Military historian Michael D. Doubler focused entirely on American learning under fire as the United States and its allies advanced into France, while military historian Russell A. Hart offered a comparative analysis of Allied ground forces as they fought against the Germans.[34] The Vietnam conflict spawned critical studies about the U.S. Army's failure to recognize and absorb lessons, including that of the now-retired Army lieutenant colonel John Nagl in *Learning to Eat Soup with a Knife*. Nagl's comparative assessment about Britain's successful adaptation in Malaya during the 1950s—in contrast to the U.S. Army's struggle to alter its battlefield efforts to include the warfighting skills demanded in the Vietnam War—is a significant effort.[35]

Today the academic community is seriously focused on this issue, and a recent surge in such literature has rectified some of the long-standing gaps in our understanding. In *On Flexibility*, retired Israeli brigadier general Meir Finkel notes that military force planners face an increasingly difficult challenge of anticipating or predicting the future battlefield.[36] Rather than predicating future success on the ability to forecast accurately, Finkel seeks to generate an advantage by identifying which factors contribute to "the ability to recuperate swiftly from the initial surprise."[37] He accepts that uncertainty pervades warfare, so the need to recover from an opponent's actions is not an anomaly in warfare. Using an array of historical case studies from World War II to the Yom Kippur War of 1973, Finkel examines the implementation of entirely new solutions and technologies forged in the crucible of combat. He hypothesizes a suite of underlying institutional characteristics that have allowed successful forces to overcome shortcomings in planning or intelligence failure quickly.[38] Relevant to this book, Finkel links critical organizational factors as enablers of rapid organizational change and flexibility in battle. Even so, his valuable work overlooks other possible factors—organizational cultures and the rigorous education of commanders, for example.

Finkel's findings are reinforced by another historical assessment. In *Military Adaptation: A Fear of Change*, Williamson Murray concludes, "Over the course of the past century and a half, adaptation in one form or another has been a characteristic of successful military institutions and human societies under the pressures of war."[39] Yet, Murray notes a pattern of behavior on the part of military leaders that begins with a picture or mental frame about what future war will look like. In Murray's research, he notices that senior leaders stubbornly cling to their prewar conceptions and try to impose assumptions on the war they are fighting, regardless of how well they fit the actual conflict. Unlike Finkel's analytical framework with institutional attributes, Murray's review focuses on senior leaders and their role in promoting change.

Two newer studies examine more systemic elements of change deriving from contemporary cases of irregular warfare. In *Innovation, Transformation and War*, Russell conclusively undercuts the simplistic top-down-driven narrative of American counterinsurgency innovation in Iraq.[40] Russell demonstrates that well before U.S. president George W. Bush directed the first surge in Iraq, Army and Marine Corps units had evolved organically and were implementing counterinsurgency techniques quite successfully at the tactical level. They did so without top-down guidance or campaign directives from higher headquarters. As Russell shows with convincing evidence, the tide already had been turned in Al Anbar as a result of these bottom-up initiatives—all in the absence of help from the "rear echelon."[41]

Russell concludes that an iterative process of organically generated tactical adaptation and innovation unfolded over time in a distinctive progression of trial and error, culminating in altered standard operating procedures and innovative practices in the units that he studied. Other recent scholarship also has identified bottom-up adaptation from tactical units as the primary source of organizational learning in contemporary conflict. Political scientist Chad C. Serena's work, *A Revolution in Military Adaptation*, reinforces many of Russell's conclusions and criticizes the institutional Army for its sluggish responses in Iraq.[42]

More recently, other comprehensive studies of adaption in war have emerged, particularly from the effort to stabilize Afghanistan. An analytical framework in one multinational assessment defined a set of drivers and shapers of military adaption in the extended counterinsurgency campaign conducted by NATO.[43] In a new twist, the shaping factors listed in that study included four external elements—domestic politics, coalition politics, strategic culture, and civil-military relations. The analysis demonstrates the dynamic interplay of the factors that shaped or limited adaptation among the members of the International Security Assistance Force (ISAF) and the way that adaptation was manifested in behavioral outputs (changes in strategy, force design, doctrine, training, and operations).[44]

Although the study offered a valuable lens on that conflict, this effort seeks to do the same with an analytical framework based on *internal* shapers and processes, across a different set of cases. The contribution of endogenous organizational factors sheds insights on the central question of this book.

The Central Issue

This book builds on the innovation literature with a focus on wartime learning and adaptation. The objective is to explore the character and process of military change *during wartime*. The study hones in more narrowly on military change when in contact with an enemy. The scale of military change can be disruptive or revolutionary—as with an entirely new way of fighting, supported by a breakthrough technology—or simply an organizational innovation that creates a new capability for an institution. Given the challenge posed by Grissom to explore bottom-up-generated forms of innovation, this book explores the internal institutional factors that promote and enable military adaptation. Building on recent scholarship, a theoretical suite of organizational elements is identified and defined as contributing to effective adaptation. The absence of such enabling factors should inhibit or retard successful organizational change in combat.

With the growing importance of conducting levels of change during conflict, senior leaders should want to understand more fully how change occurs in military organizations and what can be done to manage or stimulate it when necessary. Adaptivity—a predisposition or capacity to change while in contact—may produce strategic and operational advantage.[45] Therefore, understanding what abets or retards institutional and organizational change in the crucible of conflict has potential value in enhancing the performance of military organizations in wartime.

The book aims to resolve gaps in the current literature in this field, which include:

- Exploring bottom-up military change in wartime.
- Further examining Organizational Learning Theory as a military change theory and exploring how it bridges the innovation and adaptation literature.
- Identifying the general process and critical internal institutional factors that accelerate or block military change during wartime and explaining their role in the promotion or retardation of effective change.

To explore the crucial research questions that frames this book, we used case studies ranging across different physical domains of war and several U.S. military services over disparate generations that together served as a framework for evaluating how well each service evolved in conflict. The missions and tasks with which each institution was involved were sufficiently broad enough and long enough to provide critical insights into the character of adaptation. Although the cases all involved U.S. military forces, it is expected that these insights can be generalized to inform future research and suggest implications for policymakers and senior military leaders.

These cases include:

- U.S. Navy adaptation in undersea warfare in World War II, 1942–44.
- The U.S. Air Force's multiple adaptations in the Korean War, 1950–53.
- The U.S. Army adaptation to warfare in Vietnam, 1964–68.
- U.S. Marine Corps' adaptations to complex counterinsurgency in Iraq, 2003–7.

These cases were chosen because they involved extensive campaigns over several years with multiple cycles of action and counteraction, and because they incorporated opportunities to examine various forms of military change—doctrinal approaches, organizational changes, and new technologies. Based on the Organizational Learning literature, it was hypothesized that over the course of the war the respective institutions were both physically fighting and conducting an Organizational Learning Cycle or process of learning. The cases were critical to this study, since they have become foundations for major scholars in the military innovation and learning literature.[46] Although the cases are comprehensive, they involve only U.S. military forces, and generalizations from these cases to other strategic or military cultures may not be warranted. If there are national styles of learning or unique foreign military cultures, applying insights from our cases without due caution would be inappropriate.

In each of these cases the military force entered the war with existing capabilities and a mental model of what kind of wars and enemy they were expected to fight. The U.S. Navy had prepared for two decades to defeat the Imperial Navy of Japan and had developed innovative approaches employing modern carrier-based aviation. The war eventually demonstrated that while America had prepared well to meet its projected adversary in a symmetrical battle, significant adaptation was required to cripple Japan's economic lifelines. In particular, the U.S. submarine force evolved from a reconnaissance and screening force into a lethal underwater threat against Japanese commercial shipping. The U.S. Air Force emerged from World War II convinced that strategic bombing had been decisive in the European and Pacific campaigns and would be a key deterrent in the Cold War with the Soviet bloc. It also regarded that mission as critical in bolstering its case for being severed from the Army and established as a separate service. Similarly, in the Vietnam War, the Army brought its own institutional history to bear, fully prepared to employ technology and massive amounts of firepower to impose its will on its opponent; yet, that mindset and skill-set were not overly productive against an elusive force that blended into the jungles and villages of Vietnam. In the final case, the highly disciplined U.S. Marine Corps had focused on its amphibious mission in the post-Vietnam and post-Beirut eras; it still believed that it had the right capabilities and doctrine to counter the incipient insurgency that emerged in Iraq in 2004, and that its experiences in the 1920s and 1930s gave it a unique appreciation for modern small wars. The case study bears out the distinction between tacit institutional knowledge and actual competency on the battlefield.

More important to this effort, each institution had to adapt its predispositions and alter its repertoire of competencies—in doctrine, organization, and equipment—in order to adapt to the shifting circumstances of a conflict that was not well anticipated. It had to adjust, adapt, and innovate under duress. It is through these four cases that a greater understanding of the process of learning that leads to wartime adaptation and innovation will be sought. The critical role of institutional culture, strong leaders, and the choice of proper metrics all influenced this cognitive issue and the subsequent effort to alter tactics, seek creative shifts in operational methods, or develop new capabilities.

The structure of this project is straightforward. Chapter 2 presents an overview of theories on military innovation. A key feature is an argument for including Organizational Learning Theory as a major conceptual approach to studying military innovation in general and change during wartime in particular. It also presents a theory about military change in wartime that incorporates a synthesized process model drawn and adapted from the Organizational Learning literature. A four-stage Organizational Learning Cycle is presented as an analytical framework for researching how organizations perceive their environment, how they acquire knowledge, and how they learn new tasks or skills, to identify and validate the institutional attributes and processes that facilitate or retard learning. The Learning and Change Cycle and four institutional attributes—*leadership, organizational culture, learning mechanisms*, and *dissemination mechanisms*—constitute a proposed theory entitled Organizational Learning Capacity.

The case studies are presented in chapters 3 through 6. Each case study covers multiple campaigns over years of combat experience in a historical narrative that also captures official and informal lessons or insights drawn from each war. Within each case we discuss the contributions or influence of each of the hypothesized internal enablers or facilitating institutional elements. In all of these I find that the leaders of each military organization had reason to believe that their strategy and weapons were sound. Although these leaders were confident initially, events proved that their confidence and expectations were misplaced. They eventually had to alter strategy, devise new doctrines, and adjust weapons and technologies in order to obtain success. Their Organizational Learning Capacity was tested and found wanting in some cases. The dynamic interplay of institutional enablers shaped their ability to perceive and respond appropriately in response to the opponent or new environmental conditions.

The concluding chapter assesses the Organizational Learning Capacity Theory and the learning process model within the cases. A set of implications for promoting innovations is drawn out by inductive analysis. The chapter concludes with implications for policymakers and the military force-development community. By this time, the answer to the ultimate question of this book—"what makes a military organization more adaptive than another?"—should be clearer.

By the end of the book, I hope to convince the reader that:

- Organizational Learning Theory is valuable to better understand *adaptation* and *innovation*.
- *Adaptation* is best understood through Organizational Learning Theory as a unique process model that incorporates both *adaptation* and *innovation*, which captures how learning from the individual level to the *institutional* level is achieved.

- Organizational Learning Capacity is a useful construct for understanding military change in wartime, especially as a diagnostic tool to analyze what has happened on the battlefield.
- There are key implications for the U.S. military from Organizational Learning Capacity in terms of *leadership development* and *education* of future leaders. If military organizations want to be more successful in wartime in recognizing and responding appropriately to the demands of both *adaptations* and *innovation*, understanding the basic processes and underlying mechanisms from the start should be useful.

Military change in the midst of fighting presents some unique challenges worthy of serious study. The need both to adapt and innovate has been evident throughout the past century. The record also suggests that some institutions have difficulty with managing change. As Murray notes, "military institutions have proven resistant to change throughout the twentieth century even during times of conflict; and more often than not they have paid for adaptation in the blood of their maimed and dead rather than through the exercise of their minds and mental agility."[47] If history and security studies are to offer anything to policymakers, it should be the ability to exercise the mind in order to minimize the blood.

CHAPTER 2

On Changes

*Knowing how and why innovation flourished or lagged is an
essential step toward understanding the enduring dynamics of military
innovation and the challenges of military reform.*

—MILITARY HISTORIAN ALLAN R. MILLETT [1]

T he subject of military innovation has been a topic of serious research
and debate in the security studies community for close to two decades.
There are many competing theories about what drives and inspires military
organizations to adopt new fighting methods and invent new technologies for the
battlefield. This chapter will offer a framework to arrange these theories according to some key parameters. The potential drivers and sources of different military
technologies, methods, and doctrine are many and varied. Is innovation spurred
by top-down direction or is it sourced from the bottom up? Are new ideas forced
on recalcitrant and rigid military bureaucracies from the outside or from within?
If new ideas are driven by external sources, are the sources civilian leaders or
technocrats? When ideas are sourced from within the services themselves, is the
change being pushed by credible military leaders in responsible positions or by
visionary mavericks who create internal consensus from the bottom up?

What is the most effective process by which military institutions seek out creative solutions to emerging problems? Do certain organizational attributes facilitate or enhance the ability of a military institution to anticipate revolutionary
developments or to adapt quickly new concepts of operations generated from
within other militaries? What is the role of strategic or military culture, as opposed

18

to the specific culture of a particular military service? There are no widely accepted answers to these questions.

After a brief review of innovation theories, I have used this chapter to examine an adaptation process model and to offer a substitute that derives from Organizational Learning studies rather than from International Relations Theory. With that in mind, the final section of the chapter develops a suite of facilitating organizational attributes that promote organizational learning.

Innovation Theories

Our review of the literature covers the dominant theories about military change and innovation, which comprise four principal schools or approaches:

- Interventionists
- Institutionalists
- Intra-Organizational Politics
- Interservice Competition

After reviewing these theories and their supporting arguments within a common framework, I reintroduce Organizational Learning Theory, an older, but less acclaimed approach that is already represented in business management literature. This framework is not alien to students of military innovation. It has not been rigorously compared to other theories, but it has been increasingly employed by scholars of military innovation and adaptation. Here is a summary of the competing theories that we have considered:

The Interventionists

One canonical theorist is political scientist Barry R. Posen, author of *The Sources of Military Doctrine*. He is the principal proponent of the externally directed, top-down-driven school of military innovation that I term the Interventionist Approach. According to Posen, "[Organizations innovate] when they are pressured from outside . . . [Civilian] intervention is often responsible for the level of innovation."[2]

Posen argues that military bureaucracies seldom innovate on their own, especially in exploring new intellectual domains such as military doctrine. Service bureaucracies abhor the uncertainty generated by new ideas and because of their leadership structure and hierarchy they are likely to resist change and to inhibit the free flow of information. Having mastered the current doctrine and paradigm, Posen contends that leaders have no interest in encouraging the kind of change that would bring in new technologies, relevant doctrine, or weapons and would further accelerate the leader's own obsolescence. Posen asserts that because of the process of socialization or institutionalization major innovations in military doctrine are rare—doubly so because innovation increases operational uncertainty, which is anathema to the military.

To define the principal variables that drive the development of military doctrine, whether offensive or defensive, Posen explores a number of explanatory variables or theories—involving geography, organization theory, technology, and structural realism. In this case, he defines doctrine as the steps that a military organization takes to operationalize its fundamental approach to fighting. Posen cites military doctrine as a key component of a state's grand strategy and something properly within the purview of civilian leaders.

The Interventionist Approach is based on International Relations Theory and treats military organizations as subordinate agencies of the state. Posen believes that realism, or Balance-of-Power Theory, provides a better explanation of why governments are more likely to develop and adhere to offensive or defensive strategies. Posen finds that external threats from other countries' foreign policies are more often the major determinant of military postures and doctrine. The competitive logic governing the current international system creates a powerful incentive for states to adopt new military methods, primarily by emulating the military practices of the most successful states in the system. To stay competitive they must adopt the most successful forms and practices. Posen posits that because organizations seek to reduce uncertainty, increase their autonomy, and expand their budgets, they will favor offensive doctrines. Although this theory is oriented largely toward identifying types of drivers and sources of innovation, the Interventionist school does explore the process of change to a degree. To Posen, externally driven civilian intervention can be positive and significant. He also believes that outside intervention is most effective when it is supported from the inside by a leader who is willing to buck the system and work within a coalition of civilian policymakers. These are officers capable of generating and pushing for innovative solutions, who take public positions and seek coalition partners outside the service. Posen calls such individuals "military mavericks."[3]

Although Posen focuses on peacetime assessments of the threat and perceived imbalances of power between states, he does not examine wartime innovation or adaptation. Given his conditions for civilian intervention during periods of crisis or high threat, however, one can assume that he would contend that such top-down pressure would certainly be warranted and anticipated in wartime if military success were not achieved initially and if the policy aims of the state were at risk. This would seem to be particularly relevant to wartime innovation rather than to long periods of peace.

Nevertheless, Posen's theory has been criticized by historians for case-selection bias and historical misinterpretation.[4] Given this contested historical evidence, the slight preponderance that Posen awarded to neorealism and externally driven change may not be warranted.

Institutionalists

Political scientist Deborah D. Avant has presented an alternative theory, seeking to better explain *when* military organizations craft doctrine and respond effectively to the state's security goals. In this approach, the structural context and relative power of a state's institutions come into play. Avant evaluates the conventional theory that it is primarily external sources that influence military strategy and doctrine. By incorporating internal state structure as a domestic variable on top of perceptions of external threats, Avant extends the interventionist theorists. The character of the security environment and the structure and power of the state and its policy-makers are the main drivers of potential changes.

Principal Agent Theory is central to Avant's approach. This theory contends that leaders (principals) delegate authority to experts and authorities whom they supervise to conduct activities or provide services. The leaders of military organizations are agents of civilian leaders, and Avant contends that the way those civilians oversee military organizations affects how they promote changes.[5] Strategic leaders seek to stay in power, and how they perceive and employ their electoral power is the principal variable. "A domestic political actor is likely to promote institutional change in response to a changing position in the international system if the shift will augment that actor's domestic political advantage," Avant argues.[6]

This theory applies rational choice-based International Relations Theory about states to organizations. Avant contends that her theory "assumes that actors will behave so as to ensure or enhance their institutional power. Thus, we should expect that military organizations will be responsive to civilian goals when military leaders believe they will be rewarded for that responsiveness."[7] This model says more about the *when* innovation or change in doctrine is more likely to occur than *how*.

To Avant, domestic institutions hold the key to explaining the variation in military doctrine. She argues that military organizations are more likely to have *different* preferences about doctrine and reform from those of civilian leaders if they have professionalized themselves so that they are relatively free from civilian interference—a situation that is more likely to occur when civilian leadership is divided by politics or by form of government. Conversely, military institutions are more likely to have preferences that are *similar* to those of civilian leaders if the civilian leaders exercise strong control over the organization while it is professionalizing—which is more likely to occur when civilian leadership is unified.[8]

Avant's cases reflect some selection bias, however, since she only examines two cases where policymakers wanted the military to adapt to a form of warfare that their institutional cultures were not inclined to accept, given their missions or most important competencies. Her subtitle is telling—*Lessons from Peripheral Wars*. Lessons drawn from peripheral conflicts may produce temporary changes in doctrine or praxes applied in-theater, but the revisions are not likely to endure, given the lack of support for admittedly lower priority missions. Organizations will not explore or invest in a new competency when it is not likely to be repeated or when the outlook for future demand is questionable.[9] Overall, while seeking to explain why and when innovation occurs, this theory does not address the complexity of *how* innovative ideas are translated into learning.

Intra-Organizational Politics

The Intra-Organizational school is best represented by the output of political scientist Stephen P. Rosen in *Winning the Next War*. Rosen's work focuses on the sources, scale, and direction of successful innovation. He also isolates technology as a variable. His case studies offer a range of domains (air, sea, and land) over the breadth of the twentieth century. Like Posen, Rosen is pessimistic about military innovation, noting that "in bureaucracies the absence of innovation is the rule, the natural state."[10] Yet, while noting that bureaucracies are inherently stable and specialized, Rosen notes that they can innovate. He finds that when military institutions do create new ways of war, senior visionary leaders often are the main source and drivers of that change.

Rosen asserts that peacetime and war present different environments and conditions for successful innovation. Peacetime innovation is evolutionary and is heavily influenced by both the uncertainty of the changing character of future conflict and the nature of new technological development. Leaders cannot determine with any certainty which combat arms, innovative concepts, or emerging weapons will be most effective. Innovation is inhibited by the routines of peacetime—normal tour lengths and promotion practices, stable intra-organizational power structures, and ambiguity about the future.

Wars, on the other hand, usually resolve the ambiguity challenge, offering feedback and demonstrable evidence about strategic and operational effectiveness. However, although the justification for change is evident—allowing leaders to adapt their current combat structure and operational concepts—there often is not enough time and intelligence available to determine what alternatives might be more effective. Fog and friction remain fundamental considerations. Rosen suggests that centralized command and new measures of strategic effectiveness are needed for leaders to interpret and react to the demands of actual wartime operations.[11]

With respect to scale, Rosen focuses on significant changes in military practice—major innovations. A major innovation is defined as a change in one of the primary combat arms of a service in the way it fights or, alternatively, as the creation of a new combat arm.[12] First, innovation requires "a new theory of victory," which often results in an ideological struggle within a particular service. Hence, internal competition over power, promotions, and organizational priorities are central to this theory. In this, the internal composition of armed forces is very relevant. Navies are organized in fleets comprising a variety of ships and combat arms, surface ships, submarines, and aviation units. Armies are organized around a number of combat arms and branches (artillery, infantry, armor, helicopters, etc.), which represent sub-organizational communities that are a source of identity, socialization, and status. Rosen's cases emphasize operational innovations in or between these branches, much as they are employed to win campaigns. But, as

Rosen asserts, *major* innovation results primarily when a new theory of victory results in an intraservice ideological struggle. This adds a significant twist to his definition about major innovations—by incorporating shifts in the creation of new military branches and altered personnel policy. Rosen observes, "Peacetime innovation has been possible when senior military officers with traditional credentials, reacting not to intelligence about the enemy but to a structural change in the security environment, have acted to create a new promotion pathway for junior officers practicing a new way of war."[13]

Second, this ideological struggle must produce new, concrete, and critical tasks. This is a high bar, but it offers a unique distinction about the scale of change under study.

But wartime innovation is another matter. Effective reform during combat operations is a function of a redefinition in measures of strategic effectiveness used by commanders or the institution. In all of Rosen's cases, innovation was internal to the military, abetted by civilians and specialists, but driven by credible military leaders.

In Rosen's view, peacetime military innovation is inherently a redistribution of power between services or their internal branches. He finds that the process by which new ideas are instilled and sustained involves the creation of new branches, faster promotion rates, and the surpassing of an older generation of officers by those willing to understand and associate themselves with a new vision or concept of operation. Such power shifts can be reinforced by leadership development, promotion board precepts, new career paths, etc., to raise organizational incentives or to increase the internal power of a particular branch in a service. This further reinforces the faster advancement rate for older officers, who then control resources at the service and branch level. In turn, these rising officers can legitimize and support the less-senior officers in striving to refine and introduce the new way of war at lower levels of the institution. Power is won through influence over who is promoted to senior command.[14] Rather than focusing on the state or external threat, the Intraservice Competition school of thought focuses on the internal dynamics of the communities inside each military service.

Rosen finds that "learning from wartime experience how to perform an entirely new military function was in all cases extremely difficult."[15] In particular, defining and answering the right questions about ongoing operations and alternative options proved challenging and ad hoc efforts to discern the intellectual problem and the option set took time. Also, time is at a premium during conflict, since the essence of war is a time-competitive interaction. As a result, wartime innovation is rare.

In contrast to Posen, Rosen concludes that neither civilians nor so-called mavericks are influential. Rather, he argues, civilians often play supporting roles in initiating an innovation and that senior military officials with visionary ideas but traditional backgrounds are the most successful champions of change.

Interservice Competition

A fourth approach finds that interservice competition is the driver or catalyst for innovation. This school contends that bureaucracies are involved in a constant competition for prestige and resources and that bureaucratic politics drive policy and investment decisions for large institutions. Several scholars hold that national security policymaking is usually the result of the confluence and interaction of competing players and interests. Struggles for organizational advantage and budgetary gain are the norm.[16] Over time the resulting culture generated by this process produces a competitive intra-departmental culture that conditions participants to compete through innovation or adaptation. In a zero-sum budget, service organizations compete for attention, resources, and influence and try to expand their slice of a fixed funding pie. The competition is a source for innovative ideas that enable one organization to stake a claim to missions or resources absorbed by others less efficiently or effectively. Political scientist Harvey M. Sapolsky, a leading advocate of this approach, notes that the Navy's investment in the Polaris submarine–launched ballistic missile program was partially inspired by the desire to deny the Air Force a monopoly on both the strategic deterrence mission and the funding that goes with it.[17]

Numerous studies on U.S. naval innovation stress the competitive driver of innovation, at least during peacetime.[18] The Marine Corps, which displays a degree of institutional paranoia due to its insecure position in the American national security architecture, routinely competes with the Army for missions and deployments but sees itself as a unique extension of the Navy.[19]

Proponents of interorganizational dynamics do not explicitly deal with the direction of the flow of innovation, but the theory supports a top-down method.

Due to the increased availability of information about competing systems provided by the services, it is alleged that a secondary effect of enhanced interservice rivalry is enhanced civilian oversight over the military. This is consistent with the Institutionalists, since this approach suggests that civilian principals can manipulate the individual services by employing incentives and can generate innovative solutions by competing for resources. By playing off one service against another, civilian leaders might better frame military doctrine and capability development toward their preferred outcomes.[20] As Sapolsky has argued, "With fewer dollars and more friction, the services will have to think harder about the threat and how the armed forces can meet it. There is no better incentive to candor, error correction, and creativity in defense planning than a tight budget and a few smart rivals competing for a share of the budget pie."[21]

Advocates claim that "because of competition that has prevailed among the armed services (and between the services and the intelligence agencies), the U.S. military has better attack helicopters, amphibious warfare capabilities, satellite communications, and surveillance systems and special operations forces than it would have had absent the competition."[22] For example, the Army might compete with the Air Force for base security or theater missile-defense.

This particular school is not always incorporated into formal innovation studies, but it has strong relevance to the U.S. military's bureaucratic combat and parochialism. There is little scholarship on wartime innovation or adaptation based on this theory. Moreover, national policy initiatives, such as the Goldwater-Nichols Department of Defense Reorganization Act of 1986, minimize intraservice rivalry and overt competition between services in the United States.[23]

Organizational Learning

Up to this point we have covered the traditional theories of military innovation, but one theory has been overlooked—Organizational Learning, arguably the oldest innovation theory.[24] The origins of this concept can be traced to the 1960s, but the most substantive theoretical works came largely in the 1970s and 1980s.[25] Organizational Learning Theory is drawn from sociological and economic theory and takes a more positive view of organizations. It sees organizations as rational and profit-seeking players, interacting against others in a competitive environment where constant evaluation of products and

Table 2.1. Military Change and Innovation Approaches

	Leading Scholars	Unit of Analysis	Temporal Dimension	Directionality	Driver of Innovation/ Adaptation
Interventionist	Posen	State	Interwar periods	External/ Top down	Threat perception
Institutionalist	Avant	State structure	Wartime	Delegated from top	Interplay of structure/ actors
Intra-Organizational Politics	Rosen	Military service	Largely wartime	Internal/ Top down	Internal politics
Inter-Service Competition	Sapolsky/ Cote	Service	Peacetime	Internal/Top down	Competition for resources
Organizational Learning	Bickel/ Nagl Downie/ Serena/ Davidson	Service	During and after war	Internal to service	Survival, response to gaps in per-formance

services and continuous change are required to survive and prosper. Drawn from business literature, the theory regards military services as organizations that are competing for survival and prosperity in contested environments rather than tradition-bound bureaucratic actors. It points out that businesses, which have to be competitive in a constantly changing environment with active competitors, must continually take stock of their performance—by comparing their actual performance (and the feedback they receive from actions with competitors) with their own expectations and organizational goals. When the corporation is faced with gaps between desired results and the environment, it either must adjust its current modes of practice or explore new options for increasing its performance levels or it will go out of business. The agility with which the orga-nization can identify new needs and then craft enhanced or new capabilities and transmit them across the breadth of an organization is a source of competitive advantage over competitors.

The prominence of this theory was popularized in the 1990s by systems scientist Peter Senge in his bestselling book, *The Fifth Discipline*, and his efforts did not go unnoticed by leaders and scholars in the military.[26] Senge blended Organizational Learning with discussions of systems theory and psychology. For him, "A learning organization is a place where people are continually discovering how they create their reality. And how they can change it."[27] Here the emphasis is more on the role of leaders in facilitating personal growth as a means of raising individual contributions to the organization.

In the commercial world of the 1980s knowledge management became a technology-centric approach to organizational theory rather than a holistic one. Its overemphasis on the information processes and technology aspect of gathering, storing, and distributing knowledge has limited the acceptance of Organizational Learning as an innovation theory. This has subsequently been rectified in Western military services, where knowledge-management ecologies have been established and institutionalized with some noted success.[28]

Ultimately a renewed emphasis on enhanced organizational performance became the explicit objective of Organizational Learning. The notion that a successful firm was a learning organization came to the fore. The late Harvard management expert David A. Garvin defined a learning organization as "an organization skilled at creating, acquiring, and transferring knowledge and *at modifying its behavior* [emphasis added] to reflect new knowledge and insights."[29] Scholars in the military innovation community reinforced Garvin's definition and emphasized adapting a service's organization and its practices in order to gain competitive advantage.[30]

Organizational Learning Theory offers insights into major issues raised about military innovation and adaptation. First, it defines the general process by which knowledge is shifted from new information to increased organizational capacity. Organizational Learning is more than merely collecting information; it is "the capacity (or processes) within an organization to maintain or improve performance based on experience."[31] This includes the creation of new knowledge and capability, the sharing of this knowledge, and its storage and institutionalization in an organization's memory and culture.

Second, Organizational Learning Theory is relevant to what this book has discussed as both scale and direction. Theorists contend that learning begins with individuals and that any process of learning progresses from teams or groups and ultimately up to institutions. Both theoretical and field research in Organizational Learning Theory emphasizes far more bottom-up approaches from individuals closest to business activity and problems rather than those directed from top management.

The direction of knowledge creation in Organizational Learning starts with individuals, whether it originates at the bottom or the top of the institution. This element is in contrast to most military innovation theories. RAND Corporation strategic studies scholar Adam Grissom argues that "all of the major models of military innovation operate from the top down" so that the senior officers and civilians are the drivers or agents of innovation.[32] They recognize the need for change, formulate a new way of warfare, position their organization to seize the opportunity, and culturally manipulate or create a new consensus to push the organization forward. In discussing key scholars in the field, Naval Postgraduate School professor James A. Russell notes that they all "assume that authority flows down the governmental hierarchy in a reasonably predictable process."[33] In contrast, Organizational Learning Theory acknowledges that information and ideas flow from contact between smaller units of the organization and its operating environment and that creative ideas and solutions flow up to larger teams and higher levels of the organizations. This makes it a more relevant theory for exploitation than the existing predominant theories, particularly for incremental adaptation during conflict.

Theorists make consistent observations about the scale of change in Organizational Learning Theory. Most of the major contributors describe two distinctive levels of change and differentiate between adapting current competencies or learning entirely new skills and capabilities. The late American business theorist Chris Argyris initially made a distinction between what he called single-loop and double-loop learning. Argyris later amplified the theory to relate it to organizational frames of reference. To Argyris, single-loop learning relates to immediate and routine matters, where the group improves its skills, doing better within its existing organizational values; double-loop learning involves adopting new competencies and operating outside preexisting policies and governing values.[34] This categorization matches well with our broader definition of military change, encompassing innovation with new competencies and changes to missions, values, and belief systems of a greater degree of novelty than adaptation requires.

Senge built on Argyris's concept, labeling the two levels as Adaptive versus Generative learning, with the former equated to merely coping and the latter as a creative response to the changing environment.[35] Other scholars make a distinction between lower- and higher-level learning.[36] Still others emphasize the scale of innovation by incremental learning, manifested by minor changes in behavior rather than by transformational learning represented by bolder changes.[37] Later in this chapter, in our discussion on the process of adaptation, this tiered concept will be central to the framework applied to the case studies.

Grissom has written off Organizational Learning Theory and its place in innovation studies as "mere information-gathering."[38] This critique, explicitly referring to the work of military historians Richard Downie and John Nagl, is understandable but incorrect. Both Downie and Nagl explicitly embraced Organizational Learning Theory, writing after Senge's *Fifth Discipline* had repopularized the theory. Downie stressed post-conflict learning and equated institutional learning with formal doctrinal publications. To Downie, doctrine was represented by institutional memory and learning. Although this suggests a focus on the accumulation of knowledge, Downie regards organizational learning not as a product but rather as "a process by which an organization uses new knowledge or understanding gained from experience or study to adjust institutional norms, doctrine, and procedures in ways designed to *minimize previous gaps in performance* and maximize future successes."[39] (Emphasis added.)

Grissom's dismissal of Organizational Learning Theory is understandable, given the way Downie and Nagl depicted the theory—as a deliberative, centralized, and top-down approach to organizational change. On detailed examination, however, Organizational Learning Theory is not just about information-gathering; it is also about knowledge creation and sharing. A learning organization is an entity that is continuously interacting with its environment, absorbing feedback and altering its routines, codes, and actions. It is one that is capable of using what it has learned to improve its performance. It is an institution that can learn from both its mistakes and successes by continually changing or self-organizing its structure, processes, and performance by better harvesting, interpreting, and applying knowledge for enhanced chances of success. The hallmark of any learning organization is a sustained capacity both to learn and change. It is more than mere information-gathering. In Garvin's terms, "Learning organizations are able to develop an organizational capacity for doing something new."[40] The emphasis on learning in Organizational Learning Theory is about changed behavior, not merely the acquisition of knowledge. Thus, it affords a framework for thinking about collective learning by organizations as they sense and respond to their environment.

Organizational Learning captures the processes that an organization uses to improve its performance through observation and experience. Converting that experience into improved levels of proficiency relative to the environment is the essence of adaptation. Organizational Learning Theory has been widely used by scholars seeking to refine prescriptions for faster organizational learning and enhanced performance by militaries.[41] Because of its basis in experiential learning and its ability to improve fitness from interaction with the external environment, it is clearly applicable to studies of military change.

Organizational Learning Capacity
Political scientist Herbert Simon once offered two stark options for organizational success. "If we want an organism or mechanism to behave effectively in a complex and changing environment," he noted, "we can design into it adaptive mechanisms that allow it to respond flexibly to the demands the environment places on it. Alternatively, we can try to simplify and stabilize the environment."[42] Since stabilizing the environment is beyond the scope of most institutions, being able to respond flexibly or adaptively becomes necessary for survival. Human institutions inevitably must find a balance-point between sustaining the capabilities and norms that served them in the past and adapting those skill-sets to meet emerging challenges. Can we identify and create adaptive mechanisms for military organizations that will help ensure organizational survival in the complex and changing environments that occur in wartime?

This book seeks to determine what makes some military organizations better able to change than others. This section synthesizes the existing literature on the process of organizational learning to better understand how change and adaptation occur in institutions. It begins by evaluating the learning process or cycle that is common in the Organizational Learning approach. It then seeks to define the attributes or mechanisms that can be designed into organizations that are engaged in armed conflict, to enhance their competitive performance. The discussion establishes a general theory about the utility of these mechanisms or attributes in abetting or retarding change within a military context.

Innovation theories from political scientists and the International Relations community focus on external sources and drivers of changes to military practice but largely overlook organizational processes or capacity for doing something new. Instead, they establish the *why* over the *how*. As a result, my intent is to develop a theory that bridges those questions and identifies the organizational factors and interaction that result in an increased capacity for learning and greater effectiveness.

Leveraging key elements of Organization Learning Theory, this book will develop, apply, and assess Organizational Learning Capacity.[43] This builds on quite a body of work in the management field as well as political scientist Michael C. Horowitz's Adoption Capacity Theory. Horowitz examines the spread or diffusion of new military innovations and argues that two factors affect a state's ability to absorb innovations—financial intensity and organizational capital for adoption. His Organizational Capital concept estimates the potential change capacity of a military organization. Horowitz defines organizational capital as "an intangible asset that allows organizations to change in response to perceived shifts in the underlying environment. For militaries, organizational capital represents *a virtual stockpile of change assets* needed to respond to changes in the character of warfare."[44]

Where Horowitz was interested in understanding why some actors are more successful than others in *adopting* the major military innovations of other states (emulation), this study focuses on why some actors are better than others at creatively developing and implementing new solutions on their own. Thus, the notion of change assets, coupled with an organizational culture inclined to test, assess, and implement novel solutions, is relevant. The concept of Organizational Capital can be extended and applied to studies of change within military organizations during wartime. This concept includes an organization's longevity (presumed to be more rigid with encultured mental frames), dedicated experimentation resources (indicative of an interest in new ideas), and focus (that is, how narrowly or broadly the institution defined its critical tasks). The more specialized or narrowly the organization defines its role or mission, the less interest or capacity is invested in possible change. This reflects a useful start point for exploring change assets and institutional capacity.

Whether a military organization can construct a more tangible capacity and process to alter its practices in relation to a dynamic environmental context is germane to this inquiry. Organizational Learning Theory presumes the creation of formal and informal learning mechanisms and suggests the possibility of creating a cultural ability (if not a predisposition) to learn, to change practices and routines, or to adapt to changing circumstances. Organizational Learning theorists recognize the "absorptive capacity" of organizations to develop and assimilate new knowledge and competencies.[45] Organizational Learning Capacity also is recognized in recent scholarship in military effectiveness by research professor Matthew Alan Tattar.[46] Tattar stresses the importance of "resources and the ability to undertake an organizational response," such as a dedicated "organizational sub-unit" to tackle the problem posed by adversary innovation. He notes that "without an effective organizational arrangement, an adapting military will likely flounder," and that "organizational structure affects every step of solving the adaptation problems, recognition, analysis, creation of a solution, and implementation of that solution."[47] The emphasis on creating specific cells or structured teams to help better understand a problem and to better understand potential solutions has promise but may not be sufficient in itself in initiating or implementing change.

To learn, organizations must be able to recognize problems, errors, or gaps in performance. It is one thing to be able to recognize the need to change and to envision possible solutions. Recognizing changes in the ever-evolving character of any conflict is a constant cognitive challenge.[48] It is an entirely different challenge to be able to design and implement that change at either the group or theater level or to institutionalize that new competency across the entire service if needed. The translation of novel ideas into new operational praxes involves two major tests and involves different functions that test the leadership of an organization with different challenges.[49]

This distinction—that recognition and response are the two institutional-level challenges, with different attributes or organizational characteristics—is key to taking advantage of organizational learning and translating the practice of learning into increased operational effectiveness.

Organizational Learning includes adjustments to extant institutional competencies or to entirely new functional competencies needed to resolve capability shortfalls. Organizations with high adaptation capacity exploit their organic learning capacity to resolve performance shortfalls, disseminate solutions, and institutionalize those solutions. This requires the ability to absorb, assess, and learn from the periphery of the organization into the formal decision-making process of an institution. If the required changes do not affect current norms, values, and competencies, such adaptation may be quickly absorbed and distributed. When completely new competencies are needed and basic core values and mental models are disturbed, learning must overcome resistance and organizational defense mechanisms.

Thus, for this book Organizational Learning Capacity is defined as "the aggregate ability of a military organization to recognize and respond to performance gaps generated by campaign pressures, unexpected adversary actions, or unanticipated aspects of the operating environment via adaptation or innovation." [50]

Institutions with such a high Organizational Learning Capacity invariably will have a discrete set of attributes or mechanisms that facilitate adaptation under fire. It may be a formal process driven externally or from the very top of the military hierarchy.[51] But learning either can take place at lower levels and flow upward or else can be facilitated by higher headquarters.[52] Others note the slow response of higher headquarters to absorb and institutionalize lessons derived from subordinate and lower-level sources.[53] Russell recently has demonstrated thoroughly the role of inputs and adaptations from tactical units in contemporary conflict, yet he concludes that tactical adaptation is necessary but not sufficient. Organizational Learning is exploiting the insights and initiatives at lower levels and doing it for the benefit of the larger institution. As military historian Peter Mansoor notes, "Unless the larger institution adapts, what you will have is individual units finding individual solutions, some of which might be right and some of which be wrong but none of which gets transferred. And so you end up learning the same lessons over and over again."[54]

Institutional Learning

Why do some organizations flourish over time and others flounder? Students of bureaucracies and military historians observe that history is littered with cases where military organizations faced defeat (if not extinction) as a result of rigid devotion to the present and their orthodoxies instead of exploring new ideas.[55]

Effectiveness over time requires the ability to learn and adapt to the evolving environment in some manner. Organizational theorists posit the need for institutions to continually balance two competing drives within an institution—exploitation and exploration.[56] Exploitation involves the application of current core competencies, while exploration involves the examination of new solutions or competencies. Any successful institution must address the balance of benefiting from its present skills and competencies while staying relevant to its external context by altering those competencies or learning new ones. The late political scientist James G. March noted, pessimistically, that "adaptation requires a balance between exploration and exploitation but is continually threatened by the tendency of each to extinguish the other."[57] This balance or tension must be a constant for organizations that cannot live solely in the present lest they risk ceding market share to those with new ideas and competitors. They must exploit their current competencies while being open to new ideas and opportunities as well.

Within the Organizational Learning literature, this need both to sustain relevant organizational skills and evolve additional competencies over time—to be ambidextrous, if you will—is well-established.[58] Most organizations contain a number of core competencies central to their success in their current vision of the operating environment. Bureaucracies cling to these competencies and task-sets, even in the face of repeated failure or obvious obsolescence. [59]

In a time of conflict, where information is ambiguous and where alternative solutions to performance shortfalls exist—such as improving execution, redeployment of assets, more leadership attention, or greater resources—institutions may persist in employing extant capabilities rather than building new ones. Yet, an overemphasis on exploitation of current skills and practice in the face of dynamic changes can result in existential challenges to a military organization—defeat in battle, or worse.

Alternatively, institutions will devote some resources to *exploration*. Exploration includes learning from experience and developing new routines, practices, or competencies. Exploration embraces the development of new methods requiring innovation—*higher-level learning* or *double-loop* learning. We now turn to examine exactly how this learning occurs.

Translating Learning Capacity into Competencies

The analytical framework for this research draws on a number of adaptation process cycles found in the Organizational Learning literature. Most theorists employ some sort of learning cycle to describe, test, and apply Organizational Learning Theory. Such models range from simple stimulus or reaction models to action or reaction cycles. This section begins with a discussion of a popular innovation or adaptation model. This model will be examined against new insights from the past decade of the Organizational Learning literature, as well as insights from military theorists, including military strategist John Boyd's observe, orient, decide, and act (OODA) loop construct and the Australian military version of that action and the *adaption* cycle.[60] Both of these military applications were grounded explicitly in Organizational Learning Theory. We then propose an alternative model with the hope of exploring what processes, functions, or attributes such organizations require to be adaptive. If learning organizations are organizations that embed learning mechanisms within an open and curious learning culture, then identifying and validating these learning mechanisms is useful.[61]

A well-known model has been employed by several U.S. scholars, including military historian Richard Downie in his post-conflict learning study.[62] The same model was leveraged by John Nagl in his comparison of British and American learning in *Counterinsurgency Lessons from Malaya and Vietnam*.[63] Nagl's study was a comparative analysis and focused on alteration of military practice during conflicts. Nagl's evaluation found that top-down changes from British senior officials produced a new plan and associated tactics to better address the insurgency in Malaya. Yet, their model does not recognize that learning may have to occur in numerous cycles of campaigns, battles, or engagements over a longer period of time rather than a single grand formal observation and learning period.[64]

Some theorists, such as Downie, stay at the macro or institutional level in describing organizational decision-making and behavior. But others believe that learning and change are best sourced at the lowest level of the organization and by individuals and small groups through a series of cyclical steps, continually testing ongoing programs or combat operations against the organization's values and tenets. These steps progressively incorporate and assess individual insights as consensus is built and transmitted on what norms, practices, or competencies need to be altered.

Like Downie, Nagl explicitly based his study on Organizational Learning Theory and concluded that the British had the better learning organization.

They learned from their experience in Malay and changed their in-country training, structures, and practices. Ultimately, their culture and leadership resulted in dramatically improved performance. "The British army was far better at making those changes than was the U.S. Army," Nagl observed.[65] Nagl does not identify mechanisms for this improved performance, but he does conclude that organizational culture was a decisive attribute. In contrast to Downie, Nagl focuses more on in-theater improvements during the conflict—what we call *operational adaptation*—while Downie concentrates on formal service-wide doctrinal changes that were made after the battle ended. This temporal dimension is important.

Operational adaptation, the focus of much interest in the U.S. Army and the larger joint military community now, is similarly focused. But such lower-level learning is insufficient if the acquired improved insights and practices remain isolated within a single tactical or operational entity. To have an impact on the structure, training, and mental preparation of follow-on units, operational success in sustained wartime operations must be shared and incorporated into larger or higher-level processes or else shared horizontally with other units, ships, or squadrons that are engaged in the same conflict.

Both scholars stress the *process* of assessing context, evaluating solutions, and adaptation, using the same generic model. Nagl incisively notes the directionality of learning, writing that "identifying organizational performance gaps in COIN [counterinsurgency] is a task most often performed by relatively junior officers . . . in close proximity to both the people threatened by the insurgency and the small military units most often engaging in pursuing the insurgents."[66] Downie, on the other hand, does not address directionality and presumes that higher authority must eventually create the consensus and approve doctrinal change.

This assessment also points out the need for a more nuanced understanding about the distinction between organizational learning "under fire" and institutional learning at home installations that are responsible for sustaining organizational performance and for preparing others for operational employment. A comprehensive theory would capture that and incorporate individual learning with a larger process of translating new knowledge into improved performance across the larger institution.

A Multilevel Model

There are models in the literature that avoid the mechanistic and hierarchical impression produced by Downie's model. One of these models from the Organizational Learning literature, developed by Canadian management specialist Mary Crossan, incorporates bottom-up learning from individuals with a transition to collective learning and eventually to the institutionalization of knowledge into actionable behavior. This framework is multilevel and dynamic and incorporates four distinct steps to capture the transition in learning from individuals to teams, larger groups, and the institution as a whole.

This model, known as the "4-I" framework, has not been employed in the military literature but it offers promise. The basic steps are detailed in the first column of table 2.2. The intuiting and interpreting steps of this approach fits well with the concept that problem-recognition, and problem-solving must begin with the individuals who recognize that a challenge or opportunity exists as a gap in performance. These men and women start to realize an impression based on their prior experience and on the organizational model or mental framework in which they have been trained. This intuition is then subjected to inputs from others on the team or staff as they begin engaging in a group discourse to explore and interpret the problem or performance gap.

Over a number of events—battles, campaigns, patrols, etc.—a shared understanding of the problem can emerge and the group begins to explore solutions. Over time, this process can generate lessons, ideas, and solutions that are fed forward to be integrated with supporting or enabling mechanisms—such as new hardware or weapons, training, and command-and-control systems. Crossan's model, however, takes a large leap between interpreting and integrating. It lacks any appreciation for the function of exploration or experimentation in developing solutions. For this reason, the step of *investigation* has been incorporated into this study's model.

Eventually, if exploration supports formal adaptation, the learning can be formally institutionalized—that is, fed back from the institution to the individual level through training and education, doctrine, and personnel changes. In military terms, formal doctrine, educational support systems, and appropriate incentives would be adjusted to reinforce, teach, and sustain the newly learned practices, changes to skill-sets, and improved organizational capability. In short, what was once an acknowledged problem has systemically become a new, recognizable, and sustained organizational response and a capacity to perform differently (although not always better). That institutionalization then serves as feedback to current and future individual members as they receive feedback regarding new norms, routines, practices, and related incentives or cues.

The Crossan model is compared to Downie's in table 2.2, along with the widely known Boyd OODA loop, for illustrative purposes. Boyd's theory was grounded in the importance of adaptation and explicitly based on Organizational Learning Theory.[67] The overall objective in conflict, Boyd asserted, is "to diminish the adversary's capacity to adapt, while improving our capacity to adapt as an organic whole."[68] As Dutch military studies professor Frans P. B. Osinga, evaluating Boyd's theory, concluded:

> Boyd's theory is about interacting *processes* of thought, about anticipation and feedback loops, about learning and adaptation, and about the fatal consequences of not learning or being constrained in one's efforts. The OODA loop stands for a process of learning, of evolving. Using this construct, the crux of winning rather than losing becomes the relational movement of opponents through their respective OODA loops, *their organizational learning and adaptation processes.*[69] (Emphasis added)

As shown in table 2.2 below, there is clearly a great degree of commonality in these approaches that can be synthesized. The synthesis used in this book is detailed in the final column, labeled as Synthesis. The first two steps, *inquiry* and *interpretation*, relate to problem recognition. These processes begin generally at the individual level, but they can include tactical commanders at the tactical and operational level. Ultimately, insights and increased comprehension about gaps between desired outcomes and organizational performance produce a recognized problem and set off a search for solutions. This search function is captured in the proposed third step, which is labeled *investigation*. In this step, the capacity to analyze, test, and refine possible solutions is incorporated as an explicit step. The *integration* task has been combined with *institutionalization*. The integration task has been combined with institutionalization since the coordinated integration of doctrine, training, and acquisition of new equipment involved in adapting is required to institutionalize change properly in a military organization.

Table 2.2. Alternative Learning Process Models

Crossan "4-I"	Downie/Nagl	Boyd	Synthesis
Intuit	Perception	Observe	Inquire
Interpret	Inquiry	Orient	Interpret
Integrate	Solution Consensus Building	Decide	Investigate
Institutionalize	Distribution	Act	Integrate & Institutionalize

This modified model seeks to overcome the criticisms levied at the Downie and Nagl approach and is detailed briefly below:

1. Inquire. In this stage, individuals at the tactical level collect observations from ongoing operations and experiences. They make comparisons of expectations to ongoing actions and operations, over time. They may initiate acts of discovery to confirm the initial experiences. This is an individual level of activity. Whether at the top or bottom, "organizations learn though individuals acting as agents for them."[70] The comparison between expectations and actual experience from the environment poses gaps or shortfalls. Gaps become the subject of inquiry and directed evidence-gathering at the unit leader and command level.

2. Interpret. Here both individuals and staffs try to reconcile expectations with actual measureable results. In interpretation, groups of individuals try to give meaning to collected inputs. This work can be achieved by commanders and traditional staff processes of assessment or by designated "learning teams" and may produce new metrics or measures of effectiveness. Organizational commanders may begin to seek adjustments to current competencies or efforts to increase capacity out of the current organization's repertoire.

3. Investigate. In the investigation stage, commands or units in the field begin reconciling desired outputs and results. This can also be conducted by experimentation with alternative practices, and commanders and staffs

in–theater or back at the institutional level begin evaluating proposed changes in the level of effort or additional resources. It may result in simple adjustments to extant doctrine or organizational and material means. At this point, organizations face the decision to continue exploiting existing practices in original or adapted form or begin the validation process for changing norms, practices, and techniques involved in double-loop learning. This step may require ad hoc or dedicated experimentation capacity to complete the investigation phase and gain consensus on solutions in order to improve performance. This stage can also involve engaging institutional leaders and their staffs outside of theater that are responsible for force-generation and for resources.

4. Integrate and Institutionalize. The formal creation of new competencies through the approval and distribution of doctrine and organizational changes, the establishment of educational and training programs, and the dissemination of lessons across the entire institution. This may include personnel changes and incentives to reinforce desired behaviors. The need to consider the integration of these, and the resources and timelines required for materiel (weapons, vehicles, and other military hardware), generally require institutional intervention and longer timelines.

A representation of the model is displayed in figure 2.1. The process represents the initiation of inquiry at the individual level and its processing up higher into the organization. It also reflects two loops of learning and change. The first cycle is single-loop learning, which is occurring at unit and command levels (represented in steps 1, 2, and 3a). The second is a slower and longer loop that reflects both the deeper investigation and higher authority generally required to investigate, decide, and institutionalize change at the larger institutional level (Army, Marine Corps, Navy, and Air Force). Both single-loop and double-loop changes go through an investigation phase, and both can be cycled up higher into the institution, where the revised competency and associated knowledge is integrated with other force-generation processes and institutionalized.

This model is consistent with the approaches of both Argyris and Senge. Argyris focuses his concepts around decision-making, more accurately the detection and correction of error.[71] Put another way, his theory of organizational

Figure 2.1. Organizational Adaptation Model

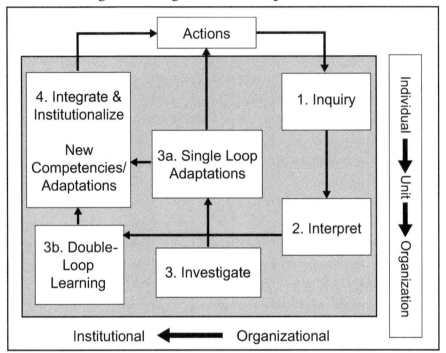

learning involves using information processing and problem-solving to close the gap between actual and desired capability. This is not at odds with military contexts. He notes that leaders and their teams face personal difficulties in acquiring and sharing information that could be uncomfortable to face up to, including errors and apparent failures. As a long-standing student of organizational behavior, Argyris was cognizant of barriers or what he called "defensive routines," which are dysfunctional behaviors or forms of resistance that act as "systems of denial," in the words of some scholars.[72] Another reason that Argyris is relevant is his finding that learning and changes in organizational effectiveness occur from collections of individuals acting in team or group settings. His theory depends on open leadership and team discourse to assess and test the prevailing assumptions or the "theory in action." What Senge called frames and mental models and what Argyris called "theories in use" inhibit double-loop learning, which has to be overcome by senior organizational leaders.[73] There are distinctions between the scholars who use dual-scale typologies, and this inquiry employs the single- versus double-loop distinction for consistency.[74]

Organizational Learning Theory-based studies can support our examination of both the scale or breadth of innovation (double-loop learning) and adaptation (single-loop learning). There are varied perspectives on these levels.[75] The proposed model incorporates the scale issue by indicating that bottom-up actions that do not alter the values or competencies of the institution can be quickly adjusted at local levels, but are not necessarily institutionalized or shared either vertically up the chain of command or horizontally to friendly units. This captures the numerous smaller forms of operational adaptation that take place in field units on the battlefield.

Enabling Attributes of Learning Organizations

Where recent efforts demonstrate how *external* drivers shape military adaptation during war, this study explores *internal* shapers that facilitate or inhibit adaptation and innovation—specifically, whether an organization can construct a more tangible adaptation capacity and process to change in response to unexpected developments in ongoing operations.[76] That requires us to define the factors that contribute to what Horowitz called "organizational capital"—that is, what this book calls Organizational Learning Capacity.

Since this book focuses on defining why some institutions are better than others at developing and implementing new solutions rapidly to increase their chances of battlefield success, an organizational model is merely a beginning. This model helps frame the process by which institutions recognize and respond to challenges that they did not anticipate. The delineation of the various process steps by itself helps our understanding, but it does not make adaptation more likely or more successful. Each step of the process—and every individual within the process—is influenced by the character of the institution and the culture, perspectives, and mental models that are encoded by that military service. Moreover, each step in the process of adaptation has supporting attributes or mechanisms needed to make change possible.

These attributes or mechanisms—processes, staff elements, and educational systems—comprise political scientist Michael Horowitz's "stockpile of change assets" that organizations must possess to evolve, survive, and prosper. The innovation literature presents some insights on critical factors and processes to abet innovation, particularly resources for experimentation. But the military literature is much thinner on other institutional mechanisms that retard or enable adaptive behavior. Organizational Theory once again offers insights into the enabling conditions or facilitating factors that support adaptation.[77] Such facilitating factors or enabling conditions promote learning in the organizational context. The more that each is present, the greater the odds that learning and effective adaptation will occur. Collectively, these represent the organization's potential capacity for learning.

The Organizational Learning Theory and Military Adaptation literature have not ignored institutional attributes, and in fact show a strong correlation about the most critical factors. In this work, these attributes include leadership, organizational culture, learning mechanisms, and dissemination mechanisms.

This section examines the literature and defines those attributes and factors to justify their incorporation into an analytical framework.

Leadership

The most clearly noted attribute or variable in the literature involves the role played by leaders. Past theorists have recognized the role of leaders as designers and stewards of the adaptation process.[78] Whether civilian policymakers working from Downing Street, Whitehall, or the White House, or military leaders atop or in the bowels of the bureaucracy, strong leadership working to identify and resolve potential or actual performance shortfalls is the dominant characteristic of successful innovation. Posen contends that civilian leaders are principally responsible for this function, at the behest of the state's security interests. Rosen argues the opposite—that in his cases of major innovation, military leaders are the major actors responsible for initiating innovation ideas and bringing about a change in effectiveness. Their principal function is to choose credible leaders at lower levels and to generate alternative career paths to abet major innovations.[79] Posen would admit that necessary technical information and credibility can come from military "mavericks" willing to work inside and outside the normal bureaucracy to advance new military capabilities.[80]

The Interservice Competition school suggests that leaders need only identify key mission areas for institutional gain to acquire resources and abet the development of new competencies. All the centralized and top-down theories emphasize the role of great captains or influential civilians in driving change; British military figures J. F. C. Fuller, Basil Liddell Hart, Hugh Trenchard, and Hugh Dowding, and German general Heinz Guderian, etc., demonstrate the "great man" theory of innovation, which focuses on the role of a singular senior leader as the driving force behind a major change.

Organizational Learning theory is thin on the role of institutional leaders. For Senge, leaders are designers of learning processes, teachers, and stewards of an organization's prevailing frames or mental models.[81] Senge emphasized the role of creating a "shared vision," and Garvin argued that the ultimate role of leadership is to create a learning organization "skilled at creating, acquiring, and transferring knowledge, and at modifying its behavior to reflect new knowledge and insights."[82] The study of strategic leadership and organizational learning has been disconnected in the past, but should not be. Leadership and organizational learning are disconnected and overly focused at the very top of the organization.[83] In truth, leaders have a role in promoting learning at each level of the institution.

The literature is mixed on where the locus of leadership resides during wartime innovation. Doubler and British historian Paul Kennedy find evidence of leadership involvement at lower and medium levels of the force, including bottom-up, from World War II cases, as when the U.S. Army faced tenacious German defenses in the Battle of Villers-Bocage in Normandy.[84] "All throughout the First Army during June and July," Doubler found that "officers, NCOs, and enlisted men contemplated methods to overcome the German defense."[85] Doubler shows how bottom-up ideas from junior officers and enlisted personnel were quickly pushed up to the division and to Army Gen. Omar Bradley and the Joint Chiefs of Staff, for support. The Americans placed no restrictions on where they got good ideas, and they were decentralized and non-directive in terms of best practices: ideas were generated from the bottom up but moved rapidly in both the vertical and horizontal directions.[86]

Of interest, military historian Robert T. Foley suggests that strong leadership roles or "ownership" of original solutions impedes the adoption of adaptations and their dissemination.[87] A decentralized approach delegates authority for solutions to lower levels, where ideas can be rapidly discovered and implemented. Doubler reinforces this point from his study of U.S. Army adaptation in Normandy in 1944:

The Battle of the Bulge in 1944–45 illustrates one of the great advantages of a decentralized approach to organizational adaption—the rapid development of solutions to immediate, unexpected problems. Soldiers learned and adapted in combat during a period of great uncertainty and confusion, and their capacity for independent thinking in action served the Army well during the December battles.[88]

Reinforcing Doubler's research, Murray and Finkel both emphasize decentralized command as well, in order to maximize inputs and minimize time lags in trying new ideas.[89]

Additionally, more current research suggests that a personal leadership attribute of openness is invaluable. This is manifested in a strong intellectual curiosity, creativity, and a degree of comfort with novelty and variety. Leaders high in openness search for relevant and conflicting perspectives.[90] The Organizational Learning Theory literature also emphasizes openness, as well as the creation of climates of openness in work environments, where problem-solving is shared and inputs valued.[91] This study hypothesizes that leaders who embrace a more decentralized mode of command style, exhibit personal openness, and cultivate a climate of evidenced-based inquiry will be better at adaptation.

Organizational Culture

The role of strategic culture is widely contested in International Relations Theory, but the narrower construct of institutional or organizational culture is less controversial.[92] While strategic culture may be germane to the conduct of combat operations and may shape learning, this book is oriented on the organic capacity to adapt and innovate, and organizational culture is appropriately within the scope of this inquiry.

Several scholars emphasize the importance of culture and its impact on how organizations innovate or adapt. Murray went so far as to observe, "Military culture may be the most important factor not only in military effectiveness, but also in the processes involved in military innovation."[93] There are numerous definitions of culture, including American psychologist Edgar Schein's suggestion: "A pattern of shared basic assumptions that the group learned as it solved its problems, that has worked well enough to be considered valid, and is passed on to new members as the correct way to perceive, think, and feel in relation to those problems."[94] Schein later emphasized that this pattern of assumptions are "invented, discovered or developed by a given group as it learns" and that these are "taught to new members as the correct way to perceive, think and feel."[95]

Theo Farrell's definition is the most concise and will be the basis in this book's study of the contributions that culture makes: "Organizational [C]ulture consists of beliefs, symbols, rituals and practices which give meaning to the activity of an organization."[96] Murray defines military culture similarly as representing "the ethos and professional attributes, both in terms of experience and intellectual study that contribute to a common core understanding of the nature of war within military organizations."[97] This matches Schein's view that "culture is what a group learns over a period of time as that group solves its problems of survival in an external environment and its problems of internal integration."[98] Culture is a well-recognized filter or barrier to innovation in bureaucratic organizations. The notion of culture as a set of beliefs and values that are inculcated into members of a professional military organization has obvious implications when it comes to their outlook on preparing for war and conducting military operations. However, the major innovation approaches that are based in political science tend to overlook it. Political scientist Elizabeth Kier has injected organizational or military culture into her study of peacetime innovation.[99] Numerous other scholars stress the importance of culture when it comes to changing military organizations and their practices.[100]

The notion that a military service has a distinctive set of values that create its personality or DNA and that this frames its mental framework on organizational purpose and performance is fairly well-accepted and understood.[101] Culture is not a driver or a prescriptive barrier, but it does serve as a prism for how organizations view problems and establishes limits to acceptable solutions. Thus, culture cuts both ways: it can be both a barrier and a facilitator of change and adaptation.[102] Any theory will have to take account of how policymakers or institutional leaders have crafted changes to culture or worked to overcome cultural barriers.[103]

Other Organizational Learning-based studies recognize that learning depends heavily on the culture variable. Nagl's emphasis is notable: The organizational culture of military forces is a decisive determinant in their effectiveness and helps to determine the course of international politics. The ability of military organizations to adapt to change is an important component of a state's ability to guarantee its own security.[104]

The internalized character of service institutions also influences their ability to consider new practices and, thus, adapt under fire. "A service's culture is a complex aggregate of its attitudes toward a variety of issues including its role in war, its promotion system, its relation to other services, and its place in the society it serves," write military historians Harold R. Winton and David R. Mets.[105]

The literature suggests that certain cultural factors explain the greater flexibility and adaptability of military organizations—a finding contained in numerous studies of U.S. and German militaries in combat.[106] Hart argues that prevailing U.S. military culture profoundly influenced institutional capacity to adapt in World War II, and that the Americans exhibited a managerial and scientific approach to war that positively affected their ability to solve problems with speed, while the Germans demonstrated their value of individual initiative and flexible command tradition.[107] Students of German military history credit their culture with supporting an ethos of critical thinking and analysis within the concept of *ausbildung* (professional development).[108] Murray and Millett's work in military innovation during peacetime certainly supports the notion that climates of critical thinking, intellectual curiosity, and objective analysis are key to supporting the rigorous evaluation of innovative doctrine or supporting weapons systems.[109] Such cultural attributes can be crucial for the consensus-building that is necessary for any significant shift in institutional beliefs and values that undergird the cohesion and identity of a military institution.

Defense studies scholar Carl H. Builder's notion that a military service has a "mask" that it puts on to face the world is also relevant to understanding what a military service thinks of itself and what it values and rewards.[110] His analytical framework of these five elements offers some utility and will be employed in this book:

1. What characteristics and icons do they value as "altars for worship?"
2. What inputs or outputs do they self-measure?
3. The focus in the institution between hardware or technology and people, or "toys versus the arts" of war.

4. The degree and extent of intraservice or branch distinction.

5. The degree of insecurity about service legitimacy and relevancy.

Military institutions are not monolithic; they do not necessarily all wear the same mask; and within each service there may be sub-schools or "tribes." Military historian Brian M. Linn has identified three specific archetypes or sub-schools within the Army.[111] Both the Navy and Air Force have branches with distinctive subcultures, uniforms, and rituals that mark each branch—such as surface fleet, submarines, fighter pilots, and support personnel.

Within the potential range of influences that culture imposes is the degree of hierarchy and control within an organization, whether it frames its mission and purpose very narrowly, whether it exerts expectations about conformity and compliance with rules, routines, and operational praxes, and how rigid and narrow its doctrine is. Highly centralized and controlling cultures do not generate the conditions for creative problem-solving.

An organizational culture inclined to test, assess, and implement novel solutions is most relevant, and the literature in both military innovation and learning theory recognizes the powerful influence of culture. Thus, while the influence of organizational culture is difficult to isolate, it will be examined in this book.

Learning Mechanisms

An adaptive culture capable of inquiry and demonstrating some curiosity must be augmented with mechanisms that help leaders and operational commanders make sense of ongoing operations. As Murray has argued, "Without a coherent system of analyzing what is actually happening, military organizations have no means of adapting to the conditions they face except doggedly to impose assumptions on reality or, even more dubiously, to adapt by guessing."[112] In reviewing the literature, I identified a number of learning mechanisms involving special personnel, after-action reporting, and structured staff for investigations as potential examples of such mechanisms.

In peacetime, experimentation and gaming are employed to explore the unknown. Although time during ongoing combat operations is a precious commodity, there is evidence that the need for investigation and even experimentation continues on during war. But structures and processes must enable an institution or its fighting forces to conduct an exploration in the present tense and not just the future. Peacetime innovation has been correlated with cultures of critical inquiry augmented by these exercises and experiments. Success in the interwar era was certainly achieved by a rigorous exploration of options through live experiments of various scale.[113] In wartime, however, the laboratory is moved to the battlefield and success depends on being able to sense, interpret, and respond faster than the opponent can. Not all of the experimentation will be conducted in a centralized manner by the larger institution—it can and has been generated on the battlefield by training or operational units "in contact."[114]

History shows a pattern of World War II operational commanders benefiting from teams of operations research analysts (or technical "boffins") to help think through the operational challenges they face. The British began this practice in coming to grips with the Luftwaffe and the U-boat challenge.[115] The practice of employing technical and quantitative analysis came across the Atlantic in short order. Subsequently, the American naval commander, Adm. Ernest J. King, turned to operational analysis to support his antisubmarine warfare challenges in the North Atlantic. Ultimately, in April 1942, the Navy stood up the Antisubmarine Warfare Operations Research Group, or ASWORG, led by physicist Philip Morse. This became the first official operations research entity in the United States. It was responsible for helping Admiral King and the Navy understand the enemy's tactics and capabilities. It also helped devise, test, and refine submarine tactics, as well as best practices for sonar and convoy techniques.

By August of 1942, ASWORG was making a real contribution.[116] After the war, King, then a Fleet Admiral, credited the operations research group with recommendations that "increased the effectiveness of weapons by factors of three or five."[117] In fact, King found this learning and research support critical to success:

In the see-saw of techniques the side which countered quickly, before the opponent had time to perfect the new tactics and weapons, offered a decided advantage. Operations research, bringing scientists in to analyze the technical import of the fluctuations between measure and countermeasure, made it possible to speed up our reaction rate in several critical cases.[118]

Working at lower levels and within a decentralized command style did not always succeed when it came to larger challenges, such as effective planning of combined arms and the introduction of close air support. Here, more top-down and integrated investigation was needed. But Doubler makes it clear in his assessment that the Army "used a more informal approach that eschewed centralized control" and instead exploited an "entrepreneurial spirit" that pragmatically absorbed potential solutions from credible sources.[119]

This practice of formally involving technical experts in operations research has been institutionalized in most military organizations. Much of this analytical capacity was miscast in contemporary conflicts, since it was devoted to traditional military missions and physical inputs and outputs, which were largely irrelevant to the kinds of complex sociopolitical considerations that pertain in insurgencies. But military organizations are now routinely equipped with such staff assistance. Of late, there has been a recognized military-wide shortfall in staff activity related to "red-teaming" adversary reactions. In response to this shortfall, the Army has established a course dedicated to educating a cadre of staff officers in how best to test and critique operational plans from an adversary's perspective.[120] The course helps commanders anticipate opponent reactions in both their planning and assessments. Formal government studies in the United States suggest that this function will take on increased urgency in the future.[121] In our cases, we will test for this element to see whether it is supportive of adaptation in varied circumstances.

During World War II, armies and navies began the formal collection of after-action reports, often labeled as "lessons-learned" or tactical bulletins, to collect and synthesize best practices. The Germans had required such processes going back to World War I, when *erfahrungsberichte* (lessons-learned reports) were required and were readily seized on by operating units, not just the general staff.[122] Doubler believes that the U.S. Army absorbed the same orientation in World War II. "Perhaps the greatest lesson the Army learned from World War II was that the learning process itself is an integral part of any conflict and can spell the difference between victory and defeat," he writes.[123] In the proposed Organizational Learning model, the after-action process is considered a potentially invaluable learning mechanism to support the process of *interpretation*.

Finally, structural adaptation or the use of special task forces should also be considered a learning mechanism.[124] Some historical examples, including the development of infiltration tactics by the German army, were facilitated by designating special units for experimental tactics. Some other examples with the Israeli Defense Force also have used designated units as incubators to test new ideas and create knowledge under operational conditions.[125] These kinds of units provide "proof" and generate internal political consensus for the diffusion of new ideas, particularly when the search for solutions reaches the point of new competencies and innovation in wartime. Such mechanisms will be explored for their contribution to the *investigation* function in the organizational learning cycles in the four cases studied herein.

Dissemination Mechanisms

After a military organization has experienced combat operations for a time, it begins to gather information about the conduct of operations, the geography, and the geometry of the competition and create an assessment of where it own forces stand in relation to the real context of the environment. If the *interpretation* phase produces insights, commanders often try to share the gaps and solutions across the enterprise, both vertically up the chain of command, and ideally, horizontally to other members of the service.

Most military organizations have entities and processes dedicated to this function. The Organizational Learning literature extensively covers techniques about gathering, storing, and sharing knowledge. Within the military *innovation* literature the focus is on the production of doctrine and on lessons learned. Much of this information is gained in-theater and distributed both to enhance ongoing operations and to generate follow-on units. In wartime there is a need to rapidly acquire, process, and distribute new tactical lessons and techniques to units that have not yet experienced combat.[126]

Foley recognized this element in German adaptation in World War I, where experiments and tactical experiences were quickly shared horizontally.[127] During World War II this appears to have been a standard practice in the U.S. Navy. To enhance their effectiveness against German U-boats, the Allies sponsored a number of information-sharing conferences and bulletins to exchange information about the changing submarine threat.[128] In addition, after a less-than-spectacular success against Japanese naval surface forces near Guadalcanal, one commander pulled back his forces for two weeks, studied the most recent battle, and put out a consolidated pamphlet on night-fighting that materially aided the performance of U.S. naval forces in the next battle.[129]

Dissemination of new ideas was a constant to the U.S. Army as well. As Doubler noted:

> If the army excelled in tactical and technical improvisation, it performed equally well in disseminating new ideas and lessons learned. Formal and informal channels carried information between units. Within battalions and regiments, new ideas probably traveled best by word of mouth. Divisions constantly produced training bulletins to get information to soldiers about methods and techniques that worked well in battle.[130]

These bulletins were issued in a number of formats, including the first Army *Battle Experiences* booklets. These ultimately have grown over time into formal historical after-action reports, often produced by large staffs and historians, as well as modern lessons-learned systems. The lessons that were produced were more "observed" than learned. Some modern examples suggest that the requirement to acquire and distribute fresh insights is not universally recognized. Osinga and Russell report limited lessons gathering and dissemination capacity in German and Dutch units in Afghanistan, further reinforced by rigid military cultures.[131]

The role of informal networks is more prominent in recent studies and is worth considering in supporting the rapid transfer of new knowledge.[132] In modern conflicts, tactical leaders have begun sharing horizontally through computer and internet-based learning systems, with or without institutional approval.[133] The efficacy of these networked systems is seen by junior officers as highly beneficial, even though this is not always appreciated by higher echelons that want to control changes to techniques and praxes.

Until now, the dissemination mechanisms have dealt with in-theater methods of transmitting new tactics or insights from operational or tactical adaptations. But the military services also have potent institutional-level systems of education and training that can absorb adaptations into the formal doctrine and learning processes of the military. The longer a war endures, the more important it is to feed battlefield lessons back to the classrooms and exercises of future leaders and their units so that they are better prepared than their predecessors. More important, for lessons to be truly learned they have to be institutionalized, not just perpetually relearned at bloody expense on the battlefield.

The essence of Organizational Learning Theory is to turn the acquisition, management, and sharing of knowledge into new organizational competencies. Hence, any sound theory must incorporate this into the institution. This book hypothesizes that the dissemination of new techniques and practices is a major contributor to Organizational Learning Capacity. It is a critical capacity of Organizational Learning, the rapid sharing of ideas and the distribution of new knowledge. Too often lessons identified are not shared or absorbed beyond the operational or tactical unit that observed or experimented with creative solutions. Thus, operational knowledge and lessons-learned efforts that collect and share information have implications for military organizations.[134] We expect to show that adaptive organizations exploit methods to routinely capture lessons from current operations for use in rapid horizontal sharing. In recent years, the U.S. Army and British military have evolved more systematic learning-collection methods to facilitate learning and institutionalization of better practices.[135]

Although recent scholarship notes the value and historic roots of horizontal sharing, modern information technology tools can now ensure a faster and more consistent diffusion of knowledge and enhanced praxis both horizontally and vertically.[136]

Collectively these four attributes or facilitators constitute the most important elements of Organizational Learning Capacity and the execution of the discrete steps of the learning cycle adapted for this study.

Conclusion

This chapter presented both a theory and process model of military adaptation. It argued for greater consideration of Organizational Learning Theory to establish an analytical framework. The proposed model is not original but rather is predicated on a multidisciplinary synthesis of the Organizational Learning literature by several theorists and military historians. This diagnostic tool can be used to assess case studies and to analyze the processes that an organization employs to change appropriately in response to alterations in its environment or identified performance gaps.

A better understanding of the process by which institutions have learned and changed in the past in the competition of combat should be illuminating. It should shed light on the institutional attributes that facilitate the process of adaptation. Some military organizations mastered this competition in the past and, if history offers any lessons, institutional "adaptivity" will be an enduring contributor to success in future war. This dynamic model captures the role of leaders, the influence of culture, and the process of transitioning information and lessons from knowledge to professional practice and application.

We now turn to our case histories to begin trying to test that model.

CHAPTER 3

Adapting under the Sea

The U.S. Submarine Offensive in World War II

As the captain squinted through his periscope, he could hardly contain his emotion. His primitive radar alerted him to three large blips, and he maneuvered closer to a good position to attack. Before him loomed three huge Japanese ships, perhaps two aircraft carriers and an oceangoing freighter. Lt. Cdr. John A. Scott, commanding officer of the USS *Tunny* (SS 282), was about to sink his first enemy warship. He identified the bigger target as the Japanese carrier *Hiyo*. He had a perfect firing position, with a range of less than one thousand yards. He quietly gave commands to prepare to fire.[1]

Years of education, training, and wargaming were about to be unleashed on the unsuspecting Japanese. Here was an opportunity of which many a sub skipper had dreamed: sitting undetected in the midst of enemy carriers. Sandwiched between two major targets, Scott might well become famous in naval annals if he could capitalize on this chance. He decided to fire all six bow tubes at the larger carrier, and the four stern tubes at the other one. It was almost a textbook firing situation, one that he had worked out a hundred times in drills.

Scott focused on the closest carrier. He tersely ordered, "Fire one! Fire two!" A slight rushing sound, and two torpedoes raced off to their target, a little over eight hundred yards off. Scott ordered another two torpedoes fired to ensure that the entire periscope image of the *Hiyo* would be covered. At this range, it was impossible to miss. The radarman reported that all four torpedoes were running "hot and true." The *Tunny*'s executive officer looked at his stopwatch to estimate the running time it would take until they would hear the explosions that would signify success. Scott fired four torpedoes at the next carrier. The first set completed their short run, and the entire crew of the *Tunny* heard four detonations. A number of other explosions indicated hits on the second target. Within minutes Scott had shot ten torpedoes at two ships and believed he had heard seven hits. The crew was elated, and Scott dived to avoid the escorts.[2]

But success was not his. The three carriers, the *Hiyō*, the *Jun'yō*, and the escort carrier *Taiyō*, escaped that night. Although the *Taiyō* was slightly damaged, the warships did not even slow their speed. Later, intelligence interceptions from Japanese transmissions reported that six of the seven explosions were premature—about fifty meters short of the target. Faulty torpedoes had denied Scott and his crew a great victory.

The *Tunny*'s ability to launch a surprise undersea attack against enemy warships was the sort of situation that the U.S. Navy had imagined as a possible role for its submarines in World War II. Two generations of naval officers had prepared to prevail against the Imperial Japanese Navy from 1907 to 1941, focusing their efforts on creating a war plan to defeat the Empire of Japan at sea. They considered submarines useful as scouts, valuable in screening for the fleet, and good for occasionally ambushing Japanese combatants, as the *Tunny* did in her missed opportunity. But submarines were just a smaller part of a powerful fleet design that the Navy planned to use to ensure victory if and when war broke out.

After the Japanese attack on Pearl Harbor on December 7, 1941, the Navy had the opportunity to demonstrate that its longstanding preparations for such a contest were suited to the actual character of the conflict. But the *Tunny*'s story demonstrated that in key respects, the service was not nearly as prepared as it could have been, and that it would need to adapt. Overall, the interwar Navy was a complex adaptive system that promoted evolution and initiative in response to dramatic changes in its external environment. Its capacity for adaptability and fail-safe experimentation set the path for its future success.[3] This case study presents why and how that adaptation was brought about.

Strategic Context and Interwar Plans

To appreciate the degree of adaptation that occurred in the Pacific in World War II, one must understand the strategic planning that preceded the war. A joint military planning board developed U.S. plans for potential contingencies against possible opponents.[4] More than a dozen such plans existed—color-coded with red for England, black for Germany, etc. But from the beginning, Navy planners focused on the possibility of a war against Japan—the so-called War Plan Orange.[5] The U.S. focus was on how to counter Japan's empire. The planning evolved over time, producing a lot of debate and many iterations about how a war in the Pacific could best be won. For more than three decades, America's finest strategic and military minds labored over the tyranny of time and distance in a war against Japan. War Plan Orange was not the only plan, but it was the Navy's principal framework for thinking about the future.

Although the planners lacked policy guidance from the nation's civilian leaders, both the Army and the Navy recognized the difficulties of a transpacific test of arms. The vast geography and lack of supporting bases and infrastructure were particularly challenging. Much of the naval planning was influenced by the theories of early twentieth-century U.S. naval strategist Alfred Thayer Mahan and his belief that a war against Japan would be decided by a clash of capital ships.[6] At the same time, planners recognized that setting the stage for such a clash required the development of a capable naval aviation component, as well as logistical bases seized by amphibious forces to support a long campaign.[7] Over many debates and revisions, the culminating phase invariably began with a major battle between the opposing fleets, followed by "a progressively tightening blockade that would sever Japanese oceanic trade."[8] The end-state in all versions of the plan was a blockade that would choke off Japan's economy.

The interwar planning effort was extensive and involved various planning staffs from the Navy and Army arguing about the relative merits of different approaches to gain U.S. objectives. Throughout the 1930s, the Navy staff naturally had focused on the Pacific and its preferred Orange Plan. Not surprisingly, the Army and Navy had disagreements on the relative merits of different strategic concepts to defend the Pacific. As events in Europe turned bad in 1938 and 1939—with British prime minister Neville Chamberlain's deal with German führer Adolf Hitler, the seizure of Czechoslovakia, attacks on Norway, and the invasion of Poland—U.S. military strategists decided that they needed to coordinate more closely and to provide for clear guidance about Washington's priorities. American planners also recognized the potential for global war, including Europe, and the necessity of employing coalition warfare against an enemy alliance.[9]

To keep up with geopolitical shifts and the uncertainty regarding U.S. policy, the Joint Planning Committee was tasked with formulating a fresh set of plans, called the "Rainbow" plans. These contained specific and more detailed prescriptions for addressing different combinations of allies and adversaries. Initial priority was given to Rainbow 1, a defensive plan completed in October of 1939, which centered on American fighting alone to defend the United States and the Western hemisphere.[10]

Each new Rainbow plan was impacted by real-world events in Europe. In Rainbow 3, the Navy's Plan Orange would be the centerpiece after the Western hemisphere was secured. In this scenario, a surge of submarines would deploy out of Hawaii to seek out significant Japanese naval targets and to screen U.S.-held islands and bases. Rainbow 3 was displaced by a new urgent need to readdress American priorities after the fall of France in the summer of 1940. Some naval forces were redirected to the Atlantic, which made major naval operations in the Pacific risky, if not impossible to execute. This propelled the rapid development of Rainbow 4, approved by President Franklin Delano Roosevelt on August 14, 1940.[11] That plan retained a strong defensive orientation.

Rainbow 5 was developed last, and initially assumed that the United States was part of an alliance with Great Britain and was predicated on a Europe-first priority. The final version of Rainbow 5 (modified), approved by the president less than a month before Pearl Harbor, retained the defeat of Germany as the first priority, but also assigned the Navy with missions in both oceans. In the Pacific, the Navy was tasked to divert Axis strength away from the Malay Barrier through capture of the Marshall Islands and raids on Japanese sea communications. The second task hinted at events to come: "Destroy Axis sea communications by capturing or destroying vessels trading directly or indirectly with the enemy."[12]

Wargames and Exercises
In the interwar era, the U.S. Naval War College, with its distinguished faculty and students, played a key role in testing the assumptions and parameters of Plan Orange. It conducted 136 wargames at the strategic and operational level, using

the floor of the gaming center at Sims Hall in Newport.[13] Some 97 percent of these games were played against Plan Orange. From this focus emerged a clear grasp of the geopolitical and military realities of war in the Pacific. Over time, the gaming produced a mental model of how such a war would be fought, and what the Navy's role would be. As a result of the games, War Plan Orange was "genetically encoded" into the Navy's thought processes and belief system.[14] Wargaming Plan Orange became part of a liturgy that was drummed into the Navy's officer corps and into its operational culture.[15]

Submarines did not play a significant part in the Newport wargames. The undersea boats were to be used as scouts, to identify the enemy's battle fleet so the dreadnoughts or the new carriers could attack.[16] Given the limits of international law regarding commercial shipping, more aggressive thinking about using submarines against Japan's merchant fleet or resources did not find traction until the Pacific war loomed near. Gaming suggested that attacks on trade would not be decisive, but that they could impose costs on the Japanese navy and force it to detach its naval and air power to defend Japan's lines of communication.[17] To be sure, overall submarines were not ignored, and many games reflected the use of submarines as part of a balanced fleet approach.[18] In truth, however, since Mahan eschewed war against commerce or *guerre de course* in his lectures, one would not have expected significant roles for submarines. Mahan's ghost haunted the lecture halls at Newport, which was imbued with his views about a concentrated battle fleet and archetypal "decisive battles."[19]

Part of the cultural encoding of the Navy's way of war was conducted by large-scale annual exercises that served to link strategic vision and innovation with the realities faced by fleet commanders. The interaction between the fleet and the Naval War College served to test innovative ideas between theorists, strategists, and operators. A tight process of concepts, simulation, and exercises with actual forces served to link innovative ideas with the realities of naval warfare. The exercises in the fleet, conceptually framed by the wargames in Sims Hall, became the "enforcers of strategic realism."[20] They also were enforcing and reinforcing the Navy's mental model of what war at sea entailed and the belief systems that the Navy held most dear. This mental model would frame the roles of various branches of the Navy.[21]

The Navy's fleet exercises were a combination of training and experimentation in innovative tactics and technologies.[22] Held once a year, they were designed to confront a clear and explicit operational problem but were conducted under free-play or unscripted conditions. Rules were established for evaluating performance and effectiveness, and umpires were assigned to regulate the contest and gauge success. The events were bounded by the rule set and supervised by senior umpires. Brutally candid post-exercise critiques occurred, in open forums and in published reports, in which junior and senior officers examined moves and countermoves. The system reflected the Navy's culture of tackling operational problems in an intellectual and transparent manner.

These fleet problems reinforced the Navy's impressive learning culture and its extensive set of components. The free-play battle exercises were a form of investigation in peacetime, where fleet performance and decision-making were rigorously explored, critiqued, and ultimately refined.[23] The Navy benefited from the low-cost experimentation that relied on gaming and exercises.[24] The activities formed the principal elements of the Navy's learning system, which promoted detailed and collective study in an open and collaborative manner.[25]

Naturally, the training exercises focused on the Navy's principal challenge—a war against Japan. Just as in Newport, Plan Orange was the usual context for the maneuvers.[26] More than the games at Newport, they provided the service's operational leaders with a realistic laboratory in which participants maneuvered steel ships at sea instead of using cardboard ships on the floor at Newport. Just like Newport's games, the waterborne exercises "provided a medium that facilitated the transmission of lessons learned, nurtured organizational memory, and reinforced the Navy's organizational ethos."[27] But they also enforced some unrealistic conclusions about submarines. Due to safety concerns, the submarines were assigned entirely to one side of the problem, leaving the opposing fleet with imaginary submarines to eliminate the chance of collisions. Operating at night was deemed unsafe, and night attack training was nonexistent.[28]

Moreover, a widespread belief that aircraft could easily detect submarines limited an accurate appreciation for what the boats could contribute and impeded the development of submarine tactics. The importance of avoiding detection became paramount. In the run-up to the war, the Asiatic Squadron commander threatened to relieve any commanding officers of subs whose periscopes were sighted in exercises or drills.[29] This led to a reliance on submerged attack techniques that required submarine commanders to identify and attack target ships from underwater, based entirely on sound-bearings. Given the poor quality of sound detection and sonar technologies of the time, this was a precariously limited tactic of dubious effectiveness.

Overall, the exercises and constrictions induced a degree of conservative tactics and risk-avoidance that was at odds with what the Navy would eventually need. As military historian Craig C. Felker wrote:

> Submarines were to be confined to serving as scouts and "ambushers." They were placed under restrictive operating conditions when exercising with surface ships. Years of neglect led to the erosion of tactical expertise and the "calculated recklessness" needed in a successful submarine commander. In its place emerged a pandemic of excessive cautiousness, which spread from the operational realm into the psychology of the submarine community.[30]

The peacetime limits governing employment of undersea vessels severely limited Navy submarines' offensive operations in the early part of World War II.[31] The submarine community's official history found that the "lack of night experience saddled the American submariners entering the war with a heavy cargo of unsolved combat problems."[32] That baggage would create the need for urgent adaptation from the very start of the war.

Ultimately, when conflict began to look likely, with a correlation of forces not in America's favor, students and faculty members at Newport broached the need to use the submarine's offensive striking power to attack Japan's merchant marine.[33] Unrestricted warfare against commercial shipping had been considered illegal, with little consideration given to targeting the critical resources of which Japan was striving to gain control. During the spring semester of 1939, strategists at Newport argued for the establishment of "war zones" around the fleet as soon as war began. The zones were a form of diplomatic exclusion zone, ostensibly to support fleet defense during war. However, it is clear that the proponents' intent was to conduct unrestricted warfare aimed at Japan's trade vulnerabilities.[34]

This was a change to earlier versions of War Plan Orange—one that changed the underlying mental framework under which the fleet and the submarine force operated. However, the Navy did not act on the implications of this change in the brief period before Pearl Harbor—a factor that helped create the conditions that would force operational adaptation under fire later. The crucible of combat in 1941 would be the ultimate confirmation of the Navy's plans, games, and exercises.

Submarine Developments

The Navy had a superior organizational approach to designing and refining its fleet. Strategic plans were analytically developed and thoroughly tested by students and strategists at the Naval War College in iterations of wargames conducted over two decades. These plans and games produced an understanding of the strategic and operational context of future campaigns, as well as the kind of Navy that was needed to execute the plans. A senior group of naval officers that made up the General Board of the Navy met regularly to evaluate and propose the quantity of ships and their specific characteristics. Its recommendations dominated the design and technology base of the Navy built in the 1930s, which fought in World War II.[35]

Although the Navy's understanding of the potential contribution of submarines was limited in the 1930s, the American submarine community created a truly lethal underwater instrument. The parameters of war in the Pacific, with its scale and lack of supporting bases, pushed the community for endurance and crew habitability. Yet, the development of the fleet submarine with the speed and range to provide scouting and screening missions for the battle fleet was not without debate and controversy. The General Board made substantive contributions to ensuring that submarine technology was not ignored.[36]

In 1937, the annual submarine officers' conference met to debate the specifications for a fleet submarine. There were two different schools of thought. One, led by Capt. Thomas Hart, argued for small boats of about eight hundred tons, about the same size as the German Mark VII.[37] Such craft would be cheaper and thus more boats could be produced. The other camp was led by Cdr. Charles A. Lockwood. Members of Lockwood's team argued to stretch the limits of production and fought for a boat almost twice as large as the existing S-boat series of submarines.[38] They wanted to support the execution of War Plan Orange and patrol deep into the Pacific, ahead of the fleet. This role would require building a platform with engines powerful enough to provide the surface speed and endurance needed to keep up with the fleet. Lockwood's team won the debate, leading to the development of a unique American fighting platform, the fleet submarine. Those boats arrived just in the nick of time, in early 1942, and they turned out to be ideal for their role as hunters.[39]

At the beginning of the war the Navy had 111 undersea boats—mostly antiquated vessels that were small and limited in range. When the war began the Navy had taken possession of only 16 of the newer fleet submarines, the *Tambor* class.[40] The USS *Tambor* (SS 198) was a long-range boat, almost 300 feet long, with a displacement of 1,500 tons and a range of 11,000 miles. For armament, it carried 24 torpedoes, with 6 firing launchers forward and 4 aft. The *Tambor's* fire-control unit was an electromechanical computing device known as the torpedo data computer (TDC). The development of submarines continued throughout the war as the *Tambor* class was succeeded by the large-scale production of the *Gato* and *Balao* classes, which incorporated stronger hulls and a deeper diving depth. The evolution of U.S. submarines employed in the war is displayed in table 3.1.[41]

The war began with fifty-one U.S. submarines in the Pacific, divided into two units. The smaller component was with the U. S. Pacific Fleet, headquartered at Pearl Harbor. The Pacific Fleet submarine force initially was commanded by Rear Adm. Thomas C. Withers, with twenty-two boats at Pearl Harbor. In addition, Rear Adm. Thomas Hart commanded the smaller U.S. Asiatic Fleet at Manila Bay and small bases in the Philippines. The Manila Bay force was battered in December 1941 and ultimately withdrew to Australia. Hart's small submarine force was led by Capt. John E. Wilkes, with twenty-nine boats nominally in his command, many of them old and incapable of long-range offensive operations.

The American Torpedo
In addition to a superb fleet boat, the Navy began the war with an updated torpedo. The steam-driven Mark 14 was developed during the interwar period by the Torpedo Section at Newport. The Mark 14 was capable of speeds up to 46 miles an hour and a range of 4,000 meters. It initially packed 500 pounds of explosive in its warhead and came equipped with two different exploders in its nose. The Mark 6 exploder mechanism was a secret device with great potential. It could be set to detonate on contact with the side of a ship. But the unique aspect of the Mark 6 was an exploder "pistol" that was detonated by the magnetic influence of passing near (or preferably under) the hull of a warship. In theory, the explosion of a torpedo underneath the keel of a ship would be magnified by the

Table 3.1. U.S. World War II Submarine Classes and Capabilities

Sub Class Names	Sargo/Salmon	Tambor	Gato	Balao
Crew (Officers/enlisted)	5/54	6/54	6/54	10/70
Length (feet)	300	307	311	311
Displacement (tons)	1450	1475	1525	1526
Speed (Knots surface/submerged)	21/9	20/9	20/9	20/9
Diving Depth	250	250	300	400
Armament (Tubes Fore/Aft, all w/ 24 torpedoes, save Balao class)	4/4, 3" gun	6/4, 3" gun	6/4, 5" gun, 20mm/40mm	6/4, 28 torpedoes, 5" gun, 20/40mm gun
Sensors	Air Radar Sonar	Air Radar Sonar	Air and SJ Surface Radar, QB Sonar, Periscope-mounted radar	Air and SJ Surface Radar, QB Sonar, Periscope-mounted radar
Range (nautical miles)	11,000	11,000	11,000	11,000
Number Commissioned	16	12	77	124

Adapted from Mick Ryan, "Submarine Operations in the Pacific," *Australian Defence Journal*, 2013)

compounding pressure-effect so that the submarine would be able to break the ship's back with a single torpedo.[42] However, the device was so sophisticated and unknown to the Navy's ordnance community that when it was fielded initially few knew how to install, calibrate, and maintain the sensitive system. There had been no live trials of the torpedo or exploder—or any firings from a real submarine. The bureau responsible for ship production would not authorize the use of a deactivated Navy destroyer for a live test. Such parsimony would later prove to be a false economy of great import.[43] Defective mechanisms and poorly designed features would cause major problems with the submarine's major weapon.[44] More critically, a generation of submariners grew up without ever firing a real torpedo, hearing one explode, or conducting any realistic training.[45]

Learning under Fire

After the attack on Pearl Harbor, the United States reacted by initiating a defensive war of attrition against Japan. Strategic adaptation began just a few hours after the report of the attack at Pearl Harbor. On hearing about the Japanese strike, Admiral Hart in Manila issued an order to the U.S. Asiatic Fleet—"Execute unrestricted air and submarine warfare against Japan"[46]—an action based on discussions in the prior year between the Chief of Naval Operations and naval planners.[47] A few hours later, the CNO, Adm. Harold R. Stark, after conferring with President Roosevelt, issued the same order to the entire Navy. The war in the Pacific no longer was a game.

But this was a mission for which the Navy was operationally and tactically unprepared.[48] Newport's senior naval planners and lawyers had prepared conceptually to employ the meager submarine fleet in a much more aggressive way to attrit Japanese forays and conduct economic warfare. However, they had not really used the time to move beyond the planning stage and to put the strategic adjustment into operation. At the same time, the Navy had not thought out the necessary components of such a campaign, such as targeting priorities, increased torpedo production, increased technical support, etc. The poor results in the first year of the campaign bore out this assessment as the fleet struggled to become proficient at unrestricted warfare.[49] Even so, members of the Navy's senior leadership had been exposed to submarine warfare early in their careers, and thus both Adm. Ernest J. King, commander-in-chief, U.S. Fleet, and Adm. Chester W. Nimitz, commander-in-chief, U.S. Pacific Fleet, had an appreciation for the challenges of submarine operations.[50]

Although submarine innovation was not ignored, at least in a technological sense, campaign pressures and operational realities would force the Navy to adapt.[51] This case study examines three overlapping cycles of adaptation in the submarine fleet.

Tactical Adaptation: 1941–1942

The adaptation itself produced a lot of early frustration in the crews of the fledgling boats of the U.S. Asiatic fleet, on whom the early defense of the Philippines and Australia fell. The story of the USS *Sargo* (SS 188) in her first war patrol captures this frustration. The *Sargo* was captained by Lt. Cdr. Tyrell D. Jacobs, class of 1927 at Annapolis. He had departed on December 8 and patrolled off French Indochina, where intelligence had identified three Japanese cruisers. Jacobs could not get in position to attack the warships, but he waited a night and found a loaded freighter. He fired a single torpedo, but it exploded prematurely—only eighteen seconds after launch. He later found two targets on December 24, 1941. The *Sargo* fired eight torpedoes at them, with no results. When two new merchantmen came in view, the captain took extra pains to get into a good position within easy range. He double-checked all his bearings on the TDC and personally examined all torpedo settings. He then fired two torpedoes at each ship from a distance of a thousand yards; all missed.[52]

Suspecting that the torpedoes were running too deep, Jacobs took matters into his own hands and set his torpedoes to run shallower and to detonate on contact. The deactivation was in violation of standing orders.[53] Jacobs' extensive education as a torpedo specialist gave him insights into the performance of the Mark 14. He then found another large, slow tanker. He again planned and executed a deliberate and meticulous approach and tactical firing-solution—a single torpedo at a reasonable 1,200 yards. Once again, he did not register a hit. He had made six attacks and taken thirteen shots, with no explosions.[54] In utter frustration, Jacobs broke radio silence and questioned the Mark 14's reliability. Jacobs concluded his patrol report with the statement that he was "of the opinion that the Mark 14 torpedoes are faulty in two respects. First that the influence exploder mechanism cannot be relied on to function as designed. Second that set depth is not being obtained within 2,000 yards ... It is believed that a change of rudder-throws to give more up rudder should be given careful consideration and that test-firings, with a tube depth of at least 45 feet, be conducted to determine the depth performance of these torpedoes."[55] Jacobs later requested a test shot through a fishnet but was denied due to the limited torpedoes available.[56] This kind of false economy repeatedly plagued the Navy.

It would be another six months before someone actually investigated these initial shortfalls and made the sort of adaptations that early patrols suggested were needed to assure operational success. It would be almost another eighteen months before enough evidence was generated to show that Jacobs' challenge was correct.

Within days of Pearl Harbor, on December 9, the USS *Skipjack* (SS 184), captained by Cdr. Charles L. Freeman, left the Philippines for her first war patrol off the east coast of Samar. The submarine conducted two torpedo attacks during this patrol. On December 25, the *Skipjack* attacked a Japanese aircraft carrier and a single escort. Following prewar doctrine, Freeman had submerged and used his sonar bearings to fire three torpedoes at the large target, but without any observed results. The utility of submerged sonar bearings compared to observations from periscope or surface attacks was debatable.[57] It was proving nearly impossible, and possibly unnecessary, especially for merchant targets or away from air cover. Freeman returned to port later and was replaced. The U.S. Asiatic fleet was forced to flee south to Java and Australia, losing valuable torpedoes, spare parts, and maintenance equipment with the fall of its naval bases in the Philippines.

Numerous ships were having teething problems.[58] On June 4, 1942, Lt. Cdr. James W. Coe, the new skipper of the *Skipjack,* completed a fifty-day patrol. He had had some clear success early, sinking four boats. He had carefully documented his torpedo usage and approach tactics. He, too, was convinced that the torpedoes were malfunctioning and running deep. He filed an extensive post–patrol critique.[59] "To make a round trip of 8,500 miles into enemy waters, to gain attack position undetected within 800 yards of enemy ships," he wrote, "only to find that the torpedoes run deep and over half the time will fail to explode, seems to me to be an undesirable manner of gaining information" that could easily have been found at Newport in a test.[60] Coe recommended a test-fire into a net but was refused due to the paucity of munitions for experiments.[61] But that didn't end the skipper's efforts to change the Navy's mind. The notion of challenging the efficacy of the powerful Bureau of Ordnance might have cowed some Navy officers, but not Coe.

The process of inquiry and interpretation occurred at the tactical and operational level. Other submarine commanders reported what appeared to be direct hits with observed explosions, with little or no damage to enemy ships. It appeared to boat commanders that the magnetic exploders were almost on top of the target but were being triggered prematurely before getting a strike. When questioned, the bureau staff and the Newport Torpedo Station suggested that either poor target solutions were causing misses or that inadequate maintenance on the torpedoes was to blame. Interpreting the results was more difficult for higher levels of command, given a wide disparity in observed data. Despite the inputs of commanders at sea, the reporting chain and the Bureau of Ordnance believed that the problems lay more with poor training or the limited experience of captains and tactical firing teams than with the weapons systems themselves.

Deployments out of Australia were constrained by the insistence that captains follow prescribed prewar doctrine, which had been learned from prewar exercises. Before the war, "Skippers and their attack teams practiced and repracticed the art of the blind submerged sound bearing attack. The peacetime training system praised procedure and punished any digression."[62] Capt. John E. Wilkes, commander of submarines in the Asiatic Fleet, emphasized hiding from air observation, making attacks based solely on sonar for final bearings, and operating without communications that could be traced back to each boat.[63] Decades of training without realism, combined with Wilkes' enforcement of outdated tactics, had compounded the problems of faulty weapons. Many captains were taking a cautious approach to attacks, unwilling to risk detection by airplane or destroyer escort.[64]

Withers, commanding submarine forces for the Pacific Fleet, based at Pearl Harbor, was more willing to adapt tactics, but he wanted a "one-shot, one-kill" ratio due to the shortage of torpedoes. He pressed his officers to be more aggressive with attacks and to take greater risks.[65] Despite almost all his skippers' recorded suspicions about the torpedoes, Withers refused to deactivate the torpedo's Mark 6 exploder or to explore alternative methods to increase their effectiveness. Withers continued to question his own officers, and the veracity of their reports, while failing to question prewar learning or Newport on the quality of their torpedoes. The system could not be at fault since it had been tested so thoroughly by the fleet exercises.

For the first six months of the war, the submarines failed to meet expectations for taking the war to the enemy. New leadership was called forth. Both of the submarine force commanders, Wilkes in Australia and Withers in Pearl Harbor, were replaced at the same time, enabling the next generation to step forward with more realistic and aggressive tactics that a war of attrition demanded.

Rear Admiral Lockwood took over for Wilkes in Australia in May 1942, and, after investigating the situation, was equally critical of his crews and their weapons. "Why they didn't get more enemy ships is a highly controversial point," he

observed, "but my reading of all war diaries has convinced me that among the
causes were bad choice of stations, bad torpedo performance, buck fever, lack
or misunderstanding of aggressiveness."[66] This assessment noted far more than
just bad "fish" [torpedoes]. Back at Pearl Harbor, Rear Adm. Robert H. English, commander of all Pacific fleet submarines, produced a report in mid-1942
detailing the submarine force's limited performance. Like Lockwood, English
identified numerous reasons that the campaign was not gaining the desired results.
His list impugned his own crews and captains more than the torpedoes.[67] A formal inquiry at higher levels did not agree with the fleet's tactical commanders, and
change and adaptation were not authorized.

The contingent of American subs in Australia was divided. One force, based
on the continent's west coast, reported to Lockwood, while another, in Brisbane,
served under Capt. Ralph Christie, who directed his boats with a more centralized
command style. Even more disconcerting, Christie did not like to hear bad news
about the quality of the torpedoes and forbade his officers to document weapons failures in their post-patrol after-action reports. When commanders reported
accurately the pitiful performance of their weapons, they got strongly negative
endorsements that publicly criticized their decisions, courage, or both.[68] Christie
chastised critics of his torpedoes and transferred one skipper back to the United
States for "rest" after the captain made negative comments about the weapons in a
patrol report.[69] Christie continued to accuse his skippers of being tired and missing their targets repeatedly.[70]

The interpretation phase of the adaptation remained confused, if not conflicted.
In examining the inputs of crews, with the expert assistance from the ordnance
experts, commanders at the operational level were hard pressed to interpret the conflicting data. Were the crews well trained? Were the captains conducting the attacks
according to doctrine? Were the torpedoes running too deep, or were they going
off prematurely because of faulty maintenance? Were the magnetic influence devices
being properly set, even though the technicians who were doing so had never seen
the complicated device before? It was not clear whether the problem stemmed from
an erroneous setting in the influence device or whether Japanese warships were
emitting some sort of magnetic signal designed to set off the torpedoes early.

Still, adaptation did occur. Shortly after replacing Wilkes in Fremantle in May
1942, the recently promoted Lockwood noted in war patrol reports that many

torpedoes appeared to be on target, running hot and straight, but were passing below their targets. With progress so limited, Lockwood attended a May meeting in Australia with as many officers and boat skippers as possible to help pinpoint the problem. Tactics and complaints about torpedoes dominated the conversation. Afterward, Lockwood asked his chief of staff, Capt. James Fife, "Would it be feasible to run some depth tests with exercise heads setting to represent warheads?"[71] Here again, a culture of learning based on evidence appears evident.

As Jacobs had noted in December of 1941, some torpedoes were evidently running deeper than set. The Navy moved into the investigation phase. Very shortly Lockwood wrote to the Bureau of Ordnance, led by Rear Adm. William H. P. Blandy, about the torpedoes.[72] Within a week, he acquired a net for tests.[73] Lockwood then informed Blandy of his planned tests and his concern that torpedoes were running far deeper than designed.[74] He bought a large fishing net and ordered a firing test at Frenchman Bay, aiming at the net as a way to verify the set depths. The somewhat unscientific test was conducted on June 20, 1942.[75] The *Skipjack*, still commanded by Lieutenant Commander Coe, did the honors. Coe fired a shot with an exercise head, set at 10 feet, from just 850 yards. The torpedoes hit and went through the net at a depth of twenty-five feet. The next day, two more test shots were fired, and when the net was pulled up, the staff concluded that the weapons ran at least eleven feet deeper than the depth at which they had been set. Lockwood reported this assessment in a message up the chain of command and to Newport the next day.[76]

Newport responded with indignation and challenged the test with criticism about its integrity and conduct. Lockwood adapted his test and reconducted his validation exercise, and got the same result. The word was passed throughout the fleet, no doubt confirming what many suspected and others already understood. Within nine weeks of taking command down at Freemantle, Lockwood had investigated the Mark 14's most obvious deficiency.[77]

The operators in the fleet were upset, and so was Admiral King, who "lit a blowtorch under the Bureau of Ordnance."[78] No fewer than eight hundred torpedoes had already been fired in combat, a full year's production out of Newport, and the idea that something as fundamental as the proper testing of the depth-setting mechanism had gone wrong was hard to fathom. The lost opportunities for increased hits and additional sunk ships were not hard to grasp. Working with a degree of alacrity inspired by Admiral King's wrath, the bureau evaluated the data, checked its instruments, and concluded that the fleet operators were correct. Only belatedly would they admit that their infamous product was indeed running deeper than set. Fundamental flaws in basic design, development, and testing of the Mark 14 torpedo were all working against the submarines.

The notion that the problem was easily fixed was a relief to many of the senior submarine leaders, who wanted to continue to use the magnetic exploder to generate maximum enemy losses with the fewest torpedoes. This would maximize their measure of effectiveness—the total amount of tonnage sunk. This goal, what they called "the bag," was their designated metric. After hearing of the problem, most submarine skippers simply set their torpedoes' running depth to zero. But this solution caused torpedoes to broach the surface, which both gave away the submarine's location and generated more premature detonations. Now, with the depth-setting problem solved, it appeared that more hits were being achieved, but another problem arose. More shots were striking ships, but the number of duds increased. Despite the corrections, many missed opportunities occurred and commanders still experienced poor torpedo performance.[79]

Like the submariners' operations, learning became decentralized. Since higher headquarters was putting its head in the sand (or in deep water, as it were), some sub commanders took the initiative on their own, deactivating the magnetic exploders or altering the depth setting on the torpedoes. Despite standing operating procedures, some captains deactivated the magnetic influence feature and swore their crews and officers to secrecy. Other captains would overstate the size of a target ship to justify their decision to shoot more than a single torpedo. There is a suggestion that patrol reports did not always accurately reflect tactics exactly, which complicated both horizontal learning at that time and the task of assessing results today.[80]

Other components for submarine operations were missing as well. The Navy lacked the doctrine, tactics, and training for offensive submarine warfare.[81] The wargames and fleet exercises had not enforced operational or tactical realism for the sub crews. In fact, a generation of crews never heard a live torpedo detonated—a perfect match for a generation of torpedoes that were never tested.[82] Nor had the Navy practiced night attacks in peacetime, although it was evident that the German practice of night surface attacks was effective.[83]

During the long interwar era, American naval doctrine emphasized a reliance on sonar to determine a target's range, bearing, and angle. Navy theorists believed that new detection systems and antisubmarine weapons had made it suicidal to expose a periscope in daylight. To support its tactics, the Navy placed highly advanced sonar and hydrophone suites in the new fleet submarines. These systems, along with TDCs that were more advanced than those used in any other navy, were to give American submariners an edge. Here innovative technologies begot creative but not realistic tactics. In fact, submerged sonar attacks were staggeringly ineffective under actual wartime conditions. The submarine fleet quickly figured this out and moved away from sonar toward shallow submerged attacks at daytime with the periscope up. The skippers, pressed for results and criticized for lack of aggressiveness in closing on their attacks, came to realize that sonar alone was ineffective. Thus, while American senior commanders struggled with the torpedo problems, the submerged sonar attack was eliminated in short order once the war began. Research after the war found little evidence of success using sonar.[84]

Patrol endorsements were a vehicle for establishing policy and reinforcing norms in the force.[85] Force-level commanders occasionally would criticize boat captains for expenditure rates against smaller targets, or for not conducting more aggressive patrols. Positive endorsements would reflect great credit on a captain and crew. These endorsements served a dual bridging function: they fed back best practices to the rest of the fleet and also lifted lower-level learning forward to the schoolhouses and bureaus that produced the boats and weapons. Such feedback and interpretation is useful as a synthesis and a confirmation of inputs to the process.

For example, the Pacific Fleet endorsement on the USS *Gudgeon* (SS 211) criticized that boat for its slow pace underwater during the day and for not making aggressive night attacks on the surface. But the *Gudgeon* was actually complying with existing submarine doctrine and its predeployment training, designed and conducted by the Pacific Fleet. "Here is an indication of the rapidity with which tactical concepts can shed peacetime theory for wartime practice," the submarine force's history notes. "Within 51 days, Commander Submarines Pacific [COMSUBPAC] was able to criticize adversely a patrol carried out in conformance with original operational instructions."[86] The submarine force was learning to learn.

Historians frequently cite the history of one particular submarine, the USS *Wahoo* (SS 238), as representative of the growth and adaptation required by the

Navy. The *Wahoo* was a new *Gato*-class boat, commanded by Cdr. Paul Kennedy. She began her maiden patrol on August 23, 1942, assigned to attack Japanese shipping west of Truk. On September 6, on just her third day in the area, the *Wahoo* found a freighter and fired three torpedoes. Kennedy was tentative in his approach and fired from long distance, with three misses. Rather than press forward, he was afraid of being observed from the air, and dove deep to avoid detection. He then withdrew from the area.

The *Wahoo* continued to patrol the Truk area for two weeks, until September 20. Under a bright moon and clear sky, the submarine sighted a medium-sized Japanese freighter, escorted by a small corvette. Kennedy got into a submerged firing position and launched three torpedoes; again, all three missed. A fourth hit the target, which was reported to be listing and settling. The *Wahoo* heard numerous underwater explosions but was chased by the escort. The U.S. sub escaped, but without a confirmed kill. Here again, a night surface attack was possible.

Two weeks later, on October 4, 1942, the *Wahoo* missed two of the best targets of the war. It proved unable to reach a firing position against a seaplane tender, the *Chiyoda*. The next day, Kennedy sighted an aircraft carrier, believed to be the *Ryūjō*, escorted by two destroyers.[87] The *Wahoo* was seven thousand yards off but failed to surface and give chase. The target escaped untouched. The *Wahoo* proceeded to Pearl Harbor, ending her first patrol on October 17, 1942. Kennedy damned himself in his own report:

> Sighted aircraft carrier RYUJO accompanied by two AMAGIRI class destroyers bearing 220dT. Angle on the bow 60d starboard, range 11,000 yards, speed 14 knots. One DD was leading and second was trailing carrier. Made approach which, on final analysis, lacked aggressiveness and skill, and closed range to about 7,000 yards. Watched the best target we could ever hope to find go over the hill untouched at 0800. A normal approach course at time of sighting and full speed for the whole twenty minutes would have brought us in to 3,000 yards and a fair shot.[88]

Battle-tested captains were in short supply, and Kennedy was given a second chance. On November 8, 1942, the *Wahoo* got underway for her second patrol. An additional officer was now present: Lt. Cdr. Dudley Morton, on his prospective commanding officer tour. The *Wahoo* arrived at her assigned area around the Solomon Islands, where the Marines were still holding on at Guadalcanal and the Japanese navy was attacking their support at sea. On November 30, the submarine spotted a freighter or transport with a destroyer escort. The *Wahoo*'s approach was tentative, and she never got a shot off. On December 10, the *Wahoo* ran across a convoy of three heavily loaded cargo ships. Kennedy chose the largest tanker for the first target and fired a spread of four torpedoes at a range of a mere seven hundred yards. Although three hit, it took two hours for the *Kamoi Maru* to sink. An escorting destroyer made the *Wahoo* pay a price, dropping more than forty depth charges. Four days later, the *Wahoo* sank a careless Japanese submarine. The submarine returned back to Brisbane on December 26 for refit and a crew rest. Kennedy was relieved for lack of aggressiveness in prosecuting attacks, and Morton took command.[89]

The *Wahoo*'s experience is representative of a year of combat for many boats. In 1942, experience was processed from the bottom up to higher commands. Here the process of learning and the politics of adaptation came into clash—at least for a while. In short order, however, peacetime doctrine, which had been developed in an artificial context, gave way to what really worked in wartime. Commanders learned how to change their routines and practices. The more senior of them, who clung to more centralized direction and to antiquated practices despite the evidence produced at sea, ultimately were moved to other commands. So, too, were overly cautious boat commanders. Not every Navy officer could step up the learning curve and meet the pressure. In the first year of the war, the Navy fired 40 of its 145 sub captains, many at their own request.[90] The average age of the sub skippers in 1941 was forty-two, and they proved too cautious and ingrained with the old doctrine. Within the first year the average age dropped to thirty-five as the Navy relieved or shunted these officers aside.[91]

This younger generation took over, schooled in combat and incentivized to be less risk-averse than their predecessors. The submarine force's lessons-learned were shared and absorbed. The Navy provided generous incentives for success, commensurate with the risk—Navy Crosses to skippers for sinking five ships in a patrol, with lower awards for other officers of each sub. Submarine equipment was altered to account for combat needs that peacetime design and development had missed. Changes in both weapons and tactics were made, and old practices unlearned. Outdated or inadequate practices, such as submerged sonar shots, were quickly shelved. "Contrary to accepted professional opinion prior to the war, sound attacks conducted from deep submergence proved to be of negligible importance," one account declared.[92] Night surface attacks became more frequent, and submarine skippers learned that they could use their radar to avoid air surveillance.

By the end of 1942, the Pacific Fleet had sent out a total of 350 patrols. Not all of these patrols were offensively oriented; some were required for intelligence and security of the fleet or the defense of Australia. Postwar analyses credit these patrols with 180 ships sunk, displacing a total of 725,000 tons.[93] Yet, that total, achieved over twelve months, was the same amount that Germany's U-boats had bagged in only two months in the North Atlantic. Since this level of damage had no impact on Japan's import of critical resources and commodities, the campaign cannot be seen as a success. Lockwood himself admitted that the sub force operated at its nadir in 1942.[94]

But the adaptation from surveillance and "hiding" to hunting was a success. A combination of bottom-up observation and operational authority ultimately led to the conclusion that reversed habits that had been developed in peacetime.[95] In fact, the operational history of the force recognizes the organic nature of the adaptation. "By late summer of 1942," it conceded, "a submarine commander who conducted his patrol in accordance with the accepted late 1941 doctrine would undoubtedly have been relieved of his command."[96]

Technical Adaptation: Torpedo Defects

Having altered the orientation of the submarine force toward a more offensive strategic approach mandating more aggressive tactics to generate greater attrition of the opponent's lines of communication, the Navy began the next adaptation cycle—adjusting its weapons to fit the task at hand. Rosen's critique dismissed this aspect of the submarine offensive as a "reform."[97] He was correct that it certainly was not a major innovation, but it does meet the criteria for learned adaptation.

At this point in the war, there were many suspicions about the Mark 6 exploder device, but there were many conflicting data points and the fleet was expanding rapidly. Moreover, there were important personnel changes. Rear Admiral English, commander of the submarine forces Pacific at Pearl Harbor, died in an airplane crash in the United States on January 19, 1943, while touring submarine bases. Lockwood replaced him and arrived in Pearl Harbor in mid-February of 1943. He would remain in this post until the war ended. Lockwood needed some time to familiarize himself with his command and its operations. Faulty torpedoes were only part of his headaches; cementing command relations with the Pacific Fleet, resolving personnel shortfalls for the many new boats, dealing with production shortfalls in weapons and spare parts, building up submarine bases and maintenance facilities throughout the Pacific theater, and keeping an eye out for new technology required significant attention. All this kept Lockwood and his staff busy.

Again, the *Wahoo* experience demonstrates that the adaptation cycle has to go through several iterations before sufficient evidence is available to demonstrate both the need for change and the nature of that change.[98] The *Wahoo* made ready for her third patrol and departed out of Australia on January 16, 1943.[99] On January 24 she went north of Kairiru Island and boldly penetrated Victoria Bay. There the captain, Dudley Morton, sighted the Japanese destroyer *Harusame*. The *Harusame* was getting underway, so the *Wahoo* fired a spread of 3 torpedoes from 1,200 yards; all missed. The *Wahoo* fired another torpedo, but it, too, missed. The destroyer was no longer the prey, it had become the hunter. Morton fired again at a range of just eight hundred yards, using a torpedo with the magnetic influence device activated. This torpedo struck the *Harusame*, making Morton a firm believer in the new device.[100]

The next day the *Wahoo* headed for Palau. On January 26, the submarine sighted two merchant vessels and launched two torpedoes at each. Morton attacked, and damaged the *Fukuei Maru*. Two more targets appeared, and the *Wahoo* attacked, scoring two hits. Morton had hit three ships with five torpedoes from a total of seven shots. The *Wahoo* then chased the two fleeing ships. With only four torpedoes left, Morton had to be economical and accurate. He hit and sank both. The submarine left station and arrived at Pearl Harbor on February 7, only twenty-three days after leaving Brisbane. In his report, Morton reported a tactical adaptation in which the CO and XO split the duties of conning the boat and running the attack team. Morton felt that this adaptation enhanced tactical proficiency and resulted in a better team. Before entering port, the *Wahoo* had celebrated her success by lashing a straw broom to her periscope mast to indicate a "clean sweep." From her signal halyard the crew hung eight small Japanese flags, one for each ship they believed they had sunk. This was the kind of aggressiveness that the Pacific Fleet leadership wanted.

On February 23, 1943, the *Wahoo* got underway for her fourth patrol. Morton was assigned to the northern Yellow Sea, an area never before patrolled by U.S. submarines.[101] On March 11, the *Wahoo* arrived in her assigned area, which appeared devoid of shipping. Morton had mixed results, sinking four ships with eight torpedoes, including an obvious dud. On March 20 the *Wahoo* sighted a freighter. She launched two torpedoes, but they exploded prematurely. Out of frustration, Morton had the *Wahoo* "battle-surface" to employ her deck guns. She raked the freighter with 20-mm and 4-inch shells. The target caught fire in several places and sank. The *Wahoo* headed home, again claiming eight victims, concluding a patrol that topped the record to date. The submarine community was happy to see aggressive tactics that used surface or periscope-directed attacks, pressed home with boldness bordering on recklessness. Since the *Wahoo*'s success was attributed to hits that employed the magnetic exploder, these patrols strongly influenced Lockwood's confidence in the weapon and prompted him to seek alternative theories.[102] Lockwood periodically published tactical bulletins to promote best practices, in particular to highlight the success of aggressive officers such as Morton who delivered results.[103] Reviewing the archived bulletins, Lockwood used them as a means of communicating lessons horizontally across the expanding submarine force.

The *Wahoo* began her fifth war patrol on April 25, departing Midway for patrol areas via the Kuril Islands.[104] By early May 4, the boat was in her assigned patrol area. Morton made a total of three attacks and fired seven torpedoes, with two hits, but he only sank one ship. He later sighted a three-ship convoy and attacked. He fired three torpedoes; two exploded prematurely, and the third failed to explode at all. On the night of May 9, 1943, the *Wahoo* picked up two targets on radar, making a run between ports in the dark without escort. The submarine conducted a night surface attack and fired three torpedoes at each. The *Wahoo* had only two hits of six shots, yet still sunk its prey. All told Morton had four hits from seventeen shots, far below average.

The *Wahoo* cleared the area to the northeast to patrol the Tokyo-Paramushiro route. Morton found two freighters on May 12 and gained a position for an attack. He fired a total of six torpedoes from 1,200 yards but got only two hits, and the last of these was a dud—no explosion. The boat sailed for home, arriving May 21, 1943. In less than two weeks, the *Wahoo* had conducted ten attacks on eight different targets. However, faulty torpedo performance cut deeply into the results achieved. Morton went to see Lockwood again and had a few strong words to say to his commander about the quality of torpedoes.[105]

Lockwood had more than eighteen months' worth of evidence by this point that the torpedoes were faulty, but he still thought that the depth mechanism rather than the exploder was the problem. That turned out to be incorrect. Only in May 1943, after his favorite ace, Morton, had finished an unsatisfactory patrol with a blank sheet and no sinkings, did the commander of submarine forces, Pacific begin to question whether the Mark 6 device was inherently faulty. Despite his reputation for problem-solving, Lockwood hesitated to take action himself. He wrote to the Bureau of Ordnance, led by Rear Admiral Blandy, to see if they ultimately might salvage the potential in magnetic influence devices. Lockwood asked whether they should deactivate the exploder and reported the low hit rates his boats were getting. He readily admitted that many causes were possible and said he believed that the problem was the flooding of the exploder in the warhead. He urged Blandy to "pull a rabbit out of his hat."[106] But Blandy's answer was not optimistic, and he asked for more help from the submarine community rather than complaints.[107] Then the Bureau of Ships chimed in, with a negative assessment on the overall value of magnetic exploders. As the builder of ships, and responsible for tests on ship armor and torpedo defense, it concluded that regular contact detonations on hulls would be just as effective as under-the-keel kills. Then Lockwood's own staff completed a formal assessment of torpedo effectiveness in July 1943 and concluded that the device needed to be deactivated. Finally, a Royal Navy liaison officer augmented the staff's work with a report noting how Britain's efforts with magnetic influence devices had failed.

Lockwood, again reflecting a measured and evidence-based approach, approved an experiment of eight patrols with the exploder device deactivated. He wrote again to Blandy in exasperation, saying he was loath to deactivate the influence mechanism, but he needed results quickly since the submarine force was now "0-for-4 on a carrier" thanks to duds.[108] Lockwood realized that his force was not operating at maximum effectiveness and he was still reluctant to adapt to the contact exploder. He also seemed to have a strongly embedded conception that the Japanese had developed a countermeasure that caused the premature detonations. Why he suspected this, relevant only to large warships, is unclear, but his personal correspondence and memoirs reflected this belief.[109]

His investigatory stage completed, Lockwood decided, ever so reluctantly, that he must act. Armed with all this information, he felt he needed approval from higher headquarters. He went to Nimitz to ask permission to deactivate his magnetic exploders, which Nimitz provided on July 24, 1943.[110] Lockwood directed his boats to use only the contact pistol.[111] But he took this step only after he had a year's worth of evidence, four months in command at Pearl Harbor, and the results of an empirical investigation. In essence, it had taken eighteen months for the Navy leadership to come to the same conclusion in 1943 that the younger officers had suggested back in late 1941.

Even after the deactivation, Lockwood did not take credit for the decision. He wrote Blandy that he only "regretfully" agreed with Nimitz's decision to deactivate the detonator. He added a statement that he firmly believed the Japanese had a countermeasure, which would have absolved Newport and the Bureau of blame for a poorly engineered weapon that was ill-suited for wartime conditions.[112]

The bureaucrats at Newport blasted back a detailed analytical report noting that they had found that 93 percent of all torpedoes fired during the war had run "hot and true"—a very odd argument that suggests just how out of touch the institution was with the operational changes faced by tactical units.[113] The mechanics of torpedo propulsion was never an issue; they almost always launched properly and ran straight. The problem is that they went at the wrong depth or else broached the surface, making them explode prematurely; or that their warheads did not detonate even when the torpedoes hit the target. Not surprisingly, institutional learning in the United States lagged behind that of the operational forces concerning what the context and problem were and how desperately the submarine force needed help.

Now that the fleet boats were past the exploder problem, both Navy leaders and the subs' crews expected a greater number of sinkings. However, the force still reported many duds, even under attacks against stationary or slow-moving targets under nearly ideal conditions. Attention turned to the basic contact exploder, which seemed to be malfunctioning. Another critical design flaw had been overlooked. This was perplexing, since the essence of the design was the same as the combat-tested Mark 3 exploder, which had been deployed since World War I.

The evidence that promoted problem recognition was provided by the USS *Tinosa* (SS 283), captained by Cdr. Lawrence R. Daspit. The *Tinosa* departed

Midway on July 9, 1943, on her second war patrol, ordered to cover the Caroline Islands area. She sailed with her magnetic exploder deactivated as an approved experiment. Daspit torpedoed and damaged the Japanese armed merchant cruiser *Aikoku Maru* on July 15, 1943, north of Truk. He then attacked and damaged a Japanese oiler west of Truk on July 24. He then carefully planned and meticulously documented his follow-up attack on a 19,000-ton freighter. Daspit fired a spread of four torpedoes from long distance (four thousand yards) and got the ship to a dead stop. Then he closed in and fired another two shots, and observed both hit, but there were no detonations of the torpedoes' warheads. With no enemy combatants in sight, Daspit then took time to carefully maneuver into a textbook position, 875 yards off the target's beam, where he fired 9 Mark 14s and observed all 9 shots from his periscope. All evidently were duds.[114]

The *Tinosa* had fired no fewer than fifteen torpedoes, with only two detonations from ten observed hits. The target was heavily damaged but still managed to get into Truk. Believing that the entire load was flawed, Daspit retained his last torpedo for analysis at port. The *Tinosa* returned to Pearl Harbor, but nothing out of the ordinary was found with that torpedo.[115]

The *Wahoo's* sixth patrol contributed to another cycle of learning and adjustment. On August 14 the *Wahoo* entered the dangerous Sea of Japan and sighted three medium-sized freighters headed south. The submarine launched one torpedo, apparently a miss. The next day, the *Wahoo* sighted a large freighter, gave chase, and fired one torpedo; it struck the ship, but was a dud. Two follow-up torpedoes also missed, and a third broached and exploded before the end of the run.[116] The *Wahoo's* next three attacks on August 16 and 17 produced no success. Within four days, twelve Japanese vessels were sighted and nine attacked. Yet, no fewer than ten torpedoes broached, or were duds; another ten were unexplained misses. The commander, submarine forces, Pacific ordered the *Wahoo* to return to base. Lockwood's staff found itself forced into investigative action again.[117]

Here again, input from the bottom up fed into the middle of the organization, where formal investigatory testing was done. Lockwood advised Rear Adm. Richard S. Edwards on King's staff that he planned tests to follow up on contact problems in late August.[118] His torpedo officer, Capt. Art Taylor, conducted these tests, aided by Capt. Charles B. Momsen, a submarine squadron commander well known for his innovations in undersea rescue gear and weaponry.[119] They fired several live torpedoes into the cliffs of Kaho'olawe Island in Hawaii, on August 31. One was a dud, and the warhead was carefully raised and examined. The evaluation determined that the warhead housing had collapsed faster than the firing-pin could drive a charge into the explosive to detonate the weapon.

After the tests, Lockwood wrote to Blandy and informed him about the cliff shots and his other testing plans.[120] Blandy's response suggests that the bureau did not appreciate the implied criticism about the torpedo and its production.[121] Lockwood's team designed a unique test using a trailer-mounted boom-lift (a "cherry-picker" truck) to raise a torpedo to a height of almost one hundred feet and let it drop to the ground—a distance that propelled the warheads to a speed of about forty-six miles an hour. Serving as targets were a pair of steel plates—a square flat one and a second set at a 45-degree angle.[122] The flat plate, which represented a perfect perpendicular target, produced a failure rate of almost 70 percent. The off-beam (or glancing plate) shots resulted in a failure rate of only 35 percent. Lockwood sent a message to the ordnance bureaucracy outlining his findings and immediately warned his boats to avoid perpendicular or classic 90-degree angles of attack. In any event, the torpedo contact device clearly was flawed.

Meanwhile, the Navy mechanics at Pearl Harbor designed a simple fix—a stronger firing-pin—which was easier than reconfiguring the contact housing or designing a new exploder. The firing-pin adjustments were tested at Pearl Harbor and found to be satisfactory.[123] Still, Lockwood felt that he needed permission before sending out his boats with the modified pin, and both of his superiors, admirals Nimitz and King, just happened to be attending a conference in Hawaii at this time. Lockwood approached them and was instantly granted permission to proceed.[124] By this step, Lockwood ensured rapid institutionalization of his results throughout the Navy. In this instance, tactical adaptation was fed backward to the institution.

Just in case the Bureau of Ordnance still did not trust the tests, COMSUBPAC did a redo of the cliff experiment, using seven shots detonated by the modified firing-pin, and experienced only a single dud. The USS *Halibut* (SS 232), which had recently returned from a patrol replete with duds, participated in these cliff shots.[125] The new firing-pin was produced at Pearl Harbor—ironically, with quality Japanese metal.[126]

The institutionalization of adaptation outside the Pacific went better this time. Newport swiftly incorporated the firing-pin alterations into American models, and the BuOrd experts delivered the newly improved contact pistols to the fleet by October 1943. The result: submarine crews could now deploy with weapons worthy of their risk-taking. U.S. submarines no longer were toothless wolves, with little thanks to the technicians at the institutional level. As journalist and author Clay Blair noted, "After twenty-one months of war, the three major defects of the Mark 14 torpedo had at last been isolated. . . . Each defect had been discovered and fixed in the field—always over the stubborn opposition of the Bureau of Ordnance."[127] Bureau leaders openly chastised themselves and their personnel when the poor design and testing ramifications became obvious.[128]

The adaptations directed by Lockwood enhanced submarine performance in the second full year of the war. The *Gato*-class boat arrived, and roughly 350 patrols in 1943 almost doubled the levels of the previous year. A total of 335 ships and more than 1.5 million tons went to the bottom. Commodity imports to the Japanese home islands decreased by 15 percent, and her total tonnage had been trimmed by 20 percent to just 4.1 million tons.[129] It was not until the summer of 1943 that Lockwood became aware that Japan's shortage of tanker assets was a great vulnerability and that targeting these tankers would curtail Japanese military operations.[130]

The adaptation in targeting proved critical to intensifying the impact of the submarine campaign on the war. In September of 1943 Lockwood was able to claim far greater success and shared the results with his force. In a bulletin, he commented that "Japan is no longer able to maintain a continuous flow of goods necessary to the Empire's economy and at the same time meet the demands of the Army and Navy in their strategic operations."[131] In the last four months of 1943, the Japanese lost fifteen tankers—more than the two prior years.[132]

Still, ship performance could vary wildly, particularly since commanders were rotated out after several patrols. The *Gudgeon* received an outstanding endorsement for sinking five ships for a total of 35,000 tons, with eleven hits out of seventeen torpedoes fired on one patrol in 1943.[133] Several patrols later, the same ship with a different commander missed twelve consecutive shots at two stationary targets.[134]

But the torpedo trouble was cured by the end of 1943. It had been "a tragically expensive muddle" of incalculable proportions.[135] The Navy carefully followed a slow cycle of learning, with many reports and actions supporting the interpret and investigate functions. Finally, solutions were created that were fed back to the fleet and incorporated into shared practice. The magnetic influence device was rejected and the contact exploders were now redesigned. The sea wolves no longer were bound by poor doctrine, outdated tactics, and abominably designed weapons. They were toothless no longer.

This level of success was not free. Greater results demanded greater risk and they were achieved, but not without cost. The American Navy lost fifteen boats in 1943, including the famous *Wahoo*, in October.[136]

Late 1943 Onward: Operational Adaptation—Wolfpacks

Nonetheless, tasked with the ruthless elimination of Japanese shipping, the Pacific fleet was not producing results fast enough. Accordingly, in early 1943, the top of the Navy directed a new approach. This third adaptation was tactical in nature, and unlike previous aspects of this case study, it did not emanate from the bottom. Instead it was directed from six thousand miles away in a message from the Navy's top leadership. King wrote to Nimitz at Pearl Harbor on April 1, 1943, noting that:

> Effectiveness of operations and availability of submarines indicate desirability, even necessity, to form a tactical group of 4 to 6 submarines trained and indoctrinated in coordinated action for operations such as now set up in Solomons, to be stationed singly or in groups in enemy ship approaches to critical areas.[137]

Nimitz agreed with King's "suggestion" and ordered that it be implemented.[138] There is no record of debate at Pacific Fleet or at Submarine Force Pacific about this shift in method, nor was there any recorded resistance to using the subs in collective tactical groupings as ambushers. Apparently, King was still oriented on the employment of submarines against Japanese naval combatants. But the U.S. submarine force was following a strategy of attrition against merchant shipping, and its culture had always emphasized individual patrols and independent command. So far the submariners had not been very successful in dealing with Japanese warships, but King felt they could be if they were properly "trained and indoctrinated in coordinated action."

In early 1943, King was fully engaged with responding to German Kriegsmarine wolfpack tactics, or *rudeltaktik*. He was painfully aware how effective they were, and he was getting strong encouragement from both President Roosevelt and British prime minister Winston Churchill to adopt defensive measures. U-boats had critically impaired Great Britain's own war effort.[139] Moreover, King was aware that the U.S. Navy was not generating the same aggregate tonnage results that the German Navy was getting. King may have concluded that emulating the Germans could produce better results from his own submarine force.[140] Lockwood was certainly well aware of the comparisons; in mid-1942 he wrote that "Germans getting 3 ships a day, Pac not getting one ship."[141] He was not alone. In January 1943 his predecessor at Submarine Forces Pacific headquarters distributed a bulletin containing a five-page summary of German wolfpack tactics.[142]

Meanwhile, the operational and tactical context facing the submarine force was becoming more complex. By 1943 Japanese convoys were larger, more organized, and better-protected than ever before. If a group of several submarines operating against an escorted Japanese convoy could mass its firepower on concentrations of shipping, the multiple threat would distract the convoy's protective screen and provide more opportunities.

Lockwood noted in his memoirs that the concept of collective action was not unknown to the submarine force. Before the war, experiments had attempted simultaneous attacks by several submarines, but communications between boats were not good enough then to ensure safety in peacetime operations. Now conditions were different: radar had been perfected, boats were equipped with high-frequency radiotelephones, and communications were vastly improved. No longer did the fleet use the old, slow, toilsome method of coding and decoding messages.[143] Coordination could be achieved, but the American submarines had had little practice at it. In addition, a year and half of operating as individual hunter-killers in their own isolated patrol areas had reinforced a culture of independence at sea consistent with the Navy culture.

King's command cut short the inquiry phase. But the Pacific submarine fleet took time to interpret the doctrinal and tactical implications of the new approach fully. As a result, the American Navy did not employ the same approach as the Germans. U-boat wolfpacks in the Kriegsmarine were ad hoc and fluid. They had a common doctrinal approach, but the packs themselves were formed on the fly after the boats had deployed. They were not teams, nor did they conduct any practice exercises together. When Adm. Karl Dönitz received intelligence about the location and character of a convoy, he would order several boats to converge on an area where he expected the convoy to be. He would thus direct the assembly of the wolfpack and coordinate its attack from long distance. There was no on-scene commander or collective attack.[144] The U-boats were simply sharks. They would swarm and attack at will, or swarm to designated areas when directed. Since the Atlantic convoys were rather large—thirty or more ships each—the U-boat wolfpacks might total as many as a dozen boats swarming around a big convoy.[145] A single U-boat could be easily driven off, but not a pack.

In its investigation phase, the U.S. Navy did not embrace German wolfpack doctrine or terminology. The accepted term was "coordinated attack group" (CAG), to preclude association with the Nazis. An innovative submariner, Captain Momsen, developed the original tactics and commanded the initial American wolfpack in the early fall of 1943.[146] American CAGs would have a senior commander on scene, but not because of necessity. Lockwood's note to Nimitz on wolfpacks mentioned a desire to use senior officers serving as division commanders (groupings of six boats per division) or as commanders of the action groups, to help them get wartime experience in boats.[147]

The investigative phase was exhaustive and deliberate over several months. Actual submarine commanders developed the required tactics and communication techniques. Discussions evolved into small wargames on the floor of a converted hotel, which conveniently had a chessboard floor of black and white tiles. The officers who would conduct these patrols developed their own doctrine and tactics.[148] The staff and prospective boat captains tested various ways both to scout for targets and then combine into a fighting force once a convoy was detected. Wargames, drills, and ultimately at-sea trials were conducted to refine a formal doctrine. Momsen drilled his captains in tactics, planning to have three boats attack successively, with one boat making the first attack on a convoy and then acting as "trailer" while the other two attacked alternatively on either flank afterward. He also developed a simple code for use on their new Talk Between Ships (TBS) system so that boats could communicate with each other without being detected or intercepted by the Japanese.

The American approach rejected the rigid, centralized command philosophy and flexible structure of German wolfpacks. The Navy took the opposite approach, consistent with its culture and practice. Coordinated attack groups comprised three to four boats under a common tactical commander who was present on the scene. Unlike those of the Germans, the U.S. attack groups trained and deployed together as a distinctive element. They patrolled in a designated area under a senior commander and followed a generic attack plan. This tactical doctrine called for successive rather than swarming attacks.[149] Other than intelligence regarding potential target convoys, orders came from the tactical commander, not from the fleet commander.

There was no urgency behind the doctrinal and organizational adaptation of the Pacific submarine fleet. Lockwood appears to be guilty of delaying tactics, but captains Momsen and John H. Brown Jr. convinced him to agree to a change of heart.[150] Here top-down adaptation from afar appears to have been resisted until it was met with bottom-up pressure or growing evidence.

Lockwood and the submarine force took their time to work out the required doctrine and tactics in an intensive investigatory phase. The first attack group, finally formed in the summer of 1943, comprised the USS *Cero* (SS 225), the USS *Shad* (SS 235), and the USS *Grayback* (SS 208). Momsen, who had never been on a combat patrol, was the commodore and rode in the *Cero*. The group finished its preparations and deployed from Pearl Harbor in late September on a combat patrol from Midway on October 1, 1943—exactly six months to the day from King's message suggesting that the Navy set up its first wolfpacks. That does not display rapid learning, given both the German success story in the Atlantic and the lack of success in the Pacific. But CAGs were not going to solve the torpedo problem, which was Lockwood's major concern that summer.

Despite possible reservations, the initial cruise was fruitful. Momsen's pack arrived in the East China Sea on October 6, 1943. It made a single collective attack on a convoy and was credited with sinking 5 Japanese ships for 88,000 tons and damaging eight more with a gross tonnage of 63,000 tons. Although this met the measures of success that Lockwood wanted, the commanders involved were less than enthusiastic. The comments and lessons from the participating captains were generally mixed, with many preferring to hunt alone rather than as a member of a group. They felt that the problems of communication were technologically unsolvable and that the risk of fratricide was unavoidable. They did not want to risk sinking a friendly submarine in the fog of combat. Moreover, commanders preferred operating and attacking alone, consistent with the Navy's overall

culture and the submarine community's preference for independent action and
the rewards that came with it. Momsen recommended centralized command from
Pearl Harbor rather than an on-scene commander afloat—a suggestion that Lockwood immediately overruled.[151]

Indeed, Lockwood did not merely take King's guidance or directive at face
value and implement it. He did assign groups of four to six boats in his packs.
Although they did develop the doctrine that King tasked them to create, they did
not apply it as King had desired, against military shipping or approaches to critical
operational areas. Instead, Lockwood deployed the CAGs to his ruthless campaign
of attrition against Japanese commerce. The developmental process was entirely
consistent with bottom-up adaptation, since the Navy's senior leadership allowed
the Pacific Fleet to develop its own tactics. Theater commanders injected their
own preferences about directed command from long distance, which reflected
both Navy culture and Lockwood's appreciation for how Allied direction-finding
equipment and signals intelligence in the Atlantic were fed by Doenitz's devotion
to centralized control and extensive communications. So this anomaly of adaptation remains consistent with the theory hypothesized in this book. The requirement was directed from the top, but the senior Navy leadership was patient in
letting local leaders figure out the "how." It then was carried out by commanders
such as Lockwood. Whatever reservations he and his staff may have held, submarine attack groups continued during the remainder of the year and were a common tactic during 1944. And Lockwood carefully planned larger combinations of
multiple attack groups to infiltrate the Sea of Japan, a vital trade artery.

Unlike Germany, in Dönitz's Operation Paukenschlag ("Drumbeat") in the
Atlantic, the United States was winning the war of attrition in the Pacific. Lockwood noted in a tactical bulletin that for the first time the tonnage comparisons
between the German effort and that of the American submarine force "now compare favorably."[152]

Lockwood took attack groups to a new level in 1945. He deliberately planned
a major projection of nine boats, operating in three packs, to enter into the heavily mined entrances of the Sea of Japan. The development of an early version of
sonar enabled boats to detect mines at seven hundred yards and bypass them. Submarines could now enter mined waters such as the Strait of Tsushima serendipi-
tously and operate in an area that the Japanese mistakenly believed was a private

lake. The Sea of Japan was where ships carrying crucial foodstuffs and coal shipments transited from Korea. The operation suggested to Japan's leaders that the noose around the islands was tightening.[153] Lockwood's staff meticulously planned this operation, which was partially motivated by his desire to revenge the loss of Commander Morton and the *Wahoo*. In Operation Barney, nine boats led by Capt. Earl Hydeman surprised the Japanese and sank twenty-seven vessels in their backyard.[154] What may have been an unwelcomed new tactic ultimately became a thoroughly developed form of naval adaptation. But it cost Lockwood one of his own—the USS *Bonefish* (SS 223), sunk with all hands. Lockwood later would promote the results of this operation in another bulletin, but omitted any mention of the loss of the *Bonefish*.[155]

Without King's intervention, this adaptation never would have been initiated. The success of its changes may be a function of having permitted commanders to develop their own doctrine. By the end of the war, Lockwood was more enthusiastic about the prospects of packs, and after the war even wrote a book on the subject.[156] A total of sixty-five different attack groups deployed from Hawaii, and additional packs patrolled out of Australia as well.[157] They never focused on King's original intent of serving as ambushers against naval combatants. Instead, the packs remained true to Lockwood's *guerre de course* against Japan's economy.

After mid-1944 there were no major adaptations in submarine warfare during the remainder of the Pacific campaign. Ships, doctrine, training, and weapons were now highly effective. In a sense, the U.S. submarine war did not truly begin until the middle of 1943. Until then it "had been a learning period, a time of testing, of weeding out, of fixing defects in weapons, strategy, and tactics, of waiting for sufficient numbers of submarines and workable torpedoes."[158] By the end of the summer, Japan's economic lifeline was in tatters. The submarine force had perfected its doctrine, its captains were relentlessly aggressive, and more important, their weapons worked reliably. The period of learning and adaptation was over at this point. The sea wolves were numerous, trained, and well-armed. In 1944, the full vengeful force of the American sub fleet fell on the Japanese.

The results for 1944 were impressive. Exploiting an increase in the total number of boats, and the shorter patrol distances afforded by advanced bases in Guam and Saipan, U.S. patrol numbers increased by 50 percent to 520 patrols. These patrols fired more than six thousand torpedoes, which were now both functional and plentiful. They sank more than 600 ships, for almost 3 million tons of shipping. They reduced Japan's critical imports by 36 percent, by cutting the merchant fleet in half (from 4.1 million tons to 2 million tons). Japan reacted belatedly to the targeting of oil tankers by building 200 ships with a gross tonnage over 600,000 tons. Although oil tanker production kept up with a high rate of destruction, oil imports dropped severely.[159] Again, success came at a cost, as Japanese adaptations increased their antisubmarine capability. During this period, the U.S. submarine fleet sustained higher losses, with a total of nineteen boats lost with almost all hands.

There was little for U.S. submarines to achieve in 1945, since the target set was largely eliminated. This did not stop Lockwood from sending his boats into harm's way inside the Sea of Japan to eradicate any remaining economic activity.[160] The U.S. Navy now had more than 120 operational boats in the Pacific, and their effectiveness was improved by new, closer operating bases at Subic Bay in the Philippines and by Lockwood's force, which operated out of Guam. The shorter distances into hostile waters gave each boat days to patiently await traffic along coastal trade lanes. In what became the culminating year, the submarine force initiated 300 patrols but sank "only" 190 ships for 1.2 million tons. Japan had lost 88 percent of its merchant fleet by this point, with only 650,000 tons of capacity left—well below what was needed merely for civilian consumption, much less for a continued defense of the imperial islands.[161] By the end of the war, oil stocks were severely constrained, limiting the ability of the Japanese navy to train pilots or conduct naval operations.[162] Likewise, the economic productivity of the Japanese empire was grinding to a halt. Lockwood could brag at the end of the war that his force had sunk 116 oil tankers.[163] Japanese tankers delivered only one-tenth of the oil produced during 1944–45.[164] The oil dependency itself spelled Japan's defeat.[165]

The torpedo problems were behind as far as the submarine force was concerned. It now had the right doctrine, updated tactics, aggressive leaders, and experienced crews. Despite the risky operations being conducted in shallow waters near Japan, and the riskier task of surfacing for extended periods of daylight to pick up survivors from downed aircraft in the open ocean, the Pacific force lost only eight boats in the final year of the conflict.[166]

Overall, the statistical and strategic results are impressive. Over the course of World War II, covering both major theaters, some 465 officers captained 263

American submarines and conducted 1,736 patrols.[167] The lion's share of the effort was in the Pacific. The sailors of the submarine fleet comprised just 2 percent of the total of U.S. naval manpower, but their boats accounted for 55 percent of all Japanese shipping losses in the war. The sinkings included 1,300 ships, among them 20 major naval combatants (8 carriers, 1 battleship, and 11 cruisers). Japanese merchant shipping losses included 5.5 million tons of shipping, or about 85 percent of the country's total wartime production.[168] This exceeded the total sunk by the Navy's surface vessels, its carrier-based aircraft, and the U.S. Army Air Corps' bombers combined. By August of 1944, the Japanese merchant marine was in tatters and was unable to fulfill its minimum requirements to support the civilian economy.[169] These successes represent three overlapping, but not concurrent, adaptation cycles. Each was complicated by the pressures of conflict against a thinking adversary. Adaptation was either directed from the top or finally approved at the operational level, but the doctrine, tactics, and command techniques all derived from operators at the tactical level. Here again, hard-earned information derived by combat was pushed forward from the bottom to higher headquarters levels, which provided the necessary momentum at the institutional level. This level also authorized the learning that was distributed horizontally to other units and to the institution.

Organizational Learning Capacity

How did the U.S. Navy come to undertake these concurrent adaptive cycles of the U.S. submarine force? Our theoretical foundation has hypothesized the need for four components of Organizational Learning Capacity, including: (a) credible leadership; (b) an organizational culture conducive to learning; (c) problem-recognition mechanisms, or learning teams; and (d) learning dissemination mechanisms.

Credible Leadership

There are numerous strong leaders in this case study, all of whom possessed credible credentials in submarine warfare and had open minds, willing to test existing methods and doctrine. Admirals King and Nimitz were intimately familiar with submarines, both having commanded boats as young officers. King was an ambitious and demanding professional, with a brusque manner that brooked few arguments.[170] He had had experience with submarines early in his career and commanded a division of boats as well as the U.S. submarine base at New London.[171] He also completed aviation training late in his career as a captain, earning his pilot's wings at age fifty so that he could command the USS *Lexington* (CV 2).[172] He wrote articles for the naval professional journal, the Naval Institute's *Proceedings*, and continued to promote innovative ideas during his career. As a junior officer, King once claimed the Navy was "clinging to things that are old because they are old."[173] King claimed to be a proponent of decentralized leadership, recognizing that the coming war would require "the initiative of the subordinate," with less detail in orders on how to do something and more emphasis on the "what" needed to be done.[174] Admittedly, he would often lapse from this practice himself.[175]

Nimitz had a different style of leadership. He exuded calm and competence.[176] And he was known for fostering collaborative decision-making.[177] He, too, had early experience in submarines, having been drafted involuntarily into boats before World War I. Overall, Nimitz commanded six boats as a junior officer, led a submarine division, and created the submarine base at Pearl Harbor. A quiet professional, who survived a court of inquiry for having grounded his destroyer as a junior officer, Nimitz was an expert in diesel engines, having visited German manufacturing plants and served a tour at Navy headquarters pushing the introduction of diesels. He, too, would write in the naval professional journal. Both King and Nimitz lectured about the potential offensive opportunities presented by fleet submarines—well ahead of the technology of the day.[178]

The principal actors at the operational level in this case study are admirals Lockwood and Christie. Both spent the majority of their careers in submarines. Both were considered advocates and leaders in submarine development during the interwar period. Lockwood was called "Mr. Submarine," famous for his advocacy of the long-range fleet boat.[179] Christie, his peer, was known as "Mr. Torpedo." Postwar reports comment positively on Lockwood's operational command. Known for an informal style of leadership and for being a gentle critic and dedicated mentor, he defended subordinates and reflected "loyalty down" rather than just demanding compliance.[180] He deferred to his commanders and understood that they had the best insights, once noting:

> I run the show from a desk in Pearl Harbor, with occasional trips to the front. I make my decisions based on reports from boat commanders sent through

their superiors, not from intuitive estimates or guesses. I rely heavily on the judgments of those in command of the submarines on the spot, and whole-heartedly support their decisions because they are there.[181]

Lockwood was open to new ideas and actively sought out commanders like Morton for personal interviews. He read and commented on the reports written by the skippers after each patrol. Lockwood attempted to ensure that he had the best information from the fighting units of his command. He would personally meet each boat as it returned to port and would go over reports with the commanders.[182] In addition to formal endorsements, Lockwood sent personal notes to commanders, to avoid any stigma from formal and public endorsements or criticisms. He also repeatedly sought to get operating time inside the more modern boats that were being deployed with new technologies such as the TDCs and sonar and radar. He collected insights and evidence from many sources and even sought contradictory information.

His subordinates described him as "not conformist and against rule-book thinking."[183] As we have seen in at least three occasions, Lockwood was willing to experiment when necessary. He was also willing to press hard to get needed changes and once confronted Nimitz to get a sub base built at Midway.[184] While it can be said that Lockwood was persistent in trying to enhance the effectiveness of his force, he was also deferential to higher headquarters and to the Bureau of Ordnance, despite its abominable torpedo design and its testing failures.

Lockwood comes off well in comparison to Christie, who retarded learning in his command. He overcentralized his operations in Australia and created a command climate in which he had stifled critical inquiry and adaptation. His adamant insistence that commanders not criticize faulty or suspect weapons in their patrol reports closed out the possibility of learning in his command. He persisted in defending a faulty torpedo, due to his personal involvement and bias. As late as March 1944 Christie still had ships out trying to perfect the flawed exploder.[185] Christie's blind commitment to the Mark 6 exploder did not help his boats, and his refusal to learn from operating boats in his command or from other boats in the theater is in marked contrast to Lockwood. In short, Mr. Torpedo had credibility, but he failed to create or sustain a collaborative or learning climate conducive to adaptation. Lockwood sustained a more open and tolerant command style that allowed officers to challenge doctrine and make independent judgments. He him-self, however, never felt empowered to alter depth-setting mechanisms, exploder devices, or firing-pins without approval from higher authority. He could have done more to enable his subordinates to be better-armed and more effective by resolving the torpedo defects earlier. But what Dönitz did in a few months with torpedoes took Lockwood and the Navy more than eighteen months to resolve. Although there was a lot of ambiguity in patrol reports and the war, there was lit-tle fog in the fact that the Navy's torpedoes were not ineffective.

Organizational Culture

At an Organizational Culture level, the submarine community had to comport its specialty within the Navy's dominant sense of traditionalism. Its mask or "way of war" and Mahan's conception of sea control were the prevailing mental models.[186] War Plan Orange remained the embodied set of beliefs about the Navy's princi-pal operational challenge and how the fleet would fight. Thus, the submarine had to fit and conform to this vision of a transoceanic drive across the Pacific to meet and defeat the Imperial Japanese Navy. During the interwar era, the Navy intellec-tually wrestled with the relative importance of surface gunships and carrier avia-tion. This pitted the battleship Gun Club against the rising advocates of airpower.

Carl Builder's framework for service culture in the United States underscores the unique aspects of the Navy within the American armed forces.[187] The char-acteristics, icons, and "altars for worship" of the Navy involve its traditions, its rise to global preeminence, its technological skills, and its notion of institutional inde-pendence. Self-measurement, Builder's second element, focuses on the size of the fleet and how many capital ships or submarines were operating. Related to self-measurement in this case study is the extensive interest in quantitative measure-ments of ships sunk and the total tonnage of ships sunk or damaged. Every letter and bulletin is replete with comments about monthly and quarterly tabulations of sinkings, and constant references to increasing the "bag," or tally, of vessels sunk by each ship. Certainly the Navy had a preoccupation with hardware and technol-ogy. It was a capital-intensive institution that operated in an unforgiving domain. Builder's distinction about the degree and extent of intraservice or branch distinc-tion is also appropriate, especially in this era, as the "blackshoe" (or surface) Navy faced competition for influence from the growing aviation branch (whose members wore brown shoes to underscore their branch's identity). Finally, the Navy brooked no insecurity over its legitimacy or relevancy. It would have been happy to conduct the entire Pacific campaign without the U.S. Army.[188]

The role of Navy schools, including the U.S. Naval Academy in Annapolis, as a form of acculturation is evident. "With its isolated environment, highly ritualized and severe rites of passage, and demanding emphasis on fellowship," one student observed, "the Navy created for its officer corps the foundation of a separate society: an embracing ethos."[189] "Above all, Annapolis functioned as an engine of assimilation. It tossed out those who could not or would not fit."[190] They were the product of a common worldview, a common warfighting philosophy, inbred on purpose and inculcated with a corporate identity as U.S. Naval Academy graduates and naval officers. Many had technical degrees, and they were competent seamen first and "Apostles of American Sea Power" second. The Naval Academy established the ethos, while Newport's "granite-girded" halls provided the doctrine and the intellectual foundations for the Navy's mission. The Naval War College reinforced the Navy's identity and mission, as well as providing a common naval doctrine. At the dawn of World War II, 99 percent of all Navy admirals were graduates of the year-long course.[191] Commanders came from a common background but were not a uniform product.[192]

Aside from its corporate identity and the Navywide operating culture of independent command at sea, the submarine branch itself was more competitive, engineering-based, and problem-solving oriented. The submariners were by necessity a rules-based group and subjected to a common operating doctrine and procedures. They were not incentivized to deviate from this core operating procedure, and the older officers were the most-indoctrinated to play by the rules-based system. It is clear that there was a generational tension between the less flexible older officers, who were more comfortable with rigid doctrine and structured roles than the younger officers, who were more competitive. The former were comfortable in a control-based culture, whereas the latter were results-driven and more at ease with flexible command styles and initiative. The nature of the new operating code for submarine warfare in the Pacific required a more creative or risk-taking culture.

Learning Mechanisms

The Navy's submarine service had possibly the best after-action and lessons-learned gathering process of any branch of the Allied military. Early in the war, the Navy tasked each boat captain with preparing a formal patrol report. While each boat was on the last leg of returning from a combat patrol, its captain generally would be working full time on making a formal record of the patrol and any combat actions in which the boat had taken part. These reports included tactical maps of each firing solution on each target. On return to port, each captain would formally submit the patrol report to his immediate superior, and copies were disseminated horizontally to other boats in the same squadron. This provided a means of feeding forward valuable information about the operating environment, new tactics, and techniques employed during the mission, and on what needed to be enhanced with respect to materiel such as periscopes, radar, and torpedoes. Commanders were not beyond modifying their torpedoes in order to enhance their chances of success, not reflecting these changes in patrol reports, and swearing their officers and crews to secrecy.[193]

In addition to the reports, each commander in the chain of command would review and append a formal written endorsement. These endorsements would assess each patrol as successful or not and often publicly commend a commander for aggressiveness or rebuke one for prolificacy with torpedoes. Endorsements of the war patrol reports became a tool for reinforcing best practices and produced a collective understanding.[194] Lockwood encouraged frank criticisms by officers in endorsements, and some veterans believe the endorsements and comments were as important as the basic report.[195] Down in Australia, Christie praised his officers if they were productive but curtailed honest assessments of torpedo deficiencies, which limited sharing and learning.

In a sense the submarine force patrol reports were the equivalent of the large forums that had critiqued the peacetime fleet exercises. Lockwood and his staff would examine every patrol report closely, would summon both operational commanders and technicians for questioning, and strove to meet and interview each returning boat captain to gain the latest intelligence directly from the source without filters.[196] In recognition of the possible adverse reaction to negative comments in endorsements, Lockwood developed a habit of sending private letters to each skipper. These were intended to enhance the fleet overall, constructively, rather than to issue depersonalized comments fleetwide.

Endorsements proved to be a way for the submarine community at large to learn how officialdom viewed each new combat lesson, and how others might view initiatives and overall boat performance. Such endorsements were crucial in framing new lessons across the enterprise. Naval historians and former commanders described them as the principal policymaking documents for the submarine fleet, by which the force's doctrinally approved "way of war" was disseminated.[197]

As a whole, the Navy did not have formal mechanisms for gathering operational experience or lessons from its operational forces aside from the operating results garnered by the fleet in the war diaries and patrol reports. Its intellectual capital and assets were heavily focused on strategy, wargaming, and naval history and were centered at the Naval War College.[198] Thanks to a culture of learning, the Navy refocused itself to learn from actual experience at sea very quickly. As one recent historical account of the early stages of naval warfare in the Pacific notes:

> Combat was a hard and unforgiving school, but the Navy was taking its lessons to heart. If the service did one thing right after the debacle of December 7, it was to become collectively obsessed with learning, and improving. Each new encounter with the enemy was mined for all the wisdom and insights it had to offer. Every after-action report included a section of analysis and recommendations, and those nuggets of hard-won knowledge were absorbed into future command decisions, doctrine, planning, and training throughout the service.[199]

There is a structural component to support learning in this case. Because Lockwood had served in London at the U.S. embassy and had participated in intelligence and technical exchanges between the British and U.S. navies, he was aware of how much operations research in Britain had contributed to the effectiveness of its efforts, including the reapplication of convoy operations and search techniques. When Lockwood replaced Rear Admiral English at Pearl Harbor, Admiral King offered him access to his Submarine Operations Research Group (SORG). That group had proven its value in the Battle of the Atlantic and was already connecting naval problems to operational research techniques. Ultimately, Lockwood decided to set up his own operations research shop at Pearl Harbor, complete with crude IBM processing machines.[200] This team was slow to get started and to adapt itself from antisubmarine work to submarine warfare. He also accessed naval research and development assets from the University of California, San Diego, which proved instrumental in bringing new technologies such as sonar to the submarine force.[201]

Lockwood pushed for his operations research teams and scientists to get on patrol boats so that they could better understand the operational context the submarines had to face. Intelligently, Lockwood located his operations research staff in the same complex that his strategic planners used. The relationship ensured that insights from analyses of tactical data were systemically captured and studied. Their insights were quickly cycled back through special reports or synthesized into tactical bulletins to the fleet.[202]

The submarine leadership came to value the objective and independent analysis provided by the civilians and gave them uniforms and allowed them to use officer quarters and have access to the officers' clubs. It was not long after his staff was augmented with the SORG that Lockwood issued his first campaign plan and raised the priority placed on targeting oil tankers.[203] Lockwood used the SORG members well beyond just their scientific disciplines and found their insights as a Red Team—a sort of devil's advocate—invaluable. For example, the SORG reviewed the classified plans for Operation Barney in 1945 and recommended against the operation due to the level of risk it posed. Lockwood read that report carefully but ordered the mission anyway.[204] Had the Navy wargamed unrestricted warfare or studied Japan's economy better, or employed these analysts in 1942, it could have targeted Japan's energy lifelines much earlier and more effectively.

The adjustments required to rectify the defects in the Navy's tactics and torpedoes took time to get fed forward into the hierarchy and its supporting bureaucracies. A major lesson from this case is the need for institutional adaptation to be energized by closer relation to the challenges faced by the combat forces. Even today, without the fidelity and urgency of operational pressures, these supporting institutions, such as Newport's Torpedo Station, may not be able to understand the challenges of the operating environment. Thus they will not learn what they need to learn, or more accurately unlearn, to promote larger institutional changes.

As noted in one historical assessment, "The lessons of prewar exercises had to be unlearned in the heat of combat."[205] Adaptation may be as much unlearning the outdated or irrelevant as it is learning new tactics or competencies.

Dissemination Mechanisms

The patrol report process included feedback loops that cycled lessons and best practices to both tactical and institutional organizations in the United States. During the course of the war, the submarine community shared its patrol reports with schools, training commands, and submarine and torpedo production facilities to give them a better sense of how their work materially aided the submarines in combat at sea. Not only were these war patrol reports used to feed better practices horizontally, but they were sent to the classrooms of the Submarine School back at New London.[206] This proved to be an effective mechanism of relating combat-tested field inputs to organizational goals and to force-generation activities as new crews were developed.

It also shortened the feedback loops between design, employment, and refinement of submarine components, especially alterations to optimize communications and radar gear. In this way, the institutional side of the Navy became aware of the single-loop adjustments made by the operating or tactical level of the organization. Lockwood even took steps to provide his officers with copies of the war patrol reports while they were resting at the Royal Hawaiian Hotel.[207] Reading patrol reports became a form of self-improvement or pastime reading while at sea.[208] This supports the idea that social and informal methods of distributed learning occur that reinforce formal learning mechanisms.

Finally, the Navy fed back lessons learned and new techniques to the fleet through short doctrine reports called submarine bulletins. The Submarine Force Pacific published numerous tactical submarine bulletins over the course of the war. The Australian sub force also issued bulletins. These became an official means of recording and sharing best practices and semi-official doctrine within the theater and the force. It was in the bulletins that radar employment techniques and improved wolfpack tactics were fed back to the larger force after trial and error at sea. The entire system—patrol reports, distributed endorsements, and doctrinally oriented submarine bulletins—made up a classic learning system based on an open feedback loop.[209] The patrol report fed forward fresh insights and the endorsements or bulletins fed back approvals and new doctrine.[210] Postwar memoirs explicitly note that these reports were written with an emphasis on content, but also with some literary flair, to share with the submarine community.[211]

This conclusion runs counter to that of Rosen, who argues that the Navy achieved adaptation largely by a change in the composition of the officer cadre, not by any form of collective learning.[212] Rosen's argument is supported by a single observation from one submariner, Richard O'Kane, and the fact that 30 percent of the sub commanders were relieved the first year. But the vast majority of officers (70 percent) adjusted to the complexity of unrestricted warfare and new tactics over time in 1942, and even more did so in later years. Rosen's position does not account for the overwhelming empirical evidence after 1942 or the perspectives of many boat captains, such as James F. Calvert and Eugene B. Fluckey, who contend that the adaptation was organic and promoted by Lockwood's endorsements and bulletins.[213]

All told, the U.S. submarine force adapted over a relatively long period of time. It made tactical changes organically and quickly, perfecting tactics and techniques in periscope and night surface attacks. Simple adjustments and significant changes to torpedoes should have occurred much faster. Organizational culture abetted adjustments in techniques, since the Navy was competitive, engineering oriented, and blessed with a problem-solving culture. However, the bureaucratic character of the larger institutional Navy retarded the support that the submarines should have gotten from the Bureau of Ordnance.

The initial absence of dedicated learning teams slowed organizational adaptation. They later proved to be useful, and if they had existed prior to 1944 they would have been even more valuable. Lockwood's lack of on-hand technical "learning teams" may account partially for the slow investigation phases of adaptation when the problem and possible solutions remained unclear. The most significant attribute for adaptation was the Navy's learning-dissemination mechanisms. The detailed war patrol reports and endorsements of higher command levels promoted robust information sharing and exploitation. The fleet came to recognize how to exploit these to push new ideas and problems forward.

The necessary adjustments for effective submarine operations ultimately relied on the adaptive capacity of the submarine force, which had an engineer's eye for problem identification and for technical evaluation of hardware. The entire Navy had been imbued with collaborative learning through exercise, games, and conferences.[214] The submarine force also reflected this collective process of engaged reflection and inputs into a constantly evolving way of fighting. Strong organizational leadership, which worked to find hard data and "ground truth" at sea, assisted the learning and adaptation process. A superior learning information and dissemination system through widely shared war patrol diaries facilitated the process of learning. A process of analysis and synthesis resulted in lessons and new tactics being fed backward into the force and fed up into higher-level learning at the submarine schools.

Adaptation was much slower than needed, especially the corrections to the defects in torpedo design. Once problems were identified (depth setting and contact exploders), they were rather easily adjusted. The exploder problem was more difficult, and the evidence more mixed. This analysis suggests that the Navy's bureaucratic structure retarded adaptation, while its leadership and culture were positive shapers. The independent and results-oriented culture of the submarine officer corps was a major contributor to the implementation of change.

The four internal attributes effectively support the Navy's Organizational Learning Capacity. Submarine patrols generated experiences that were shared and fed forward routinely as part of routine reports or inquiry. They were systematically reviewed and endorsed. Compilations of success and failed practices were examined and interpreted. The endorsements of such reports constituted the interpretation phase of the model, as well as feedback to lower levels as to what changes in practice were approved. Deficiencies or performance gaps were regularly noted, and work-arounds or solutions were proposed and tested by higher organizational levels. The persistent reports of torpedo failure required investigation by Lockwood in Australia and in Hawaii through carefully executed experiments. These efforts were valuable in confirming torpedo shortfalls identified very early in the war. Ultimately, the investigation conducted by the Submarine Force Pacific resulted in directed adaptive learning fixes to tactics and to the torpedo depth-settings, the deactivation of the magnetic exploder, and to Hawaii's firing-pin fixes. These results were eventually forwarded to be integrated into the force generation activities of the Navy for institutionalization.

The introduction of wolfpack tactics can also be examined within the model. Even in this one case of directed, top-down learning, the operational level force thoroughly investigated the nature of the problem and explored options for command-and-control, organizational arrangements, and doctrine over a period of several months. The doctrine and tactics were tested and then applied at sea. The first patrols were documented and the insights of all commanders were assimilated into further changes. Commanders found that the collective-action group was useful in searching out targets but generated lots of radio traffic once attacks began.[215] Senior Navy commanders directed the need for Submarine Force Pacific to change tactics, but the command investigated the doctrine and technology from the bottom up.

Conclusion

Looking back after the war, many Navy officers believe that their prewar planning was superb. "War Plan Orange persevered for forty years and eventually won the war," notes Miller, "What more can one ask of a great plan?"[216] War Plan Orange animated the Navy's thinking and framed the way Navy leaders approached the Pacific war. It remained the Navy's mental model of war, which shaped how submarines would be employed. It was the embodiment of the Navy's culture and ethos and still animates most of the Navy's thinking about future conflict.

There is no doubt that the American Navy was effective, eventually. Although the Navy got the strategy right, its surface force tactics were described as ritualistic and left the service unprepared for the pace and uncertainty of battle at sea, particularly night actions.[217]

But the ultimate victory was not due entirely to the strategic planning of War Plan Orange and the fleet design or doctrine that it justified. Some success must be credited to the adaptation of the small submarine community. War Plan Orange's envisioned blockade began much earlier than originally designed. It preceded rather than followed the Mahanian clashes long sought by the American Navy. Because the Americans did not anticipate the future of the submarine with great foresight, they had to learn under fire. They eventually learned and adapted tactics, training, and techniques and fixed their torpedoes.

This case study shows that Rosen's conception about the difficulty of innovating or adapting during war is correct.[218] Information was hard to come by, confounded by human failings and new technologies. Internal factors, including leaders, bureaucracies, and culture, all came into play. One problem masked another.

Torpedoes running too deep obscured the fact that the magnetic exploder was not working. The emphasis on getting "keel-breaker" shots and one-shot-one-kill efficiency did not help the Navy realize that the contact exploders were outdated.

Ultimately, the U.S. submarine force made a major contribution, one for which the Navy had not originally designed it. The postwar assessment from inside the submarine community was telling: "Neither by training nor indoctrination was the U.S. Submarine Force readied for unrestricted warfare."[219] Rather than a campaign of cataclysmic salvos by battleships or sorties of dive bombers between opposing battle lines of carrier groups, it was a war of attrition. The submarines learned and adapted, generally from the bottom up. Ironically, a Navy that had dismissed commerce raiding and invested little intellectual effort in studying it, proved to be ruthlessly effective at it.[220] Yet, it took adjustments, adaptation, and learning to create those competencies.

Overall, the competition in naval combat and learning dominated the Pacific war. The U.S. Navy and Japanese navy had their respective strengths and weaknesses, and the United States had substantial industrial and technological advantages that came into play as the war progressed. But this case study and other studies suggest that a significant "learning gap" was exposed after Midway in both surface and subsurface warfare.[221] That gap grew wider and wider as the U.S. submarines adjusted to new demands, technologies, and roles. The Japanese began to adapt later in the war, but not nearly at the same rate. The U.S. Navy achieved "organizational learning dominance."[222] In the end, while painfully slow at times, its Organizational Learning Capacity contributed to its ultimate success.

CHAPTER 4

Airpower

Adaptation over Korea

*All human institutions must inevitably deal with the tension between
continuity and change, between preserving that which has met the
needs of the past and adapting to the challenge of change in a
confusing present and uncertain future.*

—MILITARY HISTORIAN HAROLD WINTON [1]

A s it had many times before, the United States went to war in 1950 woe-
fully unprepared.[2] Policymakers can take the blame for some of this, and
perhaps the intelligence community can as well. The nation as a whole
was converting guns into plowshares and enjoying the peace that World War II
supposedly had earned. The principal concern was Europe's recovery and the protracted standoff between the United States and the Communist Bloc that would
become known as the Cold War.

In some respects, the Air Force was better-postured at the beginning of the
conflict than the Army was. It was a new institution, established only in 1947. It
was surely not on a war footing, but it was making enormous strides to create the
requisite organization and extend its competencies in strategic bombing, nuclear
systems, and modern jets. Overall, the postwar period was a dynamic one for the
Air Force that included dramatic technological changes.

The one thing on which the Air Force had not focused was the kind of war
that broke out in the summer of 1950, when the sturdy T-34 tanks of the North
Korean People's Army began driving south. The brave but poor performance of
America's Task Force Smith in the early stages of the war suggest that General of

the Army Douglas MacArthur, Supreme Allied Commander, and the U.S. Army did not take the prospects of heavy combat seriously. As in most of America's first battles, surprises occurred that required major adaptations. The changes were acquired the hard way, and under adverse conditions. The Korean War shows how quickly a combat-proven military establishment can be surprised, and what the costs of getting it wrong could be.[3]

The principal subject of this book is the challenge of recognizing that one's pre-conceptions of the next war are rarely accurate. As Williamson Murray has noted, all military institutions get the next war wrong in some way, no matter how rigorously they explore emerging trends. The issue is really how quickly they perceive the gaps between their preparations and actual conditions on the battlefield. This chapter will answer that question about the U.S. Air Force in the Korean conflict.

The Air Force had had some experience at recognizing the importance of sound intellectual preparation in response to military and technological developments in both peace and war. During the interwar period instructors at the Air Corps Tactical School developed and advocated a doctrine based on independent air operations and long-range bombing. The school was home for members of the "Bomber Mafia," which developed and proselytized strategic bombing theory.[4] Future wars, they contended, would be won by bombers—by striking directly at the "vital centers" of the opponent's war production capacity and economic infrastructure.[5] There were advocates for pursuit aircraft and fighters at the school as well—in particular Claire Chennault, then a captain in the Air Force. But once Chennault left to fight for the Chinese, the bomber community dominated the school's curricula, forming a monopoly on high-altitude, unescorted precision bombing.[6] To understand the scope of adaptation inside an institution truly, one must begin with understanding what the prior experiences of that particular armed force were and what critical lessons the organization absorbed. For the Air Force in 1950 that meant coming to terms with its perceptions about World War II.

Europe

In the crucial campaigns in Europe, "virtually nothing happened the way prewar air champions had predicted," Murray and military historian Allan R. Millett observed.[7] Airpower advocates had spent the interwar years "proving" the value of independent, unescorted, precision daylight bombing. Combat in Poland and France did not deter their pursuit, and when the Army Air Corps finally got to Europe itself it insisted on implementing its doctrine regardless of evidence. The Eighth Air Force conducted tests of its doctrine and capabilities in late 1942 in missions flown from England against German-occupied marshalling yards in France. Maj. Gen. Ira Eaker, the group's deputy commander, believed that the tests affirmed Army Air Forces doctrine. "Three hundred heavy bombers can attack any target in Germany by daylight with less than 4 percent losses." He wrote, "The daylight bombing of Germany with planes of the B-17 and B-24 type is feasible, practicable, and economical."[8] Based on this limited test in an escorted mission, it appears that the disciples of airpower remained bent on proving their theory.

Several air raids in 1943 focused on bombing German industrial targets. Air Force targeting analysis identified ball-bearing production as a potential weak link in the German industrial system. Missions over Schweinfurt targeted these facilities, but the raids, with more than three hundred planes, had loss rates of almost 15 percent. On August 17 the 1st Bombardment Wing launched 183 B-17s at Schweinfurt. Thirty-six of those planes were destroyed by the German Luftwaffe. Another 127 bombers went after German airplane-manufacturing plants that same day, and the command lost 24 more B-17s. On September 6 another 260 bombers targeted Stuttgart and 45 were shot down. In October the Eighth Air Force began bombing operations to break down the German defenses. In just 10 days, the Luftwaffe had a feast and shot down 164 American bombers.[9] Overall crew losses from April to October 1943 totaled more than 30 percent.[10] These significant losses did not deter Army Air Forces leaders.

Thus, while the Air Force leaders insisted on high-altitude, precision daylight bombing, it came at great cost because they did not anticipate possible adversary adaptations such as radar-directed antiaircraft batteries, early-warning radar, and proficient interceptors with powerful cannon.[11] Results over Germany forced the Eighth Air Force into rethinking targeting, escorts, and high-altitude targeting.[12] By 1944, targeting was focused more on aircraft manufacturing plants, which did not cause a major drop in German fighter plane outputs. The campaigns became essentially a war of aero-attrition, designed to wear down the Luftwaffe by killing pilots to gain air superiority. Eventually, the German fighters came to the aid of their own industrial base, and then attacked aggressively. Through this attrition "U.S. long-range fighters broke the back of German airpower."[13]

The air superiority that resulted from the bombing campaign was also an advantage to the Allied ground campaigns as British and American divisions broke out of Normandy and began their offensive to liberate France.[14] Daylight bombing continued for the rest of the war, with focus on the oil resources. The fuel losses impeded Luftwaffe training and German armor production. Overall, Allied bombing devastated German industry as the Allied armies converged in Germany.[15] The overall combined bomber offensive in Europe, while neither efficient nor elegant, was ruthlessly decisive.[16] Both the U.S. Strategic Bombing Survey and recent scholarship have found that airpower was decisive in the Allied victory.[17]

In the Pacific

Many of the same lessons were learned in the vast reaches of the Pacific theater.[18] By 1944 the Allies finally were getting meaningful results from massive bombing raids against Japan's economic and industrial infrastructure. Operations in the Pacific benefited from the introduction of the newer bomber, the long-awaited B-29 Superfortress. With a speed of 350 miles an hour and a ceiling of 30,000 feet, the Superfortress was less vulnerable to Japanese air defenses than the slower B-17. Moreover, it carried three times the bomb load and had twice the range—critical factors, considering the vast expanse of the theater.[19]

Centralized control of air forces by airmen became a reality in April 1944 with the creation of the Twentieth Air Force, a strategic bombing force directly under Gen. Henry H. (Hap) Arnold in Washington, where he served as executive agent for the Joint Chiefs of Staff. The Twentieth's mission was to take the war to the Japanese by conducting a long-range bombing campaign against the Home Islands. This arrangement, in effect, gave the Army Air Forces equality with the ground and naval forces in the Pacific.[20]

However, the 20th Bomber Command, flying B-29 missions from China, was not achieving the desired results. The bombers were operating at their maximum range, at high altitudes against stiff headwinds, with their target areas often enshrouded in clouds. Arnold brought in Maj. Gen. Curtis E. LeMay, with recent experience in Europe, to enhance bombing operations. LeMay expanded the concept of operations to include flying at lower altitudes and flying at night, with bombloads of incendiaries.[21] This extended the range of the planes but reduced the survival rate for crews that flew within range of Japan's defenses. LeMay targeted Japan's widely dispersed industrial sector by fire-bombing Japanese cities. From March to August 1945 he waged a relentless campaign, with improved radar, enhanced navigation, and altered bombing tactics that reduced Japan's major urban areas to ash. It was still not enough to force Tokyo to capitulate, as noted by two historians:

> With argument, the bombing crushed the Japanese aviation industry and contributed to the decline of power-generation and industrial production within Japan. The fire-bombing brought the war home to the Home Islands in ways that no other Allied operation could have, but it did not in itself persuade the Japanese political elite to give up the war.[22]

Ultimately, Truman's decision to use the nuclear bomb ended the war. While the new Air Force had staked its future on an untested prewar doctrine, the bomber thesis proved untenable in the face of a determined opponent and the actual conditions of combat. The underlying assumptions about unescorted, high-altitude, precision daylight bombing were mauled in the skies over Japan and Germany. The impact of enemy defenses, both pursuit and radar-directed antiaircraft defenses, proved formidable. Air Force adaptations were needed, in particular the introduction of the long-distance escort, the famed P-51 Mustang.[23] Airpower shortened the war in each theater and made Allied operations more effective by decreasing the materiel readiness and sustaining supplies to German and Japanese defenders. This did not occur without cost. The butcher's bill for the air war against Germany was 26,000 airmen—more than the Marines lost in the entire Pacific—and the air attacks against Japan cost 2,148 airmen in 14 months.[24]

These wars "defined the organizational culture of the USAF, laying down foundational attitudes that have characterized how the organization has fought wars across its existence," says military affairs scholar Robert Farley.[25] The Air Force kept to its Douhetian beliefs and its fundamental theory of centrally controlled precision-bombing.[26] The Air Force insisted that its fundamental doctrine, which called for high-altitude, daylight precision bombing, would work. As one Air Force historian noted, "On no point was American air doctrine more clear-cut. On no point was it to prove so wrong."[27]

Despite the evidence of combat, Air Force leaders convinced themselves that their approach had brought about total victory. Their fervor made strategic bombing an article of faith proven by two total wars fought to clear victory. The Air Force generals who held senior posts by 1950 had an indelible conviction about the role of airpower, as captured by one researcher:

> The emotional intensity of combat . . . amplifies the imprint on the memory and behavior of the future military leader. . . . The generals who would rule America's Air Force for its first three decades developed some lasting perspectives on warfare, airpower, and leadership early in their careers. Their pioneering experience in aerial warfare centered around the airplane and its attempt to return decisiveness to wars of the mid-twentieth century.[28]

There were multiple motivations for the intensity of the airpower ideology. One clear motivation, developed deep in the Air Force, was to establish itself as an independent service.[29] To the Air Force, it had "purchased its birthright with the blood and sacrifice of innumerable air and ground crews in combat around the world."[30] Although much of its prewar theory was severely questioned, the Air Force proved to be an adaptive organization that made a major contribution to the war effort. It was not as decisive in strategic bombing as the Bomber Mafia initially conceived it, but airpower was surely vital to victory in both theaters.[31]

Prewar Posture and Order of Battle

Command of U.S. forces in the Pacific theater was assigned to Douglas MacArthur, commander of the Far East Command. The air component of MacArthur's command was the Far East Air Forces (FEAF), born out of the campaigns in the Pacific during World War II. The FEAF was commanded by Lt. Gen. George Stratemeyer, a veteran of the India-Burma theater. His force was responsible for the defense of Japan and also oversaw U.S. military activities on Guam, Formosa, and the Philippines. Stratemeyer's principal airpower component was the Fifth Air Force, led by Maj. Gen. Earle Partridge, who had overseen operations in the North African theater and served as chief of staff of XII Bomber Command in World War II. The Fifth Air Force had air bases and flying squadrons distributed in Japan, the Philippines, and Guam. The laydown or base assignments of the force and their associated aircraft are listed in table 4.1. The combat forces initially assigned to the Fifth Air Force included 365 F-80C Shooting Star jet interceptors, 32 F-82 all-weather fighters, and 16 RF-80 photo reconnaissance planes. The force also included a mix of light and medium bombers, twenty-six of the venerable B-26 and twenty-two newer (and longer-range) B-29 Superfortresses. The FEAF also had cargo and utility aircraft to support the movement of troops and supplies in-theater.[32]

The largest component of the FEAF was the Fifth Air Force, which had the principal mission of defending Japan from attack. It had eight squadrons of aging F-80C fighters, intended for air defense, but they lacked the under-the-wing pylons necessary for carrying bombs, and their range was short. Once the war began, the small bomber force was augmented and became an ad hoc unit designated Bomber Command (Provisional), led by Maj. Gen. Emmett O'Donnell. It clearly outmatched the less-advanced Korean air force, but it initially had to work up from a peacetime posture to its distant and distributed air bases.

The force order of battle and base laydown is presented in table 4.1.

The Phases of the Korean War

Since a detailed history of the Korean War is beyond the scope of this chapter, the reader will need to understand the ebbs, flows, and sudden shifts of this war. The Korean conflict evolved radically in five distinctive stages:

Table 4.1. Air Force Order of Battle in the Pacific Theater, 1950

Command/Groups	Type of Aircraft	Location
8th Fighter/Bomber Wing	F-80C	Itazuke, Japan
68th All Weather Fighter Squadron	F-82 Twin Mustang	Itazuke
49th Fighter/Bomber Wing	F-80C	Misawa
35th Fighter Interceptor Wing	F-80C	Yokata
3d Bomber Wing Light	B-26	Johnson
51st Fighter Interceptor Wing	F-80C	Naha
4th All Weather Fighter Squadron	F-82	Naha
19th Bomber Wing	B-29	Guam
18th Fighter Bomber Wing	F-80C	Clark

1. The first phase began with the sudden North Korean invasion of its southern neighbor (June 25–September 15 1950), during which the North seized Seoul and penetrated the South in a series of thrusts over two months. It was finally stopped by stout defenses in a small area along the southeastern coast from Taegu to Pusan. By mid-September the Pusan Perimeter had stabilized, with the introduction of U.S. forces and the application of American airpower flying from Japan.

2. The second phase began with MacArthur's bold flanking maneuver from the sea at Inchon. The Inchon landing and quick thrust into Seoul cut off the enemy's lines of communication and supply. The UN counterattack (September–October 1950), including forces pushing north from the besieged Pusan Perimeter, produced a rout of the North's forces. South Korea was cleared of enemy troops, and U.S. forces crossed the 38th parallel and moved deep into North Korea. MacArthur received approval to seize the North Korean capital, Pyongyang, which he soon captured. UN troops continued to advance north toward the Yalu River in two major thrusts, despite the late stage of the campaign and approaching winter weather.

3. In the third phase, China intervened in the war (October 19, 1950). Since the People's Liberation Army crossed the Yalu in massive numbers, it threw back the U.S. forces, which did not expect massed attacks from well-armed (albeit poorly clothed) Chinese troops. By the end of November, U.S. forces withdrew and took up defensive positions south of the 38th parallel.

4. In the fourth phase (December 1950 until 1951), Gen. Matthew B. Ridgway assumed command of the Eighth Army after the death of Gen. Walton H. Walker, who was killed in a jeep accident. Ridgway's leadership helped the Eighth recover its morale and assume a strong defensive position. In April 1951 President Truman relieved MacArthur of his posts as commander of UN forces in Korea and of the U.S. Far East Command for having publicly opposed presidential war policies, and Ridgway replaced MacArthur. The war settled into a protracted "war of posts" along opposing lines.

5. Protracted negotiations, from the spring of 1951 to 1953. For almost two years a war that had seen wide swings in offensive and defense positions became very static. Through years of tense negotiations the U.S. applied coercive diplomacy, using airpower in search of a diplomatic arrangement.

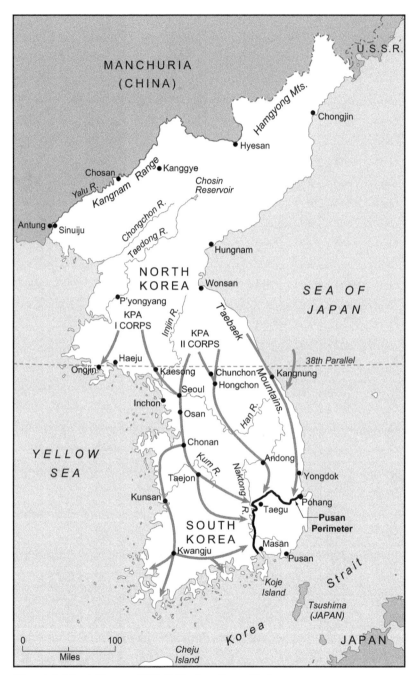

Map 4.1. North Korean 1950 Offensives, Pusan Perimeter
Adapted from https://www.westpoint.edu/sites/default/files/inline-images
/academics/academic _departments/history/Korean%20War/Korea10.pdf.

In each of these phases, the Air Force was tasked to execute widely different missions with widely different priorities, depending on the progress or distress that UN forces were facing at the time. Unlike the other chapters in this book, the ebb and flow of the air war complicates the use of a chronological overview. As a result, this chapter is functionally organized around the Air Force's major missions (close air support, air superiority, and interdiction and bombing). Such an approach offers more focus and visibility to an impressive number of adaptations.

Close Air Support
American military historian I. B. Holley Jr. once noted that interservice operations inescapably pose difficulties. The differences in equipment, doctrine, institutional priorities, and experience complicate harmonious interaction. Holley also found that armed forces often are slow in hammering out their differences and accepting necessary procedures. Often the requisite solutions occur only through repeated crises on the battlefield. "In no area of interservice operations has this phenomenon been more pronounced than in the matter of close air support," he concluded.[33]

The U.S. Air Force's time in Korea underscores Holley's conclusions. The service entered the Korean War with a rich heritage of combat experience. Unfortunately, however, both the Army and the airpower community forgot the lessons in close air support (CAS) that the Ninth Air Force had learned at great expense over France and Germany. Further, it made little effort to preserve the lessons learned beyond written doctrine. The Air Force had numerous strategic priorities during the post–World War II period, but CAS was last on that list. Although the USAF made numerous innovations in its strategic capabilities and introduced organizational changes and technological systems, it relegated the preservation of tactical air to the backwater of the Air Force. Gen. O. P. Weyland, who became commander of the FEAF later in the conflict, admitted that "what was remembered from World War II was not written down, or if written down was not disseminated, or if disseminated was not read or understood."[34]

Although the Air Force had not advanced its tactical air capabilities during the interwar period, when hostilities on the peninsula broke out it began an intense period of adaptation during the Korean conflict. As the ROK (South Korean) forces reeled back in late June, the FEAF found itself poorly positioned to offer immediate help. It had more than 550 aircraft in-theater, but almost none in Korea. Its planes, including 365 F-80C fighters, were designed for air defense, not for ground support. The F-80 Shooting Star was obsolete for air superiority or fighter intercept, and it was a poor airframe for supporting ground troops in modern combat. Its five-inch rocket system was inaccurate; it did not have pylons for attaching bombs. Due to a lack of basing options and the F-80's extensive support requirements, its sorties had to originate from Japan, where the United States had more fully developed bases with longer runways. But flying from Japan consumed the combat range of the jets, leaving little time to coordinate with ground forces or find good targets. The Air Force quickly adapted to the situation by building external fuel tanks in-theater to increase the aircraft's range. But its sorties still were limited to ten to fifteen minutes over their target areas, which reduced their capacity for coordinated strikes on targets in proximity to threatened UN forces.[35]

Senior Army theater and ground force commanders were unimpressed with the Air Force's initial contributions to the fight. Many commanders were conditioned by the more-responsive close air support received in Europe in 1944–1945.[36] In the initial days of the war, Army commanders desperately sought to repel the North Koreans and hold on to the Pusan Perimeter. Their position was in extremis, given the limited readiness of the U.S. Army and its relatively lightly armed forces. Instead of criticizing Army readiness, MacArthur's command headquarters (joint in name only, essentially all Army) preferred to impose its preferences on the Air Force.[37] Moreover, the Far East Command's director of operations, Gen. Edward M. Almond, a graduate of the Air Tactical Operations School, believed that he understood the Air Force's bias against tactical support operations.[38]

The Air Force doctrine was founded on World War II experience, embodied in *FM 31–35, Air Ground Operations.* The doctrine rested on clear Air Force institutional preferences and combat lessons about centralized control (by the senior Air Force commander) and very deliberately planned and coordinated allocation of sorties based on the air commander's assessment of priorities. This doctrinal and cultural predisposition clashed continuously with that of American ground commanders, both Army and Marine Corps, over the course of the war.[39] The Army's lack of investment in this area and the Air Force's lack of interest in it following World War II produced a lot of friction early in the Korean War.[40]

Initially ground commanders were largely dissatisfied with the support they got from the Air Force. The Army emphasized CAS shortfalls in a memorandum to the Army chief of staff. Gen. Mark W. Clark, then chief of Army field forces, outlined the Army opinion, writing in November 1950 during a dark period in Korea, "There is an indispensable requirement for adequate, effective air support for ground operations at all times. This requirement is currently not being met satisfactorily."[41]

The differences between the two services were difficult to reconcile. The Army thought that troops in close contact merited a high priority for support, and believed that its own commanders should have more control over that support. But the Air Force believed that strategic attack and then interdiction of the enemy fielded force and lines of communications were better priorities for reducing pressure on fielded forces. Air Force thinking held that airpower was best applied in concentrated efforts against decisive targets. It relegated CAS to the lowest priority on the list, considering it to be the least-efficient method of applying airpower assets. At several dire points during the Korean War, especially early in the conflict, when North Korea came close to pushing the U.S. 24th Infantry Division off the peninsula entirely, the Army called for concentrated CAS, and the Far East Air Force command only grudgingly supplied it.

The Marine air-ground coordination—evidenced in epic fights such as the first battle for the Nakdong Bulge—certainly left an impression on adjacent Army commanders. Col. Paul L. Freeman, commanding the Army's 23d Infantry Regiment, later wrote to Ridgway:

We must have Tac Air in direct support of infantry regiments just as we have artillery; and communications must be direct and simplified. . . . The Marines on our left were a sight to behold. Not only was their equipment superior or equal to ours, but they had squadrons of air in direct support. They used it like artillery.[42]

General Walker later noted that "the vast majority of officers of the Army feel strongly that the Marine system of close air support has much to commend it." He added the ultimate punch: "I feel strongly that the Army would be well advised to emulate the Marine Corps and have its own tactical support aviation."[43] These complaints misdiagnosed the systemic problem. Neither service was prepared to implement the current system well—because the staffing and communications requirements for the joint operations centers (JOCs) were undermanned and underequipped.[44] Even if target prioritizations had been amended, the limits of the F-80C and bombers to implement CAS still would have persisted.[45] It would have taken time to reconstitute the system and the efficiency that had existed in Europe. Overall, despite complaints about priorities, the FEAF executed 13,800 CAS sorties with devastating impact early in the war, when the Army was reeling.[46] That support preserved the troops around Pusan, with the use of napalm on armor targets—an example of early adaptation.[47]

Much of the criticism from Army officers was the result of comparisons to the responsiveness that Marine commanders enjoyed with their organic airpower. Marine ground commanders were able to count on dedicated sorties to specific units and received support within just a few hours when needed. Army officers wanted that kind of support. It is unfair, however, to compare Air Force CAS evolutions directly to the purpose-built force and performance of the Marines. The Marines' force structure had less artillery and their air-ground coordination was by necessity a narrower mission. The Marine Corps' doctrine used its organic aviation solely to support the ground force and its officers were trained and educated together.[48] They practiced their skills at CAS far more than most air forces, and they had no higher priority. Therefore, the Marines sustained the doctrine, skills, and communications gear needed to execute CAS with proficiency. By contrast the fledgling Air Force had an expanding set of strategic missions and lacked time and resources for tactical aviation. It had to husband its resources during the demobilization era that followed World War II.

Although many U.S. Army officers in Tokyo groused about the Air Force's organizational and doctrinal demands, field commanders eventually were generous with praise. Maj. Gen. William B. Kean wrote that "the close air support strikes rendered by the Fifth Air Force again saved this division, as they have many times before." General Walker, the commander of the ground forces defending Pusan, said: "I will gladly lay my cards right on the table and state that if it had not been for the air support that we received from the Fifth Air Force, we would not have been able to stay in Korea." Walker, who later died in a jeep accident, confirmed "that no commander ever had better air support than has been furnished the

Eighth Army by the Fifth Air Force."[49] Such comments reflect a recognition that airpower was crucial to helping U.S. ground forces to preserve the Pusan Perimeter, and later in covering MacArthur's retreat after the Chinese army entered.

Although CAS capabilities were deficient, from both planning and coordinating to actual platforms, the Air Force recognized the problem and took dramatic actions to improve its support. The FEAF requested a significant number of jet aircraft, which the Air Force refused to supply given priorities in Europe and the defense of the continental United States. In a top-down and somewhat counterintuitive adaptation, the Air Force directed the reconversion of jet fighter squadrons back to the rugged and combat-proven F-51 Mustangs, propeller-driven aircraft that were scraped together from Air National Guard units in the United States. The Mustangs were rushed to theater and sent to austere air fields in Korea, from which their range and carrying load could be applied suitably to responsive CAS missions. The trusty planes were familiar to many veterans of World War II, but these aircraft were slow compared to jets and vulnerable to antiaircraft fire. The location of the air cooler undernearth the Mustang was great for long-range missions but made the plane susceptible to ground fire when it was used as a CAS platform. The F-51s were a mixed blessing.[50] Yet, ground commanders were happy with their longer loiter-time and support. What was particularly remarkable was the alacrity of the decision and its implementation; the last of the F-51s swung into action by August 11.[51] To gather and ship 150 aircraft to Japan and Korea—with pilots and maintenance teams—in less than a month was a remarkable feat.

The FEAF would field some 187 Mustangs, as well as 250 F-80s for use as fighter-interceptors, escort missions, and bombing tasks. The Mustang, which had saved the Army Air Forces over Germany, was a necessity imposed on the FEAF. Without exploiting the stocks of stored F-51s to support the CAS demand, the Air Force would not have been able to support the ebb and flow of the UN's subsequent drives north to recover the South Korean capital or to save the UN command when China entered the war. However, an objective evaluation of F-51 attributes and its value relative to the North Koreans' growing antiaircraft capabilities shows the vulnerability of the Mustang, which took the heaviest aircraft losses during the war.

As important as the aircraft themselves were, the Air Force supporting doctrine and structure was also deficient. Although official doctrine called for the service to provide Tactical Air Control Parties (TACPs) for each Army regiment engaged, there were no standing and prepared TACPs. The Air Force rushed some ad hoc TACPs to the front, but their communications gear was limited and they were exposed to North Korean artillery fires along the front. Few experienced personnel were available to man these units with their Army brethren, and the services had to relearn lessons of the last war.

At the same time, the Air Force quickly adapted in providing airborne forward air controllers (FACs), an Air Force mission that had eroded in practice. Initially, the Air Force had tried to bridge the gap by using the Army's L-5, a light, propeller-driven plane. Rather quickly, however, these were replaced by the rugged T-6 Texan, training aircraft used in the States that could carry the radio gear needed to maintain connectivity to the JOC and to ground units.[52] By the late summer of 1950, the Air Force stood up the 6147th Tactical Air Control Squadron, known as the "Mosquitoes," for the FAC mission. Over the course of the war, the Mosquitoes excelled in coordinating air strikes.[53]

One unpopular Air Force adaptation was the use of its largest bombers against tactical targets or for CAS during nighttime. Although the Air Force leaders strenuously argued that the best use of the heavy B-29s was in long-range interdiction or strategic bombing tasks against cities such as Wonsan and Pyongyang, MacArthur insisted that so long as the North Koreans were pressing on the defensive lines around Pusan he would intrude into airpower targeting guidance. At one point, when the North Koreans were crossing the Nakdong River in mid-August and trying to seize a critical piece of terrain at Taegu, MacArthur directed Stratemeyer to use the heavy bombers to bomb a specific area through which NPRK (North Korean) reinforcements were streaming.

Bomber Command was directed to execute the mission, and it ordered a full squadron to drop its load into each of a dozen target boxes. The bombers dropped almost 1,000 tons of high-explosive bombs from 10,000 feet into a long narrow strip near the river. The results were hard to measure, but MacArthur asked for a repeat mission, and the Air Force again balked at the use of B-29s against vaguely defined area targets.[54] This was the sort of adaptation that the Air Force had wanted to avoid, but it would relent under extreme conditions or when ordered to do so.[55]

Another adaptation, again relearning from the past, was night bombing with the use of radar beacons along the forward edge of the frontline Army positions. This was a skill developed in the European theater and had atrophied. The Eighth Army increasingly asked that Air Force planes hit concentrations of North Korean troops massing to attack UN lines under all weather and light conditions. Conducting missions at night was considered highly risky, but Bomber Command ultimately applied radar-directed strikes to its list of learned competencies, although measuring results was very difficult.[56] In Operation Killer, nighttime CAS operations by B-26s were described as "highly effective."[57]

Likewise, the employment of proximity fuses on bombs to rain shrapnel on troop formations had to be rediscovered in-theater. During the early part of the war, premature detonations were being attributed to aged munitions that had been improperly stored after the Pacific campaigns, but it turned out that the Air Force had forgotten World War II experiences about the use of delays to prevent the detonation of bombs by dense clouds. An Air Force evaluation team had to point out to the harried Air Force bomb-loading crews in Korea how to better employ such fuses.[58]

Demand for close air support remained steady, and the Air Force adapted in-theater with specialized training and by increasing the number of pilots released to serve as ground FACs. It also extended the tours of FACs from three to eight weeks, which increased their proficiency as FACs (but not as pilots).[59] As the war continued, significant turnover occurred in both ground and air units, and the Air Force established theater schools for air-ground operations in both Korea and

Table 4.2. FEAF Sortie Totals and Percentages, July 1950 to June 1951

	Jul-Sept 50	Oct-Dec 50	Jan-Mar 51	Apr-Jun 51
Close Air Support	1,996 (13.6)	2,646 (13.2)	3,140 (13.5)	3,347 (12.5)
Bombing/ Interdiction	11,176 (75.8)	14,819 (76.1)	17,584 (75.7)	18,742 (77.5)
Air Superiority	1,597 (10.6)	2,117 (10.7)	2,513 (10.8)	2,677 (10.0)
Total	14,769	19,582	23,237	26,766

Adapted from Thomas Hone, "Korea," in Benjamin Cooling, ed., *Case Studies in the Achievement of Air Superiority* (Washington, D.C.: Air Force History Program, 1994), 475.

Japan and sent groups of pilots on three-day tours with ground units to appreciate their perspectives and operational needs better.[60]

Despite the heroic efforts of the FEAF, the tensions over CAS represented a persistent clash of Army and Air Force cultures.[61] The ground forces should also take some of the blame, since the bottom line is that neither the Air Force nor the Army had prepared for air-ground operations.[62] To provide some perspective, in a costly war the FEAF executed just over 721,000 sorties, of which 57,665 were labeled as CAS, which is just 8 percent overall.[63] The Army never appreciated the importance of strategic bombing or interdiction because it never saw the immediate results, but it should have appreciated the fact that its adversaries came to the battlefield exhausted by night marches, hungry, and with reduced capacity to fight.

The major adaptation early in the war was the Air Force decision to revert to the piston-driven Mustang.[64] Adapting to the combat-tested F-51 was remarkable in "heat of battle"—and not without costs.[65] Of the 351 Mustangs lost, 172 were downed by ground fire.[66] In this case, the institutional perspective dominated the preferred operational commanders' desire to have jets for the mission. In this dialectic between command levels, the higher missions in Europe and the need to be prepared for the defense of the U.S. homeland overruled the FEAF's request. What is remarkable about this adaptation was both its reversion in a technological sense, which makes it countercultural, and how quickly Air Force leaders made the decision. The Air Force recognized and responded with a clear order before the end of July 1950. This occurred in a matter of weeks, not a year, which is in marked contrast to other major adaptations in this book.

Air Superiority

Once the Air Force had swept aside the hand-me-down North Korean air force in the summer of 1950, the UN command enjoyed air superiority for most of the war.[67] That does not mean that the Communists did not try to contest it at times. The Fifth Air Force scored its first victory on June 27, 1950, when 1st Lt. William Hudson, in an F-82G (and his radar operator, 1st Lt. Carl Fraser) downed a North Korean plane (a Yak–11 or a Yak–7U) over Kimpo.[68] With the exception of the northwest corridor near the Yalu known as MiG Alley, the United States enjoyed control of the air and could apply its forces and air assets where and when it wanted to.

The most significant enemy initiative was the introduction of the swept-wing MiG-15 jet in November 1950. For months the UN force maintained air superiority after defeating the outdated and poorly trained North Korean air force. Now it appeared that the Chinese were introducing advanced fighter jets that the Russians were known to be supplying. The MiGs were based just inside Chinese territory across the Yalu River and were able to jump across the North Korean border to ambush UN aircraft. Not realized at the time was that many of these planes were being flown by Russian pilots who had had combat experience in World War II.

The introduction of the MiG-15 required adaptation from the Air Force in organization, tactics, and technology. The single-pilot MiG represented a major change in the contest for air dominance. It was designed as an interceptor to defeat bombers such as the B-29. Built around a British engine, the jet had a swept-wing design that afforded distinctive advantages. It had a higher ceiling than U.S. jets, which enabled it to climb above 50,000 feet—much beyond the F-80s and F-84 escorts.[69] Yet, the MiG-15s had a range of only two hundred miles, which kept them concentrated up north along the border area, and they rarely penetrated far into UN territory.[70]

In addition to its greater ceiling, the MiG had a higher speed and climbing rate, almost 20 percent greater than the F-86 Sabre. The U.S. planes sacrificed speed for endurance and range, which they needed to patrol deep into North Korea from their bases in Japan or south of the 38th parallel that divided North and South Korea. A critical factor in this competition was the difference in their firepower. The MiGs were armed with cannon capable of hitting a target in short bursts from a distance of one thousand meters. The Sabre's armament consisted of six .50-caliber M3 machine guns built into the nose of the fuselage. The greater punching power of cannon over machine guns was important to the pilots.[71] In effect, the U.S. fighters had to close in behind their speedier opponents and get a position long enough for their own, less-powerful guns to produce enough damage to down the MiG-15.

The Russians provided more than a thousand MiGs to the Chinese (along with Russian training and pilots). During the course of the conflict, U.S. pilots would note the appearance of aggressive enemy flyers who appeared to be superior in their flying and gunnery to the average Chinese aviators. These pilots developed unique tactics to apply the MiGs advantages and limitations. The MiGs would climb higher than U.S. bomber formations and conduct slashing attacks against the slow B-29 Superfortresses that were sent north to interdict reinforcements and supplies from reaching the North Korean forces. The MiGs adopted an ambush position at their higher ceiling levels, above U.S. bomber or fighter formations, and would "yo-yo" down into American patrols or bomber formations and escape back up, confident that U.S. aircraft could not follow them at their higher altitude.[72] This development posed a serious challenge to the strategic bombing campaign if the MiG could not be suppressed or screened from interfering with bombing formations.

The FEAF and the Air Force responded quickly when the MiG appeared. Within days, the Air Force sent two squadrons of F-86 Sabres, which arrived at Kimpo airfield near Seoul on December 15, 1950. Their first flights in Korea occurred on December 17, less than a month after their deployment orders. The first MiG-Sabre duel occurred the same day. In that contest, Lt. Col. Bruce N. Hinton, squadron leader of the 336th Fighter Interceptor Squadron, led a four-plane patrol that dueled with a flight of MiGs. Hinton scored the first kill for the Sabres.[73]

But simply matching the MiGs with a few equally fast jets would not be sufficient to recover air superiority. The Soviet-made fighters, which were able to fly more than one hundred miles an hour faster than the F-80s and F-84s—and had superior turning rates and firepower—easily outclassed the American aircraft; thus, the Sabres would have to be used in areas where the MiGs were concentrated. The introduction of the F-86 Sabre negated the significant materiel advantage conferred by the MiG-15, and the American pilots retained an edge due to their higher skill-level—except where they encountered Russian instructor pilots (what U.S. pilots called the "honchos"), who flew with more skill and aggressiveness. Overall, American pilots were better-trained, flew in more-disciplined formations, and were more aggressive. But the quality and quantity of U.S. jet aircraft were not adequate at first, and the F-86 Sabre had to be introduced into the theater quickly.

The Sabre initially was designed as a high-altitude day fighter. After the aircraft began operating over Korea, the Air Force continuously sought improvements. To increase all-weather capability, the Air Force introduced the F-86D, which had a more powerful engine and improved gunsights. The later F-86H incorporated design fixes to improve the Sabre's flexibility as a fighter-bomber. Even later models had a revolutionary horizontal tail section that gave the plane great maneuverability at high altitudes. In addition, the flight controls were operated by a new hydraulic system that eliminated the heavy effort that had been needed during high-speed turns against the MiGs. Wing slats on the leading edge of each wing— a design element first introduced by German engineers in the Me 262—gave the plane great control at high speeds.[74]

Gunsight Adaptations

A particularly interesting adaptation during the war involved the Sabre's gunsights. The initial F-86 variants used the K-18 gunsight, based on a Navy innovation that had been developed during World War II. The F-86Es were equipped with the A-1CM gunsight linked to a ranging AN/APG-30 radar. This device used radar to compute a target's range automatically and display it with the pilot's aiming reticle.[75] This equipment adaptation responded to a known deficiency. As Lt. Col. James Jabara, an Air Force ace who shot down 15 MiGs over Korea, put it:

> The original fire-control system of the F-86 was one of our greatest deficiencies. We had a World War II gunsight and World War II guns. Hitting a MiG at angles off of more than 15 degrees and range of 1,300 feet was nearly impossible with the short firing time available in high-speed jet combat. The later acquisition of the radar gunsight in the F-86 was probably the greatest single improvement of the airplane during the Korean War.[76]

Not everyone accepted the new gunsight in Korea—especially veteran pilots who had logged many hours with the manual system. Newer and younger pilots were more positive. Nevertheless, the introduction of the A-1C gunsight was a step-change in fire-control needed for air-to-air combat in the jet age. The new gunsight helped pilots improve their gunnery results appreciably by dynamically computing range and speed. This enabled more pilots with less combat experience to sustain performance in the very brief duels brought about by the increased speed of jet aircraft. Both gunsight and radar were beset with maintenance problems and with a dearth of trained personnel to keep the system operational. All of these factors, combined with a general lack of pilot training, led many of the Sabre pilots to become disenchanted with the A-1C gunsight. Some favored the inferior but dependable K-18 sight. Problems with the A-1C sight proliferated, and complaints arose to the point where the Fifth Air Force declared it was "too complicated to be maintained."

Yet, General Weyland felt that the sight had not received a fair trial. At his request, the Air Force launched Project Jaybird to rectify shortfalls. A team from the Air Training Command arrived in Korea in April 1952 to resolve the issues and upgrade all A-1C sights.[77] Still, the improved maintenance and upgrades did not satisfy the entire fighter community. More than a dozen Korea aces later met with Gen. Hoyt S. Vandenberg, then Air Force chief of staff, to argue for returning to the World War II system. Gun tapes from competitive tests conducted among aces back in the United States showed conclusively that the modern radar-enhanced site was superior, which settled the issue.[78] In this case, experts with both theater- and service-level perspectives conducted an investigations phase to determine how to adapt the equipment. In this case, the adaptations influenced the institutionalization of the new system throughout the Air Force.

Fighter Armaments

The firepower of the Sabre remained an issue. The F-86, with its smaller-caliber firepower, was not able to score enough hits against the elusive MiG-15. The Navy's F-9 Panther and the British Meteor (both in-theater) also were armed with cannon, like the MiG-15. Yet, the Air Force had not fielded cannon on its aircraft. Stratemeyer reported in his diary that his pilots thought they would be more successful with cannon.[79]

This led to an in-theater experiment. The Air Force deployed a team from the United States to experiment with a number of F-86s modified with an automated 30-mm cannon. Eight were shipped to Japan in December 1952 and deployed to Kimpo Airfield as Project GunVal in early 1953 for a sixteen-week trial under combat conditions.[80] Each of the aircraft was modified with four 20-mm cannon and flew 284 combat missions and 41 engagements with MiGs, which resulted in 6 victories for the Sabres and another 3 "probable" kills. However, the installed system generated a serious problem with compressor stalls at high altitude. Two planes were lost to engine compressor stalls after ingesting excessive propellant gases from the cannon.[81] The experiment was disappointing, and the Air Force concluded that it preferred the reliability of machine guns over the slower firing cannon. The Air Force learned to live with its existing combat-proven system during the course of the conflict and only late in the war matched the firepower of the MiG-15. It was not until the F-86H model was introduced in the last months of the war that the Sabre had cannon.

Night-Fighting Adaptations

The F-82 Twin Mustang was the Air Force's principal all-weather night fighter. This unusual twin-fuselage airframe had great speed and range and was a good long-range escort for bombers until the 1960s, when the introduction of jet-powered interceptors made it obsolete. When the Korean War began, the FEAF had one radar-equipped squadron for the defense of Japan's airspace. During the early part of the conflict, Japan-based F-82s were among the first USAF aircraft to operate over Korea. The first three North Korean aircraft destroyed by U.S. forces were shot down by F-82s. The first North Korean victim was a Yak-11, downed over Kimpo Airfield. Yet, the appearance of MiG-15 jets over Seoul in 1951 raised concerns in the FEAF, which ordered dedicated fighter-intruder coverage to preclude sudden attacks. The result was the introduction of a new fighter, the F-94, which arrived in Japan in March 1951 and was deployed to South Korea as a jet air-defense umbrella over Seoul in 1953. When the F-94 appeared, it was the first operational U.S. Air Force fighter equipped with an afterburner and was the first jet-powered, all-weather fighter to enter combat during the Korean War. The F-82s and F-94s had their tradeoffs. The F-82Fs proved to be good day and night interceptors, with excellent range, but they lacked spare parts and were difficult to maintain. The jet-powered F-94s, however, had a shorter combat range than the F-82s and relied more on ground-control interception radar to detect and intercept intruders. Both airplanes mounted .50-caliber machine guns.[82]

On the night of May 10, 1951, Air Force Capt. John R. Phillips, with his radar observer, 1st Lt. Billy J. Atto, destroyed the first MiG-15 at night using the F-94. They entered MiG Alley and climbed to 40,000 feet, then started looking for targets. Atto detected two fast-moving blips on his radar, and the team moved behind the suspected pair of MiGs to check for the aircrafts' distinctive tailpipe burner. Phillips selected his target and fired twice, and the MiG exploded.[83] Other intercepts would occur over North Korea, and the F-94 was credited with several victories.[84]

The Air Force also conducted tests with operational aircraft, using jet-assisted takeoff (JATO) rocket pods on some of its fighters to enable them to use the short fields in South Korea while carrying a full combat load of bombs and rockets. As with the GunVal trials, the Air Force did some limited testing in the United States and in-theater but preferred to use the prototypes in live-combat sorties. The JATO tests included 140 flights and 16 engagements with 6 kills. Pilots reported that the center of gravity of their planes (and thus their stability under high maneuver) had shifted dangerously. Furthermore, the rocket-assisted airframes required substantially more maintenance time to recycle the plane between missions. Due to both pilot complaints and high maintenance costs, this was a short-lived experiment.

Air superiority was the primary consideration for the FEAF during the war, since all other missions depended on keeping the skies clear and North Korean airfields closed. The results produced by the FEAF had provided a lot of freedom of action for the interdiction and bombing missions—until the MiGs appeared.

Fortunately, the Air Force had a solution on hand with the Sabre, and it quickly adapted. The agile F-86 turned the tide of the air war in Korea and resulted in the destruction of 792 MiGs, compared to a loss of 78 Sabres.[85] These totals and ratios are contested by some historians (and by former Soviet pilots), and some current experts contend that the actual ratio was closer to seven-to-one overall and even closer for engagements between Soviet veterans and U.S. pilots.[86] But out of the forty U.S. pilots who earned the title of ace, thirty-nine flew the Sabre. It was a plane worthy of the skill and valor of the Air Force pilots.

Bombs Away

The Air Force's overall readiness in 1950 was demonstrated by its prompt response to the emergency—in sharp relief compared to that of the U.S. Army. On the night of June 27, the first airpower response to the North Korean invasion was carried out by a flight of medium B-26 bombers. The Far East Air Force had already conducted an intelligence study of Korea, which became the foundation for its ability to target the industrial and transportation networks. Overall, however, Stratemeyer's force was designed and equipped to defend Japan's air space, not to project power for the scale of the war that emerged. It possessed only twelve heavy bombers and twenty-two medium-lift bombers, augmented by fifteen F-82 fighter-bombers.

The Joint Staff recognized the lack of bombing capacity and initially ordered the Air Force to send ten conventional B-29s immediately to Japan. General LeMay, the head of the Air Force's Strategic Air Command, objected to having his precious assets "pissed away in the Korean War," but was overruled in Washington, and was ordered to reinforce Stratemeyer with two entire B-29 bomber groups, totaling ninety medium bombers.[87]

As the Air Force shifted from a defensive posture to conventional war, it adapted its leadership and organization. O'Donnell was sent to take command of the operational side of the bombing campaign. The FEAF's new Bomber Command was activated on July 8, with O'Donnell immediately at work developing target lists. His first B-29 units to arrive in Japan carried out a maximum bombing effort in Korea only nine days after receiving their orders to deploy and thirty-six hours after the first B-29 had arrived in Japan. To reduce pressure on the Pusan Perimeter, O'Donnell personally led ninety-eight B-29s on a bombing mission near Wonsan.[88]

MacArthur's staff attempted to inject explicit directives and target lists for the FEAF, which Stratemeyer strenuously resisted. He wanted to control all aviation assets in a deliberate and coordinated manner to apply the Air Force's doctrine for centralized planning and weighted priorities. Although Stratemeyer ultimately won the right to not be micromanaged by an Army-dominated staff in Tokyo, the deteriorating situation in Korea forced him to apply his medium B-29s in tactical missions to help the beleaguered remnants of the South Korean army and General Walker's Eighth Army throughout July.

O'Donnell had hoped to replicate the bombing of major urban areas with incendiary bombs, given how successful it had been five years earlier in Japan, but MacArthur overruled him and directed the FEAF to employ explosive and fragmentation bombs instead. O'Donnell was even more exasperated when on July 11 he was directed to make close air support his principal priority. Weyland had retorted that focusing on just CAS "is just like trying to dam up a river at the bottom of a waterfall."[89] O'Donnell argued strenuously that B-29s should not be assigned "aimless[ly] flying in the general battle area in search of targets of opportunity" or radio directives from the ground, which "[was] not an efficient way to utilize the weapon."[90] Yet MacArthur needed to protect his beleaguered ground forces in the first months of the Korean War. Success mandated that MacArthur insist on using B-29s as "flying artillery" when circumstances dictated an emergency. Stratemeyer felt obliged to support MacArthur but carefully reported back to Washington and the Air Force that this was an exception:

> CINCFE [commander-in-chief, Far East forces] considers and I agree ground situation in Korea so critical that every possible effort must be used to break up motorized concentrations on roads in battle areas. He fully understands that this is emergency procedure only. He is most enthusiastic about the results obtained from the Far East Air Forces since our commitment to combat.[91]

MacArthur finally allowed the FEAF to start attacking interdiction targets north of the 38th parallel on July 26. At the same time, the Joint Staff concurred with the FEAF recommendations for additional bombing aircraft and ordered two additional groups (the 98th and 307th) for a thirty-day campaign against strategic targets. These units proved just as professional as the Far East units, and they conducted a combat mission just five days after departing the United States. The campaign was effective and neutralized all but one strategic target in a month, under good weather conditions.[92] At one point, the Bomber Command executed a close air support mission, using almost one hundred B-29s to bomb an area where North Korean troops were concentrated. The FEAF regarded the results from these saturation missions as minimal and counseled against further employment of the B-29s in such a role. Stratemeyer's diary reveals his support on the "improper" use of B-29s—because the ground situation was desperate.[93]

Since the North Korean Army was making most of its movements at night, Partridge decided to do the same with his B-26 interdiction effort. But the Air Force had not practiced such intruder missions recently, so Partridge had his units conduct experiments with flares and got help from the Navy and the Royal Air Force in modifying racks to dispense them. It was an early adaptation to enhance the effectiveness of the Bomber Command.

In September MacArthur executed his brilliant amphibious operation at Inchon, and North Korea forces retreated. Bomber resources were employed tactically again during this operation, much to the consternation of the FEAF. On October 7 the UN authorized its commander to initiate operations north of the 38th parallel to sweep out the Communist forces and unite Korea. MacArthur's forces struck deep into North Korea. The UN's success was now seen as foregone, and both the strategic bombing and interdiction campaigns were scaled down and ultimately suspended. Commanders were so confident that two bomber groups, the 22nd and 92nd, were directed to return to the United States on October 25.

China's direct intervention in the ground war in November made that move appear premature. The massive Chinese foray into the Korean civil war had always been a possible consequence, but it was not considered likely. U.S. intelligence did not provide early warning, and MacArthur's previous assessment about the potential for direct intervention by China turned out to be very wrong. Moreover, the Chinese divisions moved only at night to avoid detection and UN air attacks. Because the situation was so desperate, U.S. leaders quickly removed the restrictions on targeting bridges, cities, and hydroelectric plants (except for the Sui-ho generating facility near the border). As commander of UN and U.S. forces, MacArthur believed that his airpower could interdict significant reinforcements from entering the theater and severely retard their supply chain. What he overlooked, however, was that the Chinese had already entered the country en masse and were adept at hiding their movements.

The FEAF was ordered to regain the transferred bomber groups and reattack major targets in the north. MacArthur ordered his air arm to "destroy every means of communication and every installation, factory, city, and village" that had military value in North Korea.[94] The FEAF responded promptly by striking the town of Kanggye on November 4. The bombers used incendiary bombs on urban targets for the first time in the war.

The most significant enemy reaction to the bombing was the introduction of the swept-wing MiG-15 jet, on Nov. 1, 1950. The MiGs conducted brief, high-speed, slashing attacks against the slower B-29 Superfortresses just south of the Yalu River. The introduction of the superior MiG and the advantages that U.S. policymakers granted to Chinese sovereignty put the Bomber Command

at a severe disadvantage. Once the Chinese invaded, the FEAF was authorized
to destroy bridges over the Yalu in order to cut off Chinese reinforcements. But
its orders limited targeting to the Korean side of the border, in a vain attempt to
interdict supplies and troops without antagonizing China.

The Chinese units pushed the UN south and forced the evacuation of airfields
around Pyongyang and Seoul. The loss of the airfields around Seoul in December
restricted the FEAF's ability to generate enough fighter escort sorties to protect
the lumbering Bomber Command planes on their interdiction attacks.

Air Force leaders continued to believe in the power of interdiction, continuing
to display their deeply rooted interpretation of World War II. Weyland asserted
that "in a long-term war, tactical airpower will contribute more to the success of
the ground forces and to [the] overall mission of the theater commander through
a well-planned interdiction campaign than any other mission."[95] Weyland's command put that hypothesis to the test over a series of different campaigns that
adapted principally by shifting to different target sets for destruction. By the summer of 1951 the conflict had bogged down into a ground war of attrition, or a
"war of posts" with little maneuver. The Air Force adaptation sought to apply
airpower to coerce the stalemated armistice negotiations to a conclusion. As in the
major campaigns over Germany, Air Force planners and targeters tried to identify
key industrial targets for destruction to pressure the Koreans and their sponsors
to end the war.

In the summer of 1951 the Air Force's devotion to interdiction was on full
display in Operation Strangle.[96] UN forces faced off against the Chinese in static
trench lines and mountain outposts. There were few decent targets for fighter-
bombers. The Air Force shifted its emphasis to cutting off the Communist supply
lines by interdiction.[97] Air Force commanders believed that they could make the
railroad system inoperable, and that this would substantially reduce North Korean
logistics and operational effectiveness. The FEAF continued to adapt in order to
improve its ability to attack trains and trucks at night. It introduced a number of
tactical changes and technological twists to enhance its performance. As an example, the FEAF locally fabricated metal tetrahedron-shaped tire tacks that would be
air-dropped over road networks in order to puncture tires. The disabled vehicles,
it was hoped, would bottle up roads and leave long columns of trucks for easier
strafing attacks at dawn.[98]

The Air Force believed that Operation Strangle would hit valued targets and choke off any supplies to the front. It conducted 87,552 interdiction sorties and claimed that it had destroyed 276 locomotives, 3,820 railroad cars, more than 34,000 trucks and vehicles, and 19,000 rail cuts. Many of these missions were conducted at night, and the accuracy of its reporting has been questioned. The Air Force did not claim that this was fully successful, since by late December 1951 the Communists were repairing destroyed bridge spans and rail cuts within hours or a few days. By the end of 1951 the FEAF admitted that the North Koreans had "broken our railroad blockade of Pyongyang and won the use of all key rail arteries."[99] As noted in a postwar study by the RAND Corporation, interdiction programs persistently followed a cycle: initial success, enemy countermeasures, and reduced UN effectiveness as the enemy found ways to offset the U.S. measures.[100]

Thus, although the targeting and strikes were well-executed, Operation Strangle did not create the desired strategic effect. It did not impress ground commanders, who noted that the enemy still seemed well-supplied, as measured by enemy artillery shelling employed in May 1952. The Army believed that it was a failure. Clark, later commander of UN forces in Korea, observed that "as in Italy, where we learned the same bitter lesson in the same kind of rugged country, our airpower could not keep a steady stream of enemy supplies and reinforcements from reaching the battleline. Air could not isolate the front."[101] According to one author, the operation "fizzled," and to the Air Force historians it "was not successful, due to the flexibility of the Communist logistics system."[102] Weyland thought that Operation Strangle was "an unqualified success in achieving its stated purpose, which was to deny the enemy the capability to launch and sustain a general offensive."[103]

The results achieved in Operation Saturate, conducted in the spring of 1952, were no better. Nor was there a Communist offensive in 1952.

A new challenge faced the Bomber Command on October 23, 1951. A formation of B-29s and Allied fighter-bombers from the 207th Wing were attacking an airfield at Namsi when they were struck by a swarm of 140 MiGs. Despite Allied fighter escorts, including Sabres, the MiGs shot down three of the U.S. bombers and heavily damaged five more. Most of the returning bombers had casualties on board. The Bomber Command conducted a stand-down for a few days to assess its tactics. It concluded that the more advanced Sabres were best employed as a

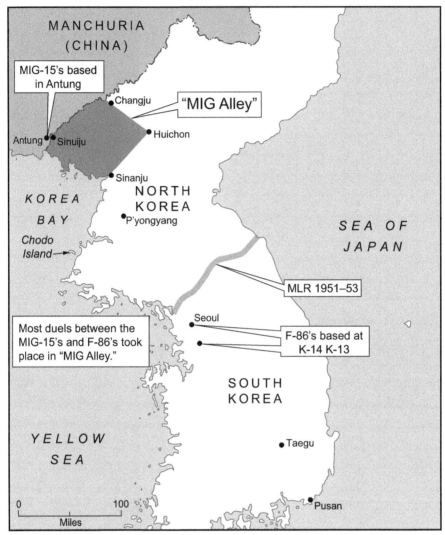

Map 4.2. Korean Air Bases and MiG Alley
Adapted from https://dpaa.secure.force.com/dpaaFamWebInKoreanAirBattles

screening force above the bombers but realized that ground targets near Manchuria in the so-called MiG Alley would always overwhelm their airborne protection. The Bomber Command needed to avoid losing in a war of attrition in conditions that favored the MiGs—such as the battle over Namsi.[104]

To preclude such losses, Brig. Gen. Joe W. Kelly, now leading the Bomber Command, proposed to shift entirely to night missions.[105] The Air Force could not provide sufficient replacement bombers and gave Kelly's proposal serious consideration. In response, two adaptations were made in short order. First, Weyland decided to cease daylight missions to minimize losses that could not be replaced. Second, the Air Force reinforced the FEAF with additional F-84s and F-86s—an adaptation that Vandenberg had rejected earlier due to other priorities. The acquisition of these two new wings brought the command's complement of Sabres to 150. The interrelationship between effective bombing and air superiority was evident now, as was the dialectic tension between the Air Force and the FEAF over priorities.

The FEAF recognized the need to enhance the precision of its interdiction strikes, particularly to destroy bridges from greater altitude, with fewer sorties and with fewer losses. It asked that special ordnance called the Razon bomb, developed at the end of World War II, be shipped to the Pacific.[106] Bombers could steer these 1,000-pound bombs by radio control from the bomber but would have to stay over the target area to guide the ordnance to the designated spot. But technical difficulties and malfunctioning radio gear frustrated the test. Of 228 bombs dropped during the project, only half of the drops were controlled by the bombers. Even so, the technicians did seem to overcome the initial obstacles. The last 150 bombs that the bombers dropped had a reliability rate of 96 percent. Overall, the experiment employed almost five hundred bombs and successfully attacked fifteen bridges. Despite the evolving success of the Razon, the Air Force switched to an even larger bomb, the 12,000-pound Tarzon ASM-A-1. It, too, required that the crew steer the bomb by radio control signals and track it through a small flare in the bomb's tail to maintain visual acquisition from above. The FEAF used thirty Tarzons in an experiment, gaining just seven hits. The command terminated the investigation in late 1951, since few of the remaining targets would require that scale of explosive power. Stratemeyer expressed great disappointment with the tests.[107]

Night Bombing

With Bomber Command pushed away from the northern areas and restricted to night missions, adaptation opportunities were at a premium. The Air Force was unprepared for night missions, and especially night precision-bombing or interdiction. Operations analysis suggested that the FEAF was destroying fewer than two trucks for every one hundred bombs that it dropped. By the summer of 1951 there were two wings fully dedicated to night operations—without improved performance. Over time, better training and new hunter-killer tactics doubled the truck metric.[108] The FEAF also tried improving flare drops, deploying aircraft with flare parachutes and mounting planes with searchlights to illuminate roads.[109] These slowed down North Korean supply rates materially, but they failed to isolate the battlefield.

A major adaptation for night-bombing operations relied on a radar beacon system known as Shoran. Air Force bombing missions were based on the ability of the B-29 crews to use their plane's AN/APQ-13 radar to ascertain their own location and that of the targets. However, before 1951 the results were disappointing, due to low skill proficiency, outdated equipment, a lack of spare parts, and poor map accuracy.[110] Shoran was not effective in late 1950, but it was redeployed in early 1951 with better results due to additional crew training and better maps.[111]

The Air Force was aware of its nighttime shortfalls as early as July 1950, when the 3rd Bomber Group began night intruder sorties. The unit lacked radar, Shoran, or AN/APQ-13 systems that would permit blind bombing by radar. Vandenberg admitted that night attack interdiction was an Air Force weakness, and the FEAF adapted by dedicating a group to night operations to build more proficiency.[112] Experiments in September used cooperative formations of B-26 and B-29s using M26 parachute flares in a buddy system and conducting a trial with British flares.[113] Both trials were terminated and a search for better flares continued. In January 1951 the 3rd Bomber Wing tested the use of a C-47 cargo plane with 'chute flares. The flares floated for four to five minutes to enable bombers to identify and attack targets.[114]

In addition, in March 1951 ground-based Tactical Air Control Parties found an innovative way to begin using the MPQ-2 radar for night drops. The Air Force ground team would guide a flight of bombers toward the target, assess the planes' speed and direction, and calculate a bomb-release point that had been given to the airborne bombardier. However, such missions were limited in range to locations along the UN's main battle lines, where the ground-based radars were deployed. For deeper operations they had to rely on the Shoran system. The downside of Shoran was that it relied on signals that the Communists could and did detect. Optimally, to reach and attack their targets, the bombers would have to follow the triangulated radar signal arcs. The enemy counteradapted by focusing its radar and antiaircraft defenses accordingly to find the signals that the system emitted and then directing its fighters to intercept them. In one such ambush, in June 1952, a dozen Chinese jets jumped a Shoran-directed night mission and successfully shot down three bombers while severely damaging the remaining aircraft.[115]

The Air Force tried numerous other adjustments. To improve its ability to counter the fast-moving MiGs, the command enhanced its gunnery training to help bomber crews defend themselves. The maintenance crews painted the bottom of bombers black to offset adversaries' flak batteries.[116] Some proposed adaptations were constrained by decisions to conceal key capabilities from Russian and Chinese observers. Senior Air Force officials had resisted introducing the best jamming technologies for fear that the systems might reveal U.S. capabilities that would be more valuable in a "real" war against the Soviets. But after a short debate, the FEAF was authorized to apply better electronic countermeasures to jam radar-directed antiaircraft systems. Even so, the FEAF ultimately used the advanced jamming systems to thwart increasingly more-sophisticated and lethal defenses.[117] In June 1952, the command was authorized to use chaff to spoof searchlight radars and antiaircraft flak systems. These adaptations, along with improved electronic countermeasures, improved bombing effectiveness.

New Interdiction Campaigns: Air-Pressure Strategy

Although the Air Force could not use its favored bombing theory against industrial production nodes and airfields outside of Korea, the FEAF planning staff consistently did its best to try to help end the war. In April 1952 a pair of Air Force officers wrote a study arguing for what they called an "air-pressure strategy" to force North Korean leaders to accept a political agreement based on the existing lines along the 38th parallel.[118] Their work presumed the existence of "lucrative targets" that could be selectively targeted for destruction to influence enemy decision-makers. Their immediate superior, Brig. Gen. Jacob E. Smart, the deputy for operations at the FEAF, believed that targets of military significance could be successful and "have a deleterious effect on the morale of the civilian population actively engaged in the logistic support of the enemy forces."[119]

This new strategy had roots in the pre–World War II "industrial web" targeting theory and sought to raise the stakes for the North Koreans. The study team identified North Korea's electricity production as a high-value vulnerability to use in pressuring the Communists. Much of the North's electrical power was sold to Russia or China, and the loss of the power might influence them. The two planners recommended focusing on these production facilities, and the the FEAF commander readily endorsed the adaptation. Ridgway feared that hitting such targets would upset the delicate negotiations in Panmunjom and tabled the proposal, but when Clark replaced Ridgway in May 1952, he accepted it and got the Joint Chiefs of Staff to support it.

On June 23, 1952, the Allies began a four-day campaign to knock out the Sui-ho generating facility, the world's fourth-largest power plant. Much of the facility's output went to China. More than one thousand sorties were executed, including strikes from four Navy aircraft carriers positioned off the coast. It was estimated that the fighter-bombers had destroyed 90 percent of the North's electricity production, which the Chinese rushed to repair.[120] The operation then shifted toward attacking the North Korean capital of Pyongyang to inflict destruction on any logistical support to the front. In July, more than 1,250 sorties by the entire UN force were directed in an all-out offensive on Pyongyang in Operation Pressure Pump. On August 29 another 1,400 sorties rained bombs on the capital while Chinese and Russian officials were meeting in Moscow.

Nevertheless, the war continued on into the next year, and the Air Force persisted in applying strategic bombing to pressure the North. In March 1953, the FEAF staff identified another target set that it believed would force North Korea to accept peace terms.[121] About a dozen dams in North Korea controlled two-thirds of the country's irrigation system, which was linked to its agricultural and food production. The campaign planned to attack the dams, which were deemed critical to rice production and hence to the ability of North Korea to feed its troops along the front.[122] On May 13, 1953, some 54 F-84s attacked the earthen dam complex north of Pyongyang, dropping 100 tons of explosives. There was no immediate effect, but during the night the dam collapsed entirely from the pressure. The resulting torrents wiped out miles of rail lines, five bridges, and one airfield. The flooded acreage also included five square miles of planted rice. Similar attacks occurred against other dams on May 15–16 and May 21–22. The latter strike was conducted by B-29s instead of fighter-bombers. However, the North Koreans had reduced the water levels behind the dam, easing the pressure there and this time precluding the dam's collapse. Strikes at the Namsi and Taechan dams flooded out two airfields. Russian and Chinese aid was immediate.

Nevertheless, the results exceeded expectations. Clark was enthusiastic about the rail lines and bridging that were destroyed, claiming in a message to Washington that the raids were "as effective as weeks of rail interdiction."[123] After an excruciating negotiation, the Korean armistice was signed on July 23.

Did the bombing missions produce the armistice? Weyland found the "pressure campaign" decisive. The official Air Force history supports him, and concluded:

> During the last year of the Korean hostilities, American airpower executed the dominant role in the achievement of the military objectives of the United States and of the United Nations. . . . No single air operation so gravely affected the Communists as the simple destruction of two agricultural irrigation dams, for this operation, too terrible to execute in its entirety, portended the devastation of the most important segment of the North Korean agricultural economy.[124]

Air Force Adaptation

Two clear conclusions come from the foregoing three sub-cases of Air Force adaptation. First, there is little doubt the North Koreans and Chinese took a terrible pounding from Allied airpower. The FEAF, without question, took the fight to the farthest reaches of North Korea and into China several times and established air superiority. It was no easy feat, given the Korean weather and terrain. The FEAF could point to an impressive total of enemy targets—enemy ground forces, vehicles, and aircraft—that they had destroyed.

Second, while one may see the war as a stalemate that merely restored the status quo at great cost, the Air Force effort was effective. Advocates of airpower can claim that it made the difference between victory and defeat in the initial defense of the Pusan Perimeter. Overall, the FEAF also could be credited with having eliminated the North Korean Air Force and significantly reduced North Korean and Chinese combat power. Air attacks stanched North Korean and Chinese offensives in 1950 and 1951 and created the time and space for the UN forces to defend South Korea successfully. Moreover, the Air Force that brought about these positive results was not the World War II–rooted institution that it had been when the war began. Success was a byproduct of continuous adaptation.

Table 4.3. Airpower Contributions in Korea

	Air Force	Navy/Marines	Foreign Forces
Counter-Air	66,997	2,096	3, 025
Interdiction	192,581	47,873	15,359
CAS	57,665	32,482	6,063
Cargo	181,659	–	6,578
Other (training, observation, recon.)	222,078	24,852	13,848
Total	721,000	274, 858[1]	44, 873

[1] The Navy never recorded sortie types, but this total includes their aggregate of 167,000 sorties. Actual numbers in the column are Marine data only.

There was no doubt that the Air Force had tried to apply its preferred paradigm—strategic bombing and interdiction—against a target set that had few parallels with Germany in World War II. From the number of sorties flown in the war, one can see that the Air Force preference for interdiction over close air support prevailed by a large margin. The data contrasts with the Navy and Marine Corps aviation components, which lacked long-range bombing aircraft, and with the Marine air wing, whose doctrine and culture were aimed at supporting Marines on the ground.

Outputs are more difficult to assess, but they still appear impressive. The FEAF aircraft dropped 476,000 tons of ordnance, while the Navy and Marines added 200,000 tons' worth. Combined, the airpower claimed 987 adversary aircraft destroyed, as well as the loss of 1, 327 tanks, more than 80,000 vehicles, 963 locomotives, and more than 10,000 rail cars as a result of air attack. Bombing attacks on infrastructure claimed 1,153 bridges, almost 9,000 gun positions, and close to 29,000 railroad line cuts.

The Air Force's success was not without losses. The FEAF lost 1,466 airplanes of all types in Korea. The rest of the UN air force—Allies, Navy, and Marine Corps—lost another 520 planes. Just over half the aircraft downings—1,041—were due to combat action. Some eight hundred airframes were shot by enemy ground fire, which says something about the risks borne by crews in both interdiction and CAS missions. It also reveals the enemy's skill in antiaircraft gunnery. Air superiority was a clear advantage, but the FEAF's losses included 147 fighters downed by air-to-air combat.[125]

Table 4.4 U.S. Air Force Adaptations

	Close Air Support	Air Superiority	Bombing
Single Loop	Airborne TAC F-80 modifications Night operations Bombers in night CAS	Design changes to swept wing jet fighters Night fighters Jet assisted take off Fighter upgrades including gunsites and cannon	Night bombing via SHORAN and radar Precision-guided Bombs via Razon/Tarzon Flares for night bombing Various tactical changes for night interdiction Electronic warfare/jamming
Double Loop	F-51s for CAS B-29s for close air support		

The results were not the culmination of Air Force investments and doc-trine changes developed during the brief interwar period. The lion's share of the intellectual development and procurement between conflicts had favored LeMay's Strategic Air Command. Rather, the advances during the early 1950s resulted primarily from actions by airmen in-theater, in both Japan and Korea, who developed and executed the FEAF campaigns. Those campaigns required numerous adaptations and innovations for the success of the air war and of UN mission in general.

The adaptations reflected in table 4.4 above are listed as single- or double-loop changes. Most were single-loop adaptations, simple fixes to shift tactics or meth-ods within existing competencies. Only a few challenged basic values or cherished myths, the barrier for double-loop adaption. All were uniformly both generated by and investigated by the FEAF. There were significant changes or adaptions, such as the in extremis employment of B-29s for close air support, that were not readily supported or derived from the bottom up. But these occurred quickly, and they were directed from the top down, with deep protests from the Bomber Command.

Overall, the development of airborne close air support, precision-bombing by radar, night stalking, night bombing, and fighter adaptations during the war reflect favorably on the Air Force. The bulk of these adaptations had been Air Force competencies before, but many of the skills that they involved had eroded after 1945. In some areas, such as electronic warfare, the Air Force relearned older lessons using newer technology.

The most impressive institutional changes were the Air Force's recognition of its shortfalls in close air support, and its "reverse modernization" using F-51 Mustang squadrons. These represented a cultural shift, given the technological revolution that had been occurring with the onset of jet aircraft. It was not easy for pilots who had been trained to fly modern jets to revert back to propeller-driven aircraft. The fact that many of them were combat veterans with experience flying Mustangs made the shift feasible, but it still was a step backward for an Air Force with a technological bent.

This may not be a totally positive example of flexibility. As early as July 12, 1950, the FEAF was aware that it was getting 150 F-51s and an equal number of pilots. But it was not the FEAF's decision; it was Vandenberg's decision back in Washington. Stratemeyer had asked for 150 jets, and his request apparently was denied. The Air Force was only willing to provide excess (though operationally ready) Mustangs. As early as August 1950, the commander of the FEAF was commenting in his diary that the F-80 remained his preferred CAS aircraft, observing that "[t]he F-80 can do more things and better than F-51."[126] Given Cold War–priorities for homeland defense and the security of Europe, the Air Force's institutional leader insisted on providing his theater commander with the Mustangs.

Yet, the fact that the Air Force recognized the gap in performance potential and took immediate steps to close it was commendable. Indeed, the *interpretation-investigation* cycle on these decisions was far faster than the Navy's efforts to fix its torpedo deficiency at the start of World War II. Among all four case studies in this book, the Air Force experience in Korea is the only example of an internally initiated double-loop adaptation—a change that is implemented even though it contradicts a service's basic value or belief. Yet it is also additional evidence of a dialectic tension between the larger institution—the U.S. Air Force—and its theater commanders. This sort of tension is seen in all four of the cases that we present in this book.

The shift seems to have been a case of competing perspectives and priorities between the two levels of command. It is clear that the FEAF and Stratemeyer, its commander, wanted more jets, not the worn-out Mustangs that they ultimately got. But the Air Force leadership had higher priorities for the squadrons that Stratemeyer had wanted for Korea. So it may not have been a case of belated recognition about poor decisions made after World War II, or even a suddenly rejuvenated awareness about the venerable Mustang. When presented with this historical and institutional anomaly, current Air Force officers account for this rapid shift as having been acceptable to their service because it did not have any impact on the institution's strategic-bombing priority. Indeed, one interviewee attributed the agility behind the seeming double-loop change entirely to the irrelevance of CAS to strategic bombing, which was the basis for the Air Force's institutional status.[127] Yes, the shift from jet backward to a propeller-driven aircraft was countercultural, but this officer thought that the adaptation was acceptable because CAS was not a central mission to the Air Force. Rather, using bombers for CAS was more of a *cultural* challenge to the Air Force's sense of its role and doctrine.

In retrospect, Air Force leaders probably should be credited with both rapid recognition of the divergent conditions in Korea's operating environment and their prewar assumptions. They also should be praised for swiftly organizing the FEAF for bombing and for the introduction of F-51s. Although the Air Force leadership was inclined to apply institutional preferences for bombing to the war, it also was open to rapid adaptation. Indeed, Air Force leaders made this shift without orders from the Joint Staff or above. On the other end of the scale, the inability to develop a more powerful armament suite for the F-86 series stands out as rare case of failed adaptation, although the service clearly made an effort to field both cannon and better sights during the war.

Organizational Learning Capacity: Leadership

The post–World War II generation of Air Force leaders was heavily influenced by bomber pilots. The two groups shared distinctive common career paths. Eighty percent had fought in the Pacific, with 75 percent serving in the 20th Air Force. There, far away from Washington, they demonstrated a high level of operational competency and practiced their religion without interference. They were, in the words of one Air Force scholar, "a natural product of the traditions of their romantic promises (decisiveness), their most destructive and singular means (strategic bombing), and their unconditional ends (total victory)."[128]

The spirit of the Air Force was well captured by defense studies scholar Carl H. Builder in *The Icarus Syndrome*. Builder argued that the Air Force had fought for service independence in World War II based on a theory of airpower as a decisive instrument, and that its unaltered subscription to that theory fueled the intellectual engine of the newly minted USAF as it matured.[129] "The experiences of World War II had branded lessons on the consciousness of the now-independent USAF," Builder noted. Ironically, the new service's first chief of staff, Gen. Carl A. Spaatz, said when he took office that "the major lesson of the war was that prolonged ground wars of attrition would now be relegated to the past."[130]

These were not the conditions that Air Force commanders found in Korea. Nor was it a conflict that embraced a strategy of annihilation by the unlimited use of bombers. Airpower and strategic-bombing absolutists believed that precision strategic bombing was decisive in and of itself. Their faith in centralized, focused, and strategic airpower remained unbridled. General Arnold was part of the Bomber Mafia, if not its institutional leader; he failed to appreciate the need for fighter escorts, and "[in] his doctrinal myopia and almost religious faith in strategic bombardment, he failed to appreciate the comparable advances that were being accomplished in devising defenses against the bombers."[131]

The senior Air Force leadership was combat-credible and had had significant organizational management experience in creating and applying the tools of the world's largest airpower institution. There were numerous background elements in the Air Force's post–World War II leadership. Most were West Point graduates, and all had gravitated early to aviation by choice. Their interest in novel technologies and leadership of new but continually evolving organizations is noteworthy. Many had experiences in teaching and were products of the Army Air Corps' premier education program, as well as graduates of the Army's top schools. All received early promotions, rose through the ranks quickly, and took on major organizational leadership roles at a relatively early age. Their staff and leadership positions involved considerable wartime responsibility, and they faced evolving technological developments. With few exceptions, their career patterns involved development within the Air Force. Unlike the Navy officers in the previous case study, few went on to graduate schools in the academic world, and even fewer sought technical degrees the way their Navy counterparts did. They acquired expertise in the technological side from outside the Air Force, through boards and commercial contracts from the rapidly expanding aeronautical industries. The Air Force also acquired human capital from former German scientists who had expertise in long-range rocketry and jet engine design.

The leadership cadre that led the Air Force during the Korean War was the direct product of that institution's birth and of a common experience in the pre–World War II Army Air Corps. These officers emerged from the large-scale bombing campaigns of both the European and Far East campaigns, where U.S. forces pounded the major industrial and urban areas of Germany and Japan. This same officer cadre emerged as the leaders of a new service after the war—a gestation that had been long overdue, but not obtained without debate by the existing power centers in the U.S. national security architecture. They were supremely confident in their leadership at both the national and theater levels of war. They also were supremely focused on establishing their branch as a separate and independent service.

The leadership styles of these commanders varied, but in general they were masters of their profession in terms of an acute appreciation of the value of airpower and a desire to apply airpower efficiently. To a man, these leaders were combat-tested and were credible advocates for the contributions that airpower could bring to bear in war. They shared a common conviction about the necessity of the Air Force as a separate institution. They had proven themselves to be masters of the air as well, with firmly held core principles about how airpower was best employed.[132]

If there was an anomaly in the Korean War, it was Weyland, whose expertise was in tactical airpower. Weyland had commanded the XIX Tactical Air Command and supported Patton's aggressive armored thrusts against German forces.[133] Patton expressed deep appreciation for the air support supplied by Weyland's command and called Weyland "the best damn general in the Air Corps."[134]

There is a strong common background in this set of leaders:

Fifty-nine percent of them participated in the debate and ultimate canonization of airpower theories by attending the Air Corps Tactical School (ACTS) before World War II. There the gospel professed the efficacy of strategic bombing,

which promised a decisive alternative in warfare to the slaughter of World
War I. Bomber pilots accounted for 69 percent of this generation, and 86 percent of those attending the ACTS before World War II were bomber pilots and
commanders in that war. In addition, 88 percent of the pilots in this group
would command a squadron or wing in combat in the Second World War.[135]

Overall, the nature of the rapidly developing field of aviation made these officers
flexible and open to new ways of executing missions. The constantly evolving character of aviation, new engines, new weapons, and novel enabling systems for navigation, targeting, radar, etc., made them acutely aware of the role of technology in
warfare. All had studied and experienced war. This reservoir of credible experience
allowed them to address performance shortfalls with an open mind and to focus on
organizational performance. Operationally, the officers were uniformly pragmatic
and well-versed in the challenges of managing fleets of aircraft as well as the complicated logistics and maintenance involved in applying airpower in wartime. They
had spent their formative years learning how to operate iterations of technology,
and then, under enormous pressure, how to operate organizations against thinking
opponents in harsh conditions. Where Air Force leaders were inflexible was in their
ideological stance about the value of airpower, the importance of centralized planning to maximize its value, and their unalterable insistence on an independent air
arm. With the service finally having gained its independence in 1947, no Air Force
officer wanted to see its status or independence reduced.

There was a strong element of both self-selection and common nurturing among
Air Force leaders. They were all early adapters who were attracted to an entirely
new domain of warfare, with its emerging technology. Their chosen field of interest pitted them against existing doctrines, modes of fighting, and long-standing
institutions. They were not passive or evolutionary by nature. They went against
the grain, questioned conventional doctrine (except their own), and crafted their
own institutions and processes. Collectively, they faced a constant development
of new doctrine and tactics as technology evolved. They graduated from decades
of debate by the searing experience of global war, large-scale innovation, and the
demands of total war on two continents.

Representative of the culture of openness of the Air Force leadership was Brigadier General Smart, especially in his relationship with Weyland in Korea, whom he

served as chief planner. They bounced ideas off one another and understood that innovation flourished only in an atmosphere that encouraged it, and that learning required the recognition that "an optimum course of action has to be discovered, weighed, amended, and accepted with prayers and the full realization that the adopted course could be wrong."[136]

Air Force Culture
The Air Force was established on precepts and doctrine based on the belief that airpower can be decisive in war and that it is best managed and applied by an independent branch of the armed forces.[137] The Air Force's culture remains an area of intense study today.[138]

Altars for Worship
The Air Force sense of self rests on the technology that it employs. In *The Masks of War*, Carl Builder writes that the Air Force worships at the "altar of technology" and measures itself in terms of having the newest and best. What distinguishes the Air Force from the other services, he says, is its belief that technological advances continually can provide an entirely new manner of waging war. The Air Force gained its independence to manage better the unique military capabilities made possible by aircraft technology, and it developed doctrines and strategies to exploit its unique capabilities. The history of airpower has remained focused on ways to use and improve technology, and its research and development and acquisition initiatives continue to search for better technologies.

The different pilot communities use different measurements of success. For the air-superiority fighter pilots, their most important measure has been the number of enemy planes downed—and becoming an "ace" by destroying five or more planes. For the bombers, it is the number of missions flown, first, and then some measure of results achieved—how many bridges, factories, and airfields were destroyed. The air-interdiction mission quite naturally has taken to counting tanks, trucks, and troops destroyed.

Toys
More than an institution, the Air Force is an "embodiment of an idea, a concept of warfare, a strategy made possible and sustained by modern technology."[139] It

worships technology, rather than the institution itself or a professional identity such as peacemakers or warriors. "The prospect of combat is not the essential draw," Builder wrote. "It is simply the justification for having and flying these splendid machines."[140] Airmen (and now women) tend to identify with their plane or weapon system over their service.[141] He continued: "The pride of association is with a machine, even before the institution."[142] Air Force pilots, the dominant personality or group in the institution, "identify themselves as pilots first—they just happen to employ their occupational skills and competencies for the USAF."[143]

Some officers find that the Air Force prioritizes the "primacy of technology over warfighting theory." Thomas argues that this is the natural result of an institution born from the development of technology instead of a warfighting doctrine. The Air Force embraces a theory of victory that stresses a way of applying superior technology and is less enthralled with historical cases and centuries-old theoreticians. It is not too much of a stretch to suggest that in its current state, the Air Force "seeks technology as an end not just a means."[144] When assessing its technological health, the Air Force does so with an eye toward sophistication rather than numerical largess.[145] Being outnumbered may be tolerable, but to be beaten by better technology, more advanced systems, or heaven forbid, outflown by the enemy is not.[146] Decades ago, one student of aviation said that the Air Force embraces a "Toys R Us" approach to technology.[147] Even today, Air Force officers sense that they are most comfortable with technology. Looking back from today, modern students of Air Force culture still assess technology as a principal driver of beliefs, since the service was created to exploit a disruptive technology and still retains "an abiding faith in the potential for new technologies to change the face of warfare."[148] This focus does not stunt the capacity of the Air Force to adapt over time; if anything, it promotes more openness toward continuous change and evolution, since technology changed so often from the interwar era through World War II and Korea.

Branch Distinctions

Combat pilots claim the clearest and proudest identity within the force and dominate both its leadership and its legends.[149] Military sociologist James Burk notes that pilots represent a romantic holdout of military fighting form—"individual warriors, each fighting for his [or her] own reputation and honor." While the modern military emphasizes a strict adherence to fighting with a collective team, the fighter pilot continues a tradition of individual glory in the midst of modern war.[150] Heroes in the Air Force have "the ability to single-handedly wield an advanced technological machine in combat."[151]

Today the Air Force is an organization in which "small, often technology-based, subcultures flourish," a condition that requires a common, servicewide understanding of the Air Force mission to hold things together "and creates an identity and cohesion problem involving tribes such as strategic bombing crews, fighter pilots, missileers, space or missile defense specialists, cyber defense experts, etc."[152] The Air Force leadership has attempted to remedy the identity problem through a consciously produced rally around a common unifying label. Men and women in the Army are soldiers and Marines are Marines, but the Air Force has lived institutionally divided—between pilots and all others.[153]

Confidence in Mission

A key aspect of the Air Force culture in this period has been its relative insecurity. In 1989, Builder assessed that the Air Force was "supremely confident about its relevance, [and] about the decisiveness of airpower as an instrument of war."[154] That was not true forty years earlier. The young force had yet to claim the sorts of celebrated norms and deeply rooted values that feed and sustain identity. In the Korean War era, the Air Force had the most limited historical basis for its identity, not just in the sense of temporal formation as a distinct service but conceptually as well. The Army, Navy, and Marine Corps have progenitors for their craft stretching back centuries. Warriors have fought on land and at sea on ships, and strategists theorized about them across all of that time. Even now, Air Force advocates recognize that it "can trace its conceptual history only to the beginning of the twentieth century, when aircraft were invented, and its identity as a separate service only to 1947."[155]

The flip side of not having hundreds of years of tradition and historical baggage is an openness to new ways of doing things. Some current Air Force officers believe that an ongoing commitment to searching for creative solutions over conventional approaches is a central element of their service's culture.[156] At the institutional level, at the time of the Korean War, it stressed the "strategic" dimensions of aerial combat over "tactical" support for ground forces to buttress its case for autonomy.[157] The fight for autonomy was long and hard. Thus airmen feel deeply insecure about rolling back to an identity founded in servicing U.S. ground and naval forces.[158] This was seen during the Korean War, when the Army and Marines were calling for more control over the close air support mission.

For institutional security and reasons of sheer pride, the Air Force strongly prefers a scheme of warfare in which it makes autonomous contributions to "war at the high end of the spectrum." Wishful thinking of this sort has demanded a continued institutional focus "almost exclusively on major combat operations or situations where [the Air Force] alone can be decisive" and neglect of "situations where it serves primarily in a supporting role."[159] Evidence of this neglect in CAS proficiency and investment manifested itself in Korea and repeated again in Vietnam.

Despite the intensive motivation of its embrace of technology and its rigid defense of its independent status, the Air Force's culture did not prevent the counterintuitive reversion of jet fighter squadrons to the low-tech F-51 Mustangs. The Air Force temporarily raised the importance of CAS in Korea, but it did not institutionalize the lessons that it had learned from the war or create dedicated platforms for the mission. As a result, it had to relearn many of the same lessons in the Vietnam War a decade and a half later. The invincibility of strategic bombing that formed the priority mission and soul of the Air Force in 1950—and rationalized its *raison d'être* in the post–World War II era—was diminished in Korea and certainly challenged in Vietnam.[160]

As this case study shows, military culture certainly matters. It has an impact on the way a service views its mission, how rigorously it prepares for war, and how quickly it is willing to jettison its preconceptions for reality.[161] In Korea, commanders realized that the enemy had a vote in the process and that "tactics that are successful in the morning may be obsolete in the afternoon."[162]

Learning Mechanisms

The Air Force's Korean War experience spawned a recognition—at both the theater operational level and at the institutional level—of the need to record the performance of the FEAF. The Strategic Bombing Survey conducted after World War II, which supported the value of airpower's contribution to the conclusion of the war, heightened the interest of the fledgling service in measuring its performance metrics, as a means of both enhancing its performance and of succeeding in public debates about defense priorities.

The Air Force was an early adopter of operations research, with General Arnold establishing a Committee on Operations Analysts at Headquarters, Army Air Forces, in mid-1942.[163] Although the Army Air Forces may have been a nascent organization, it employed well-established formal learning mechanisms. During World War II, the Eighth Air Force had an extensive operations research effort and employed that office to carry out detailed studies of bombing operations, gunnery, and targets.[164] These included field studies and examinations of targets after cities were recovered, in order to assess their results. This practice continued after the war, and operations research offices existed at both the FEC and the FEAF.[165]

Secretary of the Air Force Thomas K. Finletter asked Dr. Robert L. Stearns, the president of the University of Colorado, to assess the effectiveness of the Air Force during the Korean War objectively. Stearns began that investigation in November 1950 and produced a preliminary report two months later—in time for Senate Armed Services Committee hearings scheduled for January 1951—titled the "Korean Evaluation Project: Report on Air Operations." The document noted some deficiencies in TACP training and night-attack capability, but it largely lauded the support being provided by the Air Force in Korea.[166]

Another initiative to promote investigation from the institutional perspective was a larger evaluation project headed by Maj. Gen. Glenn O. Barcus. He was tasked to "make an evaluation of the performance of the Far East Air Forces in the Korean war with particular emphasis on the tactical support of ground forces." Usually referred to as the Barcus Commission, the group spent the latter part of 1950 in-theater, gathering inputs on how the Fifth Air Force was executing its missions, with an emphasis on ground-support roles. Although the panel evidently was established to counter criticisms of the Air Force's dedication to close air support, it gathered extensive documentation of the conflict. The final report, a seven-volume product, was issued in March of 1951. The chief of staff of the Air Force also sent a special assistant from Washington to Tokyo to provide insights on what lessons the institution should draw for the future about the employment of airpower. The special assistant, Col. Ethelred Sykes, would later lead a standing cell on the Air Force staff (called the Korea Evaluation Group) to synthesize all the studies and operational assessments being drawn up and provide data to support Air Force accomplishments.

In theater, the FEAF established other investigation mechanisms. At the Fifth Air Force in Korea, the commander set up a Tactical Airpower Evaluation (TAPE) section. This cell, which comprised staff officers with operational analysis skills, collected empirical data on the effectiveness and efficiency of the bombing, inter-diction, and close air support missions being executed by the Fifth Air Force. Its work also eventually would feed the production of regular evaluation and his-, torical products from Korea and from the Far East Command.[167] The Air Force established similar operational analysis sections stood up in Korea to collect and analyze air operations.

These reports were both a data collection learning mechanism and a means of disseminating Air Force achievements in interdiction and strategic impact. Many of the learning mechanisms were initially sparked to fend off attacks and criticisms about the Air Force's effectiveness.

In fact, more even than the previous case study in this book, the Air Force employed post-mission washups, intelligence debriefs, gun-camera film, and photo reconnaissance pictures to assess mission effectiveness. At more operational and tactical levels, Air Force units had formal processes for debriefing pilots and crews after major missions. Intelligence officers typically conducted these reports, in addition to the work done by operational analysts. Moreover, in addition to intelligence reports, pilots would review their tactics and replay gun cameras to assess adversary actions and Air Force tactics. The cycle of plan, execute, and assess was built into the aviation culture and operational cycles. The cycle of mission analysis, planning, execution, and assessment was ingrained in Air Force operations and culture and processes by the nature of wartime operations.[168]

In the case of the F-86 gunsight debate, the Air Force used focus groups of experts in-theater and special competitive experiments back in the United States, using combat aces to compare various sights. These mechanisms helped both insti-tutional and organizational leaders settle on the advanced radar-ranging attributes of the AC-1M sight over the simpler K-18 sight.

Dissemination Systems

The FEAF squadrons and wings routinely captured lessons and combat informa-tion that were shared within their command, but the study on which this book is based did not find extensive formal documentation of adaptation transition-ing back to the institutional level. Most major commands used an informal pilot-indoctrination process to ease new pilots into combat situations. Eventually, a more

formal training program, called the Clobber Course, was created to enhance learning after crews or pilots arrived in-theater.[169] This terminology was likely a carry-
over from the officers who had been based in Great Britain or who, like General
Weyland, had served in the European Theater of Operations from 1944 to 1945.

In other cases, such the Navy submarine force, one can see links from veterans
and from patrol reports being almost immediately brought back to formal schools
and training centers in the United States. Certainly, some training material on air-
to-air combat techniques and some of the tricks of the trade in executing CAS
tasks found their way back to Air Force training activities, even if only vicariously
through veterans returning from the war. Yet, this study found no documentary
evidence of linkages between field operational reports and changes in doctrine or
in training and educational programs in the institutional Air Force. The Air Force
did establish informal learning mechanisms for social and horizontal learning
using ready-room discussions of tactics and observations and the well-established
technique of a senior-pilot-and-lead-wingman relationship.

Starting as early as the summer of 1950, the *Air University Quarterly Review*, the
official U.S. Air Force professional journal, began a formal series on Korea. For
four years, the Air Force maintained a continuous dialogue on aviation's contributions in the conflict. More directly, the Air Force established an in-theater
Air-Ground Operations School, which ran three-to-five-day courses in tactical
air operations. This was the best venue for ensuring a common understanding of
what airpower could do. Near the end of the war, the Army routinely sent officers
to the course to improve their understanding of combined arms.[170] Since many
ground officers at this point in Korea were not veterans of World War II, the move
to use in-theater learning as a dissemination mechanism was necessary. In addition, as Air Force combat experience from World War II faded away, the institution assigned Korean combat pilots and crews at the newly formed Combat Crew
Training Course at Nellis, Nevada, to enhance dissemination of lessons learned.[171]

Conclusion

Like most wars, the "Forgotten War" in Korea was one of constant adaptation,
either in response to the enemy's moves or to unexpected environmental conditions. The culture of the nascent Air Force, with roots going back to World War I, set
the conditions for an adaptive mindset but also framed its desire for independence.

This was manifested in its heavy identification with strategic bombing, but it did not help prepare the new service for the missions that it faced in Korea. As noted in a recent historical study, "Culture is a key determinant in organizational effectiveness and plays an enormous role in the birth, life, and death of military organizations."[172] The Air Force's orientation toward the strategic attack of industrial states and their critical nodes was not as relevant in the limited war that it found in North Korea. With its "air-pressure" strategies the Air Force tried to revive its "industrial web" theory of targeting, with varying degrees of success.[173] The problem was that Korea was hardly the kind of advanced industrial state that the Air Force theories were established to destroy. Yet, in numerous critical aspects, the Air Force excelled in the competition to out-adapt the North Koreans and their sponsors. The Air Force pressed forward the development of new tactics and technologies such as the swept-wing fighter, night-fighting abilities, and improved precision-attack systems. It readily proved able to move backward a generation with the employment of the venerable F-51 Mustang. But it neglected the air-ground coordination that it had honed to a remarkable degree in Europe, and, as Holley observed, "hard-won lessons were lost and had to be acquired all over again."[174]

Somewhere in the acrimonious debates about Air Force interest in close air support should be the recognition that the Air Force materially saved the ground force at least twice in the most extreme periods in Korea—along the Pusan Perimeter and after the Chinese army intervened. The FEAF's posture and readiness for a limited war in Korea was admittedly less than ideal, but it was ready to respond with lethal force.

Compared to other services, the Air Force was prepared to respond more quickly. Its culture of problem-solving and innovation demonstrated a considerable ability to adapt under fire. It may not have prioritized certain missions the way that other services believed would be most desirable, but it could execute those missions. That success was not solely the result of institutional preparation but also of the willingness of the Air Force leadership to adapt to conditions in the air and on the ground. If the critical challenge in wartime is really about how quickly commanders perceive gaps between their original concepts and tactics and actual conditions on the battlefield, the Air Force was decisive because it was adaptive.

CHAPTER 5

The Army in Vietnam

The Caissons Keep Rolling Along

The noise of the helicopters and the wind from the open troop doors drowned out any chance of communicating. The battalion commander was left to his thoughts as they flew the fifteen miles toward Landing Zone X-Ray. The initial assault lift comprised only sixteen UH-1 Hueys, with four additional gunships for fire support. It was a cool Sunday morning, November 14, 1965. At two thousand feet, the American infantrymen were well above the rolling plains of Vietnam's central highlands. The fog cleared as they approached the landing zone, and the impact from the preplanned artillery support hitting the area was visible.[1] As they got within a few miles, the helicopters dropped to tree-top-level flight. Now the intricate symphony of an air-assault operation was in the hands of the fire-support coordinator. His job was to ensure that the artillery and helicopter gunships prepped the edges of the landing area. A minute before the troops arrived, helicopter gunships strafed the tree line around the zone with rockets and machine guns. The supporting fire lifted just as the vulnerable troop-carrying helos came racing in to drop off the soldiers.

The first of the helicopters touched down at Landing Zone X-Ray just before eleven o'clock. On alighting, the battalion commander hopped off and set up his command group in the five-foot-high brown elephant grass that covered the landing zone. His troops spread out to secure the area. The terrain was lightly wooded, with thin twenty-to-fifty-foot-high trees, and dotted with large red-colored dirt

mounds. Just west of the landing site were the thousand-foot slopes of Chu Pong
Mountain, where Army intelligence thought that at least one North Vietnamese
regiment was hiding. The landing zone had to be secured, and the 1st Battalion,
7th Cavalry quickly assembled in the soccer-pitch-sized zone before the North
Vietnamese could react with overwhelming numbers.

By noon the battle had begun. The 450 men of the battalion never got out of
the landing zone, surrounded by 2,000 enemy soldiers, pitted in an epic contest
of wills that lasted almost three days. The U.S. Army wanted to apply the new air-
assault tactics against an elusive enemy. The North wanted to test its mettle against
the Americans. Both sides got their wish, and took away critical lessons.[2]

"Vietnam was a war that cried out for innovation and adaptation," an American
government official who served in Southeast Asia observed.[3] Instead, the bureaucracy simply executed its repertoire and institutionally failed to adapt to the character of the conflict. This is part of a strong narrative among historians—that
American forces simply did not adapt during the Vietnam War. The charge is
often directed at the Army in particular, since that service provided the leadership
and bulk of the American forces during the conflict.

The following case study will explore the evidence of the Army's adaptation in
the face of the challenges that it encountered in Vietnam, from 1965 to the Tet
Offensive of 1968. In a tripart review, we will present a cross-section of the principal Army operations in Vietnam during that period under the three-phase plan set
down by Gen. William C. Westmoreland, commander of U.S. forces in that theater,
to defeat the combined efforts of the Democratic Republic of Vietnam and the
insurgents of National Liberation Front. The study includes the key lessons and
insights pulled from Army units, from Army historical and doctrinal records, and
from the major U.S. headquarters units in Vietnam. As with the first and second
case studies in this book, the chapter concludes with an assessment of how the
Army's efforts reflected what we define as Organizational Learning Capacity.

The Context
The U.S. Army had been involved in Vietnam since 1950, and the Military Assistance Advisory Group (MAAG) had been headquartered in Saigon for the entire
time.[4] By 1960, when the Kennedy administration came into office, the MAAG
had grown to 685 military persons. President John F. Kennedy believed that the

U.S. military needed to be better prepared for low-intensity conflicts, and had supported the creation of the Green Berets special operations force.[5] The MAAG was training and helping to equip the Army of the Republic of [South] Vietnam (ARVN).[6] Much of that effort was focused on molding the ARVN in the image of a Western military to help it hold off an invasion from the North. The MAAG expanded threefold after 1960 and in 1962 became the Military Assistance Command, Vietnam (MACV), designed to manage the increased support that was needed then. MACV continued to expand, reaching five thousand U.S. military personnel by 1964.

By then Hanoi had begun sending regular North Vietnamese units to infiltrate the South. One battalion arrived in 1963 and a second came in during the spring of 1964. Rather than building up and arming an organic guerrilla force, North Vietnam was injecting its own infantry forces into the fight and also re-equipping People's Army of Vietnam main force units (PAVN) with Chinese versions of the AK-47 assault rifle and lethal mortars, rocket-launchers, and machine guns that enhanced their firepower markedly.

In the summer of 1964, as the situation in South Vietnam deteriorated, General Westmoreland took command of MACV.[7] Westmoreland recognized the North's efforts and viewed the decline in ARVN performance with growing concern. As Army historian Dale Andradé, one of his modern defenders, points out, "What had been primarily a guerrilla war in 1961 evolved into the use of increasingly formidable units in 1963, and two years later it was moving toward even-larger armed confrontations with the introduction of North Vietnamese units."[8] By mid-1965, the North had seven regular regiments in the South and the number of main force units battalions had increased from forty-six to seventy-nine.[9] They began to use these hybrid formations successfully against the ARVN. In December 1964, the Battle of Binh Gia got Westmoreland's attention. A Viet Cong force successfully attacked and seized a town, which it held for several days.[10] Instead of hit-and-run guerrilla tactics, the North Vietnamese Army (NVA), as the Viet Cong military force was known, was defeating ARVN forces in conventional battle.

U.S. commanders believed that the North was shifting into Mao's classic third stage of mobile warfare. Westmoreland's assessment was that the opposition had seized the initiative in the countryside, and that the ARVN was at a critical point. Moreover, several key support bases in the country, including the Pleiku air base, had sustained serious attacks from rocket and mortar fires as well as sapper assaults. Westmoreland requested and was granted American ground units to use for defensive purposes. In March of 1965, those forces—Marines, at first, and later conventional U.S. Army formations—began arriving.

Inside the Johnson administration the introduction of sizable U.S. ground forces was hotly debated, ultimately leading to a compromise authorization for only 18,000 to 20,000 troops for MACV. But the decision, reflected in National Security Action Memorandum 328, authorized a more active use of U.S. combat forces. The "Pentagon Papers," a study conducted for top U.S. military and civilian leaders, accurately highlighted the memorandum as "a pivotal document" that marked the first offensive use of American combat forces.[11] The training and advisory era was now over, and the insertion of U.S. combat forces constituted the first strategic adaptation in the U.S. war effort.

In response to new intelligence, Westmoreland requested 82,000 more troops, bringing U.S. force levels to 175,000 by the end of the year.[12] The question before MACV was how to employ the new forces to serve U.S. security objectives best. Westmoreland perceived the threat from the NVA and VC main force units as his most immediate challenge. As the general observed in his postwar memoirs, he did not have a Napoleonic impulse, but "the enemy had committed big units, and I ignored them at my peril."[13]

Westmoreland's strategy was predicated on a division of labor. American ground forces in division strength were to be deployed within South Vietnam in 1965 and 1966. Their mission would be to stop North Vietnamese units coming into the South and to attack and destroy "all major VC main force units." While the Americans were employed in these offensive military missions, the task of protecting the population, rooting out the guerrilla infrastructure, and conducting pacification programs was allocated to the ARVN.[14]

The die was cast. America had now entered the war with substantial amounts of force and would take on the NVA. Westmoreland's concept for operations had three steps or phases:

First, to halt the VC offensive—to stem the tide.
Second, to resume the offensive—to destroy VC and pacify selected
   high-priority areas.

Third, to restore the entire country to the control of the South
   Vietnamese progressively.[15]

It was in the second phase that Westmoreland hoped to penetrate the VC's sanctuaries and begin degrading its influence. It was the development of these tactics—particularly the emphasis on search-and-destroy operations based on limited
intelligence, supported by the unlimited application of American airpower and
seemingly limitless use of artillery—that proved controversial, particularly as the
complexity of the insurgency challenge became clear.[16] In the final phase, Westmoreland hoped to expel the NVA and secure the country by "mopping up"
residual units.

Learning and adapting were expected. "Tactics and techniques to cope with this
unique challenge are under development and will change with time and additional experience," the directive concluded.[17]

The Air Assault Concept
As in the first case study involving Navy submarines, ongoing organizational and
technological innovations were occurring that would influence the initial battles.
One of the most significant operational adaptations of the Vietnam era was the
development of the "air-assault" concept, which combined technological progress
in helicopter design and engine power with new fighting tactics and creative
organizational arrangements. As one Army history observed, "the integration of
aircraft into the organic structure of the ground force is as radical a change as the
move from the horse to the truck."[18]

The Army's interest in aviation assault stemmed from perceived shortcomings
in Korea in the 1950s. Gen. James M. Gavin, former commander of the famed
82nd Airborne Division, had lamented the lack of mobility in Korea.[19] A subcul-
ture inside the Army had been promoting the helicopter as the solution to these
deficiencies. The early advocates deliberately embraced horse cavalry analogies to
make the idea appealing to the senior Army officers who had been schooled in
the 1930s, when the cavalry was a combat arm of some prestige.

Early in his tenure as secretary of defense, Robert S. McNamara had become
disappointed with the direction of the Army's aviation program and he pushed it
to be more aggressive. In late 1961 McNamara read an Army study specifying the

service's aviation requirements. The report dissatisfied him, and he worked with Army mavericks to effect greater change. The Army helicopter advocates drafted a memorandum for McNamara's signature in April 1962 to force the pace and direction of Army efforts. The memo expressed the secretary's disappointment with the Army's report. "I have not been satisfied with Army program submissions for tactical mobility," he wrote.[20] McNamara directed the Army to reexamine the issue through a new Army Tactical Mobility Requirements Board. To spur the Army leadership into considering expanding the use of helicopters in combat, he ordered that Brig. Gen. Hamilton H. Howze, a well-known proponent of that objective, head the panel.[21]

The so-called Howze Board took only a few months of effort, reporting out on August 20, 1962. It recommended that the Army create an Air Assault Division, equipped and sized to be able to lift its assault elements in three waves. Instead of 3,452 ground vehicles and tanks in the traditional division, the Air Assault force would be assigned 459 aircraft and 1,100 light tactical vehicles. The board thought that the Army should create five Air Assault divisions, along with separate Air Cavalry brigades of 316 aircraft, of which 144 would be attack helicopters, which had an impressive antitank capability that had proven ideal in high-intensity conventional operations in Europe.[22]

The Army did not accept the full breadth of the board's recommendations, but it did quickly approve the creation of a test organization. In January 1963, the service established the 11th Air Assault Division as a test bed for further air assault work, and over the next twelve months it experimented with existing helicopter technology. Although it was an experimental effort, the prototype advanced extraordinarily fast. By the summer of 1963, the division had six infantry battalions, organized into three brigades. At the same time that the service's air assault concept was being developed, the Army's Concept Team was testing helicopters in Vietnam.[23] The team assessed the technology, developed techniques from the combat theater, and fed them forward to the Army and its test division.

The 11th Air Assault Division was formally established in February 1964.[24] Its initial commander was Maj. Gen. Harry W. O. Kinnard II, a World War II veteran. His leadership would be instrumental in getting the division's equipment, training, and doctrine integrated in short order, even though critical equipment, especially helicopters, was slow in arriving. By June 1965 the Army believed that the 11th

Air Assault Division had matured beyond the experimental stage, and proposed that it be activated as the 1st Cavalry Division. McNamara did so in July 1965, and with the activation came surprise orders to ready the division for deployment overseas. On July 28, 1965, President Lyndon B. Johnson announced that he was sending a division to Vietnam—the newly minted 1st Cavalry Division (Airmobile). It was assembled in Vietnam by the end of September and declared fully operational. Army leaders called the development of the air assault capability as "the most innovative tactical development to have come out of the war."[25]

Stemming the Tide: Phase I

This initial phase began in the fall of 1965 and ran into the summer of 1966. MACV had too few forces to use until the American ground units completed their phased arrival and had become acclimated to their new environment. As U.S. troops arrived, MACV was simultaneously creating the port facilities, airfields, and bases that would be needed to support Westmoreland's strategy. It was a remarkable logistical feat.

In November 1965 Westmoreland's strategy and the Army's air mobile concept got their first test—in the central highlands, in Operation Silver Bayonet.[26] MACV ordered General Kinnard and the 1st Air Cavalry (Airmobile) to gain the initiative with an offensive into the Pleiku area.[27]

The highlight of this campaign was the stand of Lt. Col. Harold Moore's 1st Battalion, 7th Cavalry in the Battle of the Ia Drang (November 14–16). It was a prototypical air-assault operation, one in which Moore's battalion ended up surrounded and almost overrun. For two days, Moore's under-strength unit faced off in a ferocious fight against two thousand NVA regulars. The 1st Battalion, 7th Cavalry, was battered and had to be saved by additional battalions and massive amounts of fire support, including B-52 bomber strikes on the Chu Pong. The 1st Battalion, 7th Cavalry, suffered 44 percent casualties—79 killed and 121 wounded. The NVA suffered far worse; American estimates of the damage that they afflicted were 641 dead, 1,200 wounded.[28]

The Ia Drang campaign was not over, however. On November 17 a sister battalion of Moore's outfit, the 2nd Battalion, 7th Cavalry, led by Lt. Col. Robert A. McDade, was ambushed by a VC regiment marching in parallel from the opposite direction. McDade's force was cut in half in minutes. For the rest of the day and the ensuing night, the battalion formed two tight perimeters and fought off numerous probes. It too was saved entirely by sheets of fire placed around McDade's troops. Without that support, the battalion would have been even more decimated. As it was, the casualties for the 2nd Battalion, 7th Cavalry, in the second half of the Ia Drang battle were 151 dead and 121 wounded.[29]

The U.S. Army came out of the battle convinced of some clear lessons. The ferocity of the combat and the press reaction surprised the White House and MACV. The Army press releases stressed Moore's heroic defense, while civilian news reports emphasized the near-destruction of McDade's battalion.[30] Moore crafted an after-action report (AAR), which was distributed to all Army schools. Moore's lessons were tactical, noting how close the NVA got to his lines and how important close fire support was.[31] McDade's only lessons were on the utility of firing artillery around landing zones prior to occupation, and the need for leaders to have maps and compasses.[32] The division commander, General Kinnard, wrote an extensive report and would later write and publish an extensive battle history.[33] He concluded that the battle proved the value of the airmobile concept.[34] But Kinnard's article covered only the actions of the 1st Battalion, 7th Cavalry, and ignored the grievous losses of the 2nd Battalion, 7th Cavalry, at Landing Zone Albany.

General Westmoreland declared that Ia Drang proved "the ability of the Americans to meet and defeat the best troops the enemy could put on the field" and that it certainly had validated the air mobility concept "beyond any possible doubt."[35] The perceived success of air mobile warfare tactics, particularly the heavy losses inflicted on the enemy, had confirmed that an attrition-based strategy and air mobile tactics were ideally suited to gaining an American victory in Vietnam.[36] To Westmoreland and Maj. Gen. William E. DePuy, commander of the 1st Infantry Division, "two officers who had learned their trade in the meat-grinder campaigns in World War II," American firepower had been decisive. "What they saw was a ratio of 12 North Vietnamese killed for each American. They decided that these results justified a strategy of attrition: they would bleed the enemy to death over the long haul, with a strategy of attrition."[37]

Encouraged by Ia Drang's outcome, MACV pressed on with airmobile tactics and search-and-destroy missions. Based on the lessons, the Army continued a pattern of brigade- and battalion-sized operations. The scale of the attacks was smaller than desired, but force levels had not yet reached their proper size, and the smaller-than-hoped-for number of helicopters available constrained operations.

In late December 1965, the 173rd Airborne Brigade was ordered to launch Operation Marauder, tasked to locate and destroy the 506th VC Battalion, which was reported to be near Bao Trai in the Mekong Delta. The brigade, known as the "Sky Soldiers," kicked off the operation on January 1, 1966. Here again, Westmoreland's orders were simple: locate and destroy the enemy, and establish some measure of control in the area.[38] It was a standard air-assault operation. Army intelligence suspected that there were VC units in Hau Nghia Province, thirty-five miles west of Saigon. Over a two-day period, the airborne command would conduct a series of battalion-sized air assaults in an attempt to cordon off the target area. The Sky Soldiers soon found their quarry, the 267th VC Battalion, which elected to stand and fight. A three-day battle ensued. Using classic infantry tactics, the Allies fought through a series of fortified enemy positions. The brigade's after-action report summarized the results of Operation Marauder: "The Viet Cong 267th main force battalion was engaged, out-fought and routed from its positions with 114 VC killed by body count. In addition, much of the headquarters of the 506th VC Battalion was destroyed."[39]

On January 8, 1966, Operation Marauder ended, and MACV initiated Operation Crimp, which placed a multiple-brigade force in a new area of operations in the Ho Bo Woods and Binh Duong Province. The woods were believed to contain the political-military headquarters of the Communist 4th Military Region. Pitted against the Viet Cong were about eight thousand troops of the 1st Infantry Division, under the command of Maj. Gen. Jonathan O. Seaman. The main objective of Operation Crimp was to seek out and destroy the VC headquarters—a mission that was based on some imprecise intelligence.[40] It would be the first division-sized operation, another search-and-destroy mission, with a heavy aerial bombardment followed by an airmobile assault by the 173rd Airborne Brigade (an international brigade with an Australian battalion). Meanwhile, the 3rd Infantry Brigade would seal off the area to the south. The units encountered little resistance, but they did find a vast tunnel complex. The Americans had planned to destroy the tunnels, but the Australians entered them instead and systematically gathered intelligence. The commander of the 173rd labeled Operation Crimp "one of the most successful ever conducted in RVN (Republic of Vietnam)."[41]

That may have been a stretch, but he also recognized that "the capture of the enemy documents during this operation possibly hurt the enemy more from a long-range viewpoint than did the loss of his personnel and weapons."[42] After that, the Americans adopted the Aussie tactics and created tunnel-clearance teams.[43]

Operation Crimp was regarded as a limited success, but it also revealed the basic constraints of search-and-clear operations, which became standard operating procedure for the U.S. Army in Vietnam. The Ho Bo Woods and tunnels were still in use in January 1967 and remained useful to the insurgents up to the attack on Saigon during the Tet offensive in early 1968.

As 1966 began, Westmoreland continued to focus on the conventional (main force) units, and on his large-unit war strategy. Having blunted the Communist efforts in the frontier area of the highlands, he now turned toward the coast. Army intelligence believed that it had identified the specific location of the 12th PAVN Regiment. The VC was historically strong in this area. The 1st Air Cav got the assignment to find and destroy the VC force in the Bong Son area. The Army devised a classical hammer-and-anvil operation that massed multiple divisions against the 3rd PAVN Division around the southern Quang Ngai Province of Binh Dinh. Originally code-named Operation Masher, the plan was retitled Operation White Wing after the White House objected to the aggressive name.[44]

The combat phase of the operation was kicked off on the morning of January 28, 1966. Roughly one hundred helicopters were used to lift the 7th Cavalry brigade onto the southern end of the Bong Son Plain. Kinnard's plan was to feint toward the major coastal road with one brigade and then conduct a series of air-mobile assaults on the plain to flush the enemy out of its base areas and hopefully right into its blocking positions. The town of Bong Son was eventually encircled and secured without a major fight. The Air Cavalry then maneuvered into the adjacent valleys. Over the next month, the Americans attempted to continue to "find, fix, and finish" their well-hidden enemy. They had great success initially until finally the insurgents withdrew, and Operation White Wing was officially ended on March 6, 1966. Yet, although the NVA and VC suffered 1,340 killed in action, they still maintained control over much of the province. The Americans used an impressive amount of firepower, but they did not have the men and equipment to stay and hold the area. MACV's attrition came at the cost of 228

U.S. troops killed and 834 wounded. For American leaders, the most important lesson of the operation was that air cavalry could sustain itself in major operations and in less-than-ideal weather.[45] MACV insisted that White Wing was its most "outstanding" operation of the year.[46]

Following White Wing, in April 1966, the 1st Infantry Division opened a search-and-destroy effort against VC base areas in III Corps area. Designed by Major General DePuy, Westmoreland's former deputy and now the 1st Infantry Division's commanding general, Operation Abilene was conducted by two reinforced brigades over a sixteen-day period in an area forty miles west of Saigon. The division had few contacts, except for one desperate battle on April 11 in which a company was isolated. Frustrated by the inability to find and fix elusive VC elements in this area, DePuy deployed patrols by an individual infantry company as bait to lure the local forces into making a move.[47] He believed that his surveillance systems, firepower, and helicopter mobility would mitigate any risk to his unit.

That confidence was not borne out during the subsequent battle. The "bait" unit, Charlie Company of the 2nd Battalion, 16th Infantry, was severely mauled before reinforcements and the concentrated fire of American artillery and air support could be applied effectively. The company lost thirty-five dead in short order, and the VC left forty-one bodies behind.[48] The 1st Infantry Division's lessons-learned report emphasized the operation's success and its "demonstrated ability to move and move rapidly by airmobile assault operations."[49] But in a rare expression of a need for improvement, the same "commander's analysis" indicated that the airmobility techniques for calling in massive supporting fire "quickly and accurately . . . require additional refinement and will be improved."[50]

In the wake of Operation Abilene, the U.S. 1st Infantry Division mounted a series of operations during June and July 1966 for the express purpose of opening Route 13 from Saigon to Loc Ninh in Binh Long Province and destroying elements of the 9th VC Division, which had been concentrating for an attack on An Loc. DePuy, still commanding the 1st Infantry Division, planned to spoil the expected VC offensive with his own. Although the Americans kicked off the operation, code-named El Paso II, the VC retained the tactical initiative. Five separate battles were fought, and each began with an ambush set by the VC. By this point the 1st Infantry Division had been reinforced with some armor units, and

Operation El Paso II provided Army leaders with some insight about how useful armor could be, even in terrain and tactical circumstances that they had not previously thought of as ideal for tanks. The lessons came primarily from a set of battles along Route 13, a major north-south highway in Binh Long Province.

The first major battle, the Battle of Ap Tau O, began on the morning of June 8, 1966. The "A" Troop of the 1st Squadron, 4th Cavalry, was moving north to the provincial capital of An Loc. The unit had 135 men, with 40 armored vehicles—including 9 M48 Patton tanks and 29 armored cavalry vehicles. Near midday it maneuvered right into a classic L-shaped ambush set up by the VC's 272nd Regiment. The U.S. troops used the firepower on their armored vehicles to pin down the ambushers. They did not maneuver against the attack. A firefight raged for several hours, with the Americans stuck in a perimeter, trading fire with the enemy. By late afternoon the VC commander withdrew, having absorbed a pounding, with at least one hundred killed in action at a cost of fourteen American casualties.

DePuy claimed that Ap Tau O proved the value of armored units "whose utility had been established beyond any doubt."[51] The parent brigade gave generous praise to the Air Force: "Close air support was considered the decisive factor in the success of the battle on June 8 along Highway 13." A total of eighty air sorties delivered twenty-seven tons of high explosives and napalm, six tons of fragmentation bombs and twenty-four canisters of cluster bombs in the lengthy fight. The division staff suggested that the unit should have taken a more aggressive response, despite the fact that it was outnumbered six-to-one. Fighting was not enough; enemy units were to be "finished."[52]

The 9th VC Division continued its aggressive operations. DePuy received intelligence on the movement of the VC 272nd Regiment, which was pushing toward Minh Thanh. On July 9, he laid a trap to exploit his adversary's aggressiveness by leaking information about a movement of a small escort of vehicles to the nearby ARVN Division. DePuy expected the VC spy network to learn about this "plan" quickly. He set out a small force as bait, which the VC quickly took, and the First Division applied a massive counterambush on the Minh Thanh road with four infantry battalions, half an armored cavalry squadron, and five artillery batteries.[53] The planned suppressive fires and "extremely heavy concentrations of 8-inch, 105-mm and 155-mm artillery fire were immediately called in against the attacking forces on the north side of the road."[54] By noon it was all but over, and when the infantry swept the jungle it found almost three hundred bodies.

All told, the 1st Infantry Division fought five major battles and claimed that the enemy had lost 825 dead. The United States suffered 125 killed and 424 wounded.[55] To DePuy the operation represented "an important learning process throughout the 1st Infantry Division." The importance of employing more fire-power, artillery, and airpower simultaneously was the major lesson. The division reported progress: "Communications were tightened up, [and] the coordination of air and artillery was improved by the simple means of preplanning artillery sup-port on one side of the road and air support on the other so these two decisive weapons could be used continuously and simultaneously."[56] Armor officers found that "highly effective counterambush tactics based on the firepower and mobility of armored forces were developed during three of the five engagements. These battles showed that armored cavalry with air and artillery support could more than hold its own against a numerically superior force."[57] New tactics, but the same objective—destroying the enemy's fielded forces—remained the prime directive.

At this early point in the war, Westmoreland and the Army could point to sev-eral important adaptations that the U.S. Army had implemented:

- Helicopter-borne artillery movement and the rapid construction of mutually supporting, interlocking systems of fire bases.
- The introduction of devices and techniques that permitted the rapid adjust-ment of U.S. howitzers to fire 360 degrees.[58]
- Highly refined procedures and communications equipment to ensure con-tinuous and responsive fire support.
- The introduction of the AC-47 gunship, popularly known as "Puff, the Magic Dragon," to increase precise and more massive amounts of firepower.
- "Road-runner" tactics employing high-speed dashes on roadways in antici-pated ambush areas and using machine-gun fire to trip ambushes prematurely.
- The expansion of airmobile operations to all maneuver forces, not just to the 1st Air Cavalry.
- Jungle-clearing and engineering equipment to create and expand landing zones rapidly.

- Development of long-range reconnaissance patrols that went deep into contested areas to identify VC forces clandestinely and call in supporting arms on enemy movements.
- Large protected tractors called Rome Plows for clearing trees from around villages and for clearing the sides of jungle roads to eliminate ambush sites.[59]

The Army's principal lessons in this first phase of Westmoreland's campaign involved taking maximum advantage of the mobility afforded by the 1st Air Cavalry Division and its high kill ratio of 6.6-to-1.[60] A key indication of Army thinking is reflected in an official lessons-learned report entitled "The Battle of Annihilation."[61] The document was issued to underscore the importance of intelligence and aggressiveness, as well as the validity of "Find, Fix, Fight, and Finish." It emphasized flexible maneuvering, sealing off of escape routes, and fighting to destroy the opponent. Half a year later, the same command would proudly note that its kill ratio for the last quarter of the reporting period had doubled—to 14.8-to-1, from 7.2-to-1 before.[62]

Despite that success, Westmoreland pushed for a higher operating tempo and sense of urgency. He complained that "we are not engaging the VC with sufficient frequency or effectiveness to win the war in Vietnam." In published guidance to the force, he emphasized taking the fight to the main force elements: "Our operations must be oriented toward the destruction of these forces and we must undertake *an effective war of attrition* against them. We have not yet adequately exploited our great advantage in mobility and firepower."[63] He pointed out that although American troops had shown themselves to be superb soldiers, the operational initiative was with the enemy.

Looking back at his Phase I, General Westmoreland declared that his command was still learning:

[We] were progressively developing our ability to fight an elusive enemy on an area battlefield while improving our troop and logistical capability. *It was a year of learning*: old tactics had to be modified, new tactics and techniques explored. New equipment had to be developed and new skills acquired. We had to learn the enemy's tactics and how to deal with them.[64]

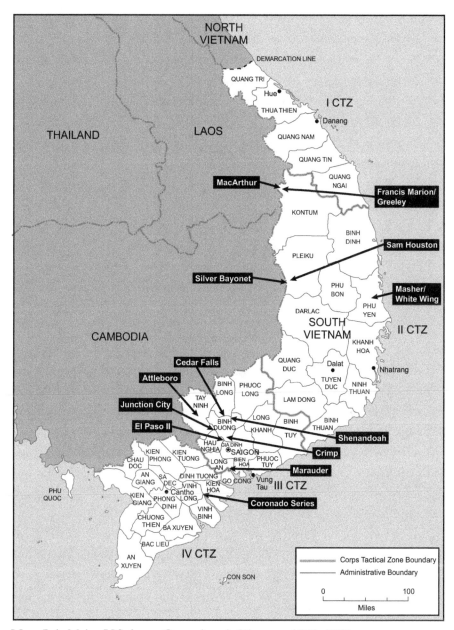

Map 5.1. Major U.S. Army Operations in Vietnam, 1965–1967

Adapted from George MacGarrigle, *The U.S. Army in Vietnam: Taking the Offensive, October 1966–October 1967*, Washington: Center of Military History, 1998, 20.

At this point in mid-1966, MACV was designing a campaign plan for 1967 that would continue efforts to destroy main force elements and base camps. The MACV staff recognized that the NLF "has been able to maintain a proportional counterbuildup to the growth of U.S. forces."[65] Thus, the logic of attrition and the "crossover" point was still apparent and had not been met.

Although the Army was learning to execute its strategy better, it also was adapting to a degree. In the next phase, the Army would strengthen that initiative by starting its own offensive operations.

Taking the Offensive: Phase II

Having staved off various potential main force incursions in Phase I, MACV now switched to the offensive. By the middle of 1966, it had built up several divisions, with their supporting infrastructure and logistics. During this phase, the Army forces designed and executed a number of large, multidivision operations.

The first operation of this phase was not really planned as much as it simply evolved. It was initially aimed at Viet Cong forces near the Cambodian border in Tay Ninh, fifty miles northwest of Saigon. The area was assigned to the untested 196th Brigade of the 25th Infantry Division. The unit had arrived mid-August and was still building a base camp. Unknown to the U.S. military, the NVA was aware that the 196th was new. It hoped to test the brigade and destroy it.[66]

Operation Attleboro began as a series of limited battalion-sized search-and-destroy missions. On October 23, a battalion uncovered one thousand tons of rice near the town of Dau Tieng. The rice was secured and patrols fanning outward found even more caches. Next, based on MACV intelligence about enemy movements, the 196th Brigade was directed to move toward Ba Hao on the morning of November 3. The brigade put together a complex insertion plan along four different routes in difficult terrain. Two air-assault companies were to be carried by helicopter into different blocking positions and two other units would maneuver on the ground in rough terrain. One battalion commander objected to the complexity of the plan.[67] Tragically, he was proven correct.

While the 196th Brigade was deploying, the commander of the 9th VC division attacked the widely dispersed Americans. In dense terrain, the U.S. forces were caught by surprise. In the melee, several units lost their commanders and were isolated. During the swirling battle, units were thrust into the fight piecemeal. The precise location of units was not clear, preventing commanders from employing artillery lest errant strikes hit friendly units. At one point, a battalion commander ended up leading eleven different rifle companies from four different battalions. Over the next few days the flaws of the battle plan and American tactics were exposed. In 2 days, the brigade lost 60 dead and suffered 159 wounded.

Major General DePuy was in the area and found the situation a "hornet's nest."[68] Taken aback by the poorly led operation, he was given charge of the entire effort. He pulled back all U.S. forces and initiated an intensive twenty-four-hour artillery and air bombardment on suspected NVA and VC positions. DePuy expanded the operation to a division-level force and amassed all the supporting fire possible. Having finally found the enemy, he started to "pile on" with everything MACV could give him. At the end, at least 20,000 U.S. and South Vietnamese troops were assigned to the effort.[69]

Reflecting a tactical adaptation that had been building inside the Army, DePuy's orders for the next nineteen-day phase of Attleboro were succinct: "Find the enemy with the least number of men and destroy them with the maximum amount of firepower."[70] Despite the huge influx of U.S. forces, the NVA still pressed forward. Once found, the enemy had to be pursued, fixed in place, and destroyed by fire. Some 22,000 troops piled on, backed up with 88 artillery pieces firing more than 100,000 rounds of supporting fire, and 1,600 air sorties—including 11 B-52 strikes—dropped 12,000 tons of ordnance. The operation ended on November 24. After more than 6 weeks of hit-and-run fighting, the VC forces sustained more than 1,100 casualties and withdrew back to Cambodia. American losses were significant—155 killed and 494 wounded.[71]

What began as a calamity evolved into a substantial victory in the after-action reports. The senior Army headquarters claimed that "Operation Attleboro inflicted heavier personnel and equipment losses on the VC than they had ever encountered in South Vietnam to that time."[72] The parent division, the 25th Infantry Division, reported (accurately) that "Indications are that Attleboro completely disrupted VC plans for a major winter offensive by the 9th Viet Cong Division and the 101st NVA Regt."[73] Attleboro became the model for DePuy's tactics in fights to come.[74]

The pattern of overly optimistic claims in after-action reports continued. However, one battalion commander was refreshingly honest: "It would be beneficial to examine the detrimental factors of the action in order to seek improvements and solutions," he wrote. He identified several:

- The inability to reconnoiter the VC positions without becoming engaged.
- The limited use of air and artillery firepower due to the closeness of the combatants.
- The piecemeal commitment of the battalion into the area of operations.
- The inability to reinforce . . . quickly because of the dense jungle.[75]

In late 1966, as his forces shifted to the strategic offensive, Westmoreland wanted to strike at major threats to South Vietnam's capital. Thus began the planning for Operation Cedar Falls, to be carried out in January. This new search-and-destroy offensive was designed to degrade insurgent operations by sweeping the so-called Iron Triangle, a sixty-square-mile area north of Saigon. Using innovative signals intelligence techniques, MACV pinpointed the command post for VC's Military Region 4. The headquarters was protected by an NVA regiment and two VC battalions, totaling around five thousand troops. This would be a massive, multidivisional operation that would surround and systematically search the Iron Triangle. Long a virtual Viet Cong stronghold, it was considered a "dagger pointed at the heart of Saigon" due to the location and shape of the area.[76]

Army leaders planned a huge operation. Some 30,000 Allied troops would participate, with 16,000 U.S. soldiers assigned from two Army divisions (the 1st and 25th infantry divisions), and three separate brigades (the 196th, the 173rd Airborne Brigade, and the 11th Armored Cavalry Regiment). This corps-sized equivalent would be joined by almost 14,000 South Vietnamese troops. The operation began on January 8, 1967, and ended on January 26. In a major shift from previous sweep operations, and indicative of some degree of organizational learning, Operation Cedar Falls called for a permanent eradication of the VC bases, a defoliation of the jungle areas within the triangle, and a relocation of the area's citizenry to New Life Villages—fortified hamlets built to relocate families of counterinsurgents who supported the South Vietnam regime. By the end of 1966, sweeping enemy-held areas for a minor or temporary gain was not considered acceptable. Instead, an area would be cleared and turned into a non-occupied zone in which all movement would be subjected to fire—in other words, a "free-fire zone."

Cedar Falls was another hammer-and-anvil operation. The "anvil" would be the 25th Infantry Division, reinforced with the 196th Light Infantry Brigade. It would assume blocking positions west of the Iron Triangle along the Saigon River, and a brigade of the 1st Infantry Division would do the same along the Song Thi Tinh River. The "hammer," provided by the 1st Infantry Division, would strike the Viet Cong by sweeping through the Iron Triangle. The plan incorporated two phases. In the preparatory phase, January 5–9, the anvil would be created along the Iron Triangle's flank, with an air assault on Ben Suc, a Viet Cong village, on January 8. Ben Suc was the considered the center of Viet Cong dominance in the area.[77] In the main phase, the encirclement would be closed, and then the hammer would sweep through the Iron Triangle from both the south and the west.

On January 8, the 2nd Brigade conducted an air assault on the village of Ben Suc. Achieving complete tactical surprise and facing surprisingly limited opposition, American forces sealed off the village and ARVN troops screened the population. They detained dozens of suspected VC and discovered their underground tunnel system. The village's six thousand residents were ultimately relocated to camps. Army bulldozers then razed Ben Suc to the ground.

U.S. forces then initiated the hammer phase. Following large-scale artillery fire and carpet bombing, the 1st Infantry Division began its sweep into the Iron Triangle, but the massive military thrust encountered empty space. Perhaps forewarned, the Viet Cong had evaded allied forces instead of defending their bases. There were no battalion-sized clashes—just a pattern of small-unit actions and snipers. Although the Army failed to destroy any significant PAVN forces, it did uncover the NLF's complex tunnel system, where it found supplies and valuable intelligence.

When Operation Cedar Falls ended—on January 26, 1967, after nineteen days—the effort had compiled what appeared to be impressive results. Again, U.S. Army estimates claimed a total of seven hundred enemy dead, despite the lack of major battles.[78] By comparison, losses were light. U.S. forces lost 72 killed and 337 wounded. Army commanders were pleased with Operation Cedar Falls. One brigade thought it was "judged by all standards . . . a major success."[79] Some of this success was ascribed to the use of specialized equipment—including bulldozers, tear gas, and acetylene for clearing underground bunkers, tunnel teams, and flame-throwers. Westmoreland found the results "very impressive."[80] The Army claimed that the operation had been lucrative.[81] The corps commander, General Seaman, called it a success, due to the sweep's disruption of Viet Cong capability and its "serious psychological impact" on a populace that had long been intimidated. General DePuy called Cedar Falls a "decisive turning-point in the III Corps area" and "a blow from which the VC in this area may never recover."[82] Despite DePuy's hope, however, the VC forces returned to the area and local peasants continued to support them.

Following Cedar Falls, the Army worked to keep up pressure on the VC with Operation Junction City (February–May 1967). The U.S. objective was to locate and destroy the COSVN (Central Office for South Vietnam), the VC central committee's headquarters.[83] Once again, U.S. leaders earmarked a significant force for this operation. All told, there would be twenty-two battalions participating. The 1st and 25th infantry divisions and the 11th Armored Cavalry Regiment would be the major fighting forces. Planners allocated four thousand strike sorties and assigned seventeen artillery battalions.[84] Using 249 helicopters, it would be the largest air assault in the history of Army aviation.

Operation Junction City was another hammer-and-anvil maneuver, where airborne forces would suddenly land to "flush out" the VC headquarters, sending them to retreat against a prepared anvil of prepositioned heavy forces. American forces kicked off the operation on February 22, 1967. The initial moves were carried out by the two infantry divisions, moving to create the anvil on which the VC would be crushed. That same day, eight battalions of airmobile infantry flew into place. On the following day, the 11th Armored Cavalry and the 2nd Brigade of the 25th Division provided the hammer, seemingly giving the enemy no chance to escape. For five days, the zone was swept and little was found. The main COSVN headquarters was not discovered, and no significant quantities of arms were seized. Having closed the trap on little more than vapor, the U.S. troops began to disengage and redeploy on March 3.

Operation Junction City claimed even more impressive results than previous operations. With a huge consumption of resources, including 366,000 rounds of artillery and 3,235 tons of bombs, the American forces reported that they had inflicted heavy losses on the enemy. By American estimates, the VC suffered 2,728 killed. Yet, the American losses were not negligible, amounting to almost 300 dead and more than 1,500 injured.[85] Westmoreland concluded that War Zone C, "an inviolate Viet Cong stronghold for many years," was "now vulnerable to allied forces any time we choose to enter."[86] He also noted that the tunnel complexes and vast underground bunkers network represented a lost investment of twenty years in its building.[87]

General DePuy noted that the enemy had initiated the major actions in Operation Junction City and that smaller units were invariably attacked by numerically superior VC forces. The U.S. commander attributed his high kill ratio to careful defensive positions, fire-support assets, adequacy of air support, and the use of armored and mechanized units to bring direct volumes of fire. By his report, the division had garnered extensive experience, defeated each regiment of the 9th VC Division and estimated 1,809 killed in action (KIA).[88]

Brig. Gen. Bernard W. Rogers, the assistant commander of the 1st Infantry Division, concluded that "a turning-point in the war had been reached."[89] Rogers also defended the scale of the operation, declaring that "multidivisional operations have a place in modern counterinsurgency warfare because they forced the insurgents to face larger forces than he could assemble."[90] His chief lesson from both operations related to firepower was:

Operations Cedar Falls and Junction City confirmed in the minds of most of us the decisive role played by artillery and air during major battles such as those fought with the 9th Viet Cong Division. They also verified the need to get as much firepower as possible on an attacking enemy without delay and . . . establish a fire coordination line and use artillery and air strikes simultaneously.[91]

A decade later, this period of operations would be assessed quite differently by members of an Army battle analysis team, including then-captain David Petraeus. To them, Operation Junction City "principally served to illustrate the shortcomings of search-and-destroy tactics and a strategy of attrition in this type conflict." They also found that "a second important lesson that was recognized but perhaps not learned was the bankruptcy of the search-and-destroy operation."[92]

Almost simultaneous with Junction City was Operation Sam Houston, a division-level operation with two brigades conducting border security tasks. The operation ran from February 12, 1967, to April 5 in the Pleiku and Kontum provinces. Like most of its predecessors, this one was a series of aggressive search-and-destroy sweeps, focused against two NVA divisions. In February, the 4th Infantry

Division had no fewer than eleven battles with the NVA. The combat consisted of a series of engagements waged under a jungle canopy that minimized American firepower while maximizing opportunities for ambush on the other side. Yet, these battles blunted a potential offensive and drove the NVA back into Cambodia. The operation was curtailed on April 5. The 4th Division claimed 733 North Vietnamese KIAs, at a cost of 169 American dead and another 700 wounded.[93]

Maj. Gen. William R. Peers, commander of the 4th Infantry Division, called Operation Sam Houston "eminently successful," and Col. James B. Adamson, the 2nd Brigade commander, pointed out that "we sought the contact and every battle was the direct result of our tactical movements."[94] Intelligence was thin, and most contacts developed by companies conducting patrols in search of the NVA, which had to be quickly reinforced with fires.[95] Destruction was sought through massive amounts of firepower. No doubt the North Vietnamese absorbed heavy casualties—a consequence of enormous quantities of artillery, some 230,647 rounds.[96] As with other American units, the principal lesson was to use more firepower, faster: "Immediate application of firepower is the decisive factor in fighting, commanders are enjoined to make immediate use of all supporting fires."[97]

In retrospect, as noted in the U.S. Army's postwar history, "Sam Houston was simply another . . . more expensive exercise in hide-and-seek with the North Vietnamese," wrote military historian George L. MacGarrigle of the Army's Center of Military History. "It was becoming clear that the enemy really controlled the fighting near the border, making it a costly proposition to send American units there."[98] The reality was that the enemy choose when he would stand and fight or when he would flee.

Imposed Adaptation

Although the Army's major combat operations did not reflect substantial adaptation, a major change did occur during this period. Instead of being sourced from the bottom, it was imposed on the Army from the top down, from Washington. In March 1967, President Johnson, reflecting his perception that economic and development assistance efforts were lagging in Vietnam, approved the establishment of the Civil Operations and Rural Development Support program (CORDS) as part of MACV through National Security Action Memorandum 362 (NSAM 362).[99] It took effect in May.[100] Former ambassador Robert W. Komer, a civilian who served as Westmoreland's deputy and was assigned as the first CORDS director, understood the value and complexity of the program this way: "As pacification is a multifaceted civil-military problem, . . . it demands a multifaceted civil-military response."[101] Westmoreland agreed, despite the objections of other staff members.[102] He called the adaptation both "major and portentous" and declared MACV now organized to pursue a "one-war" strategy.[103] Westmoreland never believed that force alone would be sufficient by itself, and had incorporated pacification into his strategy from the beginning, as noted by Erik Villard in his official Army history.[104]

CORDS expanded from a little more than 1,000 persons to almost 8,500 American advisers (civilian and military) at its peak in 1969; some 95 percent of its personnel were from the Army.[105]

In addition to organizational adaptation, some doctrinal change is evidenced by the promulgation of a draft doctrine by MACV to support pacification in May of 1967.[106] The final version would not be published for a year, but it is indicative of organic doctrine.

Despite the new emphasis on pacification and revolutionary development, combat lessons learned were continuing to emerge. The experiences of the 1st Infantry Division were incorporated into a pamphlet produced by one of its brigade commanders and disseminated throughout the Army in its professional journal. Col. Sydney B. Berry, who served under DePuy, summarized the adaptation in the changing relationship in ground maneuver and supporting fire in Vietnam:

> the brigade commander seeks to inflict maximum damage to the enemy at the least cost in lives to his own soldiers. He employs to the fullest the firepower, mobility, and mechanical advantages which U.S. forces have over the enemy. He uses his soldiers to find and fix the enemy and supporting firepower to destroy him.[107]

Echoing DePuy, Berry wrote: "Commanders at all levels should seek to find the enemy with minimum forces and then use maneuver units to block the enemy's withdrawal and supporting firepower to destroy him." The Army was advised to avoid heavy infantry contact. "The key to success," Berry went on to stress, "is the massive use of supporting firepower when the enemy is located."[108] The mantra for operations in Vietnam became "Infantry finds, artillery kills."[109]

Westmoreland could point to the "success" of his major operations and the now-integrated CORDS program as proof of progress.[110] By the end of Phase II, Westmoreland hoped to have U.S. forces poised for a year of decision.

Year of Decision: Phase III

Originally, MACV and the Army had hoped to have established a high-enough level of security for the Vietnamese people by the fall of 1967 that U.S. efforts could again be focused on training and advising the ARVN military. Yet Hanoi kept up its support, infiltrating more resources into the South, and maintaining large sanctuaries just across the border in Cambodia and Laos. The American forces continued to maintain a relatively high op tempo to keep the main force units at bay. MACV continued its basic plan and sought to make 1968 a year of decisive action. Firepower and attrition would remain the defeat-mechanism-of-choice: "Combat-induced attrition remained the central tool for degrading the enemy's capabilities," Villard wrote, "if not to win the war on the ground, then to break the enemy's will to continue."[111] In the words of the Army's latest history of this period, it would "stay the course."[112]

After Junction City, the 1st Infantry Division's next mission was to clear out VC base camps along Highway 13, which runs from Saigon north to the Cambodian border, in Operation Shenandoah II.[113] The crude highway was the main artery from the capital north to the border and had been the focus of Operation El Paso II almost a year and half before. The division planned a series of search-and-destroy missions as part of Operation Shenandoah II to fulfill that task.[114] A number of battalions were distributed across the division's area of responsibility attempting to find and destroy their persistent VC adversary.

On October 17 one of these battalions was decimated in a dramatic ambush by a VC regiment reinforced with heavy machine guns. The "Black Lions" of the 2nd Battalion, 28th Infantry were led by Lt. Col. Terry D. Allen, a West Point graduate whose father had led the 1st Infantry Division in the invasion of North Africa and Sicily in World War II. By October 15, the Black Lions had been on a search-and-destroy mission for more than a week. They were undermanned and tired, but still looking for the VC.[115] The Black Lions had several engagements with the VC on October 16 while patrolling in jungle along the Ong Thanh stream to a distance of two kilometers from their base camp. Each time, Allen pulled back his force and directed airstrikes or artillery against it. Late in the afternoon, Allen felt it best to return to base. That evening, the assistant division commander, Brig. Gen. William Coleman, visited the battalion and rebuked Allen for not having maneuvered aggressively. Allen was directed to reattack and to lead from the ground with his men the next day.[116]

As ordered, on October 17 Allen led roughly half his command on a search-and-destroy mission into the jungle. The battalion patrol left its base camp at around 8 a.m. with good intelligence that a VC regiment was in the area. In fact, the 1,200 veterans of the 271st VC Regiment were waiting in a prepared ambush. Following its standard practice, Allen's force stopped periodically to conduct brief "cloverleaf patrols" to their front and flanks.[117] But then around ten o'clock the lead company got pinned down by heavy machine-gun fire. The company commander and his artillery liaison officer were severely wounded, while the radio operators and two platoon leaders were killed.

Having rendered the first company ineffective, the VC force maneuvered toward the remaining company and Allen's command group. Allen tried to call in air and artillery support.[118] At one point, requests for artillery were blocked by higher headquarters as the units sought to clear the battlespace for airstrikes. The VC force chewed up the outnumbered Americans. Members of the battalion command group, including Allen, were all killed.[119] During two hours of fighting the battalion lost sixty-four men KIA and seventy-five wounded in action (WIA).

The Army tried to paint the disaster as a meeting engagement that produced a victory. The final line of the brigade's report succinctly captures the Army's mindset: "The mission of finding and destroying the enemy was successfully accomplished."[120] After Shenandoah, the Army identified improved defensive measures as a clear innovation from these operations. The 1st Infantry Division extolled the vaunted "DePuy" fighting position and overlooked losses from the offensive patrols. According to the division's after-action report, a night defensive position was attacked in Shenandoah II and five times the attacks were repulsed at a total loss exchange of 503 VC KIA for seven Americans.[121] The senior Army headquarters reported the Ong Thanh battle and the loss of the Black Lions in a single paragraph.[122]

After the war, Maj. James E. Shelton, a former member of the Black Lions staff, did his own evaluation, which contradicted the brigade-level assessment. "By all accounts, on October 17, 1967," he wrote, "the 'Black Lions' were out-positioned, out-gunned, out-manned and out-maneuvered."[123]

The war in the central highlands continued.[124] During the previous summer months, the 4th Division conducted a lengthy pair of operations, respectively called Francis Marion and Greeley, but the efforts were not entirely fruitful. Now the 4th Division planned Operation Paul Revere IV up along the Cambodian border. This was a division-level search-and-destroy mission aimed at enemy base areas, intended to blunt any potential offensives being planned by the B3 Front—another spoiling attack still trying to keep the NVA off balance. By the end of the operation, four brigades from two different divisions had been engaged.[125]

Probing close to enemy camps and on terrain well known to the adversary is inherently dangerous, and on November 21, a U.S. Army company paid a high price to learn that. A platoon-size patrol found itself facing a battalion from the NVA 101st Regiment and was overrun, at a cost of thirty-two Americans. The NVA next tried to overrun a firebase positioned a mere three kilometers from the border. Airpower was especially effective in blunting two human-wave assaults, despite bad weather. North Vietnamese losses were high, with at least four hundred killed trying to neutralize the artillery base. The 4th Division would claim a body count of 977 NVA, and would place American losses at 110. The loss-ratio reflected the NVA's unusually dogged effort—despite its previous abandonment of human-wave attacks—to overrun a defended position that had adequate air and artillery support.

Not everyone was impressed with the 4th Division's account of the campaign. After receiving the official after-action briefing by the division staff, one cynical veteran, Lt. Col. David H. Hackworth, assessed it far more critically:

> If the operation were measured by World War II experience it was indeed a victory. But if it was viewed as it had to be, from the perspective of the war as an insurgency that it was, then we did *not* win and we were *not* brilliant. In fact we were stupid, lethally so, and Charlie had won the day. The enemy initiated the action, used tried and true highlands methods, i.e., threatening a CIDG [Civilian Irregular Defense Group] border camp [established by the U.S. Central Intelligence Agency] and using decoys to entice U.S. forces into an airmobile operation. The enemy sucked the American units

into well-dug-in killing zones along the Cambodian border, killing 140 and wounding more than 560 of our men on terrain that favored them completely.[126]

U.S. intelligence reported that the North Vietnamese were withdrawing regiments from the Pleiku area to join those in Kontum Province. Despite the extensive attrition prompted earlier by Operation Francis Marion, the 1st PAVN Division had been reorganized and reinforced. It was tasked with the destruction of a brigade-sized U.S. unit. The North Vietnamese fed six thousand troops into the area, mounting their own search-and-destroy operation.

This intelligence led to the launching of Operation MacArthur to spoil the NVA plans. The Army ordered the 173rd Brigade back to Dak To. The immediate goal of the paratroopers was to establish a base of operations and bolster the defenses at Ben Het. They would then search for the 66th PAVN Regiment, believed to be south of Fire Support Base 12. Simultaneously, most of the 4th Infantry Division and two 1st Air Cavalry battalions moved into the area around Dak To. The stage was set for a major pitched battle.

The centerpiece became a series of hilltop fights that took place in Kontum Province and around Dak To between November 3 and 27. The battles that erupted on the hill masses south and southeast of Dak To were some of the hardest fought battles of the war. The first fighting erupted on November 3 and 4, when companies of the 4th Infantry Division came across NVA troops in defensive positions. The next day the same thing occurred with elements of the American 173rd Brigade. The U.S. forces combed the hills on foot, ran into prepared defensive positions, applied massive firepower from aircraft and artillery, and then launched ground attacks. In all of these instances, the NVA troops fought hard, inflicted casualties on the Americans, and then withdrew. The U.S. troops continued this stubborn pattern of expensive attacks.

As the Americans quickly discovered, the area had been well-prepared by the North Vietnamese. The number and elaborateness of defensive preparations indicated that they had been prepared as much as six months in advance. As General Peers noted about the enemy: "Nearly every key terrain feature was heavily fortified with elaborate bunker and trench complexes. He had moved quantities of supplies and ammunition into the area. He was prepared to stay."[127]

Peers was just as prepared to keep advancing and push them out. He ordered a number of hilltops seized, to increase artillery fire and support his sweeping patrols logistically. One small company landed at Hill 823, only to find that it was sharing the hilltop with an NVA company in tunnels and bunkers. The next day that tired company was relieved by a battalion, the 1st Battalion, 503rd Airborne. The day after that, the paratroop unit was divided into two small task forces for reconnaissance patrols. On November 11, one of those task forces was ambushed by two VC battalions and had to fight for its life. Only close air support kept it from being overrun. The Americans paid a price: there were 20 KIA and 154 WIA, representing half the battalion's fighting strength.

American forces kept pressing in search of the NVA. U.S. intelligence indicated that a PAVN regiment had slipped westward and had taken up positions on Hill 875, a prominent terrain feature in the area. A battalion was ordered to secure it. On the morning of November 20, the battalion got within three hundred meters of the crest but was driven back by heavy fire. As the Americans retreated downhill, they walked into an ambush. The U.S. troops fell back farther and evacuated their wounded. The next day the Americans called in airstrikes and a heavy artillery barrage. A fresh battalion, the 4th Battalion, 503rd Airborne, reinforced the initial force. The next afternoon, on November 21, both battalions assaulted the hill. They made it to the PAVN trenches, but could not clear them, and fell back.[128]

The division piled on the firepower instead of more troops. The Americans launched airstrikes and a heavy artillery bombardment the entire following day. On November 23, the two battalions of the 503rd swept up the hillside and found there was no fight left. Their adversaries were gone. Hill 875 cost the Americans 115 KIA, 253 WIA. Operation MacArthur was expensive—376 U.S. KIA and another 1,441 wounded. The North was able to down forty helicopters. The Americans fired 151,000 artillery rounds, used 2,096 tactical air sorties, and conducted 257 B-52 strikes. The U.S. Army claimed that 1,644 NVA soldiers had been killed.[129]

General Westmoreland declared that his command "had soundly defeated the enemy without unduly sacrificing operations in other areas. The enemy's return was nil." Speaking at the National Press Club while his troops were scaling Hill 875, he argued that the battle represented the "beginning of a great defeat for the enemy."[130] In response to a question as to why U.S. forces were fighting so far from any major population centers, he said: "We'd find ourselves in an enclave posture, which would be completely unacceptable to me because we would have surrendered the initiative."[131] Gen. Earle G. Wheeler, chairman of the Joint Chiefs of Staff, also queried MACV on such costly expenditures along the border. Westmoreland sent a lengthy reply that included this excerpt: "I can see absolutely no psychological or military advantage to a strategy that would intentionally invite the war east towards the coast. It would be retrogressive, costly in casualties and refuges, and almost certainly prolong the war."[132]

Behind these questions were issues about the Army strategy. Was the Army reacting to the enemy, continually lured into battles where it surrendered the initiative and tactical advantage in order to generate a higher degree of attrition?[133] Was it failing to adapt? Critics of the Army's approach in this campaign noted that "in the context of Westmoreland's strategy . . . the fight for Hill 875 with its attendant losses, was worth it. There was never any thought to holding the hill once the enemy had been driven from it. It was just one more place where they could be killed."[134]

Rather than adapt to the enemy's tactics, American leaders continually sought out new chances to close with the NVA under conditions more suited to benefit their opponent. Firepower was lavish, but the infantry still had to find and fix the opponent. Time and again, the opponent picked the time and the place of battle, extracted a measure of blood, and withdrew to fight another day. As the U.S. Army's history points out, these operations never decisively defeated the enemy, nor did they prevent him from returning later. Rather, it found that "no territory had been won; no enemy armies had been vanquished. Instead, a thousand firefights had worn down both sides in a hot, rain-sodden land that neither side could really claim to dominate unless physically entrenched there."[135]

The one distinctive adaptation in this period was the development of a joint riverine force to penetrate the "cradle of the insurgency" in the Mekong Delta. The delta held a third of the South's population and a majority of its food production. The U.S. Navy had created a riverine force to interdict the VC's use of the waterways in this region. Although the Navy cut down the VC's use of major river arteries, it could not penetrate the bases where the VC enjoyed sanctuary, so a Navy officer on the MACV staff developed a concept for the use of converted World War II ships as a mobile base and amphibious assault craft (LCM-6s) modified for use in the dangerous Delta.[136] DePuy briefed Westmoreland in early

December of 1965. Westmoreland found the concept to be "most imaginative" and sought support from his superiors in March 1966.

The plan was implemented in early 1967. The Mobile Riverine Force employed a U.S. Army brigade, which lived and operated on the river. The force was based on board U.S. Navy ships, including five barracks ships and two LSTs for command-and-control. Two U.S. Navy River Assault Squadrons (RAS) would provide tactical water mobility. Each RAS would be capable of lifting an infantry battalion.[137] The LSTs and barracks ships could move throughout the delta under their own power.

The 9th Infantry Division was activated in the United States in 1966 and prepared for riverine operations before deploying later that year. Trial operations began February 16 and ran until March 20, 1967.[138] The efforts evolved in Operation Palm Beach, generating a high eleven-to-one kill ratio, as recorded by the 9th Infantry Division.[139] The MRF learned how to blend riverine, air mobile, and mechanized assets in the Delta region in operations Coronado I through IX.[140] These assaults proved the concept and demonstrated the Army's capacity for adapting.[141] Westmoreland extolled the Coronado operations, based on a claimed kill ratio of fifteen-to-one.[142]

Tet Offensive of 1968

The decisive operation that Westmoreland sought occurred in early 1968, but it was not the success MACV had pursued. The "border battles" of operations Francis Marion, Greeley, and Dak To had distracted the Americans from seeing something much bigger.[143] Instead of conventional attacks along the border or against the Marines at Khe Sanh in a Dien Bien Phu scenario, the North executed a large-scale offensive in South Vietnam with all its local forces in a simultaneous uprising. The surprise offensive began during the early hours of January 31 during the annual Tet [Vietnamese lunar new year] holiday truce. Some 80,000 VC militia threw themselves at designated targets in the South's major cities. The targets in Saigon included large military bases and the American embassy.

The offensive was unexpected, which accentuated its impact in the wake of indicators from Westmoreland that the United States was making substantial progress. The South Vietnamese admirably held their own against the onslaught. The U.S. embassy walls were breached, but few U.S. installations were damaged and security was quickly restored in most cities. The major exception was the old imperial city of Hue, where the NVA seized the ancient Citadel. U.S. Marine forces methodically cleared the city at great loss.[144]

The media coverage of the Tet offensive was graphic, giving the North a strategic propaganda victory. The subsequent media firestorm stimulated a long-needed policy reassessment by President Johnson's cabinet. As captured in the Pentagon Papers, "a fork in the road had been reached and the alternatives stood out in stark reality."[145] The Johnson administration examined alternative strategies, rejected the notion of larger troop increases and chose to take the path leading away from the war. Johnson turned more of the war back over to the Vietnamese.

Westmoreland persisted with his strategy throughout 1967. He did not seek options—just more troops. In the fall of 1967, he was developing a campaign strategy for 1968 that was more of the same. "Defeat the VC/NVA main force" was the primary objective, with destruction of base areas and infrastructure, and U.S. forces sought to drive the opposition away from more populated areas where the South Vietnamese government could "protect the population."[146] Westmoreland could not accept the strategic significance of Tet. MACV's reaction to Tet was to claim a great victory, citing the utter destruction of the VC militia throughout South Vietnam. Westmoreland looked back and said, "It added up to a striking military defeat for the enemy on anybody's terms."[147]

America would go on fighting in Vietnam and expend enormous resources in what many thought was a lost cause. Indeed, the U.S. force lost more troops *after* Tet than in the years of escalation.[148] But the only major adaptation after that was turning the war over to the South Vietnamese.

On March 31, 1968, President Johnson announced he would not seek reelection in November. Tet had claimed its final casualty.

Organizational Learning Capacity
This case evidences an overall failure to adapt in-theater. How do we explain this? Having summarized the major operations and adaptations that actually occurred during the escalation years of American Army involvement in the Vietnam war, we now turn to examining how this experience matches the expected conditions for successful Organizational Learning and the four internal shapers that are associated with Organizational Learning Capacity.

Leadership

The key leadership in this case study comes from the Army, in the form of General Westmoreland and his operations officer, William E. DePuy. Westmoreland was known as the "inevitable general," the top-ranking cadet in his class at West Point and a successful combat commander in World War II.[149] His physical stature and chiseled looks marked him early in his career as a potential general. He was groomed by mentors for greater responsibility and was selected for prestigious positions that would guarantee him the greatest chance of climbing to the top.[150]

But Westmoreland was also a personification of the Army's culture. He was an organization man, more educated in corporate management than in military affairs. He did not graduate from either the Army's Command and General Staff College or the Army War College, although he was briefly on the staff of each.[151] His sole educational experience from the end of World War II to taking up his post in Saigon two decades later was a three-month management seminar at Harvard University. He was described by contemporaries as "intellectually very shallow" and appears to have made little investment in reading within his professional sphere or beyond.[152] Thus, he was undereducated by the standards of the Army's formal educational system.[153]

To his critics, "Westy was a corporation executive in uniform, a diligent, disciplined organization man who would obey orders."[154] To Westmoreland himself, the war was an exercise in management that matched the Army's cultural values and way of war. Enforcing those values and applying a mechanistic vision of industrial age war was consistent with his own career and the belief system that promoted him. Ahead of both his service and his contemporaries, he became comfortable with using statistics as a management tool.[155] Members of his staff acknowledged that "there were limits to his capacity for handling cognitive complexity."[156] This is not to suggest that he was stupid; his papers and performance in many key conferences during the war refute that. Yet rather than being open-minded and inquisitive, he was managerial, indecisive, and defensive. As described by one study on U.S. generalship, "He was an odd combination of traits, energetic and ambitious, yet strikingly incurious and prone to fabrication even as he considered himself a Boy Scout on ethics."[157] This combination of traits was not well-suited to the complexities of Vietnam, and the intellectual and political virtuosity required by theater command in such a war.

Westmoreland's chief MACV deputy in Vietnam was his operations officer, DePuy. DePuy served essentially as Westmoreland's chief of staff, authoring his strategy, very much as the Prussian general August Gneisenau was to Field Marshal Gebhard L. von Blücher. Like Westmoreland, DePuy was a veteran of the European theater of World War II. Like Westmoreland, he rose steadily in the Army ranks, but dutifully passed all the traditional Army educational gates at the Command and General Staff College in 1946, the Armed Forces Staff College, and the British Imperial Defense College in London. Still, he became the principal architect of Westmoreland's (and the U.S. Army's) approach to fighting in Vietnam.

DePuy was described by those who served under him as intense, analytical, "extraordinarily forceful," and "crisp."[158] One major described him as a commander who made his subordinates "jumpy" as well as anxious to please him.[159] He had a very tactical focus, solely interested in bringing the main force units or any organized VC unit to battle. In interviews, he made it clear that the true mission for U.S. forces was "search-and-destroy," not pacification or counterinsurgency. "It was my idea to go after the main force units wherever they could be found and to go after them with as many battalions as I could get into the fight—what was later called 'pile-on,'" he said.[160]

When DePuy was selected for promotion, he was rewarded with command of the 1st Infantry Division in March of 1966; the division employed attrition, with little regard for traditional pacification measures. DePuy did not apologize for his views. "You can sit and write extremely clever leaflets, broadcasts and appeals, and nothing will happen unless you combine it with a tremendous amount of military pressure," he said.[161] He admitted to being demanding and tactically oriented.[162] He also understood that in the case of people who could not get in line with his philosophy, who could not think that way, he should send them along to other duties. All told, during his command he relieved fifty-six commanders and senior enlisted personnel—more than all the other division commanders combined.[163] DePuy's oral history suggests that he believed he dismissed ten to twelve officers, but it was enough to produce a dispute with Gen. Harold K. Johnson, the Army chief of staff, during a battlefield visit. Although some have applauded DePuy for holding poor performers to account, from a historical perspective one wonders what sort of command climate was established in which assumptions, plans, and orders could not be challenged for their logic. Numerous subordinates recall a sense of fear when briefing DePuy or operating in the command climate of his headquarters.[164] His biographer thought that this sense of fear could have curtailed the discourse required to recognize new challenges or devise adaptive solutions.[165]

According to one close staff officer, DePuy "loved hands-on tactics at the lowest level."[166] He simply could not resist addressing tactical issues, consistently injecting himself into platoon tactics, and peers such as Gen. Alexander M. Haig Jr. would describe him as a tactical genius.[167] DePuy issued terse sets of instructions and "battle principles" about the tactics and techniques that he expected his units to employ.[168] To critics in the press, "He had been convinced of the invincibility and universal application of the system of warfare the U.S. Army had derived from World War II. The system consisted of building a killing machine that subjected an enemy to the prodigious firepower the American technology provided."[169] He also developed a marked predisposition for firepower, suppression fire, and attrition. In his assessment of American generalship, journalist Thomas Ricks is critical of DePuy's firepower-centric methods, which were "magnificent in bringing firepower to bear on the battlefield but never seeming to pause to consider whether this might be counterproductive or even irrelevant."[170] DePuy was decisive, and a problem-solver open to conceptual issues, at least within his tactical framework.[171] His chief tactical innovations involved the extensive use of artillery during operations, a "cloverleaf" patrolling movement to minimize ambushes, and the "DePuy fighting position"—a foxhole designed with frontal and overhead protection with portals to fire diagonally rather than frontally.[172]

When challenged on his views on firepower about measuring progress using the body count in Vietnam decades after the war, DePuy did not back down, noting that "body counts were a gruesome way of accounting, but there didn't seem to be any other way to keep track of the progress being made."[173]

Although DePuy was adamant about bringing the NVA or VC to battle in search-and-destroy operations, after the war he conceded that the strategy he espoused was faulty:

> We engaged the enemy on ground of his choosing. We won battles—even campaigns—but at enormous costs in time, treasured lives, and political tolerance in the United States. By opposing the enemy at every level; by organizing as a mirror image, leaving the option of fighting or evading to him; by

honoring the political sanctity of his cross-border sanctuaries until too late, we engineered ourselves into a war of attrition in which the enemy largely controlled the tempo of operations.[174]

These two leaders would shape the Army's mode of operations early in the war. Many leaders, including generals Howze, Kinnard, and Creighton W. Abrams, served with great distinction and were positive influences in shaping the way the Army viewed the war and in sustaining the command climate of the Army head-quarters and its subordinate units. Thus, they were crucial to how well or poorly the Army adapted. From 1965 to 1968, the Army's way of war in Vietnam and its learning and adapting were shaped principally by Westmoreland and DePuy.

Organizational Culture

The U.S. Army's culture comes into discussion often in the literature about Vietnam. The officer corps of the time was led by a cadre of veterans of World War II and the Korean War. Many of the senior officers had extensive, if not searing, experiences in confronting the Germans in the Normandy campaign and were considered well-qualified in the profession of arms. Although their forming experience was in the past, they extended their visions and preparation for future war forward around a prototypical conventional land war in Europe. As noted by Builder, World War II "made an impression that has persisted with remarkable tenacity."[175]

To the late military historian Russell F. Weigley, the American Army's culture and doctrine sought victory "by the means sanctioned by the most deeply rooted historical American concepts of strategy, the destruction of the enemy's armed forces, and his ability to wage war."[176] The persistence of the Army's failure to adapt, over a long period of time, and most recently, in the face of a political mandate to adapt, suggests a controlling explanation: the rigidity arises from the fundamental assumptions on which the American Army rests.[177] Thus, the fail-ure to adapt stems from the defining elements of the Army's organizational cul-ture, rooted deeply in its history and reflected in its doctrine—in particular, the assumption that there are two separable, largely autonomous spheres of action which can be labeled "political" and "military," with the latter defined in narrow, essentially technical terms.[178]

The officer corps of World War II was shaped by West Point graduates, whose cadets represented a "Long Gray Line" back into the Army's history, and which influenced its future leadership.[179] Despite West Point's origin as a school for engineers who could help develop the American frontier, the educational system at the U.S. Military Academy emphasized science and doctrine over art or creative problem-solving, and this had a profound effect on Army culture. Moreover, the system was geared to the industrial-scale production of many officers, with few opportunities for divergent experiences. As Muth described the World War II generation, the Army's professional military educational system produced "an average officer who knew the basics of his trade in theory because he had run though a number of schools," but who "longed for doctrine and prepared solutions and tried to 'manage' rather than command."[180]

Much of that culture lived on in the Vietnam era. Brian Jenkins, a U.S. Special Forces officer in Vietnam and later a planner at MACV, summarized his own assessment in late 1969, arguing that "the Army's doctrine, its tactics, its organization, its weapons—its entire repertoire of warfare was designed for conventional war in Europe. In Vietnam, the Army simply performed its repertoire even though it was frequently irrelevant to the situation." To Jenkins, it was the Army's own doctrinal rigidity that prevented it from adapting to the war.[181]

What was true and apparently effective in the two World Wars continued as Army culture: "American officers treated doctrine like dogma."[182] This attitude or value was largely at odds with the complexities of their profession and certainly with the challenges presented in Southeast Asia. A service culture bound by tradition, technology, and the dogmatic applications of firepower shaped an approach that was doomed to fail in a different context that required more restraint and discrimination.

Brian M. Linn's description of the various intellectual traditions of the U.S. Army also is insightful.[183] He describes the rise of what he terms "managers" in the Cold War era. Managers believed that future wars would require mass conscription and large-scale mobilization. They envisioned future wars being won by "the creation of a mass army, equipped with the best armaments, trained large-unit operations, and controlled by educated professionals." In Linn's apt characterization, "war is fundamentally an organizational (as opposed to an engineering) problem—the rational coordination of resources, both human and materiel."[184] As Carl Builder put it, this is a culture that values logic and linear processing to generate answers.[185]

The managers, who dominated the Vietnam-era leadership, showered over-whelming resources, superior administration, and detailed planning into that con-flict in a vain attempt to secure victory. In Linn's characterization, Westmoreland was a highly capable manager, focused on organizing the resources, infrastructure, and logistics to fight a large-unit war with high-tech firepower.[186] The most inci-sive post-Vietnam survey of the era's officer corps was titled *The War Managers*.[187] In that survey, many officers subsequently believed that U.S. Army operations, par-ticularly search-and-destroy missions, were flawed. Such attitudes were prevalent in postwar assessments but were almost never made in formal after-action reports or lessons-learned products during the war. As one Army general noted, a self-critical culture was not part of the U.S. Army's DNA at that time.[188]

The Army's embedded "way of war" accounted for its prodigious administration, vast logistics, and the accelerated incorporation of new technologies such as the helicopter, night-vision devices, sensors, and napalm. But its managerial excellence could not adjust rapidly to the character of the war. Both leadership and culture conspired to sustain this lack of operational adaptation. Put bluntly, the Army's cul-ture and leader development experiences of this period encouraged inaction over initiative, compliance instead of creativity, and adherence instead of agility.[189]

Learning Mechanisms

Adaptation may have been retarded by the lack of a viable Army intelligence sys-tem. In 1965, the Army recognized, belatedly, that it had failed to create a sound intelligence program inside Vietnam in its advisory period, and that a substantial effort would be required to change its "disjointed, floundering staff of several hundred" intelligence personnel into an effective collection and analysis capabil-ity.[190] A professional intelligence officer of general officer rank did not arrive at MACV until 1965, and it took until mid-1967 before a theater-level intelligence effort was organized.

MACV had to feed McNamara's systems-analysis machine back in the Penta-gon with the quantitative inputs that it needed, regardless of their relevance to the kind of war that was being fought. As military historian Gregory A. Daddis has noted, "McNamara's requests for both progress and statistical confirmation drove a military institution already accustomed to approach problems with an engineer-ing mentality toward the mechanical system MACV instituted."[191]

The MACV staff evolved over time to accommodate the analytical needs of the commander. Westmoreland often tasked out studies, organizational proposals and long-range assessments.[192] Much of the assessment work was done by the MACV staff, specifically the planning directorate. The Army headquarters created a Command Analysis Center to assist in conducting in-house or organic studies for their service and for Westmoreland.[193]

The Army provided study support from outside of theater. The Army chief of staff created one of his own study teams, a widely cited PROVN study by a distinguished group of officers back in Washington. The document was an assessment of how the U.S. Army was conducting the war, spurred by General Johnson's deep reservations.[194] The report included strong criticism of some aspects of MACV's approach and also recognized that security was required to establish conditions for successful pacification to take root. Pacification was identified as warranting a higher priority. Westmoreland downplayed the report and asserted that some parts were already being addressed. The significance of this sole effort to challenge MACV's operational approach is still debated today. PROVN was not shaped by MACV and had no direct role in its formulation or execution. Although the sample set was small, the PROVN case study suggests that external efforts from the top down to *feed downward* can be resisted—and all but ignored.

Inside of South Vietnam, the Army Concept Team studied aerial strike techniques, countermine activity, heavy Flying Crane helicopter lift capabilities, tactical navigation systems, and AH-1 Cobra employment.[195] In addition to the Army's own team, the RAND Corporation sent analysts to Vietnam as well. RAND produced hundreds of studies and reports on the war, both for MACV and the Pentagon.[196] However, the organization's own history of its contribution concludes that "research results that challenged how things were done or indicated failure in a program to which important officials were committed were not usually accepted."[197]

In September 1967, Westmoreland requested a larger systems analysis capability. In two months, the MACV Operational Research and Systems Analysis Office (MACEVAL) was stood up. It was tasked with conducting short-term, operational studies. MACV acknowledged that this was a belated effort in the command's efforts to formally bring in scientific solutions.[198] By this point, Westmoreland had been in command for three years. After the war, the Army concluded that operations research was employed often in Vietnam, but that it appeared to have confirmed the professional judgment of the leadership, rather than providing fresh insights.[199] The influence of the science adviser and the entire MACEVAL program on command decisions at MACV was dryly noted to be "open to question."[200]

Westmoreland and the Army were almost as lavish about learning mechanisms as they were with firepower. Reports, studies, and statistics were used like B-52s and artillery—to "finish" resistance—but ultimately they suppressed comprehension. MACV suffered from intellectual rigidity and simply continued amassing vast amounts of statistical data without considering their usefulness in helping to better prosecute a long war and difficult war.[201] Derived as it was from the physical sciences, operations research proved less valuable in capturing the more political and socioeconomic aspects of Vietnam's war.[202] The assessment of progress in Vietnam was oversimplified in one sense by body counts and kill ratios, but also confused by an overabundance of sources and myriad metrics.[203] Early in the war, the enemy body count was overemphasized. One U.S. Army officer who served in Vietnam as a brigade operations officer was fired the day after he refused to inflate VC casualties in an operation.[204] In short, the Army used statistics to justify itself and as a substitute for understanding the war.[205]

As the war became more controversial and resistance to MACV's strategy heated up in Washington, there was strong pressure to generate favorable indicators that buttressed the appearance of progress. The Army's own official MACV history concluded that "statistics and their analysis become not management tools but weapons in public relations campaigns and policy battles. Operational analysis in the Vietnam conflict too often served, to paraphrase Clausewitz, as a continuation of politics by other means."[206]

Dissemination Mechanisms

The U.S. Army has a long history with detailed after-action reports to document operations and lessons.[207] In Vietnam, the Army made extensive use of formal combat after-action reports after each major operation and of operational reports and lessons learned on a quarterly basis. These reports were laboriously compiled and include enormous details regarding enemy dispositions, U.S. intelligence, logistics, and operational details. The documents almost unanimously describe outputs entirely in terms of casualties and weapons captured. Some reports reflect results of interactions with civilian personnel and the number of refugees created

or encountered. A few reports discuss efforts at pacification or civic action projects. Most describe lessons learned about specific deficiencies concerning hardware items, including radios, vehicles, and weapons. They are long on operational
detail, but short on insights or critical recommendations for changing or adapting beyond the tactical level. Today, they form an impressive historical record for
students, but they are devoid of critical insights (with one exception noted after
Operation Attleboro).

The Army did an excellent job in distributing these reports and lessons back to its
institutional schools in the United States. It also recognized that it needed to better
capture tactical lessons, and the Army chief of staff sponsored two notable authors
to develop a primer on fighting in Vietnam. The lessons that the Army did appear
to take away were very tactical—about patrolling and conducting ambushes.[208]
The MACV staff and the Army appear to have scoured the after-action reports
regularly and synthesized them into more summary compilations.[209] The Army
did not ignore the need to incorporate lessons into its force-generation processes
back in the United States. The Army Continental Command judiciously read and
digested tactical lessons from ongoing operations and synthesized them regularly
into published pamphlets for ease of transition into various training activities and
schools.[210] This is indicative of a concerted effort to both document and interpret
combat performance and forward reports to higher headquarters. Yet, they never
challenged the extant strategy or operational mode.

In addition, the Army employed a unique technique of formally interviewing
commanding officers of major organizations through senior officer debriefing
reports. A review of these interviews in preparation for this book produced few
insights or disagreements about the conduct of Army operations in Vietnam.[211]

The Army's officer corps was feeding new ideas forward, but few challenged
the existing orthodoxy or concept of war. Fewer brigade or division commanders raised critical concerns in the formal learning mechanisms. But postwar survey accounts such as Kinnard's *The War Managers* certainly suggest that
many had doubts. The after-action review process in today's Army is touted
as "arguably one of the most successful organizational learning methods yet
devised."[212] But the Vietnam War system, which left much to be desired, was
more about documenting history than about learning or challenging operating
concepts or results.

Further adaptation is reflected in the promulgation of updated doctrine back in the United States—particularly in the crafting of counterguerrilla doctrine, but also in the production of handbooks on pacification and civil affairs.[213] The generation of doctrine is a prime indicator of institutional learning that feeds the force-generation process with fresh units with appropriate training and expertise in the relevant competencies required. Back inside the United States, the Army's institutional learning components did adapt. Educational programs at the Army's Infantry School expanded from being roughly one-third about insurgency to as much as half of the program of instruction.[214]

The four enabling elements impacted the Army's Organizational Learning Cycle in Vietnam. There was extensive operational experience between 1965 and 1967 that produced many inputs, but few insights that altered how the Army used ground forces and firepower. In essence, *inquiry* was ongoing, but *interpretation* was blocked by senior leaders in Vietnam, who insisted on imposing their own mental model of the enemy and the war on the American ground forces. In this case study there is simply a failure by leadership to recognize the importance of systematic learning and a lack of a command climate at MACV to support critical inquiry in order to adjust its strategy and operational methods. There is no dearth of reports and documented experiences, and many commanders realized that the strategy was flawed. There are hundreds of after-action reports and campaign histories typed in triplicate and forwarded up the chain. But there is little evidence of *investigation* or the absorption of organizational learning at the strategic or operational level. Both the individual leaders and the Army's hierarchical and doctrinally compliant culture appear to have frozen the service's capacity to adjust or adapt under fire.

The Army's adoption of mobile riverine warfare should be noted as an exception. The proposal to adapt ships and landing craft was developed at MACV by a junior officer, presented to higher levels for subsequent approval, and applied successfully within a year. The Army had no existing competencies in fighting afloat. The initiative's relatively rapid development is a testament to effective adaptive learning in contact, as long as it supported the Army's overarching concept of getting at the enemy.

The larger issue about Army learning in Vietnam reflects the need for higher order learning or innovation, and the failure to master a different mode of warfare.

As noted in the Pentagon Papers:

> General Westmoreland's strategy based upon exploitation of our inherent superior mobility and firepower was designed to simultaneously attrit the enemy and retain the initiative by disrupting VC or NVA operations before they completely materialized. This led to seeking engagement with enemy main force units well out into the border regions. Related to this was the notion that the important thing was to fight—to engage the enemy and create casualties. It mattered little that you accepted combat in regions with certain advantages for the enemy—the prime objective was to engage and to kill him.[215]

The establishment of CORDS is a clear example of externally directed adaptation. But it was not an adaptation that sprung forward from the Army itself. Nor did the Army alter the dominant role given to search-and-destroy operations or the central role of firepower and attrition in its concept of fighting the war. As Komer noted, pacification was simply a small complement to a "raging, big-unit war." It "remained a small tail to the very large conventional military dog."[216]

All told, this case study supports the utility of the Organizational Learning Capacity construct. The Army had an impressive array of learning mechanisms. These ensured that new insights and tactical lessons could be shared horizontally and vertically. Tactical lessons from combat were synthesized and routinely shaped new doctrine and training and educational programs. The Army could not fundamentally reassess itself at the strategic and operational level and alter its basic operating method. The Army lacked flexible leadership and was afflicted by a culture that was less willing to examine its assumptions and activities with any degree of candor. By the end of 1967, there was more than enough physical evidence to suggest that the much-talked-about "crossover" point was not simply elusive, it was illusory.

The failure to adapt was captured by RAND analyst Brian Jenkins: "Much more troubling than our apparent failures in Vietnam is our inability to learn and apply lessons from these failures."[217] Jenkins also perceptively captured the two-loop distinction between levels of learning:

Of course, there have been changes in our weapons and troop-delivery capabilities during the past few years, but these changes were made to enable our forces
do more of what they were already doing or to do it faster, without questioning the validity of what was being done in the first place. It is like two church
architects arguing the merits of the Gothic arch as opposed to the Romanesque
arch. Nobody in this case is questioning Christianity, merely architecture.[218]

That was the problem in Vietnam: no one in command was questioning the U.S.
Army's operating approach and its attrition strategy adequately. Lessons were
about architecture and tactics. Overall, the Army made many adaptations, which
enabled it to do more conventional fighting and to do it faster. However, it did not
question the validity or effectiveness of what it was doing enough and continued
to enhance the ability to do the wrong thing better at least until the immediate
threats were held back.

Conclusion

The objective of this case study is not to resolve a debate over strategy in Vietnam,
but rather to address the Army's organizational learning as it fought the critical
first three years of direct combat involvement in the conflict. The consensus is
that the Army was not a learning organization during the Vietnam era. Gen. Peter
Schoomaker, the former Army chief of staff, wrote that in Vietnam:

> The U.S. Army, predisposed to fight a conventional enemy that fought using
> conventional tactics, overpowered innovative ideas from within the Army and
> from outside it. As a result, the U.S. Army was not as effective at learning as it
> should have been, and its failures in Vietnam had grave implications for both
> the Army and the nation.[219]

The Army's theater leadership did not investigate alternative modes of fighting in
Vietnam. It is clear is that the Army *was* adaptive during the war. It had few problems with single-loop learning, improving on ways of executing its mental model
of conventional fighting. In particular, learning was arguably extensive and rapid
during the period covered in this chapter. In particular, the introduction of the

air assault and mobile riverine warfare represent substantive forms of adaptation. Yet, tragically, in both cases they went no further than to reinforce the firepower-centric approach favored by the operational commander; as such, they may not have contributed to strategic success.

The development of air mobility in both doctrine and operational praxis demonstrates just how fast the Army can adapt when it must. Although building air assault capability was strongly pushed by McNamara, it was a notable achievement. As one monograph noted, "The widespread use of the helicopter was the most significant advance of the Vietnam War. Combined with a new air-assault concept, it led to the refinement of the airmobile division that proved to be an unqualified success." An official Army history concluded that the airmobile team in Vietnam represented "the most revolutionary change in warfare since the blitzkrieg."[220] That may be hyperbole, but it clearly was a marked adaptation that generated a new competency and added a new branch to the Army.

In Vietnam, the Army stuck to its cultural approach to warfare. Counterinsurgency and pacification run against the offensive nature of the Army and its concept of taking the fight to the enemy by massed fire and maneuver. Closed-minded leaders and a heavily compliant corporate culture served to offset the value of numerous learning and dissemination mechanisms that might have better informed the inquiry and interpretation phases. Westmoreland and DePuy did not shape a culture that valued inquiry or professional reflection about alternative methods outside the warfighting strategy that had been chosen in 1965. Without the encouragement of senior leaders, inquiry and interpretation were stunted, and double-loop investigation was nonexistent.

Altering culture, routines, and practices of an organization such as the U.S. Army, which has been shaped by a long history, is never easy. But this case study suggests that it can occur, and it also strongly suggests that the right leadership and cultural attributes can support learning and enhanced performance.

CHAPTER 6

From the Halls of Fallujah to the Shores of the Euphrates

The Marines Adapting in Al Anbar

Amid the high risk and uncertainty of combat, shared experience—especially lessons hard-earned—should be promulgated laterally as quickly as possible so that the learning curve of the entire organization is elevated by the creativity or misfortune of the individual units.

—MARINE CORPS OPERATING CONCEPTS[1]

The Marines had just arrived in Iraq and were surprised to find themselves ordered to attack an armed city. Marines are not prone to backing down from a fight, and they understood orders. Four American contractors had been brutally killed, and U.S. policymakers wanted to show America's resolve. The planned operation, Valiant Resolve, represented the antithesis of what the Marines had come to Iraq to do. Instead of conducting stability tasks, they were about to attack a large, insurgent-infested urban area: Fallujah, about forty-three miles west of Baghdad.

The task was daunting, even for the aggressive Marines. Attempting to enter, much less control, a city of 285,000 residents is not to be taken lightly. Doing it in the midst of a hostile population in which hundreds of armed insurgents are embedded is more difficult. Time precluded detailed planning; the city would be quickly sealed off and attacked. The Marines would maneuver to the city's borders and then seize industrial sites inside Fallujah as bases for raids against high-value targets.

The assault force would comprise two Marine battalions. One would come down from the northern part of the city, and the other, the 1st Battalion, 5th Marines, would move in from the south and east to box the insurgents against the Euphrates River, along the city's western edge. The attack was scheduled for the morning on April 5, 2004. The Marines, who had grown mustaches to display their cultural awareness, now shaved them off and affixed bayonets to their rifles. The point was entirely psychological—to show the people of the city that the Marines meant business. The units infiltrated the city steadily until they ran into resistance in the early morning light. The attack did not lose momentum. Unit leaders did not have to give orders: their Marines leaned forward reflexively. As a journalist who was there during the fighting noted:

> It was a collective impulse—a phenomenon I would see again and again over the coming days. The idea that Marines are trained to break down doors, to seize beachheads and other territory, was an abstraction until I was there to experience it. Running into fire rather than seeking cover from it goes counter to every human survival instinct—trust me . . . I had started deluding myself that they weren't much different from me. But in one flash, as we charged across Michigan [Street] amid whistling incoming shots, I realized that they were not like me; they were Marines.[2]

Context: The Marines in Iraq

As in the last two cases, this chapter presents a historical narrative of more than three years of campaigning in Iraq, followed by the collected observations of Marines about what lessons had derived from that period. This permits us to trace how the U.S. Marine Corps adapted (or did not adapt) over time. As with the previous cases, the chapter ends with an assessment of how the elements of Organizational Learning Capacity influenced the degree of adaptation that was achieved.

This case study begins after the major combat operations phase of Operation Iraqi Freedom. In that largely conventional operation, the Marines performed admirably, demonstrating their offensive mindset and prowess, slicing north into Iraq.[3] The I Marine Expeditionary Force, led by Lt. Gen. James T. Conway, slipped around the prepared defenses of Kut and raced to Baghdad.[4] Exploiting their combined-arms skills, the Marines charged farther and faster than many thought possible.[5]

What almost all American civilian leaders and many military planners thought was the decisive phase of the campaign ended April 10, 2003. Marine Corps and coalition forces transitioned at this time to stability operations, or what was called Phase Four of the intervention. The scope of this phase was not well-anticipated, but the Marines recognized the necessity for a transition phase. However, the chaotic conditions existing in their area of operations had not been anticipated. The new "battlespace" assigned to the Marines was the overwhelmingly Shi'a-populated area of southern Iraq, contiguous with the Iranian border. The area amounted to almost the entire southern half of Iraq, with close to 40 percent of the Iraqi population. By April 24, 2003, the Marines were redeployed in Al Muthanna, Karbala, Babil, Al Qadisiyah, and An Najaf.[6]

Maj. Gen. James N. Mattis, commander of the 1st Marine Division, issued a new mission order and a new code phrase to ensure that his force made the necessary shift in mindset for stability operations. He added "do no harm" to the famous "no better friend, no worse enemy" guidance that he had provided previously.[7] By issuing this additive phrase, Mattis successfully shifted his troops from fighting an enemy to one that was fighting for a population.[8] As part of this mental shift, Mattis ordered his forces out of their heavy vehicles to conduct dismounted patrols. Body armor was reduced, commensurate with the tactical situations. Marines were ordered to remove their helmets and sunglasses. "Wave tactics" were underscored as Marines tried to interact with the local population. Tanks and heavy weapons were shipped back south to Kuwait to begin their redeployment to America; they would be unneeded in the division's adaptation to post-conflict scenarios. Ever mindful of their commander's intent, Marines of the 1st Division began to work on restoring a sense of normalcy to the lives of the average Iraqi citizen, even in the absence of any functioning public bureaucracy and in the presence of a nascent but palpable enemy.

That created challenges for the newly designated military governors who were in control of the seven provinces. For many commanders, the challenge was one of education. Some felt overwhelmed. "All the sudden I was the mayor of eight cities," Col. Ronald L. Bailey, commander of the 1st Marine Division, recalled later. "I had no idea I would be responsible for getting the water running, turning on the electricity, and running an economy."[9] There was no reliable water purification system, power grid, basic sanitation, or trash collection. One battalion

commander mused that if he had to do it all over again, he would have wished
that his predeployment training had included a week with the mayor of his local
town back at home.[10] Six months later, Mattis' Marines were ordered home, having helped steady their area during the honeymoon period between the down-
fall of Iraqi President Saddam Hussein and the rise of the subsequent insurgency.
In those six months, the "Blue Diamond" Marines, as the 1st Marine Division is
nicknamed, lost only a single Marine.[11]

The Marines Return for an Encore: 2004

In November 2003 the Marines were informed that they would be returning to
Iraq to conduct stability operations by early 2004. This time the area of operations would not be the Shi'a-dominated southern marshlands. Instead, they were
assigned to the barren tracts of Al Anbar, home of the so-called Sunni Triangle
and the epicenter of Sunni resistance. Al Anbar is a vast province in western Iraq
that borders on three countries—Syria, Jordan, and Saudi Arabia. Its most significant terrain feature is the five-hundred-kilometer run of the Euphrates River valley, running from Syria through the province to the south of Baghdad. Almost 90
percent of Al Anbar's population lives along or close to the Euphrates River.

The division organized its predeployment training program around a cadre
of Iraq veterans. It designed a security and stability operations training program
that included urban operations, dismounted patrolling, convoy operations, vehicle checkpoints, and quick-reaction force drills. Facilities and training areas were
adapted to represent Iraqi towns and increase the training's realism. The earlier experience from Iraq was brought to bear quickly. The Marines adapted by
intensifying their cultural and language classes, sending more than four thousand Marines through short courses in Arabic. The culture training was expanded,
with each Marine receiving one day's instruction in basic cultural information. An
additional package was required for small-unit leaders and senior division and regimental staff officers.

The Marines also adapted their structure for the coming deployment, making
up for a lack of manpower by tasking one artillery battalion to serve as a provisional military police battalion to augment the Corps' limited assets.[12] Each battalion assigned one officer to cover information operations and civil affairs to offset
a lack of capacity in these critical areas.

The campaign plan was based on an operational design framed by Major General Mattis. The division fully understood that both the human and physical terrain of its next area of responsibility was different. But the Marines initially believed that they would return to a benign environment.[13] Eventually, based on insights from the Army and their own intelligence staff, they understood that Al Anbar was on the verge of becoming adversarial. The insurgency had taken form, its leadership was networked, and it was launching attacks. The Marines had no formal doctrine, but they believed that the principles of the seventy-year-old *Small Wars Manual* remained valid.[14] They intimated to the media that the Army had failed by following the wrong approach, and that a velvet glove was needed.[15] Mixing a nuanced understanding of culture and psychology, they planned to provide incentives that would divide the silent majority of Iraqi civilians from the Baathist diehards and jihadists. At the same time, the credible capacity to apply force would remain persuasive.

Operation Valiant Resolve

The ambush and brutal mutilation of four U.S. contractors in Fallujah on March 31, 2004, undercut the Marines' approach. The media impact of the corpses being dragged in the streets was instantaneous, and the White House and the Coalition Provisional Authority (CPA) wanted a forceful response. On April 2 the Marines were ordered to enter the volatile city and find and punish the perpetrators.[16] Without time to collect intelligence, gather reinforcements, or shape the battlespace, the Marines argued against an immediate attack. But their reservations were overridden by the need to demonstrate resolve. The Marines dutifully obeyed and put a cordon around Fallujah on April 5, 2004.

Despite their misgivings about their orders, the Marines prepared to conduct a hasty attack into the city. Their orders from higher headquarters were clear: they were to capture or kill the murderers of coalition contractors while simultaneously conducting offensive operations to isolate and destroy the Anticoalition Forces (ACF) in order to restore law and order and build long-term stability in the city of Fallujah.

The orders for the attack, defined by Col. John A. Toolan Jr., who commanded Marine Regimental Combat Team 1 (RCT-1), were equally succinct: "On Order RCT-1 conducts offensive operations to cordon Fallujah and conduct raids and attacks against ACFs in order to capture [or] kill personnel involved in attacks against coalition forces and set the conditions for a functioning Iraqi civil administration."[17] Toolan's plan called for a four-phase attack: cordon the city of Fallujah, conduct raids against high-value targets, secure RCT objectives, and hand over the battle and city to Iraqi security forces.

They began with the cordon on April 5. The anticoalition forces were not passive. They made probing attacks using rocket-propelled grenades (RPGs), small arms, and mortars against the Marine positions blocking the city. Phase Two involved Marines teamed with American special operations forces to conduct a raid into the center of the city to seize suspects and an ACF command post. An early strike against the insurgents' nerve center was highly desirable in order to delay any planned countermoves that the insurgents or jihadists might try. The intelligence was poor, and the resistance was stiffer than expected. The raids were cancelled.

Valiant Resolve was centered on Phase Three, in which three battalions would attack in-zone to destroy the remaining combatants in the city. One battalion would attack from the northwest. This force, built around the 2nd Battalion, 1st Marines, led by Lt. Col. Gregg P. Olson, was to drive south through the Jolan district. Another battalion, the 1st Battalion, 5th Marines, commanded by Lt. Col. Brennan Byrne, would conduct a supporting attack into the southeast corner of the city. Once it arrived, another battalion was to drive in from the northeast corner. (See map 6.1 for the original scheme of maneuver.)

After establishing themselves inside the city, the plan would enter its second component. One unit, the 2d Battalion, 1st Marines, would continue its attack from the northwest in its highly populated districts. The 3rd Battalion, 4th Marines, led by Lt. Col. Bryan P. McCoy, would swing left and sweep the insurgents out toward the eastern edge of the city. Byrne's battalion would continue sweeping into the city.

The attack began at 1 a.m. on April 6, 2004, to take advantage of the darkness. The members of the 2nd Battalion, 1st Marines started from the northeast into the Jolan district and crossed the railroad tracks into the city. But they met heavy resistance, including volley fires of RPGs against armored targets as well as effective indirect fires. The enemy appeared willing to stand and fight. The battalion slowly pushed back the defenders and was reinforced by U.S. Army armor.

On April 7, the fight continued.[18] The 3rd Battalion, 4th Marines began to arrive at the edge of town. Both Marine battalions exchanged blows with the insurgents. Olson's Marines advanced into the city, working with their Iraqi commandos. The former regime elements and Arab insurgents put up a stiff resistance, counterattacking with small assaults and snipers. The insurgents used several mosques and public buildings to store weapons and as defensive positions.

The Marines had hoped to work side by side with Iraqi forces in this operation, but the uneven performance of the indigenous forces required a reassessment. Four Iraqi battalions were available, but the 2nd National Army Battalion essentially deserted. Two other battalions were able to man static blocking positions or follow Marine units to clear passed buildings. Only the Iraqi 36th Commando Battalion proved effective, reflecting its U.S. Special Forces training.[19]

The political aspects of this battle spiked immediately. Al Jazeera and other cable channels began playing up rumors of mass casualties and alleged atrocities. There were reports of innocent civilians wounded at the Fallujah hospital, reinforced by stock footage of U.S. air strikes from previous battles. All of this took hold in the international media and began to influence the Iraqi Governing Council (IGC). The CPA was not prepared for the political fallout. Key allies were openly critical of the violence employed by the Marine offensive, as perceived through Arab media. The IGC threatened to resign *en masse*, putting pressure on U.S. ambassador L. Paul Bremer to reconsider. Additional diplomatic pressure from the Allies forced the White House to seek an end to the operation.

On April 9, Lieutenant General Conway was ordered to suspend offensive operations but to keep the Marines inside the city. A cease-fire was arranged to enable the IGC to meet with local city leaders and attempt to negotiate a settlement, but the negotiation failed.

The U.S. government was in a quandary, and left the Marines hanging inside the town for well over a week. Each day the Marines absorbed fatalities from snipers. A military solution in Fallujah was attainable, but only at a steep cost. The Marines had lost twenty-four men and had more than a hundred wounded, but they did not finish the mission. Although they thought they could still secure the city, a search for a political solution was continuing at the Marine Corps headquarters.

The Marines began looking for an innovative political solution to break the stalemate. On April 11, Conway met with his staff to examine the possibility of using an Iraqi force to police the town. He later met with a group of Sunnis to discuss having them establish their own uniformed military force to secure Fallujah. The resulting Fallujah Brigade concept empowered Sunni leaders to establish law and order in their own area. It would also increase their stake in restoring order. On April 30, Gen. Muhammed J. Saleh and three hundred freshly recruited soldiers met with Conway and began taking control of their city. Yet, the Fallujah Brigade melted away in only a few days, leaving the city to the insurgents.[20] The result of this short campaign was the perception that instead of the United States' demonstrating resolve, the insurgency had successfully defended the city from the Marines.[21]

Although Fallujah drew a lot of attention, groups of insurgents thrived elsewhere and went on the attack as well. In Ramadi, the 2nd Battalion, 4th Marines, under Lt. Col. Paul J. Kennedy, was attacked several times by platoon-sized forces. That battalion found itself in a swirling three-day battle for control over the provincial capital. The unit lost twenty-seven killed and ninety wounded, restoring a minimal amount of order.[22]

Fallujah II

Marine Corps planners and intelligence officers were dismayed by the results of April 2004 but immediately turned to the inevitable second round of the bout. The cancer could not be permitted to grow, given the city's proximity to Baghdad. Inside Fallujah conditions deteriorated throughout the summer of 2004. The foreign ACF elements maintained a grip over the populace through gruesome brutality. A stream of foreign fighters, money, and weapons flowed from Syria down the Euphrates into Fallujah.

In September the Marines started serious planning to clear and retake the city. Plans called for the attack to begin sometime between the American presidential election in November 2004 and the Iraqi elections in January 2005. The 1st Marine Division was now under new leadership: Mattis had departed and was replaced by Maj. Gen. Richard F. Natonski. Conway also had been reassigned, the senior Marine was now Lt. Gen. John F. Sattler.[23]

The Marines developed a detailed operational plan for Operation Phantom Fury. Iraqi prime minister Ayad Allawi asked that it be called Operation Al Fafr (New Dawn) to give it a more Iraqi touch and to reflect a new beginning for his country. Military intelligence revealed the scope of the insurgent defense preparations, with more than three hundred identified positions. In the city there were somewhere around two thousand insurgents. The analysis showed that the defense was oriented toward the south of the city. That suggested that an attack from the south was expected—a prospect that Marine Corps planners hoped to exploit to their advantage.

In many ways, the battle plan that Sattler and his team had created was designed to be the opposite of Valiant Resolve.[24] Instead of a hastily conceived plan, this one would take two months to plan. Instead of a small force, it would employ a powerful combination of ground and air units. The organization for the attack included seven U.S. Army and Marine Corps battalions and six Iraqi battalions, as well as Navy, Marine, and Air Force aircraft. The Army provided two mechanized battalions to give the Marines more armored shock and firepower. Allied support from British and Polish contingents also was provided. All told, Sattler would have more than 12,000 coalition troops.

Intelligence would come from numerous sources and would be carefully sifted and pushed down to the units fighting in the streets. Instead of entering a densely populated city, the Marines sought to urge the remaining civilians to evacuate the area, eventually convincing 80 percent of Fallujah's population to depart. Unlike the previous battle, the information campaign was planned in depth. Marine Corps leaders reinstituted the practice of "embedding" professional journalists with combat units in all, some ninety-one correspondents, representing sixty different news outlets, accompanied the troops.[25] They were key to overcoming distortions in the media.[26] Sattler pushed his staff to work with civil affairs officers toward the same themes and proactively brought a major news analyst inside his plans office to observe how scrupulously disciplined the targeting process was.[27] In Sattler's words, this time "we stole the strategic communications initiative from the enemy and never gave it back."[28]

Decisive operations would be conducted by the 1st Marine Division's two "fists," or major ground-maneuver elements—RCT-1 and RCT-7.[29] Each was reinforced with an Army armor-heavy battalion. RCT-1 was now led by Col. Michael A. Shupp. His regiment would drive from the northern edge of town and slice south along the western half of the city. RCT-7, commanded by Col. Craig A. Tucker, would attack in parallel through the eastern side of the city.

The attack began the night of November 7, 2004, as the Iraqi 36th Commando Battalion captured the Fallujah General Hospital to the west of the city.

The Marine 3rd Light Armored Battalion secured the two bridges south of the hospital, sealing off Fallujah from the west.

The ground assault began along a broad front in the early hours of November 8. The Army tanks and Bradley infantry fighting vehicles served as a penetrating force.[30] After they cleared the major arteries and occupied key intersections, the Marines followed through and attacked identified enemy positions. The Marines entered houses and cleared them room by room, often finding insurgents hiding in wait to ambush them. The insurgents were willing to hold their ground and die in place, and the Marines strove to oblige them. Stubborn pockets of resistance were taken under fire with air and artillery.

Numerous caches of weapons and grenades were found on each block. Insurgent tactics gave Marines the impression that they were familiar with U.S. doctrine and techniques. The fighting was the likes of which Marines had not experienced since the battle of Hue City in Vietnam.[31] Colonel Shupp explained his clearing tactics:

> We called it the squeegee. So we're clearing house by house, building by building. In many of these houses, the [stored] ammunition is so big that you would need a tractor-trailer to move it—or it would be too dangerous to move. We found over 800 caches inside the city, over 160 improvised explosive devices (IEDs), and this clearing continues systematically through all the districts.[32]

Lieutenant General Sattler had anticipated reaching the center of town within three days, but the battle progressed faster, with elements of RCT-7 crossing the road that runs from east to west through the center of Fallujah in just fourteen hours. RCT-1 encountered some of the insurgents' toughest defensive positions in the Jolan district, but they still managed to fight to Highway 10 within forty-three hours of the start of the attack. The Marines continued sweeping south on November 11. The speed and shock of the massed armor and Marines' use of firepower simply overwhelmed the defenders. The resistance became more disciplined as the Marines worked toward the southern sections of Fallujah, where foreign fighters appeared. One veteran commented, "The way these guys fight is different than the insurgents."[33]

Over a grueling week of room-to-room, face-to-face fighting, the Marines made one alteration to their tactics: after several days of slow and deliberate operations, with mounting losses sustained while fighting against prepared positions inside buildings, they shifted their tactics and increased their tempo. They increasingly relied on tanks and explosive satchel charges to destroy buildings whenever they were fired on instead of stopping and clearing the building. This was an organic adaptation made at the tactical level while the battle evolved.[34]

The street fighting continued until November 13, when coalition forces reached the southern edge of Fallujah. With fighting slowing down, coalition and Iraqi soldiers continued to go house to house, searching for arms caches and insurgents. They found thousands of AK-47s, RPGs, mortar rounds, and IEDs. More than one thousand insurgents had been killed in Fallujah and five hundred detained. On November 16 U.S. military officials announced that the city had been secured, despite sporadic insurgent activity.

That said, Marine Corps leaders were aware that how effective they could be in turning so destructive a battle into an Allied advantage and a benefit to the Iraqi people was going to depend on how quickly they could begin providing humanitarian aid and civil affairs help. Before the battle was over, the Marines began humanitarian and reconstruction activities simultaneously with the attack operations. Civil-military operations were not an afterthought, but an integral part of the overall plan.[35] The results were impressive enough for the Iraqi prime minister to reopen the city for its residents by December 23, 2004.

The violence applied in the battle was considerable. Some 2,500 tank rounds were fired, and many sections of the city were completely destroyed. In total, U.S. forces conducted 540 air strikes in support of the operation and expended more than 14,000 artillery and mortar rounds. Almost half of the city's buildings were damaged.[36] The losses for the coalition were significant, with seventy Marines and six Army soldiers killed in action. Another 425 were wounded.[37] The Marines believed they certainly cleared up any doubts about who ultimately dominated Fallujah, but the second battle did not provide a strategic victory across Al Anbar. In many respects, their job was now going to become harder.[38]

Lessons and Adaptation in 2004

The Marines showed a marked ability to make transitions in Iraq in 2004. Alternating between stability operations and high-intensity urban fighting required more agility than adaptation. The need to adapt to the enemy's efforts, such as

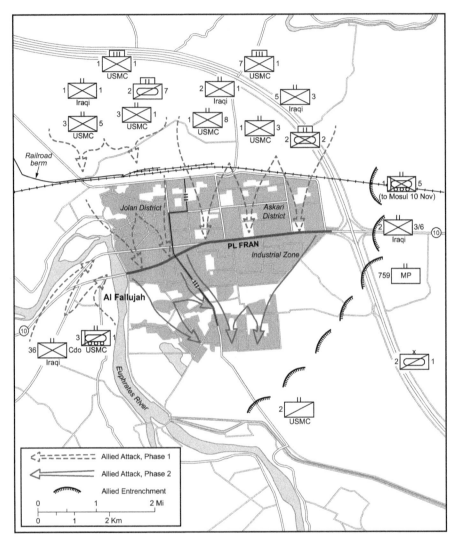

Map 6.1. The Assault on Fallujah, November 2004
Adapted from *The Army in Iraq*, Army War College Press, 2019, p. 350.

countering the IED threat, was recognized.[39] The most significant shortfalls that the Marines found in their competency repertoire in 2004 were in non-traditional military functions, especially intelligence, civil affairs, and information operations.

In 2003, the Marines realized that they had overinvested in capital-intensive collection systems designed to support division-level decisions. Intelligence processed at higher levels and sent down was often irrelevant by the time it reached tactical units.[40] In the emergent counterinsurgency environment, "those tactical commanders who require the highest resolution of the battlefield (and have the least time) are those least able to influence a very complex and highly centralized intelligence architecture."[41] The solution was the creation of a new organization, to be called the Tactical Fusion Center (TFC). The concept was to "push intelligence horsepower where it was needed most to ensure a bias for tactical action."[42] The TFC concentrated various sources of intelligence assets and removed echelons between the intelligence analysts and the commanders on the ground. The idea was to create a fused and granular picture produced from the ground up and then push it down to battlefield units. As a Marine general put it, "We learned that the less 'conventional' the conflict, the farther forward we must push our intelligence capabilities."[43] The TFC proved critical in making the shift from conventional war to stability operations, one Marine said, "The preponderance of the division-level resources were aligned to division-level decision-making. This resulted in a failure to detect, understand. and disseminate battlefield situational awareness."[44]

Marine Corps leaders understood that the training of indigenous forces was crucial in counterinsurgency, but they had had few experiences in training foreign military forces since the days of the Vietnam War. As a result, the Corps fell back to its Vietnam-era Combined Action Platoon (CAP) program—a part of Marine Corps history. In Vietnam in the 1960s, CAPs combined a squad of Marines with a platoon-sized indigenous security force. The small program proved to be an effective means of securing the local populace.[45] In Iraq in 2004, the 1st Marine Division employed a hybrid CAP concept in which each battalion was assigned one platoon for CAP duty. General Mattis had reasoned that this was a way of focusing culture and language training in the short time available.[46] Some CAPs in Iraq lived on their own bases, but others lived, ate, and fought with their Iraqi counterparts. In theory, this approach, "living with their counterparts and sharing all duties and dangers with them . . . facilitated communications and understanding, enabling both cultures to solve the complex problems faced in combat," wrote Lt. Col. Willard A. Buhl, who was a battalion commander in that battle.[47] For Marines, the CAP was a culturally accepted way to conduct this mission, exploiting their stored knowledge from Vietnam even if it was not truly a current competency.

Another non-kinetic shortfall was in civil affairs, or what came to be called civil-military operations (CMOs). The Marines define these as "the activities of a commander that establish, maintain, influence, or exploit relations between military forces, governmental and non-governmental civilian organizations and authorities, and the civilian populace . . . in order to facilitate military operations, [or] to consolidate and achieve operational U.S. objectives."[48] Given the absence of governance and the decrepit infrastructure found in Iraq in 2004, there were many civil functions that had to be performed. The Marines went to Iraq with fresh doctrine, but limited capability. They relied on two small Marine Corps Reserve civil affairs groups (CAGs) to accomplish this mission. Yet, Marines began to realize that "everything we do here . . . has a CMO component. . . . Everything." As one officer put it, "Most of what we do over here is civil affairs stuff. We spend more time on building relations with the local community than we do in actual combat."[49] Another commented, "We went back with an anemic CA force . . . we needed much greater numbers of civil administrators." Numbers mattered. "The CA mission was too big for the CAG . . . so by default, infantry units did it."[50] Nevertheless, none of their training had prepared them for this mission. In 2004 the Marines created two additional CAGs, staffed by reservists, to relieve the pressure. Many of these groups lacked experience, but the reservists brought fresh insights and few inhibitions. "The reservists figured this out because they work in the business world. Many (active-duty) uniformed guys saw kinetics," Col. David G. Reist, commander of the 1st Marine Logistics Group, recalled later. The reservists saw how business, tribes, and diminished influence for al-Qaeda were sewn together. They were very useful "due to a thought process, connections, and they are not constrained by [Marine] rules [and] regulations, like active-duty guys."[51]

Adaptations began with information operations. They are "how you dry up the swamp that's festering this plague," Mattis once said.[52] Marine campaign plans identified information operations as a major element, as did the new counterinsurgency manual.[53] But the Marines had little doctrine and no psychological operations units capable of generating messages or broadcasts. The authority to release information in any form was tightly controlled from Baghdad, and it had to be delegated to much lower levels of the force if the information was going to be useful in countering the propaganda of the insurgents.[54] New doctrine was issued in late 2003, and the Marines adapted their staffing and targeting processes to account for including desired messages in information outlets.[55] But the Marines had to create an ad hoc staff for this effort and had to rely on Army psyops detachments for production. Marines saw the influence of such efforts as reactive and limited.[56] After-action reports consistently complained about lack of newspaper and radio production capacity to get the word out to civilians, and obtaining approval of these messages was too slow and too tightly controlled.

In 2004, the Marines expected to apply a velvet glove. A force that had prepared itself to be Iraq's "best friend" instead proved to the insurgents what their worst enemy could do. The Marines found themselves engaged in ferocious combat, but also in need of the nonlethal components of effective counterinsurgency. The Marines of I MEF returned home after 2004, and their commander, Lieutenant General Sattler, bragged to reporters: "I think in the west, we have broken the back of the insurgency."[57] As the next year would show, that proved to be utterly wrong.

Clearing, But Not Holding—2005

The second assault into Fallujah established which tribe really was the strongest in Al Anbar, but it did not diminish the insurgency or al-Qaeda's continued infiltration into the Sunni heartland. Nor did it change the American strategy, which regarded Al Anbar as a sideshow to Baghdad, where the focus was on transferring authority to an elected government and handing the security burden to the Iraqi army as fast as possible. Sectarian divides still ran very deep and continued to challenge the American strategy. The Marines shifted from their application of static stability operations into a series of conventional sweep operations to offset the growing polymorphic insurgency.[58]

The new assault had come in reaction to al-Qaeda's own adaptation, which had sought to dominate Al Anbar and its tribal Sunni communities through a strategy of brutal intimidation. Although the Marines had significantly depleted the insurgent force inside Fallujah, al-Qaeda fighters and the nationalistic insurgency

still held sway over the major towns along the Euphrates river valley in Al Anbar
Province, from Ramadi all the way out to the town of Husaybah on the Syrian
border. This area belonged to RCT-2, led by Col. Stephen W. Davis, an aggressive
and able officer. His campaign plan for RCT-2 during 2005 was labeled Operation Power Sweep/Sayeed, and it called for clearing the valley from the southeast
to the northwest, culminating out toward the Syrian border in Husaybah. Davis
intended to attack the insurgents among the heavily populated river towns. In
effect, his campaign plan would maneuver directly into Al Anbar against the road
and river network that was the insurgency's line of communications to the outside world.

RCT-2 had a large area of responsibility, but few troops. They were stationed
along the valley in small bases, but not positioned inside the major cities. There
the enemy built up bases and stored its bomb-making materials. Davis did not
believe that he had sufficient forces to cover his area of responsibility adequately
or really hold the towns that he wanted to oversee.[59] The region was heavily Sunni
and holding it was not considered as important as gaining control of Baghdad and
other major Iraqi cities.

Davis was forced to allocate about a third of his three-battalion force to protecting the division's command headquarters and air base. Although his area of
responsibility covered a huge expanse, its population was compressed along the
river valley. With helicopters and light armor, Davis could concentrate his available units selectively. His campaign began with a pair of battalion-sized operations, River Bridge and Outer Banks, in the area around Hit. These operations
targeted insurgent groups and degraded their overall influence in the area. Similar
to Westmoreland's early sweeps in Vietnam, these were spoiling attacks. Davis did
not have the forces to hold terrain or to accept the risk of defending small bases
that directly supported the local Sunni population. Still, he could interdict their
supplies and keep them on the defensive.[60]

The first major sweep was Operation Matador, assigned to attack and clear
the area just north of the river around the town of Ubaydi. A task force of two
Marine rifle companies, a light armor unit, and an Army bridge company was
formed under Marine Lt. Col. Timothy S. Mundy. The operation was planned to
assist the Albu Mahal tribe gain a sense of independence and protection from the
ravages of al-Qaeda in Iraq (AQI). The combined Marine-Army force surprised

the insurgent defensive scheme by using amphibious tractors, swimming light armored vehicles and employing bridging assets to avoid using roads that were undoubtedly mined. The task force first attacked and swept New Ubaydi. The next day they crossed the river and cleared Ramana in a tough fight. Subsequently they cleared Ar Rabit but then withdrew from the area since they did not have the combat power to occupy the towns they had cleared. Operation Matador was terminated on May 14 and was considered successful, with 144 insurgents killed at a loss of 9 Marines.

Undaunted, the insurgents continued to attack the coalition. During Operation Matador, al-Qaeda in Iraq kidnapped the governor of the province, Raja Nawaf Farhan Mahalawi. His tortured body was found a few days later. He was replaced by Mamoon Sami Rashid al-Alwani, who had survived numerous assassination attempts. Abu Musab al-Zarqawi, AQI's leader, recognized that he was now competing for influence with the tribes and announced that any tribe that engaged with the "Crusaders" would be attacked. AQI effectively countered the Marines' progress by assassinating half of the leaders of the Anbar People's Committee, including the governor. The first small "awakening" of Al Anbar's tribes against AQI was crushed in the cradle.[61]

A significant adaptation was evident during Operation Iron Fist later that summer. The operation was by led by Lt. Col. Julian D. (Dale) Alford, who commanded the 3rd Battalion, 6th Marines. Alford previously had served in Afghanistan and had drawn different lessons about kinetic operations from units that had only served in Iraq. During a reconnaissance visit to the Al Qaim area in the summer of 2005, before his battalion's arrival, Alford saw that the Iraqi tribes, militias, and insurgents were fighting each other. He did not understand the faction dynamics, but he intended to exploit them. He also recognized from Afghanistan the importance of tribal culture, and he specifically requested a Marine Corps Middle East expert, Edwin O. Rueda, to serve as his cultural adviser. Drawing on his own counterinsurgency research, Alford concluded, roughly eighteen months before it became official doctrine, that the population was the prize. He intended to be innovative and operate among the district's population and partner with local Iraqi security forces.

The 3rd Battalion, 6th Marines arrived in Iraq in August and was operating from Camp Al Qaim, several miles south of the district. On October 1, 2005, Alford

Table 6.1. RCT-2 Operations in Al Anbar, 2005

Operation	Dates [2005]	Location	Mission
River Bridge	March 17	Hit/Haditha Corridor	Disrupt and Mask Relief in Place
Outer Banks	April 1	Hit/Haditha Corridor	Clear
Matador	May 17–24	Al Qaim/Ubaydi	Clear
New Market	May 24	Haditha	Clear
River Sweep	May 30	Hit/Haditha Corridor	Clear
Spear	June 15	Al Qaim	Clear
Sword	June 20	Hit	Clear
Saber	July 24	AO Denver	Disrupt
Quick Strike	August 3	Haditha	Clear
Green Light	September 21	Hit/Haditha Corridor	Clear
Lightning Strike	September 27	Anah	Clear
Iron Fist	October 1	Al Qaim	Clear
River Gate	October 4	Haditha	Clear
Steel Curtain	November 5	Husaybah/Karabilah/Ubaydi	Clear and Hold

Adapted from Kenneth W. Estes, *U.S. Marine Corps Operations in Iraq, 2003–2006* (Quantico, VA: U.S. Marine Corps Historical Division, 2009).

kicked off Operation Iron Fist, a battalion-sized plan to clear two towns, Sadah and Karabilah. They carefully cleared each building, room by room, to displace insurgents and their caches. Resistance consisted of sniper attacks and small ambushes. Rather than withdraw to his base camps, Alford created two "battle positions" in each town and placed units in each. This time the Marines were here to stay. Each battle position was manned with equal Marine and Iraqi army platoons, to bolster the Iraqis and to constantly ensure that strong partnerships were created.

By the end of October, members of the 3rd Battalion, 6th Marines had consolidated their toehold in two towns and were prepared to fulfill their assigned mission of sweeping the remainder of the district in a new Operation Steel Curtain. Colonel Davis believed that a faster and larger effort would be needed this time, and he sought reinforcements. He got help from the 2nd Battalion, 1st Marines, led by Lt. Col. Robert G. Oltman, commander of the battalion landing team, and the Army added the 4th Squadron, 14th Cavalry and the 3rd Battalion, 504th Paratroopers. With four battalions, Davis massed enough combat power to ensure a complete sweep and screen out interference from outside insurgent forces. On November 5 both Alford's and Oltman's battalions swept through Husaybah from west to east, surprising the insurgent forces, which had oriented themselves for a defense of the town against an attack from the east. The insurgents shifted quickly but had to take on the Marines in the streets instead of from prepared defensive barriers. Oltman's force encountered a lot more mines and IEDs, but at the end of the first day, it had cleared 25 percent of the town. The two units made the same amount of progress on November 6. One history described their movement: "like a slow-moving glacier leaving sediment in its wake."[62] The "sediment" was made up of the platoons that were left behind in battle positions. RCT-2 was now hold-ing, not just clearing.

The battalions changed their approach for the next assault into Karabilah. Olt-man swung his battalion below Karabilah and set up a screen south of the town, while Alford's battalion was repositioned to the north. Then the 3rd Battalion, 6th Marines drove south into the town, pushing through the eastern and central por-tions, and finally clearing the town on November 10, the 230th anniversary of the Marine Corps.[63]

Phase Two of Operation Steel Curtain involved the clearing of both old and New Ubaydi by the 2nd Battalion, 1st Marines and the Army's 3rd Battalion, 504th Paratroopers. They began their sweeps on November 14 and met stiff resis-tance from the beginning. Making extensive use of their close air support, the U.S. forces suppressed well-planned insurgent ambushes. The twin towns were finally cleared by November 20, and Alford immediately populated them with battle positions. Operation Steel Curtain ended on November 22, with RCT-2 claim-ing two hundred dead insurgents. More important, it began providing a persistent presence in order to protect the residents.

At this point the Marines had cleared out the major insurgent strongholds, reduced their influence in the area, and occupied a series of battle positions in each town. Their hold on the area remained tenuous, but at least the local Iraqi population could breathe more easily and participate in the coming December elections. Alford continued to pair Marine Corps and Iraqi units but was ham-pered by the Shi'a composition of the Iraqi army. He sought to enhance Sunni participation, but tribal leaders of the district would not support the central Iraqi government. They were willing to provide recruits for a tribal force, which the U.S. Special Forces would train. Subsequently, Gen. George W. Casey Jr., the American who commanded the Multinational Force, Iraq, authorized the establishment of an Iraqi brigade with Sunni recruits.

Alford's ideas about counterinsurgency derived from his prior tour in Afghanistan, where kinetic (lethal) operations had produced few results, and from personal research.[64] He was well ahead of the debate over the *Counterinsurgency Manual* and recognized that overemphasizing kinetic operations would be futile, if not counterproductive. In particular, he realized that ignoring the sociocultural relevance of tribal societies was a flawed strategy. "I knew that we were fighting this war wrong," he said.[65] He believed that it was necessary to work with the tribal forces in the area and empower them. Alford worked to pull these organic elements into semi-official units while also working to prevent tribal militias from spinning into rivalry.[66]

Alford then consolidated the gains that he had made with the tribes by realigning his battle positions to better match the areas that each tribe held. He sensed that stability could only be achieved through the existing tribal networks. The results were significant: Alford's force had far fewer casualties and encountered no IEDs for two months. Much of the subsequent success in Al Anbar later in 2006 and 2007 is traced to this initiative. General Casey visited numerous times, praising Alford, and made sure that the U.S. counterinsurgency academy in Iraq used the 3rd Battalion, 6th Marines' approach as a case study.[67]

Even so, the Marines' efforts were marred in Haditha, an area being held by the 3rd Battalion, 5th Marines, on November 19, 2005, when an IED went off under a Marine vehicle traveling through the town, resulting in the death of a Marine and several serious injuries. A Marine in another vehicle overreacted and shot several young Iraqis who were running away, killing five. As the Marines were removing their wounded, they took on sniper fire, and were directed to clear buildings from which they believed the fire was coming. In clearing two buildings, the Marines used violent urban fighting techniques to clear rooms. Another nineteen civilians, including women and children, were killed. Despite the significance of the incident, the regiment and battalion did not investigate. The incident reflected a poor understanding of the mission and context of an insurgency.

Subsequent investigations were critical of the Marines, their training, and the follow-up that was done by the battalion staff.[68] The battalion commander and company commander were relieved and faced disciplinary action.

While RCT-2 garnered a lot of attention in the western cities, the remaining Marines struggled to keep a lid on the growing violence in Ramadi and Fallujah. A series of operations inside those cities attempted to disrupt insurgent plans and the buildup of arms caches. But those efforts, such as Operation Sayeed, were hobbled by thin intelligence about the opponent and did not provide consistent protection to the population.

Colonel Davis' regiment knew the difference between clearing operations and protecting the population.[69] RCT-2 claimed that it had stabilized a dozen cities and towns and eliminated 889 insurgents, but its leaders knew that it had not yet truly secured them.[70] They simply did not have the forces to hold much of anything—nor did they have the non-kinetic tools.

Lessons and Adaptations

By late 2005, the Marines recognized that they needed to adapt more.[71] As had been the case in Vietnam, the Marines assigned to CAP missions were young and inexperienced. They had enthusiasm, but insufficient language skills or advisory experience to train foreign forces. Shortfalls in advising capabilities were recognized at the lowest level and pushed forward. One participant, Capt. Scott A. Cuomo, showed that he understood the level of effort, but he also was aware of the performance gap, writing later that:

> [We did not] execute the basic principles that must be applied to defeat an insurgency. We were never intimately familiar with the millions of people, languages, cultures, and terrain in any of the five provinces that we operated in for two weeks or longer. And, we did little to help indigenous security forces protect the populace from the insurgency.[72]

The Marine Corps adapted when it reviewed its civil affairs structure in light of its experience in Iraq, increasing the size of each Reserve civil affairs unit.[73] Like the rest of the Marines, CAG personnel were short on operational culture and foreign languages.[74] The Marines tasked the artillery community to absorb the mission as a secondary role. The artillery units understood the Marine operational planning processes but had little expertise with foreign populations and civic agencies, and they lacked skills that Reservists had gained in the civilian world. Part of the problem was cultural, given the Marine Corps' offensive orientation and warfighting ethos. As one seasoned CAG officer noted:

> The problem is that we think of CMO as something that the CAG does. We are all more comfortable with kinetic operations, so that's what we focus on and then leave the detailed planning for Phase [Four] operations to the CA guys, who often lack the background and expertise to make it work. We do this even though we all say that Phase [Four] on November 19, 2005, is the most important phase.[75]

Other shortfalls compounded the lack of civil affairs. For example, information operations were still limited. Young officers noted that the enemy was more sophisticated when it came to influencing perceptions. Second, U.S. efforts were not proactive enough to negate the other side's narrative. Much of this was within the authority of local commanders to change and could have made a difference in-theater.[76]

Cultural awareness was still limited, Ben Connable, a retired Marine Corps major and a RAND Corporation analyst, recalled. "We were saying the right things, we were doing all the right things. We were trying to engage with people, but we had a very immature understanding of Iraqi culture. We had a very immature understanding of the authority and the power of the tribes, the tribal leaders."[77] That lack of cultural understanding impacted alliances with the tribes. Marines like Alford recognized that they were not yet working close enough with the Iraqi people and not investing and rewarding training and advisory personnel.[78]

The Marine Corps recognized that it needed to understand better how culture and human terrain could be a force-multiplier. It rejected the Army's Human Terrain Team approach—which recruited civilian social scientists—in favor of an organic cultural competency.[79] The Corps' response would be less costly, which the ever-efficient Marines would favor. Cultural awareness was enhanced in 2005 by the establishment in Quantico of the Center for Advanced Operational Culture Learning (CAOCL), which was charged with standardizing the ad hoc language and culture training that the Marines had originally grabbed from various sources. The center created training and educational products to promote applied cultural understanding in Marine operations.[80] The original team felt that it was instituting a "radical, irregular-warfare-focused culture policy into a military organization that views itself as structured and trained to fight big 'conventional' wars."[81]

The Marines pursued numerous small institutional adaptations, including bomb-detecting dogs; a training project called Combat Hunter to enhance patrolling, tracking, and countersniper skills; and a highly realistic close-combat immersion simulator that replicated the chaos of combat.[82] The Marines started the Lioness program, which used female Marines for interfacing with Muslim females. In the spring of 2006, this expanded into a larger Female Engagement Team concept in Al Anbar province.[83]

The threat posed by IEDs was a recognized problem in Al Anbar. They adversely impacted the Marines' ability to maneuver in the province and to supply their strung-out forces. The Marines depended heavily on HMMWVs (light, four-wheel-drive utility vehicles known as "Humvees") for patrols. The need for the Marines to maintain their lines of communication between urban bases along the Euphrates valley was a vulnerability that the enemy recognized and exploited. The Marines began to adapt in 2004 by issuing armor kits that could be bolted onto their vehicles to afford them greater protection. It was an expeditionary improvisation, ineloquent to be sure. But it was the kind of 70-percent-solution that the Marine Corps' own culture could accept.

In February 2005 the I MEF staff submitted an Urgent Universal Need Statement (UUNS) for the acquisition of Mine-Resistant Ambush-Protected vehicles, known as MRAPs. MRAPs have a V-shaped hull, higher road clearance, and special seats to absorb blasts. Brig. Gen. Dennis Hejlik, who headed the Corps' newly established Special Operations Command unit, asked for 1,169 MRAPs to "increase survivability and mobility of Marines" operating in the very unstable Al Anbar province.[84] His bottom-up request was based on a study by staff officers who were familiar with foreign vehicles used in irregular warfare. Some MRAPs were already employed in theater by coalition members, and the Marines had a few in their engineering units.

The request ultimately was formally received back at the institutional level for evaluation. In the spring of 2005, a working group of Marine officers assessed the

MRAP and expressed numerous concerns. Accepting the UUNS would require that the Corps reduce existing weapons budgets to fulfill the new requirement. The group did not assess the operational risk of continuing to expose Marines to the evolving IED threat, or trends in the lethality of attacks. Instead, the senior members of the working group believed that the desired level of protection could be met with conventional vehicles that the Marines already expected to buy during the next few years. Gen. Michael W. Hagee, the Marine Corps commandant, testified in a subsequent investigation that he had decided to continue to buy the modified Humvees in the near term and consider MRAPs for the future.[85] But the MRAP was stillborn for 2005 and 2006.

The MRAP decision aside, the Marines were still conducting conventional raids from forward operating bases and not functioning under classical counterinsurgency doctrine. They could disrupt and temporarily clear areas of operation, but they had no trained or trusted Iraqi army units to which to hand off missions for the "holding" phase. Unfortunately, the Iraqi army too often was seen as a force of Shi'a oppression and instability. As a result, the effort was costly. During the series of operations in Sayeed, the Marines lost 50 killed and another 324 were wounded.[86] Moreover, 65 percent of the casualties were coming from IEDs.[87] Calls for a more comprehensive approach to civil affairs—greater presence instead of "hiding in the shadows," and increased attention to training Iraqis— were published in the *Marine Corps Gazette*. Information operations were seen as an Achilles' heel for the Marines.[88] The seeds sown in Al Qaim showed promise, but it does not appear that these insights were fed forward into the Marine Corps or absorbed or shared, despite General Casey's endorsement.[89] A cyclical pattern of "clear, clear, clear" in 2005 wore down both the Marines and AQI, and left the populace and the Marines quite frustrated.

From Transition to Engagement—2006 and 2007

Operation Sayeed and its dozen combat sweeps might simply be viewed as a series of tactical battles without strategic purpose. Yet, a spark emerged among some tribes. They were being pressed by al-Qaeda, and they sought help. Al-Qaeda recognized the tribal shift and immediately tried to dampen it, sparking more violence. In the first two months of 2006, two preeminent sheiks were killed, as well as the chairman of the Fallujah city council. A suicide bomber successfully exploded a device at a police recruiting drive in January and killed sixty recruits from one tribe. Then, on February 22, 2006, the gold-domed al-Askari Mosque of Samarra was destroyed, unleashing the retribution of the Shi'a militias throughout the rest of Iraq. It was a tipping-point that inflamed sectarian tensions and made political compromise unlikely in 2006. Thus, the ferocity of the insurgency grew to record levels of violence, and Al Anbar remained a stronghold for AQI-inspired insurgents. Some observers thought that Ramadi, a city of 250,000 people, looked a lot like Berlin in 1945.[90] There was little doubt that Al Anbar's provincial capital remained highly contested.[91]

As a result, the momentum created by RCT-2's attrition and clearing operations and Alford's example stalled in Al Anbar. A new Marine regiment arrived to relieve Davis' headquarters, and the cycle of learning resumed in the west. Alford's outposts were sustained by his replacement. But as new Marine units started rotating into Ramadi and Fallujah, they fell into a tactical pattern. Every day the Marines would leave their bases and patrol their areas by foot during the daylight hours and then return to their fortified camps by night. Efforts to train Iraqi security forces persisted, as did reconstruction projects and support for weak provincial and city governments that struggled to provide any of the most basic services. Progress was limited, despite the Marines' persistence.

Things were getting particularly ugly in Ramadi, Al Anbar's capital. Lt. Col. William M. Jurney and his battalion, the 1st Battalion, 6th Marines, had recently arrived in the summer of 2006.

> When we arrived it had been described as the most dangerous city in Iraq. We averaged 10 to 12 firefights a day, 70 to 80 [significant events] a week, very kinetic, limited freedom of movement, whole areas of the city which were predominantly insurgent controlled, population—which was thoroughly subdued by the murder and intimidation campaign of AQI. . . . There's no question that they were bona fide hard-core AQI foreign fighters who were pulling the strings.[92]

In particular, the complexity of the insurgent attacks was mounting. These included combination attacks with ambushes of twenty-five persons using vehicle-borne IEDs and rockets. They were organized and aggressive. They did not just hit and run; they *assaulted* the Marine positions—something that had not been seen in previous deployments. Marine intelligence analysts realized that the U.S. strategy was not effectively combatting the insurgency in Al Anbar. In a widely cited intelligence assessment, a Marine noted:

> The insurgency has strengthened in the past six months. Insurgent groups are better organized, increasingly achieve effective operational security, have improved their capabilities to cache and distribute weapons, and have refined and adapted their tactics. Control of criminal enterprise means the majority of insurgents are now financially self-sustainable at the lowest levels. Although it is likely that attack levels have peaked, the steady rise in attacks from mid-2003 to 2006 indicates a clear failure to defeat the insurgency in al-Anbar Province.[93]

Journalists have interpreted his assessment as an admission of failure.[94] Instead, it was really a belated recognition of a gap that called for *investigation* of a better approach. Marine headquarters, led by Maj. Gen. Richard C. Zilmer, formed a team from his staff to look for innovative ways to pacify the provincial capital of Ramadi as violence was spiking.[95] The creation of the team began a push for increased tribal engagement by the Marines. Further proof was near at hand. The Marines had assigned the city to the attached Army brigade, led by Col. Sean B. MacFarland. MacFarland's brigade had started their tour in Tal Afar, so it was familiar with the counterinsurgency fundamentals that Army Col. H. R. McMaster had employed there. His brigade consisted of a total of five battalions, which included one Marine battalion. Around July of 2006 MacFarland approached the tribal leaders about allowing their younger tribal members to join the police force, and got some positive responses.[96] Zilmer gave MacFarland and Jurney permission to improvise as they interacted in Ramadi, but they remained uncomfortable with creating tribal militias that would contravene U.S. policy for a unified Iraq. Moreover, Marine leaders were concerned that tribal leaders in Ramadi were "small fry" compared to more prominent sheiks still in Amman.[97]

At about the same time, Sheikh Abdul Sattar al-Rishawi of the Albu Risha tribe came forward and offered to broker a meeting between the tribes and the Marines. Sattar was a minor sheik with leadership skills and the courage to step forward. He formed the Anbar Salvation Council with other sheiks and worked to gain U.S. support and resources. Sattar quickly raised up his militias into "Emergency Response Units," which the Marines began training and paying.[98] Ultimately Sattar succeeded in gaining the support of a majority of the tribes and the Sahawa al Anbar ("Anbar Awakening") was formed on September 14, 2006. The next day, a Marine unit in the vicinity of Hit called to report that someone had just arrived with a message from Sheikh Ali Hatem of the Nimr tribe: he would place 350 of his tribal sons in the Iraqi police and 750 in the army. The Nimrs were now "in," which meant that al-Qaeda was out.[99] The next day more than a thousand volunteers arrived. A major shift in the environment was occurring.[100]

Al-Qaeda was aware of Sattar's moves and retaliated, but the tribes persisted. New forces and police stations appeared outside of Ramadi. This signaled a shift to the rest of the area that securing the local population could be done by the Iraqis themselves and that resistance against the American "occupier" was not desired— a turn that destigmatized cooperation with U.S. forces. On the other hand, collaboration with AQI was no longer sanctioned by tribal elites, which dried up some of their support. It was the biggest and most overt shift in Sunni attitudes toward their own future in Iraq.

But tribal forces would not be enough to expel AQI from Al Anbar. The Marines would have to continue to nurture their support into an ability to secure their tribal areas and cities. Ramadi became the epicenter of the next adaptation in Al Anbar. The Army brigade, led by Colonel MacFarland and augmented by a Marine battalion, generated a concept to clear the infested provincial capital city systemically, block by block, to sweep away the insurgent strongholds.[101]

Lieutenant Colonel Jurney, the commander of the Marine battalion in Ramadi, had picked up the same idea from discussions with Alford before he even deployed.[102] The unit before him told him that working in partnership with the Iraqi army and operating inside urban areas was too risky. Jurney disagreed, arguing that "there is even greater risk to successful accomplishment of the mission if you choose to operate from some isolated, disconnected forward operating base while conducting independent or intermittent partnered U.S. [operations] that lack permanent presence and a connection to the people."[103] Instead of creating transition teams, Jurney sought to partner with local forces, side by side, eating and sleeping together. Rather than using small specialized detachments for nontraditional counterinsurgency tasks, he pressed his whole battalion to think of itself as a combined action battalion (CAB) as it methodically swept west to east across the city.[104]

Jurney planned to clear discrete neighborhoods or zones in an expanding ink blot.[105] As each zone was cleared he would build or fortify a joint security station—a platoon-sized outpost. He emphasized partnering, as had Alford, and located his companies right along with Iraqi units. Every system, every outpost, every patrol, every operational decision would be joint. The Marines and the Army and the police would work out their problems together, side by side. He also adapted his structure to reflect the non-kinetics elements of his approach, creating an "effects cell," led by his executive officer, that combined the civil and information efforts. Information operations were deemed deficient, and, after a brief study, the battalion purchased a broadcasting system that the local mosques used to reach the city's residents.[106]

Jurney did employ traditional raids if he thought they were warranted, but knew that he would be more effective at neutralizing the insurgency by working with the Iraqi police and by creating jobs.[107] He shelved the notion that contracts should be allocated to foreign or Iraqi businesses that offered the lowest prices, and began awarding contracts for rubble- and trash-removal to the cooperating sheikhs, using the projects as "carrots" to cement the relationship with friendly leaders. Jurney clearly understood the importance of relationships—and the need to mix security measures with civil affairs and information operations.

The results were impressive. At a price of 9 million dollars, half of the city had been pacified and cleared of trash. It also acquired four soccer fields.[108] Jurney's battalion went from more than seventy significant incidents a week to zero. At one point, the unit enjoyed six weeks without having a shot fired at it. At the same time, the local police force expanded from 200 to 1,300—with tribal blessing.[109]

At the Marine headquarters, they knew that they had to exploit this opportunity quickly—before AQI would try to counter it. They started protecting the sheiks, fortifying the sheiks' homes, and training their security guards. Maj. Gen. John R. Allen, who arrived in February 2007 as deputy commander of II MEF (Forward), was focused on governance, economics, and tribal engagement. Allen quickly saw the shift in the tribes' attitude and sought to exploit it. He garnered funding from Baghdad to offer tribal leaders the resources for economic development projects—part of a deliberate plan to exploit the tribes.[110]

The Next Stage: Fallujah Flips

As the months went on, the tide that eventually became known as the Anbar Awakening movement continued to move down the Euphrates valley and created an atmosphere that led more and more Sunni leaders to realize that partnering with the Americans was in their best interests. Next would come a similar experiment in the major population center of Fallujah—a place where traditional assault tactics had secured the city initially, but where insurgents soon began to gain traction.

In the spring of 2007, Fallujah had regressed to the point of collapse. Three city council chairmen had been assassinated by AQI in three successive months, and the government was coming apart. Marines and Iraqi security forces were fighting AQI every day and night in the streets of Fallujah.[111] A new Marine battalion arrived in April 2007—the 2nd Battalion, 6th Marines, led by Lt. Col. William F. Mullen III.[112] This was Mullen's second tour in Iraq, and he was open to an unconventional strategy.[113] Mullen understood from reading Marine reports that the insurgency had increased its lethality and that U.S. progress using lethal weapons alone was doubtful. Static defensive positions by the Marines around the city, and the introduction of the Iraqi army, had not gained results. Mullen realized that a tribal-based approach in Al Anbar was anathema to democratic notions, but he wanted to see progress: "The approach used by coalition forces to that point in the city had to change," he wrote later. "It resembled something little better than the arcade game of 'whack-a-mole' and had made little progress . . . in Fallujah."[114]

Mullen was engaged in investigation at his level and dispatched his operations officer, Maj. George Benson, to Ramadi for a week to examine Jurney's battalion. He heard that the people of Ramadi were actively working with the Marines there. Benson got the most intense week of learning in his career, more from one week in Ramadi than the eight-month preparation cycle that his battalion just finished.[115] Based on Jurney's tactics, Benson developed a detailed plan for Fallujah. Mullen recognized that his area was not as tribal as Ramadi, and he would need to work with Fallujah's local leaders, the Muktars. The plan proposed to divide the city into ten precincts; each would be isolated in turn with barriers; and then the Marines would "swarm" into each precinct with an Iraqi police unit. Each precinct would build a joint security station to house a joint Marine and

Iraqi police force. Once the police force was situated, it would deputize and pay local Iraqis (150 dollars a month) to serve as a neighborhood watch and it would man checkpoints to preserve local security.

Mullen sold this concept to the Marine chain of command and to his Iraqi counterparts. His plan, Operation Allah, proved to be as effective as Jurney's efforts in Ramadi. Again, AQI responded in kind. The chairman of the city council, Sheik Sami Abdul Amir al-Jumayli, was assassinated on April 21 and a city councilman was killed on May 11. The Marines continued to work with tribal leaders, but on May 23 a third sheik was killed, and his funeral procession was hit with an IED the next day.

Mullen's plan for Fallujah was kicked off in the Khadairy neighborhood on May 29 and was fully in place by early fall. Tribal leaders returned and authorized the pairing of their forces with the Marines and the Iraqi soldiers, and they assisted those units with intelligence and by bolstering local security forces. The ten new precincts succeeded in gaining security and began to demonstrate to the local populace that their security was in their own hands, with Marine support. By September, the ten new joint security stations were operational and the overall situation had improved substantially. The numbers were impressive. Where there had been 750 incidents in the Fallujah area in March, and 650 in April, the figure fell to 520 incidents in May, 420 in June, and 260 in July. By September, when the town was completely "swarmed" and secured, total attacks had been pared to 180—a reduction of 75 percent—and that number was cut in half again by the end of October.[116]

The dramatic transformation of Fallujah from a rubble-filled town, festering with insurgents and the pungent odor of raw sewage, into a united, locally supported effort that rebuffed the worst that al-Qaeda could throw at them is a remarkable story. An appreciation for the tribal system and the area's human terrain clearly was a lesson to be learned. As General Allen noted afterward:

Once we were able to penetrate the tribes and be accepted and trusted by them, then we were able to then isolate al-Qaeda and go after them and eliminate them, and that was our goal. So the problem was penetrating the tribes and from roughly the latter part of the summer of '06 until our battle handover that process was just really getting underway.[117]

Thus began the biggest adaptation in Al Anbar. First came the recognition that the human terrain and cultural dynamics of Al Anbar were never suited for the centralized, democratic solution that the United States had sought to create in Baghdad. The Marines faced a stark choice in 2007, and the leadership was divided over what to do next.[118] The idealists within the Corps continued to push for a national and unified Iraqi state, but they risked letting al-Qaeda's hardcore insurgents take over Al Anbar. The realists were more pragmatic and recognized the inherent strength of the Anbar tribes. The realists won, and the resulting adaptation by the U.S. forces was long awaited by tribal leaders. One sheik made a telling point: "Our American friends had not understood us when they came," he wrote. "They were proud, stubborn people and so were we. They worked with the opportunists, now they have turned to the tribes, and this is as it should be."[119]

Next came the realization that AQI had created a backlash among the tribal elders in the area, that they were ripe for a major shift in alliance. At the end of 2006, the sheikhs collectively concluded that AQI wanted to destroy the tribal system.[120] Recognizing that shift was a critical step for the Marines, but so was the organic development of locally relevant tactics and practices by Jurney and Mullen.

When Allen arrived, in early 2007, he got behind the realist solution and made it the primary effort for the Marine staff. What the Marines had been calling "tribal engagement" actually had expanded into tribal exploitation. As Allen described it, "We intended not to operate *around* the tribes . . . to win this insurgency we had to operate *inside* the tribes. We had to penetrate the tribal membrane that excluded our influence."[121] Allen's ideas, collected within an overall stability plan called Anbar Dawn, was approved by Maj. Gen. Walter E. Gaskin, commander of the Multinational Forces–West and senior Marine commander in Al Anbar province, giving the concept the support and recognition that U.S. forces were taking a decidedly different approach. The Marines may not have caused the tribal shift, but they realized now that they needed to exploit it. Anbar Dawn became Allen's plan to cement the emerging alliance with the tribes.[122]

Lessons Learned from 2006 and 2007

The Marines continued to extract lessons from the ongoing campaigns. Again, the lessons focused on the elements of counterinsurgency that did not make full use of the storied fighting skills of the Corps. The same observations regarding intelligence, civil affairs, information operations, and training foreign indigenous forces were repeated. As one Marine put it:

> The kinetics are easy. We get that. The non-kinetic, civil affairs—PsyOps [psychological operations]—information operations, working with civilian leaders—that's the hard part. I'm not saying going to guns is not important—But focus your efforts of your staff, the battalion, on the non-kinetic aspect of the fight.[123]

Marine information operations were still overcentralized, and one regimental commander admitted, "the terrorists were well ahead of us when we first got on the ground in this regard."[124] External observers found Marine tactical information operations to be "almost worthless."[125] Nevertheless, in 2006 the Marines adapted to a more decentralized approach, with authority eventually delegated to lower-level units. Army assets were highly valuable in generating information leaflets and announcements, and the Marines became ingenious in communicating and getting local government leaders to broadcast on radio and TV.[126] In Ramadi, the Marines created a radio and TV station; local citizens took it over, to be replaced eventually by the city government.

Civil affairs personnel shortages persisted in 2007. The Marines resorted to using an active-duty artillery battalion staff as a civil affairs force in 2007.[127] The unit stayed for a year to give greater consistency to civil and economic projects, but it was an ad hoc solution. Information operations also remained thin. A G5-Civil Affairs section of thirty-five Marines was created to coordinate battalion efforts at governance, economic development, and tribal engagement. For the previous two years the Marines had delegated all planning and conduct of CMO to the CAGs. By attaching the CAG assets directly to the regiments for the first time, the military commanders now felt that they owned the problem.[128]

Intelligence resources were continuously evolving, with the Tactical Fusion Center accessing more national resources to support the Marines at lower levels, and the creation of company-level intelligence cells as an organizational innovation.[129] The intelligence adaptation incorporated all the lines of operation inherent to counterinsurgency, including development. "The intel fusion cell was superb," Reist observed later. He noted that the unit included "an economics assessment cell for what we were doing" in reconstruction and development.[130]

Marine shortfalls in training and advisory tasks continued, but here, too, there were continual adaptations. Military training teams (MTTs) were created to embed with Iraqi security forces. They were hastily formed, had limited guidance, and little formal training.[131] There was a learning curve in training for these teams, since their preparation was ad hoc and too general.[132] The Marines sought to get away from using pickup teams, since advisory training was still limited even as late as 2007: "We didn't do a lot of cultural or language training, nor did we train on how exactly to be an adviser. There was very little of that. We had maybe a week or two total of language and cultural training, with some advice on how to be advisers thrown in as well. I think that was a big deficiency for us."[133]

Cultural intelligence also remained limited—a shortcoming as the Marines adapted to the role and influence of Al Anbar's human terrain in 2006, especially to the realities of the tribal system. As Zilmer reflected on that year, "In my view without tribal engagement, to include in the government, we're going to have a tough road. They are absolutely essential to the social fabric of the people in Iraq and specifically in Anbar Province."[134] Brig. Gen. Robert B. Neller, deputy commanding general for operations of the Marine Expeditionary Force (Forward), made the same point when it came to recruiting for security forces. "We really didn't understand or appreciate to the extent that we do now the importance of tribal engagement—engaging the different tribes, tribal support for the people joining the army, and joining the police."[135] The senior Marines in Al Anbar came to the conclusion by 2007 that "this whole area is tribal and if you understand how important and how fundamental that tribal society is, and the influence and the position of the sheikhs, then you begin to understand how everything works. You can ignore that fact if you want to, but it's to your own peril."[136] The Marines had been overlooking it since 2004, but no longer. Within ninety days, the impact of the tribal engagement work showed a dramatic reduction in incidents, and the opportunity to substitute AQI's intimidation with government and economic development presented itself.[137] In 2007, two years of bottom-up work by the civil affairs teams finally was paying off,

when Marine leaders finally saw that economic resources could be more effective than a tank in keeping the peace.[138]

Once Marine Corps leaders realized how critical true tribal engagement could be,
the tide changed quite suddenly. The Marines claimed they had killed 1,775 insurgents in 2006 alone, doubling the 2005 total. They also captured almost five thousand more. Yet, despite removing almost seven thousand enemy fighters, Al Anbar's
violence levels doubled in 2006. General Allen summarized: "It was clear unless we
went after the underlying factors that fed the AQ insurgency we were not going to
win this war. Put differently . . . we were learning the hard way we weren't going
to kill our way out of Anbar."[139] The Marine Corps' institutional bias for action and
kinetic tools had to be "unlearned" and replaced with patience and mastery of the
human terrain, training foreign security forces, and microeconomics.[140]

A major lesson from Al Anbar was that cultural understanding and tribes matter,
and that success would occur only when "Marines are capable of gaining the trust
of tribal leadership and the tribesmen themselves."[141] In 2006, the Marines began
to realize the power of tribal networks in Al Anbar and sought to leverage those
networks. This shift ultimately was successful. The tactics and techniques of tribal
engagement and exploitation that were used in Ramadi trace back to Al Qaim in
2005, and were fed forward to Fallajuh. But it was only informally shared horizontally, not by the Marine's nascent learning mechanisms. Until AQI pushed the
tribes toward the Marines and the Marines learned how to embrace them, success was doubtful. Of all the adaptations, "tribal engagement" was paramount.[142]

As Jonathan Schroden of the Center for Naval Analyses notes, the adaptation to
tribal exploitation did not occur easily or quickly:

> There are instances throughout the war of tribal leaders coming forward to
> seek help against al-Qaeda in Iraq, and decisions by senior officials to turn
> them away. The shift from an attitude that said "tribes have no place in a mod-
> ern Iraq" to one that embraced them as an integral part of Iraqi society and as
> a source of manpower and intelligence came from the bottom up.[143]

Thus, credit really goes to the mid-level battalion commanders, who experimented and fed forward a solution to the challenge posed by AQI in Al Anbar.
This was surely bottom-up adaptation. It is also a case of horizontal learning, since

Alford's ideas influenced Jurney in Ramadi, and his experience helped Mullen in Fallujah. Noticeably, although all three battalions were successful, they passed the "novel" tactics entirely informally between themselves. They would offer their example to the battalions rotating in after their tours were over.

It took at least two years for that transformation to occur, and it was still not complete by 2007. Marine leaders were slow in appreciating the opportunity presented in late 2005, or in attempting to replicate the tactics of the 3rd Battalion, 6th Marines in Al Qaim to other areas in 2006. But by 2007 they had detected the shift in the willingness of tribal leaders to align with the coalition and sought to promote it as a key feature of their approach. They adapted their strategy to conform to the sociocultural realities of the environment.[144]

There was still a lingering retention of a kinetic and conventional mindset as late as 2007. "Many in our service seem to want to forget the lessons that we had to re-learn (from Vietnam) in Iraq and Afghanistan because the wars in those places did not fit what they thought of as 'real war,'" Reist wrote later.[145] Several Marines recognized that "we are losing because we put a kinetic face on everything and we are too slow to try others things."[146]

The IED threat in Iraq continued to take a toll. Between March 2003 and August 2007 there were 1,496 U.S. troops killed in action due to IEDs—just under 50 percent of the total of 3,037 American combat deaths in Iraq. Even with improvements in Al Anbar's security, from March 2007 on the percentage of American fatalities in Iraq due to IED incidents rose to 72 percent.[147] Aside from a handful of MRAPs purchased for explosive ordnance units, the vehicle was still not available to the Marines in 2006. To circumvent the bureaucratic block in Marine headquarters, the I MEF commander resubmitted the MRAP request from March of 2005 as a joint urgent need in the spring of 2006.[148] This pushed the proposal outside the Marine Corps, direct to Washington. Meanwhile, champions such as Franz M. Gayl, a former Marine major who served as a science and technology adviser at the Pentagon, pressed the requirement inside and outside Marine Corps circles[149]—sparking some news articles in the summer of 2007 that did not portray the Marine Corps positively.[150]

Nevertheless, in March 2007 the Marine Corps shifted its official position on the vehicle. In a letter to the chairman of the Joint Chiefs of Staff, General Conway, now the commandant of the Marine Corps, asked for help:

The MRAP vehicle has a dramatically better record of preventing fatal and serious injuries from attacks by Improvised Explosive Devices. Multinational Force–West estimates that the use of the MRAP could reduce casualties by as much as 80 percent. Since [May 21, 2006], when MNF–W issued its first urgent request for MRAP, over 150 servicemen and women have been killed and over 1,500 seriously injured in vehicle IED incidents.[151]

Conway continued: "Getting the MRAP into Al Anbar Province is my number one unfulfilled warfighting requirement at this time. I request your support in fielding this force protection capability."[152] His letter misdated the original Marine request by a full year, but it unequivocally recognized the vehicle's value. The comment that this requirement was "unfulfilled" meant that the Marines did not fund it in their budget.

External and top-down support was soon at hand. In December 2006 Robert M. Gates succeeded Donald H. Rumsfeld as secretary of defense. Gates was sensitive to the impact that increased casualties were having on public support for the war. He saw the press reports in April 2007 that revealed that the MRAP solution was not being aggressively pursued. On May 2, 2007, Gates signed a memo making the MRAP the highest-priority Defense program.[153] He then ordered a task force to report to him on progress of the program every two weeks—to reflect his urgency and overcome "bureaucratic inertia."[154]

Once the Pentagon had gotten behind the MRAP, the proposal moved forward quickly.[155] Some senior Marines were willing to admit that the response to MRAP had been delayed, "although perhaps understandable given the Marine Corps' traditional tendency to look for non-material solutions first (a legacy of their . . . limited funding)."[156] No doubt, the Corps could not have afforded the vehicles without help. As one officer observed: "To penny-pinching Marines . . . the vision of an almost 100-billion-dollar program to completely replace combat vehicle fleets was beyond the scope of what commanders thought was achievable." Instead of inertia, the same officer stated, the decision not to pursue the vehicle was "more likely a prioritization of other considerations (e.g., it's hard to practice *FM 3-24* from inside an MRAP)" than missing the demand signal.[157] Others remained skeptical about the value of MRAPs, admitting that they saved lives, but that "the answer was to get to the left of the boom by any and all means available"—including electronic jamming to counter IEDs. "The answer was not to get bigger, heavier, and better-designed and -armored vehicles, because the enemy just made bigger bombs."[158] Even looking back from a vantage point of several years, "Yes, it saved lives, but in doing so, it forced us into a set of tactics that the enemy adapted to. We would have been better off remaining with the people and being less 'buttoned up.'"[159]

Even though the Marines were now moving forward, Franz Gayl spent most of 2007 conducting a study of how the initial MRAP request was processed, and how the bureaucracy responded to it. He blamed the administrative bureaucracy for stonewalling the development of the heavy vehicle, which would ultimately save lives. His assessment was that "if the mass procurement and fielding of MRAPs had begun in 2005 in response to the known and acknowledged threats at that time . . . hundreds of deaths and injuries could have been prevented."[160] This conclusion benefits from hindsight, but it also is accurate. Secretary Gates remained undaunted and ensured the vehicles were fielded, despite criticism about its expense or the fear that it might keep troops from close contact with the civilian population.[161]

Organizational Learning Capacity
Leadership
The Marine Corps espouses a more decentralized mode of leadership, which focuses on clearly articulating a generic concept or what is called "commander's intent" while leaving the details of execution to subordinate unit commanders. Marine doctrine emphasizes decentralized leadership and high trust between senior officers and their subordinates.[162] Its philosophy is that issuing detailed instructions reduces initiative and creativity and slows timely responses to enemy actions. The argument is that using the "commander's intent" concept permits more creative expression of alternative means and induces more unit-level investigation of solutions in-theater. This leadership approach precludes excessive control or micromanagement, as was demonstrated in the previous case study of the Army in Vietnam.

Several Marine commanders have attributed success in Iraq to these doctrinal leadership qualities.[163] Looking back at Al Anbar, the role of leadership in pursuing adaptation was deemed critical. "Leadership is what it's all about," Reist has written. "The question to me is, how do you find the most innovative and adaptive leaders—and this includes how a leader might not be the best guy, but listens well. Our organizational culture breeds this."[164] As another brigadier general noted, "Far and away, leadership is the most important. Training and education serve a critical role in making an adaptation endure, but are not the source of innovations."[165] Another officer admitted that, "yes, the adaptations did take a while. It was a leadership climate issue."[166] But the underlying climate was always attributed to "Leadership—Period."[167]

Under the "commander's intent" concept, leadership and guidance are decentralized, emphasizing intent, not specific instructions. Even prototypical Marine commanders such as Conway and Mattis were satisfied with general plans and guidance like "their best friends or their worst enemy," to steer their commands. In Iraq, senior Marine Corps commanders emphasized articulating their overall purpose or intent but left the implementation details to lower levels. After the march to Baghdad, the 1st Marine Division transitioned to stability operations with detailed plans, and unit leaders devised the training regimen for subsequent rotations. Adaptive commanders such as Alford, Jurney, and Mullen operated consistently within the overall ideal envisioned by their seniors but applied that guidance to their local situations. "In this case, the innovation was championed by a respected commander, and tactical adaptation was rapid in disciplined Marine units. Leadership is the difference. Visionary and principled leaders create climates where innovation is accepted, and adaptations are swift."[168]

The adaptation from conventional warfare to the disciplined and patient mode required for irregular warfare was attributed to credible leaders and their tolerance for tailored adaptation by subordinates, rather than for strict compliance with details issued higher up. The cases of Groen's Tactical Fusion Center and the urban counterinsurgency techniques promoted by Alford, Jurney, and Mullen were all ultimately briefed to and approved by senior Marines. This is indicative of a command climate that supports good ideas getting a hearing and a chance to be demonstrated.

Culture

The Marine Corps is America's smallest military service and has the most distinctive culture. Marines explicitly imbue their recruits and young officers with certain values and teach them how to operate under the Marine belief system. Recruit training, or boot camp, and officer candidate school are the central modes of imprinting that culture.[169] The journalist Tom Ricks evaluated the Corps' institutional DNA:

> [T]he Marines are distinct even within the separate world of the U.S. military. Theirs is a culture apart. The Air Forces has its planes, the Navy its ships, the Army its obsessively written and obeyed "doctrine" that dictates how to act. Culture—that is the values and assumptions that shape its members—is all the Marines have. It is what holds them together. They are the smallest of the U.S. military services, and in many ways the most interesting. Theirs is the richest culture, formalistic, insular elitist, with a deep anchor in their own history and mythology.[170]

Insecurity about service legitimacy and relevancy can keep an institution open to new ideas and be an accelerant for entrepreneurial innovation. Because the Marines do not "own" a physical domain they are concerned with their institutional legitimacy and relevance. This insecurity stokes the Corps' paranoia and supposedly makes it less susceptible to complacency. Marines claim an expeditionary ethos— one that prepares units and individuals for rapid deployments to unexpected crises and requires a mindset that is creative and adaptive. In Marine Corps doctrine, the expeditionary mindset implies a "Spartan attitude: a certain pride in enduring hardship and austere conditions" and "versatility and adaptability to respond effectively without a great deal of preparation time to a broad variety of circumstances."[171] The Marine Corps' history and iconic heroes extol the role of innovation in the Corps' history. In *First to Fight,* legendary Marine Corps Lt. Gen. Victor H. Krulak describes the different personalities of the Corps, including the "fighters" and "innovators." To Krulak, adaptation "is a way of life for the Marines."[172]

The Marines also claim "the greatest tolerance for mavericks and outside-the-box thinkers."[173] Lecturing once to a new crop of generals, Mattis encouraged them not just to challenge conventional thinking themselves but to shield unconventional thinking. "One of your primary jobs is to take the risk and protect these people, because if they are not nurtured in your service, the enemy will bring their contrary ideas to you," Mattis said.[174]

The views from participants in Iraq about the Corps' adaptability are varied. One Marine asserted that although "the Marine Corps is a very traditional organization, individual Marines are enormously innovative." Several felt that adaptations occur most often when they are generated by individual ideas from the bottom that become accepted by credible leaders.[175] One felt that the Corps' conservative "crust" is broken only when threatened with irrelevance.[176] One general officer did not agree that the Marine Corps was a learning organization, pointing to tactics from the battle for Fallujah that he believed were not yet incorporated into doctrine.[177] Another general thought that the "Marines Corps was innovative, but at varying levels," and suggested that Reserve officers were "supremely innovative."[178]

The most distinctive element is the reduced role that doctrine plays in the Corps. A philosophy that embraces creativity and results over doctrinal compliance is well-suited for adaptation. As General Mattis quipped, "doctrine is the refuge of the unimaginative."[179] A retired Army officer remarked on the difference between the Army and Marines: "Having grown up in an Army culture, it's a breath of fresh air [to be in the Marine Corps]. It's innovative. It's a learning organization that is open to different ways of looking at a challenge. As someone who chafes under micromanagement and procedures and rules that must be adhered to, I found it [the Marine Corps] more like Special Forces."[180] Moreover, it was a culture that rewarded the attributes it espoused. The middle managers who succeeded in bringing about adaptation during Iraq—Groen, Alford, Jurney, and Mullen, for example—were all promoted and ultimately became generals.

The counterinsurgency adaptation was easier for the Marines to make than it would have been for the Army, given the Leathernecks' small wars history. The *Small Wars Manual* represented the recorded history that legitimized the necessary tactics based on the Corps' past. For Marines, "the new COIN doctrine was not substantially different . . . in principle . . . from that described years ago in the Marine Corps *Small Wars Manual*."[181] It formally accepted counterinsurgency theory, unlike the Army's doctrine, which had internalized different lessons.[182] Yet, the Marines supported only tactical forms of adaptation and ad hoc fixes. Major organizational changes and hardware priorities remained focused on the Corps' deeply rooted amphibious mission. It had no difficulty altering training and practices for Iraq's counterinsurgency operations—but only temporarily.

Overall, it appears the Marine Corps culture is suited to a greater degree of organizational learning and adaptation.[183] Recent scholarship suggests that in peacetime, Marine Corps efforts to instill creative concepts and continuous change have faltered, despite sponsorship at the very top of the service. This suggests that the Marines are not nearly as innovative as their culture and mythology depict.[184] This case study identifies the development of numerous tactical adaptions, but still the most important shifts were certainly not swift. A penchant for "can-do" pragmatism, coupled with an institutional bias for action over theory, lends itself to satisfactory solutions. Continuous inquiry and deliberative investigation can be a casualty.

Learning Mechanisms

The Marine Corps adapted its learning mechanisms substantially during the war in Iraq and Afghanistan. The most immediate mechanism was the relearning of operations assessment techniques that capture more than traditional military metrics. The ability to collect appropriate measures to evaluate progress in local governance, population attitudes, civil affairs projects, and economic development took time. Much of this recalled the U.S. experience in Vietnam.[185] Although assessment should be the foundation for interpretation in the learning cycle, leading practitioners identified a fundamental failure cycle in the conduct and use of assessments in both Iraq and Afghanistan that explain why many commanders were not cued to begin formally investigating alternative approaches.[186]

Apart from the expansion of formal assessment cells, special cells, or Red Teams were not prominent during this case. The Center for Naval Analyses provided analysts for technical operational support.[187] They produced dozens of reports with recommendations for enhancing the operational effectiveness of Marine units, but none of them was linked to critical adaptations.[188]

Next, the Marines recognized a need to learn and disseminate faster, but they did not achieve that objective in a systemic way. Before Iraq, the Marine Corps relied on a passive lessons-learned system to store observations. The system was not seen as useful or proactive and never was tied to proposed changes to tactics, personnel, doctrine, or materiel. Instead, it relied on individual Marine commands to submit reports after operations or exercises or major events. Moreover, it was infrequently used by the operating forces in peacetime.

This effort expanded in 2006 when the Marines expanded the lessons effort into a formal center and invested in an improved computer-based system. The Marine Corps Center for Lessons Learned (MCCLL) in Quantico professionalized and institutionalized the process of learning and disseminating insights across the force. The center's mission was to collect, analyze, manage, and disseminate knowledge gained through operational experiences, exercises, and supporting activities in order to enable Marines to achieve higher levels of performance and to provide information and analysis on emerging issues and trends.[189]

Marine Corps leaders created MCCLL to be the vehicle for adapting lessons learned as rapidly as possible while providing a responsive source for institutional knowledge feeding into the combat development system. As outlined by headquarters, the intent was clear: "We must learn from our successes and our mistakes. This concept is not new, but the reality is that we too often do not pay attention to the lessons of the past."[190]

The MCCLL itself was an institutional adaptation, and it faced a learning curve of its own to get established and embedded with major Marines headquarters in Iraq.[191] At the outset MCCLL representatives collected information, but analysis was not part of the effort.[192] Not satisfied with just collecting and automating reports, MCCLL authorities created compilations on specific topics.[193] They also conducted interviews and probed on key issues. To catalyze discussions on lessons, the Marines used educational venues and conferences specifically convened to garner and redistribute inputs on key lessons. While informal rather than analytical, these conferences were a deliberate strategy to generate consensus on solutions for identified problems.[194] Eventually, the analyses drawn from this database might succeed in enriching institutional adaptation, but they appear to have had little impact on operational adaptation in Iraq. Over time, MCCLL served as a collection asset for institutional learning, but it had no analytical capacity or methods for developing or testing forms operational adaptations that potentially could be used immediately. Having an information system for collecting and storing lessons is not the same as installing a mechanism that drives change. It results in a resource that commanders potentially could exploit, but does not promote learning itself.[195] Leadership and culture have to provide the genesis for learning, but they need mechanisms to sift through the fog of battle and identify ideas for investigation. As years went on, MCCLL began systemically evaluating reports from different units to glean larger insights and recommendations.[196]

One small exception is the use of cultural advisers as a learning mechanism. Mattis acquired the services of an Arab expert from the Naval Postgraduate School, and Alford "borrowed" an underemployed Marine major who spoke Arabic. Allen recruited an expert in tribal engagement, hiring him away from the Army.[197] Mullen leaned heavily on a civilian political adviser. Adaptive leaders reached out and pulled in expertise to fill in cognitive gaps and enhance their ability to generate insights or lessons.

Dissemination Mechanisms

In addition to creating the MCCLL, the Marines adapted an array of dissemination mechanisms during the conflict in Iraq. The most common were the wider use of traditional training and education.

Many adaptations from Iraq were transmitted into the mainstream institution by major educational and training changes. Many of them were spurred by the assignment of leaders who returned from Iraq to key leadership roles at Quantico. For example, the posting of Col. John A. Toolan, who served in Iraq as commander of Regimental Combat Team 1, as director of the Marine Command and Staff College was deliberately intended to revitalize unique education needs for Iraq. Toolan shifted the school's primary exercise from conventional warfare to stability and post-conflict operations. He also revamped the curriculum to include courses on how to deal with foreign cultures, interagency interactions, and foreign language instruction (over the faculty's objections). The same transition occurred with the Marine Battle Staff Training Program—to ensure that deploying staffs were integrating stability and counterinsurgency elements into their planning.[198]

Another mechanism for ensuring that observations were transitioned into lessons absorbed was the adoption of centralized predeployment training. Before that, Marine combat units had planned and conducted their own training. However, to ensure that operational praxis was updated and that rotating forces from around the entire Marine Corps were prepared to operate with one another, the Marine Corps created a formal program at its major live-fire training base, Twenty-Nine Palms, in California. This training, known as Mojave Viper, included events designed to immerse units into as realistic a context for Iraq as possible, complete with a mosque, native role-players, an "IED Alley," and other events. The majority of Marine units underwent a thirty-day training cycle with Mojave Viper before deploying. It was a great method for passing on lessons, best practices, and instilling mindsets.[199] As one originator of the program put it:

> As early as December 2004, there was a concerted effort within the training establishment to capture new developments from the battlespace and translate them quickly into updates to the predeployment training syllabus. The motto was, "if they see it in Anbar on Thursday, we want to be happening in the training here (in California), on Monday." To the degree that the information reached the trainers, this was accomplished, but it depended largely on the initiative of the training establishment to reach out for the information.[200]

With that as a goal, Major General Mattis regarded the training establishment as a "reciprocal engine," with tactics and learning flowing in both directions.[201] Garrett agreed that the predeployment training was a key learning "engine."[202] As Mojave Viper gained credibility with the assignment of credible practitioners coming back from Iraq, the Marine Corps successfully created a means for institutionalizing learning and enhancing the performance of new units before they went.[203] Yet, the capacity to distribute laterally to units already in Iraq, to disseminate insights rapidly, remained lacking.

While the MCCLL strengthened the systemic collection of lessons, the Marine Corps relied on a more informal approach to disseminate those lessons. As late as 2007, Marine veterans with multiple tours in Iraq bemoaned the Corps' limited ability to capture and share tactical lessons in real time.[204] Notably, headquarters did not institute any informal networks, such as *CompanyCommander.net*, to share insights horizontally.

As noted earlier, the Marine Corps does not focus on doctrine the way the Army does. Indeed, the Marines had not updated their counterinsurgency doctrine since 1976. Nonetheless, the service did join with the Army in early 2006 to support the development of counterinsurgency doctrine through *FM 3-24* and also updated doctrine for information operations and counter-IED tactics. It also issued "a tentative manual" on countering irregular threats.[205] The book reflected a comprehensive approach and predated *FM 3-24* by six months, but it was not issued as formal doctrine.

Table 6.2. Marine Corps Adaptation, 2004–2007

Form of Adaptation	Operational and Tactical Adaptation	Institutional Adaptation
Organizational	• Intelligence Fusion Center • Military/Police Transition Teams • Female Engagement Teams • Combat Action Program • Civil Affairs	• MCLLS Expansion • CAOCL • MCU Education changes and Mojave Viper Training Program
Doctrinal/Praxis	• Population-oriented COIN • Tribal Engagement • Combined Action Program	• Classical Counterinsurgency—FM 3-24 • Operational Culture education/manual
Technological	• Counter-IED Efforts and MRAP	

All in all, as shown in table 6.2, the Marine Corps generated numerous initiatives to adapt to the circumstances in Iraq. As shown in the first column, adaptation took multiple forms. Structural, doctrinal, and technological adaptions were all produced. Some were operational or tactical adaptations involving new methods and tactics that were organically generated in contact by the Marines that were fighting in Iraq. But to support those Marines, institutional adaptation was also needed, and MCCLL and the centralized predeployment training program were central to that. The literature and the bulk of the examples in the case studies focus on operational forms of change. Both operational and institutional adaptations were needed to sustain the high turnover of deploying Marine units and increase their operational effectiveness over the course of the numerous rotating units that came to Al Anbar. Given the importance of force-generation capacity at the service or institutional level and the desire to make units as effective as possible, the numerous institutional adaptations that emerged outside of Iraq cannot be overlooked.

The Marine case history underscores the key elements of the Organizational Learning Cycle. There are many instances of institutional change during the course of the Marine participation in Iraq. Many of these adaptive changes came from dispersed operational units and were based on their own experiences; others were captured formally by institutional forces to prepare the next rotations of units into Iraq. However, the systematic stimulation of inquiry through the collection and formal interpretation of those experiences does not appear to have occurred at higher operational headquarters. Thus, interpretation and investigation at the operational level, followed by rapid dissemination horizontally to other units, did not occur. This does not serve to improve the Marine Corps' learning capacity, but it may reflect its more-informal style of learning.

The decentralized Marine culture facilitated organic operational and tactical adaptation by separate units. Yet, they lacked a systemic learning process and true learning mechanisms at both the operational and institutional level. The Corps recognized the need for a better system when it created the Marine Corps Center for Lessons Learned, which had to go through its own growth period to "learn how to learn." Some aspects of this system, including the user-friendly computer-based information system that the Marines developed, proved valuable for acquiring and sharing information, but it only helped those who searched the data system, and it did little to promote learning across the service by itself. Organizational leadership must stimulate and encourage this kind of learning.

What the Marines lacked was a systemic structure and process to promote learning. Problem recognition was not a challenge; inquiry was constant. It was certainly evident from 2004 to 2006 that conventional operations would not suffice. Yet, the capacity to examine alternative methods or to experiment was lacking. Nor did the Marines absorb new tactics rapidly when bottom-up adaptations presented themselves as potential breakthroughs. The Marines did not move to the investigation phase of the Organizational Learning Cycle until 2006 in Ramadi to resolve the central operational challenge against the insurgents. Senior military commanders lacked mechanisms—aside from their usual staff structure—to facilitate their investigation of potential solutions to drive learning. They also had no way (besides routine changeover briefs) for sharing lessons or new adaptations. Instead, learning occurred informally and laterally at middle-management levels.

The MRAP story illustrates the tension between learning-in-theater—by forces in direct contact with a live opponent—and the institutional elements of the service, which serve longer-term issues or the most bureaucratic instincts of the larger institution. The inquiry and interpretation phases in Iraq strongly argued for better vehicles to provide force protection. Yet, when the request shifted back to the institutional side of the Marine Corps, that investigation pursued options that were consistent with the Marine Corps' culture, sense of identity, and more traditional amphibious mission. It took extended pressure, from both internal and external sources, to override the institutional resistance. In peacetime innovation, the focus and credibility is with force-development institutions. During war, the warfighting community and operational pressures have more influence—but not enough, it seems, given the MRAP history. This dialectic interaction between institutional-level decisions and operational commands has been seen in other cases in the literature.[206] In this book, tensions between the institutional perspective and the operational forces in the war are present in each case study. The Navy did not accept criticisms about torpedoes in the Navy case study, despite pleas from Lockwood; the senior leadership of the Army was critical of Westmoreland's approach in Vietnam; and the Air Force refused to allocate jets to Korea initially despite the requests from FEAF. These tensions are natural, but they can retard successful adaptation.

Marine leaders have absorbed the right lessons from Iraq with respect to their openness to adaptation. In a 2016 speech General Dunford shared an anecdote about Capt. Wayne A. Sinclair, who wrote an article in 1996 about the threat posed by small homemade bombs that eventually would force the Marines to transform their approach to transporting ground forces. Dunford called Sinclair "one of the godfathers of the MRAP," and noted that the Marines did not take advantage of that insight until Iraq. Ironically, as Dunford noted, Sinclair served in Iraq and rode in the very MRAPs he had advocated, "—but not before the IED nearly brought the world's most advanced fighting force to a halt."[207] The MRAP case underscores the complexities of making double-loop adaptations under wartime conditions.

By contrast, the Marines' shift to tribal engagement in Anbar Dawn should be classified as a single-loop adaptation for two reasons. First, the ever-present references to the *Small Wars Manual* by many Marine officers suggests that the volume's influence in the Marine Corps culture still was strong and positive.[208] Marine Corps culture and the official history capture that era as a successful period for the Corps, so the temporary return to local governance and short-term constabulary work is not antithetical to the Corps ethos. This is observed by the numerous battalion-level efforts to work with local officials, as well as the numerous references to the *Small Wars Manual*. Second, the initiative was spawned much earlier, in 2004—by Marine Corps Reserve civil affairs personnel, who were more attuned to civilian economic transitions. They appreciated the non-kinetic solutions from the start. One Marine reported that "without doctrine or strategy, we stumbled onto the informal system that defines how the sheikhs [and] tribes have worked for centuries—rewards and gains."[209] It is true that this was not a routine competency for the Marines. Permanent creation of unique units for counterinsurgency, or promulgation of Marine doctrine with greater stress on non-kinetic tools would have made it a double-loop adaptation. It is still a clear example of effective bottom-up adaptation, and a credit to the openness of selected leaders.

Conclusion

The experience of the Leathernecks in Iraq is one of classic adaptation to both unforeseen campaign pressures and the competition for learning against a thinking opponent. The Marines had to alter their default-switch from warriors seeking to close with and destroy well-defined opponents in high-intensity combat to a new setting of culturally aware nation-builders and trainers, protecting civilians, restoring services, and mentoring police.[210] The evidence of adaptation is clear, but the Marines learned more slowly than expected. As the epigram at the start of this chapter notes, hard-earned lessons from combat should be "promulgated laterally as quickly as possible so that the learning curve of the entire organization is elevated." It is clear from this case study that learning and adaptation did occur, but it did so informally and not very quickly.

Although the adaptations took time, the Organizational Learning Capacity of the Marines was evident. Kinetic predispositions, an aspect of Marine Corps culture, had to be adapted for some time, but they were overcome by 2007. The Corps' leaders and culture did not retard adaptation; rather, they created a climate in which bottom-up adaptation could emerge. The principal element shaping this adaptation was leadership from the middle, and an expeditionary culture that was open to new ways of doing business in the face of ongoing operational and tactical challenges. Unlike the Army in Vietnam, senior leaders in the Marine Corps did not enforce compliance or close down new ideas. However, they failed to identify and promote learning experiences from creative units to the rest of the Marine force. Had they been able to do so, the potential opportunities from 2005 might have been immediately identified and systematically distributed.

A second issue involves the slow adaptation of the MRAP, which reflects the strong pull of organizational culture. The Corps' identity and mission of amphibious warfare shaped the way it looked at these heavy vehicles. The vehicle could not fit aboard amphibious ships, and it competed with the prized expeditionary fighting vehicle, which had been viewed as the key to the Marine vision of future war. The MRAP was seen as a costly threat to that long-term vision. The Marine Corps' sense of identity and its mental frame of itself as "Shock Troops from the Sea" blocked rapid adaptation.[211] Here Marine culture and bureaucracy established barriers in both problem-recognition and implementation. It took a new secretary of defense to shock the bureaucracies and free up the resources. The Marines could not easily adapt their mental model and institutional priorities. The notion of cultural blind spots, where institutions disregard the consequences of action or inaction, appears apt.[212] As the late Anglo-American scholar and strategist Colin S. Gray has noted, cultures are perfectly capable of ignoring what they want to ignore.[213]

The best summation of the Marine Corps case is from then-general John R. Allen. When asked about the relevance of adaptation in Al Anbar, his response is telling: "Anbar? . . . it was *all* about adaptation."[214]

CHAPTER 7

Conclusions and Implications

War is the great auditor of institutions.

—CORRELLI BARNETT[1]

Wars inevitably become audits of military institutions, where the bloody costs of institutional failings are entered into the ledger in red ink. War tests the output of bureaucratic organizations—their leadership, prewar preparations, strategic direction, and doctrine. Yet, success in war is inherently tied to a military organization's capacity to respond to the enemy or the environment in wartime as well. Military change involves learning new routines and competencies—and adjusting old ones—in order to improve the organization's performance under wartime conditions. As the cases in this book demonstrate, learning and adapting under fire can help bring about wartime victories.

There are clear penalties when military organizations either fail to adjust or adapt too slowly to pressing demands for learning and change. The case studies that we have presented here amply reveal the human and materiel costs of not recognizing or properly reacting to unexpected campaign pressures and enemy actions. What would have been the history of the Pacific campaign against Japan if the U.S. Navy had taken only a few months rather than years to realize that its torpedoes were flawed? Conceivably, could the Navy and its intrepid submarine force have substantially decimated the Japanese tanker fleet and crippled its economy by 1944? Could the critical battle for Okinawa have been avoided, saving many thousands of lives? Could better interdiction against North Korean transportation networks, conducted at day and night, been more effective, and shortened the Korean War? The Military Assistance Command Vietnam stifled creativity and blocked much-needed changes in that conflict. Could it have implemented less-destructive large operations and applied firepower against the North Vietnamese more discriminately in the jungles of Southeast Asia, or was the epic tragedy a function of the adversary's "revolutionary mode of fighting?" The major debate about the war is whether it could have been won conventionally rather than using counterinsurgency to defeat North Vietnam—or could the United States have instituted an effective counterinsurgency program in 1967 and reduced the dramatic cost escalation that doomed sustained involvement by U.S. forces?

In Iraq, Marine leaders were approached numerous times by the Sunni tribes starting in 2005, but it took almost a year for the battalion commanders to begin to realize the power of tribal networks. It took even longer to adapt fully to counterinsurgency operations in hostile Al Anbar. Perhaps still more telling, the Corps spent more than two years before it realized that its counter-IED efforts—meant to deal with improvised explosive devices—were not effective in negating the enemy's ability to generate significant casualties. How might Iraq look today if both the Marines and their Army counterparts had been able to implement a counterinsurgency solution rapidly in 2005—instead of having to mount the "surge" operations of 2007?

As these cases show, historically military change has not been a simple matter. Rosen was right—there *are* difficulties in piercing uncertainty and dissipating friction on the battlefield. The process of interpreting the many signals coming from the battlefield—or undersea, given our case study involving the Navy—is not a simple matter. In each of these instances, the military organization took eighteen to twenty-four months to resolve gaps in operational effectiveness. In some of the cases solutions to problems appeared intractable or were unclear due to the fog of war. In others, leaders resisted altering their mental model or doctrine. Instead, they attempted to make reality fit preformed ideas and existing organizational core competencies.[2]

The need for an increased understanding about the dynamics of change is now evident. After two conflicts spanning over fifteen years, there is an increased appreciation for the importance of adaptation at the apex of the U.S. joint military community. A 2012 study sponsored by the Joint Chiefs of Staff, entitled *A Decade of War*, noted that "while units learned and adapted to their operating environments, their experiences, best practices, and lessons were not always shared, either within theater or with the larger [Defense Department] institutions."[3] The study conceded that although the services maintained many lessons-learned organizations with active collection efforts, those activities too often remained within stovepipes and rarely were shared with the larger joint force. This is an admission worth noting and working to correct.

That is why this research effort sought to gain a better understanding of the process by which institutions have learned and changed in the past. If change in wartime is critical to military organizations, what processes or attributes make one service more adaptive than another? What contributes to a predisposition to be adaptive or what generates institutional "adaptivity?"[4] History strongly suggests that some military organizations have done better than others at change, while others have failed. It would be useful if we understood why some are better and how they outperform the competition.

To answer that challenge, this final chapter is organized into three major sections: the Organizational Learning Cycle, the attributes of effective Organizational Learning Capacity, and finally, implications for theory.

Organizational Learning Cycle

The Organizational Learning Cycle postulated in this book is offered as a useful framework of a complicated heuristic process. Most Organizational Learning theorists examine change as part of a deliberate, systematic learning cycle or process. A review of the literature suggests that effective learning follows such a process, abetted by facilitators and enabling mechanisms. To test that hypothesis, a model was developed that assumed that learning was sourced from the bottom, or tactical, levels of a military organization. In this model, insights and experiences from actual military operations are assessed in relation to expectations in a step called *inquire*. Iterations of experiences are fed forward for subsequent interpretation by larger groups and then at higher staff levels. This function feeds forward observations that support a process termed *interpretation*. Interpretation is a step in organizational learning that is necessary if these leaders are to be successful over time. The complexities of assessing military performance of units in combat conditions is difficult, but interpretation (often referred to as "assessment" by military staffs) is essential to support an understanding of the environment and unit performance.

The proposed theory also details a step called *investigation*, which generates, tests, and refines potential changes to organizational practices, structure, or capabilities. At each level of the organization, the investigation leads to a decision to adjust inputs in some way and to apply changes to increase the effectiveness of the military organization and heighten its chances for success. The case studies suggest that the investigation phase can be conducted at either the organizational level in the field or at the institutional level back in the United States.

The model further postulates that a process to absorb field experience and vertically process that knowledge is a necessary aspect of an organization's capacity to learn and benefit from combat experience. Ultimately, incorporating new skills, insights, and adaptations into the wider organization—through "*integration and institutionalization*"—is a test of such institutional processes and systems.[5]

The Navy submarine case study demonstrated each element of the model. Submarine patrols generated experiences that were shared and fed forward as routine reports to support *inquiry*. They were systematically reviewed and endorsed. Compilations of success and failed practices were examined and *interpreted*. The endorsements of such reports constituted the *interpretation* phase of the model as well as feedback to lower levels concerning which changes in practice were approved. Performance gaps were regularly noted and "work-arounds" or solutions were proposed and tested by higher organizational levels. The persistent reports of torpedo failure required *investigation*—by Rear Admiral Lockwood in Australia, through experimentation in Hawaii. These efforts confirmed torpedo shortcomings that had been identified very early in the war. Conflicting information, the fog and friction of war, human failings in reporting, and bureaucratic resistance all played their part in efforts to confound the Submarine Force's attempts to enhance boat performance levels over time. Ultimately, Submarine Force Pacific's conduct of the *investigation* phase resulted in learning, albeit belatedly. Some of this was done by simple adjustments—such as fixing the torpedo depth-settings or deactivating the magnetic exploder. These did not represent an adaptation, but simply a change to existing skills or equipment. These were forwarded to the Navy's bureaus and schools to fix the technology shortfalls permanently and to institutionalize lessons at the training centers that would produce the next generation of technicians and sailors.

The Navy's wolfpack tactics also can be examined within the model. Even in this one case of directed, top-down learning, the operational force investigated the nature of the problem and over the next several months thoroughly explored options for command-and-control, organizational arrangements, and doctrine. Lockwood's shooting tests were a classical example of investigation, executed in this case by the operational forces rather than by the institutional bureau responsible for torpedo production. The doctrine and tactics were first tested and then progressively applied at sea in exercises. Senior Navy commanders may have directed this significant change to method or praxis, but the submarine command was permitted to investigate and implement the details from the bottom up.

The Air Force appears to have demonstrated a high degree of Organizational Learning Capacity in the Korean War. Its technocratic and empirical operations facilitated routine forms of inquiry, which fed into discriminating interpretation by FEAF and Fifth Air Force operations analysis. The Air Force augmented the investigation capacity of the busy headquarters in Korea by using several boards and study groups to assess particular performance gaps. The majority of the investigations or experiments were conducted in-theater and in combat, including radar-directed bombing, precision bombing, cannon test evaluations, and gunnery-sight tests. The Air Force appeared willing to interpret performance results and energetically explore options to enhance their platforms and their munitions. Although the service made some training and doctrinal adjustments during this period, most did not affect the war in Korea, since its strategic constraints were considered an anomaly. Thus, a war that initially seemed likely be ignored as an aberration compelled the Air Force a decade later to relearn many lessons about political constraints on targeting and intensive close-support tasks in Vietnam.

The model can be readily applied to the Vietnam case study as well. The Army amassed extensive operational experience from 1965 through 1967 that produced many inputs, yet the documentation resulted in few insights about changing methods to combat the Viet Cong. Instead, the critical function of interpretation was blocked by senior Army leaders in Vietnam, who insisted on imposing their own mental model of the enemy and the war on the American ground forces. In this case study, there is simply a leadership failure to recognize the importance of systematic learning and the lack of a command climate at MACV that accepted the interactive nature of war and the need to adjust its strategy and operational methods. There was no dearth of reports and documented experiences and in retrospect there were many commanders uncomfortable with the strategy and operational methods that the Army used. Hundreds of after-action reports and campaign histories were typed in triplicate and forwarded up the chain. However, there is little evidence that these insights were absorbed in the form of organizational learning. The learning mechanisms could not promote changes in performance without leadership support.

The case of the Marines in Al Anbar reflects a different kind of shortfall in the learning process. The Leathernecks belatedly recognized the need for a more systematic framework for organizational learning in 2006 when they created the Marine Corps Center for Lessons Learned in Quantico. Their peacetime system was inadequate to support the higher demand for adapting generated by operations in Iraq. There were many instances of institutional change during the Marine Corps' participation in Operation Iraqi Freedom, including language training, culture, predeployment training, and educational curricula revisions. New tactics and techniques were developed to support counterinsurgency efforts in Iraq. Many of these adaptive changes came from requests by operational units, after their own ad hoc experiences were pushed forward in 2005. However, the systematic collection of these experiences, the formal interpretation of those experiences at higher organizational levels, followed by rapid dissemination horizontally to other units, was not part of the Marine Corps system. The Corps' culture of "mission command"—decentralized execution in accordance with the commander's general intent—actually may have retarded collective learning and horizontal dissemination. This could represent either the lack of a doctrinal tradition in the Marine Corps or its more informal style of learning from role models and self-study.[6]

Other institutional changes, such as the development of counterinsurgency doctrine through *FM 3-24* or the development of the MRAP, were pushed more by the Army or by the Pentagon from outside the Marine Corps.[7] The Marine Corps' history with the MRAP is instructive because it shows how demands for change that derive directly from operational lessons and come from the bottom of the organization may not be accepted at all at higher levels. In 2005 commanders sought an effective solution to a lethal problem and gap. That challenge, the IED, continued to evolve and become more lethal. Institutional preferences, far removed from the battlefield, sought solutions that were more in keeping with the Marine Corps' culture and amphibious mission. In this case, the system did not produce the answers that those at the bottom of the chain were seeking, and senior Marines decided that the changes were not necessary or desirable at the time. The Marine Corps campaigns in Al Anbar provide numerous examples of positive organizational change and agile learning, but the MRAP is not one of them.

Attributes of Organizational Learning Capacity

The Learning Cycle is a process that is facilitated or retarded by Organizational Learning Capacity, defined as "the aggregate ability of a military organization to recognize and respond to performance gaps generated by unexpected adversary actions or unanticipated aspects of the operating environment." The four elements of Organizational Learning Capacity include: (a) credible leadership that cultivates openness, flexibility, and collaborative learning; (b) an organizational culture conducive to experimenting and learning rather than strict compliance with existing routines; (c) the existence of structured learning teams, processes, and mechanisms to support inquiry and investigation; and (d) the effective use of dissemination mechanisms to promote sharing and learning of new knowledge.

The detailed case studies indicate that the first two elements of Organizational Learning Capacity are the critical elements needed to promote *operational adaptation* in forces that are engaged in combat. These factors, *operational leadership* and *organizational culture*, create the conditions for *inquiry* and *interpretation* to occur. These factors are essential to the *recognition* process; they also create the adaptive pressures to seek solutions in the subsequent phases. However, these two shapers of adaptation are not sufficient by themselves. Ultimately they must be accompanied by *learning and dissemination mechanisms* that support the *investigation* of options and the *integration* or *institutionalization* of new tactics and techniques into a military organization's repertoire of skills and competencies. Without these mechanisms, the response steps in the learning cycle are stunted or ineffectual at enhancing organizational performance across the operational force or back into the institutional force-generating machinery of the particular armed service.

The cases collectively underscore the importance of Organizational Learning, and each case highlights how Organizational Learning Capacity shapes and enables military change in wartime.

Leadership

Failure or success in adaptation relies on both effective leadership at various levels of the organization and on a conception of command that permits learning.[8] Some recent research stresses the importance of senior leaders in mobilizing top-down organizational and doctrinal innovations by the Army.[9] There is no doubt that major changes are unlikely in hierarchical bureaucracies such as military organizations without agreement from senior leaders. Overall, however, our study found that strong leadership did not in itself generate or initiate military change. Leadership was a factor but was not necessarily sufficient by itself, since the ideas and impetus for change did not always come from the top. Rather, senior and credible leaders created climates where information and ideas could be collected, shared, and studied. These climates were conducive to inquiry, the interpretation of experiences, and the promotion of change. Leaders who were comfortable listening to and receiving inputs from junior officers at the source of contact or from learning mechanisms were then able to understand and respond to challenges in the operating environment. They also were comfortable with subordinates employing diverse ways of solving local problems.

The Navy, Air Force, and Marine Corps cases suggest that openness and decentralized leadership are useful attributes, while the negative Army experience in Vietnam displays the impact of a closed and controlling orientation at senior levels. The submarine case study juxtaposes two different leadership styles that capture the positive contribution of an open mode of leadership that seeks out insights from the tactical edge of the organization. The flip side of the ideal leadership for adaptation came from the Army in Vietnam, in the form of Westmoreland and DePuy. Their directive and controlling style produced a command atmosphere that proved counterproductive for the generation of creative problem-solving from lower levels of the organization. Such an environment was the antithesis of a command that is capable of recognizing new challenges or devising adaptive solutions to enhance unit performance. This produced a climate that was more chilling than collaborative, which impeded learning.

The Marine Corps' operations in Iraq show the benefits of decentralized authority in facilitating the development of organic solutions to local problems. The leadership philosophy of the Corps played a strong role, in the sense that senior officers did not retard the ability of commanders to try creative solutions. At the same time, however, the senior leaders did not promote the systemic exploitation of tactical lessons into an improved operational performance horizontally. The concept of "mission command," a component of the Marines' warfighting philosophy, may have limited higher headquarters from compiling and interpreting best practices from the higher-performing units. The mission command concept promotes an "entrepreneurial" spirit in subordinate commanders, which in turn promotes initiative and tactical adaptation.[10] At the same time, however, it also may inhibit higher-level commanders from seeking to absorb and disseminate these adaptations to other units.

It should be noted that as of mid-2019 an entire generation of the U.S. military had been molded by protracted conflicts in Iraq, Afghanistan, and Syria. The role of leadership in adapting to these unanticipated and different contexts appears to have been absorbed throughout the Joint Force. Gen. Joseph F. Dunford Jr., a former Marine Corps commandant who served as chairman of the Joint Chiefs of Staff through September 2019, stressed to future leaders graduating from the National Defense University:

> There's no substitute for taking a clear-eyed look at the threats we'll face, and asking how our force has to change to meet them. There is no substitute for leadership that recognizes the implications of new ideas, new technologies, and new approaches and actually anticipates and effects those changes, actually affects adaptation.[11]

General Dunford emphasized his own learning process over the past few decades and advised the next generation of leaders to "create an environment within which innovation, the questioning of conventional wisdom and creativity are not only allowed, but actually encouraged . . . and assume you don't have all the answers."[12]

Organizational Culture

These case studies also bear out the importance of organizational culture to learning and adaptation. Organizational Learning theorists generally emphasize the importance of culture.[13] Military organizations that instill professional cultures that embrace collaborative and creative problem-solving and tolerate free or critical thinking should be more successful at adapting to novel conditions. Cultures that are controlling or very doctrinally dogmatic or that reinforce conformity should not expect to be adaptive.[14] In fact, the cases suggest that culture is a double-edged sword that can be either a barrier to or a facilitator of change.[15] This reinforces the conclusions of military historians Downie, Nagl, and Murray on the role of organizational culture as a shaping influence on adaptation. In the cases studied here, Organizational Culture influenced how unit leaders saw their mission, how willing they were to ask questions or challenge assumptions, and to what extent likely alternative tactics or techniques were examined and implemented. Historical studies suggest that culture is a strong component of innovation and adaptation—and of warfighting effectiveness.[16]

The Navy's submarine force had a culture that had been framed by its unique operating environment. Aside from its corporate identity and its operating culture of independent command at sea, the submarine branch was oriented toward problem-solving. It was a rules-based group by necessity and was subject to a common operating doctrine and prescriptive practices. Submariners were not given any incentive to deviate from this core operating procedure without good reason, and the older officers particularly had been indoctrinated to play by the rules that they had practiced in peacetime. They were comfortable in a control-based culture, where the later generation of "wartime" officers was results-driven and preferred an informal command style with greater initiative. The demands of unrestricted warfare dictated that skippers become hungry "hunters" rather than the silent "hiders" that they had trained to be before the war. It took time to make this adjustment, but, under the pressures of campaigning against a thinking opponent, aggressive new tactics emerged that improved combat performance.

In the Korean War, the most significant adaptation by the Air Force was its rapid reversion from jet fighters to the piston-driven P-51 Mustang. Almost all pilots had flown propeller-driven aircraft in their training and professional careers, so it was not an inordinate difficulty. But it was not without controversy or costs. Consistent with some other cases in this book, the change was driven from the top down, in this case by the Air Force chief of staff. The episode suggests that the P-51 was chosen because so many of them were available for reversion—not because the aircraft had distinctive attributes that seemed likely to enhance pilots' performance. The Korean War was *not* the top priority of the either Air Force or the United States. As long as the relatively scarce jets in the force required long and secure airfields, the Mustang would be the best choice for expanding the number of close air support missions. The distance from Japan to Korea led one senior officer to remark that a single F-51 flying from Taegu in South Korea was worth four F-80s based in Japan.[17] General Vandenberg's decision to send 150 Mustangs so quickly—and the rapid assembly and deployment of these planes to Korea—is a testament to the Air Force organizational culture. The other double-loop adaptation—one that involves suspension or change to an institution's central ethos or values—involves the in extremis employment of B-29s in day and night bombing missions when the Pusan Perimeter was under pressure. MacArthur rightly insisted that his subordinate commanders provide any means necessary to blunt the North Korean offensive, regardless of Air Force doctrine or the inefficient character of Air Force doctrine or the inefficient results. Using bombers was very inefficient, expensive, and had limited results.

Conversely, the Army's slow adaptation in Vietnam was "the triumph of institutional culture" over strategy.[18] The service's ingrained doctrinal rigidity precluded the cognitive processing that was needed to support strategy changes and operational adaptation in the war. This was not a culture that encouraged reflection or experimentation with alternative solutions. Open criticism was rare and even more rarely appreciated or rewarded. Hence, interpretation and investigation were rarely exercised. Operational control was overly centralized and controlling well into 1968, and although reports were compiled regularly, they too often were ignored.[19]

For its part, the Marine Corps cultivates a mix of tradition and mythology to instill a set of beliefs and values. History, rituals, and the so-called "institutional DNA" of the Marines are imprinted early on recruits. In these the Corps celebrates both its "fighters" and "innovators," and reinforces a culture that is comfortable with creative ideas once they prove themselves. This makes the Marines better improvisers and adapters than true innovators. In Iraq, battalion commanders felt empowered to try alternative methods. Conformity was not imposed, and creative-but-pragmatic problem-solving remained part of the Marine mindset.

Learning Mechanisms

There appears to be a positive correlation with what this book has termed *learning mechanisms* and *military change*. Successful commanders have employed a range of techniques—including reports, studies, assessment processes, and dedicated teams—to assist in assessing operational performance and promoting change in praxis. The structural and systematic aspect of enhancing the capability to adapt is rarely examined.[20] The four cases here capture the contribution that such mechanisms have to the interpretation and investigation functions of the learning and adapting process.

The literature has focused on the development of appropriate metrics as a preceptor of adaptation. Wartime adaptation has been hindered by the difficulty in obtaining and analyzing the right information and metrics.[21] Rosen correctly pointed out that the Navy initially lacked the analytical capability to understand the strategic effect that the commerce-targeting campaign was having on Japanese economic and warmaking capacity.[22] The sea service wrestled with that for some time, engrossed in overcoming the perplexing spate of torpedo problems, much as the Army struggled in Vietnam when it was confounded with the hybrid combination of North Vietnamese troops and Viet Cong irregulars. The Air Force also found it difficult to measure the success of its interdiction efforts, both because it lacked photo-reconnaissance capabilities and because it relied too extensively on nighttime bombing, which deprived it of immediate mission assessment by aircrews. In response, the Air Force incorporated the collection of operational performance data and learning into its mission planning cycle. The combination of its operational analysis and performance monitoring kept more senior levels aware of the evolving effectiveness of the Air Force and its operations.

The Army did not lack for learning mechanisms or metrics, but it did struggle to learn and adapt. In-theater personnel produced a mountain of formal reports, studies, and after-action reports, but these did not promote learning. Instead, the Army was swamped by statistics that did little to clarify how effective their units were performing. Rather than highlighting gaps or deficiencies, the Army used the assessment process to reinforce the campaign strategy and deflect criticism—not to support interpretation and investigation of new approaches.[23] MACV suffered from intellectual rigidity and routinely collected vast quantities of statistics without interpreting data for insights about operational methods. There is more to learning than merely capturing metrics and historical details. The organization must use these actually to assess performance and to seek higher levels of effectiveness, and that includes challenging fundamental assumptions.

The Marines had assessment techniques, but they lacked the staff structures or processes to identify and investigate better practices or techniques. The Marine Corps' experience in Al Anbar suggests that organic tactical improvisation did occur as tactical commanders formulated solutions and felt free to adjust them as necessary. However, harvesting and exploiting proven solutions at the operational level was weak. Because the Marines lacked mechanisms to routinely conduct the interpretation and investigation function that would have helped identify and absorb best practices, horizontally or vertically, the Marine Corps units in Iraq could not be considered a learning organization. Gathering knowledge for future force-generation (through the Marine Corps Lessons Learned System) is not the same as exploiting new knowledge to improve the performance levels of units that already are in contact. Hope is not a preferred strategy for war, nor is it a sound Organizational Learning approach.

In all four cases, there is evidence of "learning" capacity being enhanced in wartime. In the case of the Navy, the establishment of technical advisors from the Antisubmarine Warfare Operations Research Group (ASWORG) gave the staff of the Submarine Forces Pacific better insights and more resources for investigating new technologies and doctrine. In the Vietnam case study, the Army Concept Team and MACV's analysis capability were belatedly enlarged. The unit was not effective during the timeframe examined in this book. The Marines also both increased and enhanced their learning mechanisms with the creation of both the staff and the computer software needed to document after-action reports and interviews. As in the case of the Army, the enhanced *learning capacity* did not materially contribute to learning or increased operational performance until later in the conflict.

One of the insights from this portion of the study is the need to practice learning in peacetime rather than standing up new structures and processes in extremis. Learning how to learn in wartime may not be advisable, and like other battlefield functions, it may be best to practice it in peacetime. The Navy's culture seemed to embrace this during that service's major exercises. Separately, recent research offers insights into new practices in the Israeli Defense Force that incorporate daily learning into the rhythm of each Israeli commander's daily staff processes. Such practices suggest how to institutionalize learning, but they also must be attuned to the organizational culture of each military force.[24]

Dissemination Mechanisms

These cases offer insights into the importance of capturing and sharing new tactics and operational praxis. The emphasis here was on vertical absorption from field units to the larger institution. The process of translating operational and tactical learning into institutionalized learning is the final step in the learning cycle. This is usually achieved in military schools and training activities. As Mansoor has observed, without vertical institutional absorption "you end up learning the same lessons over and over again."[25] Recent literature notes how horizontal sharing has produced timely enhancements to organizational performance in conflict.[26] This form of dissemination is relevant to enhancing combat performance in the operational force but is not sufficient by itself for institutionalization.

Dissemination mechanisms facilitate the ability of a military force to forward local learning both horizontally (to units in theater) and vertically (back to the larger institution) to gain wider acceptance and accelerate positive change. The sharing of experiences across the campaign theater can enhance operational effectiveness quickly and improve chances for significant progress. This kind of sharing is needed to exploit bottom-up-driven learning across the larger institution so that it does not have to be relearned by each arriving unit—a costly pattern of *identifying* lessons but not truly *learning* them. In all four cases, the insights and adaptations from operational field units were ultimately fed into formal learning processes at the institutional level, through training and education programs that provided sustained performance improvement for subsequent operations in each war.[27]

Not every case demonstrated horizontal learning. Clearly, the Navy promoted both methods of formal and informal systems through patrol reports and bulletins. However, the lack of lateral or horizontal sharing is an explanation for why Marine Corps adaptations resulting in better counterinsurgency practice were not captured, absorbed, or transmitted except informally between leaders at the battalion level. The failure to create knowledge or learning dissemination mechanisms slowed the rate at which adaptations were recognized and distributed. Thus, adaptations made by individual battalions were not readily absorbed into the larger Marine Corps, a factor that impeded counterinsurgency efforts across Al Anbar well into 2007.[28] Marine Corps leaders exploited informal networks, typically among peers, to gain contextually relevant information and even innovative approaches in order to compensate for weak formal learning mechanisms.[29] The Marine Corps appears to have created the management information system to store knowledge, but not the culture or practice of learning.[30]

Ultimately, institutional adaptation has to be abetted by learning and dissemination mechanisms. These mechanisms can be formalized and made consistent with the learning style or culture of an institution without being centralized. More important, such processes can be designed and employed to offset institutional inertia and promote learning.[31] They may not stimulate learning per se, but they certainly can accelerate learning, both horizontally and vertically, throughout a military organization.[32] These techniques may be better described as "enablers" rather than as shaping influences.

Overall, these cases demonstrate the existence of a dynamic process—one that captures the role of leaders, the influence of culture, and the process of transferring information and lessons from knowledge to practice. The cases also underscore the warning that merely gathering knowledge and storing experiences does not itself constitute learning. Simply recognizing a problem or performance gap per se is not enough. That has led to the old saw about "lessons identified" versus "lessons learned." The true measures of a learning organization are *actual* adaptation and *real* changes in outputs or performance. Knowledge must be translated into an enhanced level of organizational capability by either modified or new competencies. Some organizations master this competition better than others. Organizational Learning Capacity offers an explanation for how this is achieved.

An assessment of the components of Organizational Learning Capacity from the case studies is displayed in table 7.1. The table summarizes the strength and character (positive or negative) of each component in the four cases. These cases illustrate the role that the shaping and enabling attributes of Organizational Learning Capacity have on military change in war. Overall, organizational leadership and culture are invaluable contributors for adaptation in wartime and are decisive factors and key shaping influences for Organizational Learning. Yet, they are not enough by themselves. Without supporting structures and processes true organizational learning remains local and focused on the tactical rather than becoming

Table 7.1. Aggregate Assessment of Organizational Learning Capacity

	U.S. Navy Subs in Pacific	U.S. Air Force in Korea	U.S. Army in Vietnam	U.S. Marines in Al Anbar
Leadership	Strong (Positive)	Strong (Positive)	Strong (Negative)	Strong (tactical)
Organizational Culture	Strong	Strong (Positive)	Strong (Negative)	Strong (Mixed)
Learning Mechanisms	Strong	Strong	Weak (plural means but no support)	Limited
Dissemination Mechanisms	Strong	Moderate	Moderate (largely doctrine)	Limited

widespread and strategic in its scope. Without formal learning and dissemination mechanisms, institutional adaptation is slow and constantly reoccurring. As is evidenced in research drawn from Australian and British army examples, informal learning processes have both a limited reach and local influence, and they do not generate the kind of institution-wide learning that can lock in new and better methods.[33]

Implications for Military Theory

The case studies examined here, involving different armed forces conducting different kinds of warfare in different eras, confirm the general utility of organizational learning theory and argue for placing it among the major approaches to thinking about military change.

A theory that explains how individuals engage in productive problem-solving in the face of perceived organizational shortfalls or performance gaps—and how such learning is fed into more collective organizational groups and diffused across an institution as large as a military service—helps in understanding change in wartime. In particular, a theory that details how extant knowledge, mental models, and routines frame commanders' decision-making provides insights on how the education of officers might be enhanced. Any theory that explains the complexities of adjusting existing core competencies is useful and offers explanatory power if not instrumental value. More important, a theory that helps explain how organizations can effectively learn in a competitive environment and adjust competencies to increase performance levels has general prescriptive utility. Harnessing this theory to exploit the faster absorption of proven experiences into the repertoire of an institution for effective application, could have significant implications for creating military organizations that are better postured both to recognize the need to adapt and to demonstrate the ability to do so.

Organizational Learning Levels

The case studies support the construct of single- or double-loop learning from Organizational Learning theory and confirm the differentiation made in the literature between single-loop learning and double-loop learning and their utility to the understanding of change. The cases examined were of sufficient duration and robust enough to permit the examination of both levels. Most of the adaptations examined here were cases of simple lower-level learning. But each case also included an example of a major adaptation that challenged the identity or institutional belief system in some way.

Double-loop learning is inherently more difficult, reinforcing Rosen's conclusions about wartime innovation.[34] In theory, the acceptance of such adaptation would be expected to be more difficult and require more time, as well as more institutional buy-in or the application of external pressure. The cases presented here suggest that adaptation is an evolution of existing competencies to a new environment or opponent and is more than the simple correction of errors, and that adaptive learning can be institutionalized, even though double-loop learning takes longer and occurs at a much higher level of the organization.[35]

As seen in the case of submarine warfare in the Pacific and the air-assault tactics in Vietnam, adaptation can incrementally lead to major change or innovation in both means and methods.[36] Numerous adjustments to tactics and equipment were made to enhance the lethality of submarines over time and by 1943 they were a formidable weapon against Japan's shipping and lines of communication.

Table 7.2 below displays the adaptations contained in the case studies by their characterization as single-loop or double-loop.

Examining the adaptation cases this way produces a distinct finding. In each case of double-loop adaptation, the origins appear to be generally top-down driven. This may reflect the level of authority required to apply resources. In the case of submarine adaptation, the shift to wolfpack or collective-action groups probably was a reflection of the desire at the highest levels of the Navy to bring the performance of the submarine force up to the level of what the German U-boats were achieving in the Atlantic. Even when an adaptation was imposed from the top, its details were produced organically in the fleet. In the case of the MRAP, the original request came from middle-grade officers who were intimately aware of both the problem and how their proposed solution was a logical fit.

Similarly, in both Vietnam and Iraq, it appears that senior political leaders imposed the changes after military institutions failed to adapt appropriately. It took President Johnson's decision to send Robert Komer to Vietnam to get the Army to focus on the "other war"—pacification and economic aid. Yet, there is evidence that some Army leaders wanted to adopt these before Komer began his mission. Similarly, although Marines in Iraq wanted the MRAP, they could not convince the service's senior leaders to support that request. Even when Marine Corps leaders eventually agreed that they wanted the MRAP vehicle in order to enhance troop survivability, they did not allocate any budget resources. It was Defense Secretary Gates' decision that provided the resources and eliminated all the roadblocks.

Civilian Inputs to Military Change

The fact that it sometimes took civilian pressure for the services to adopt new equipment or ideas counters a major finding in the innovation literature. Rosen postulated that civilian influence in major military innovation was minimal, and suggested that civilians had no role in wartime changes.[37] This research effort suggests that the opposite may be true. There is little civilian input into most forms of adaptation during conflict, as seen in each case studied here. However, in two cases—Army helicopter doctrine and the MRAP—there is clear and significant civilian influence that was crucial to the initiation and sustainment of the innovation. There is less evidence of civilian inputs into the Navy's development of collective-action groups, although technical assistance by civilian scientists played

Table 7.2. Single- and Double-Loop Adaptations

	U.S. Navy Subs	U.S. Air Force, in Korea	U.S. Army in Vietnam	Marines in Al Anbar
Single Loop	Night surface attack tactics	Airborne TAC	Air assault tactics	Intelligence Fusion Centers
	Torpedo tests/Fixes	F-80 mods	Firepower adjustments and technologies	Culture Center/Training
	Radar/Sonar introduction	Night interdiction ops	Mobile riverine force	CAP/Training teams
	Unrestricted targeting	Bombers in CAS (night)		Non-kinetic counterinsurgency tools/tactics
		Design changes to Sabre jet fighters and gunsites		Tribal engagement
		Night fighters		
		Jet assisted take offs		
		Night bombing via SHORAN and radar		
		Precision-guided bombs Razon/Tarzon		
		Flares for night bombing		
Double Loop Learning	Wolfpack/ Collective Action Groups	F-51 Reversions	Pacification/CORDS	MRAP Vehicle
		B-29s in close air support		

a significant role in the development of ship-to-ship communications and sonar used by American wolfpacks. The civilian influence on the decision to establish CORDS within MACV and the extensive civilian support for introducing MRAPs into Iraq for the Marines is consistent with the Interventionist approach advocated by Posen, and it extends his peacetime theory about military doctrine into military change during war.[38]

Indeed, the idea that civilian political leaders do not have a significant role in promoting wartime adaptation or innovation is not supported by the cases in this book. Instead, our study suggests that both top-down military guidance *and* senior civilian involvement in pushing for adaptation actually may be necessary to alter the services' missions, roles, and sense of identity. A former secretary of defense has already absorbed this lesson based on his own experiences at the Pentagon, where he was involved with accelerating the MRAP acquisition.[39]

The Sources of Military Change

For the past decade research in the field has focused on the sources of military adaptation, with an emphasis on studying bottom-up change, initiated at the tactical level, rather than top-down-driven alterations. By contrast, most broad innovation theories tend to emphasize top-down approaches.

However, the different forms of adaptation laid out in the cases in this book suggest that crediting a single direction may not fully address the range of options. The Navy case study shows instances of both top-down and bottom-up forces. The decision to order submarines to conduct unrestricted warfare, for example, was directed from the highest echelons of the Navy and civilian government, yet the origins of the strategy shift actually began with students at the Naval War College. Furthermore, the "how" was largely determined by the Pacific submarine force and modified frequently by actual combat experience, not outside pressures. The one exception to this was the implementation of wolfpack tactics, and even in that case implementation was driven internally from the submarine force.

In Vietnam, the Army's operational methods were developed by General Westmoreland and his staff, and although they were intensely scrutinized and debated they rarely encountered interference. Apart from the approval of overall force levels in-theater, the conduct of the ground war was under Westmoreland's control. It took top-down political pressure from Washington to get MACV to absorb the concept of the pacification programs and provide appropriate resources to carry them out. Although there were always vocal advocates such as John Paul Vann pushing these ideas from the bottom, pacification efforts languished for years, and ultimately the president directed the establishment of CORDS under MACV.

Conversely, top-down direction impeded adaptation in Al Anbar for some time. Instead of supporting a comprehensive counterinsurgency, the campaign strategy under which both Army and Marine Corps forces operated prioritized the standup and transition to national Iraqi security forces. The strategy emphasized the use of fewer and bigger camps, too far away from the major urban centers for effective counterinsurgency. Well before the now-famous *FM 3-24 Counterinsurgency Field Manual* was crafted back in the United States and before President George W. Bush changed leaders and force levels for Iraq, a few commanders ignored the campaign plan and began applying appropriate tactics that produced dramatic results.[40]

Recent historical assessments by the Army suggest that the problem was not isolated to the Marine Corps. Army veterans looking back have noted that although their culture generated innovative thinking from lower-level tactical units, the institutional Army did not recognize it and in fact inhibited innovative thinking. The Army's formal lessons-learned study observed:

> Indeed, it seems that the most successful innovators were actually inverting policy rather than operating within policy, most notably in the case of the brigade and battalion-level COIN (counterinsurgency) approaches of 2005–2006. This is a fact that the Army has not really confronted, and it seems possible that the in the Iraq War the Army actually tended to penalize successful leaders who challenged their commanders.[41]

By contrast, in Iraq the Marine Corps gave its local commanders leeway to seek their own improvised solutions and did not take adverse actions. Rather, it rewarded the most adaptative; most were promoted several times over, ultimately to general officers.

The counterinsurgency doctrine developed for Iraq was certainly catalyzed by demonstrated tactical adaptation in the field, and those experiences were seized by the top of institutions to legitimize adaptations for use servicewide.[42] This suggests a more dialectic or dynamic process. The tactical concepts embedded in *FM 3-24* were the result of bottom-driven initiatives from creative commanders such as Army Lt. Gen. H. R. McMaster and Marine Corps Gen. Julian D. Alford and then assimilated by leaders such as Army Gen. David H. Petraeus and Marine Corps Gen. James N. Mattis, catalyzing a larger debate that sought to gain consensus for a solution to Iraq's insurgency from successful tactical experience. As such, the manual should be seen as the product of bottom–up driven adaptation, which was ultimately integrated by the doctrinal process and then institutionalized in both the Army and Marine Corps.[43]

This suggests a more dynamic model of adaptation that blends top-down- and bottom-up-driven perspectives, particularly in cases involving more than tactical adaptation. What is not clear is whether this is a case of a dialectic of opposing organizational actors, as cyber and innovation expert Nina A. Kollars suggests, or is merely the confluence of forces.[44]

Dynamics of Internal and External Forces

Nevertheless, the dynamics of military change involved may be more complex than the focus on direction implies. This book was oriented to internal shapers or enablers of adaptation. The underlying hypothesis of the research was that wartime pressures generate the impetus or incentives that overcome traditional resistance to change by military organizations. It was the confluence or nexus of institutional factors *internal* to the military organization that were presumed to entirely shape its recognition of the performance gap and its ability to find and implement corrective actions to adapt. Although the cases in this book confirm the importance of both formal institutional processes and intangibles like organizational culture, they suggest the involvement of *both* internal and external shapers.

Theo Farrell has demonstrated the dynamic influence of a set of external shapers on British wartime innovation in military operations in Afghanistan.[45] Although the relevance of such external sources of innovation was not originally part of this book, their impact is difficult to ignore. There was evidence in each of the cases to argue that a mix of exogenous and endogenous factors shape how military organizations respond to threats. External shapers appear to have had relatively limited influence on the conduct of the Navy's submarine offensives in the Pacific during World War II. No doubt, American strategic culture indirectly advanced U.S. submarine technology over the course of the war and framed its strategic and offensive use against Japan's economic vulnerabilities. Both strategic culture and international law constrained the Navy's prewar thinking about unrestricted warfare, since that practice violated existing treaties and moral considerations. The attack on Pearl Harbor animated domestic politics and minimized moral constraints on unrestricted warfare, and permitted the Navy to wage an offensive campaign, with little remorse for the niceties of maritime law. External shapers, particularly civil–military relations, injected some influence. The decision to pursue the defeat of Germany as the principal opponent and a strategic priority reflected U.S. strategic culture and its European roots.

External influences also had a clear impact on Army adaptations in Vietnam. American strategic culture influenced the Army's overall offensive approach and how U.S. military leaders interacted with the White House in policy deliberations.[46] While its organic Way of War induced the Army to think in conventional terms and to employ large-scale firepower, the service's adaptations in technological approaches were distinctly shaped by host nation and domestic politics. The presidential decision to create CORDS also shows the influence of civilian-military relations during the war.

The impact of external shapers or drivers is evident, if slightly more muted, in the Marine Corps case study. U.S. Marine Corps operations in Al Anbar were more isolated from Iraq's central government and U.S. attention. American support for democracy and centralized national solutions is clear: it resulted in the election of a Shi'a-dominated government in Baghdad, which precluded early consideration of tribal issues and blocked overt support to the Sunni-based population of Al Anbar province. Thus, coalition politics and U.S. strategic culture—i.e., support for elected democratic government—were distinctive shapers that limited early adoption of the tribal engagement option.

As a result, while military change may be pursued entirely by senior leaders of a military organization, external shaping factors cannot be overlooked. As anthropologist Paula Holmes-Eber has argued, "military and organizational change is not unidirectional." Rather, it stems from "an interactive process, in which external shifts and pressures from the state, society, and the battlefield are integrated and reworked into the unique internal cultural and structural patterns of the specific military organization."[47] This dynamic interaction of external shapers and internal factors was demonstrated in all four case histories under examination.

This suggests that military change in general and adaptation more specifically may best be studied as a dynamic process involving both *internal* and *external* shapers. What often might be mistaken as an inability to learn is actually a product of numerous influences, including cognitive limitations, strong or weak learning mechanisms, organizational politics, military culture, and civil-military relations that thwart accurate assessment and agile adaptation.[48] It is doubtful that a learning failure is the result of a single causal factor.

Implications

From the cases considered, there appear to be at least four implications for the joint warfighting community in the United States armed services:

1. *Leadership development.* Senior officers must be educated to understand how enhanced operational performance is tied to collaborative and open command climates, where biases, preferences, or erroneous assumptions can be challenged. Senior defense officials should continue to promote decentralized leadership techniques, but they should not let "mission command" excuse commanders from oversight or learning or from providing support or recognizing good or bad practices for absorption into praxis by other units. Educational programs should develop and promote leaders who can remain flexible, question existing paradigms, and work within teams of diverse backgrounds to generate collaboration and greater creativity.

2. *Cultural flexibility over compliance.* Military organizations should instill cultures that embrace collaborative and creative problem-solving and display a tolerance for free or critical thinking. Cultures that are controlling or doctrinally dogmatic or that strongly reinforce conformity should not be expected to be adaptive. Commanders should be educated on the need to create climates in which new ideas and their champions are more than simply tolerated. If institutions are to be successful over the long haul or adaptive in adverse circumstances, actively promoting diversity and imaginative thinking is a must.

3. *Learning mechanisms.* Commanders should be prepared to use operational assessments to allow themselves to interpret the many signals and forms of

feedback that occur in combat situations. If needed, special action teams or formalized learning teams can be used to identify, capture, and harvest examples of successful adaptation. They should codify a standard process to collect lessons from current operations for rapid horizontal sharing. They also must be prepared to translate insights laterally into modified praxis for operational forces, and not just institutionalize these lessons for future campaigns through post-conflict changes in doctrine, organization, or education.

4. *Dissemination mechanisms* can be best thought of as a key enabling factor in passing on best practices and conferring legitimacy to adaptations. It is clear that formal and informal mechanisms are crucial in the diffusion of new forms of adaptation and increasing organizational effectiveness across the larger institution. Without them, tacit knowledge at local levels cannot be shared or absorbed. Thus, operational knowledge and lessons-learned collection efforts should be improved, principally by a closer connection between operational forces and military educational centers. The rigorous validation and institutionalization of lessons and best practices is more than simply warehousing new information.

Future Research Directions

An obvious but often overlooked insight emerged in concluding this book: over the course of study it was noted that different kinds of adaptation emerge.[49] These may include organizational adjustments or new tactical structures, technological, or materiel changes in weapons or equipment, or doctrinal modifications, or Tactics, Techniques, and Procedures aids (TTPs) that constitute a shift in operational praxis. As Stuart Griffin, a U.K.-based defense scholar, has argued persuasively, there is a need for greater rigor in the military innovation studies field, and moving on to the study of change by the nature of the various forms adaptation may take is an example of where the field might expand. The current age portends major technological changes, which no doubt will impel organizational and doctrinal change as well.

One potential area for study in this field is a deeper inquiry into how leaders influence a service's culture. Military leaders (or their civilian masters) must promote organizational adaptation during wartime with different techniques, embedding mechanisms or incentives based upon the kind of adaption required. Leaders will need to identify which approaches should be used under what circumstances and match them to the task at hand. Templates or cookie-cutter solutions may not be appropriate across the range of adaptation situations encountered. This insight has implications for military leadership development and educational purposes.[50]

There are some key questions in this regard. What are the specific tools employed by successful leaders in initiating adaptive changes? What are the limits of culture and what are the most effective mechanisms for stimulating investigation and rapid adaptation? Should leaders mask or disguise adaptation or major innovations as "merely temporary" or "evolutionary" change?[51] If the culture of a service or branch is infected with resistance to the desired change, what tools or reinforcing mechanisms are suggested? Schein suggests a framework of numerous mechanisms, ranging from the allocation of rewards to "excommunication."[52]

A related area for possible exploration is the use of experimental units as a means of overcoming bureaucratic or political resistance to innovations or adaptation. Grissom identified this as a potential area of study, and a recent study of the Israeli Defense Forces depicted a heavy reliance on purpose-built units centered on a dynamic tactical leader to create and refine a possible adaptation or remedy.[53] Both Marcus and Jensen seem to agree that "incubators" are necessary. These would not likely be bottom-up initiatives, however. The authority and resources to create nonstandard formations is more associated with senior officials. It is not enough to have mavericks or entrepreneurs pushing up from the bottom; they have to have access to higher levels of the organization, where the authority and resources to make organizational decisions and acquire technological solutions is situated. As one practitioner has noted, "identifying lessons and teaching them is not enough. Authority and power are essential for learning and implementation."[54]

Conclusion

Given the fundamental nature of war as an interactive conflict between competing polities, the ability to adapt is essential to success in wartime. If true, this research is both timely and relevant.

Modern military forces need to better understand how to facilitate, if not accelerate, adaptation to increase their odds of success in future wars. The capacity to adapt to unforeseen conditions and unanticipated military and technological contexts could well be even more important to the effectiveness of military forces than was the case in the twentieth century. To be successful in the twenty-first century, armed forces will have to learn, unlearn, and relearn with some degree of alacrity. Recently a historian reinforced that conclusion, observing that "the ability to adapt at every level of war from the tactical to the strategic and political would seem to be more important . . . than any time since 1941."[55]

The accelerating technological complexity of war is certainly one factor reinforcing this conclusion.[56] Another is the broadening array of missions for which military forces must be prepared, among them homeland security, responding to Ebola-infected areas, combatting terrorists, or conducting combined-arms warfare. Given the uncertainty of the future security environment, the ability to change rapidly may, therefore, not be just a source of relative tactical advantage, but a competitive necessity of strategic importance.

This book is a response to the challenges posed by scholars such as Farrell and Grissom to examine bottom-up sources of innovation and adaptation.[57] It also responds to Foley's challenge to integrate the literatures between disciplines in business and military history, and closely examine the process of how armies and navies learn.[58] Finally it responds to Griffin's lament for more discipline and interdisciplinary approaches in innovation studies.[59]

In this effort, a more holistic and multilevel learning model was postulated and tested against four cases. These demonstrated the validity of the internal enablers that constitute Organizational Learning Capacity.

In sum, Organizational Learning Capacity is generated by a combination of factors, including an institution that promotes a deep understanding of history coupled with a decentralized leadership philosophy; a culture that promotes a flexible, realistic and nondogmatic operational doctrine; the organizational capacity to explore ideas and alternative modes of praxis; and both formal and informal information-sharing practices. This capacity ensures that bottom-up change is absorbed, and that changes with merit in the larger mission of the military service are institutionalized.

Although bottom-up ideas are often the source or impetus for change, the institutional level remains critical. Institutional adaptation is needed to sustain adaptive learning that occurs at the tactical level and exploits the learning for the benefit of the entire organization. This is true regardless of the scale or timing of change.

It is institutions that create and sustain the core values of their bureaucracy, and it is at this level that decisions and policies to educate and train the force are made. It is the institutions that create and enforce the norms, beliefs, rituals, and even the operating code of their respective operational forces. They create the mechanisms, culture, and doctrine that are the "ghost in the machine" of every military institution.[60] These factors can either promote or retard changes, and ignoring that reality only hamstrings greater organizational performance and sustained results.

Military forces have always had to learn how to learn and then use that knowledge to change in order to succeed. As Farrell reminds us, "War invariably throws up challenges that require states and their militaries to adapt. Indeed, it is virtually impossible for states and militaries to anticipate all of the problems they will face in war, however much they try to do so."[61] Force development and design in peacetime can only accomplish so much. Once the tocsin sounds, the ability of an institution to learn and adapt comes into play and often determines success. Mars must not just harvest information; it must adapt in order to win.

Notes

Chapter 1. Introduction

1. Michael Howard, "Military Science in an Age of Peace," *Journal of the Royal United Services Institute* 119 (March 1974): 3–11.

2. Victor Davis Hanson, *The Father of Us All, War and History* (New York: Bloomsbury, 2010), 123–24.

3. Quoted in Eric Schmitt, "Iraq-Bound Troops Confront Rumsfeld Over Lack of Armor," *New York Times*, December 8, 2004.

4. Carl von Clausewitz, *On War*, Michael Howard and Peter Paret, eds. (Princeton: Princeton University Press, 1984), 193.

5. Chuck Hagel, *Quadrennial Defense Review 2014* (Washington: Department of Defense, 2014), 22–25.

6. U.S. Joint Chiefs of Staff, *A Decade at War, Enduring Lessons from the Past Decade of Operations* (Suffolk, VA: June 2012), 19–21.

7. See the concluding chapter, "Military Adaptation and the War in Afghanistan," by Frans P. B. Osinga and James Russell, in Theo Farrell, Frans P. B. Osinga, and James A. Russell, eds., *Military Adaptation in Afghanistan* (Stanford: Stanford University Press, 2013).

8. Chad C. Serena, *A Revolution in Military Adaptation: The US Army in the Iraq War* (Washington: Georgetown University Press, 2011).

9. David A. Fastabend and Robert H. Simpson, "Adapt or Die: The Imperative for a Culture of Innovation in the United States Army," *Army* (February 2004): 14–25.

10. U.S. Army Training and Doctrine Command, *The Army Capstone Concept—Operational Adaptability: Operating Under Conditions of Uncertainty and Complexity in an Era of Persistent Conflict, 2016–2028* (TRADOC Pam 525–3–0) (Fort Monroe, VA: TRADOC, 2010).

11. Barry Watts and Williamson Murray, "Military Innovation in Peacetime," in Williamson Murray and Allan Millett, eds., *Innovation in the Interwar Period* (New York: Cambridge University Press, 1995), 414; Williamson Murray, *Military Adaptation in War, Fear of Change* (New York: Cambridge University Press, 2011), 5.

12. Murray, *Military Adaptation in War*, 313.

13. Jurgen E. Forster, "The Dynamics of Volksgemeinschaft: The Effectiveness of the German Military Establishment in the Second World War," especially 199–214, in Allan R. Millett and Williamson Murray, eds., *Military Effectiveness, The Second World War*, vol. 3 (New York: Cambridge University Press, 2010).

14. Rick Atkinson, *An Army at Dawn: The War in North Africa, 1942–1943* (New York: Holt, 2007), 339–92.

15. Eliot A. Cohen and John Gooch, *Military Misfortunes: The Anatomy of Failure in War* (New York: Free Press, 1996), 95–131.

16. Abraham Rabinovich, *The Yom Kippur War* (New York: Schoken, 2004), 339–440; Finkel, *On Flexibility*, 150–178; Murray, *Military Adaptation in War*, 262–304.

17. Stephen P. Rosen, *Winning the Next War, Innovation and the Modern Military* (Ithaca: Cornell University Press, 1991), 20–21.

18. Theo Farrell and Terry Terriff, *The Sources of Military Change: Culture, Politics, Technology* (London: Lynne Rienner, 2002), 6.

19. Farrell, "Introduction," Farrell, Osinga, and Russell, eds., *Military Adaptation in Afghanistan*, 2.

20. Adapted from Anthony Dibella, Edwin Nevis, and Janet Gould, "Understanding Organizational Learning Capability," *Journal of Management Studies* 33, no. 3 (October, 1996): 363.

21. Adam Grissom, "The Future of Military Innovation Studies," *Journal of Strategic Studies* 29, no. 5 (October 2006): 905–34.

22. Farrell and Terriff, *Military Change*, 6.

23. Cohen and Gooch, *Military Misfortunes*, 222.

24. Cohen and Gooch.

25. James Lacey and Kevin Woods, "Adapt or Die," U.S. Naval Institute *Proceedings* (August 2007): 16–21.

26. David E. Johnson, *Fast Tanks and Heavy Bombers: Innovation in the U.S. Army 1917–1945* (Ithaca, NY: Cornell University Press, 1998); William O. Odom, *After the Trenches: The Transformation of U.S. Army Doctrine, 1918–1939* (College Station: Texas A&M University Press, 1999); Thomas Hone, Norman Friedman, and Mark Mandeles, *American and British Aircraft Carrier Development* (Annapolis: Naval Institute Press, 1999).

27. On U.S. insights into the RMA see Admiral William A. Owens Jr. and Joseph S. Nye, "America's Information Edge," *Foreign Affairs* (March–April 1996); Richard O. Hundley, *Past Revolutions, Future Transformations* (Santa Monica: RAND, 1999); Owens, "The Once and Future American Revolution in Military Affairs," *Joint Force Quarterly* (Summer 2002): 55–61; Andrew Krepinevich Jr., "The Unfinished Revolution in Military Affairs," *Issues in Science and Technology* (Summer 2003).

28. Clayton Christenson, *Innovator's Dilemma, When New Technologies Cause Great Firms to Fail* (Cambridge, MA.: Harvard Business School, 1997). See also Terry Pierce, *Warfighting and Disruptive Technologies* (London: Frank Cass, 2004).

29. Williamson Murray, "Thinking about Revolutions in Military Affairs," *Joint Force Quarterly* (Summer 1998): 37–44.

30. Eliot A. Cohen, "Change and Transformation in Military Affairs," *Journal of Strategic Studies* 27, no. 3 (September 2004): 395–407; Fredrick W. Kagan, *Finding the Target, The Transformation of American Military Policy* (New York: Encounter Books, 2006).

31. On transformation see Andrew Krepinevich, *Transforming the American Military* (Washington: Center for Strategic and Budgetary Assessments, 1997); Andrew Krepinevich, "Why No Transformation," *Joint Force Quarterly* (Autumn/Winter 1999–2000): 97–100; Donald Rumsfeld, "Transforming the Military," *Foreign Affairs* (May–June 2002): 20–32; Donald Rumsfeld, *DOD Transformation Planning Guidance* (Washington: Department of Defense, April 2003). For an overview of both U.S. and European perspectives see Theo Farrell, Sten Rynning, and Terry Terriff, *Transforming Military Power since the Cold War: Britain, France and the United States, 1991–2012* (New York: Cambridge University Press, 2013).

32. Arguably, advanced information systems and unmanned systems were relevant to operations in both Iraq and Afghanistan. Keith L. Shimko, *The Iraq Wars and America's Military Revolution* (New York: Cambridge University Press, 2010).

33. For a detailed historical study see Bruce I. Gudmundsson, *Stormtroop Tactics, Innovation in the German Army, 1914–1918* (Westport: Praeger, 1993), 40–93; Timothy T. Lupfer, "The Dynamics of Doctrine: The Change in German Tactical Doctrine during the First World War" (Fort Leavenworth: Combat Studies Institute, July 1981).

34. Michael D. Doubler, *Closing with the Enemy: How GIs Fought the War in Europe: 1944–1945* (Lawrence: University of Kansas Press, 1994); Russell A. Hart, *Clash of Arms: How the Allies Won in Normandy* (Boulder: Lynne Reinner, 2001).

35. John Nagl, *Counterinsurgency Lessons from Malaya and Vietnam: Learning to Eat Soup with a Knife* (Westport, CT: Praeger, 2002). See also Richard Downie, *Learning from Conflict, The U.S. Military in Vietnam, El Salvador, and the Drug War* (New York: Praeger 1998).

36. Meir Finkel, *On Flexibility, Recovery from Technological and Doctrinal Surprise on the Battlefield* (Stanford: Stanford Security Studies, 2011).

37. Finkel, 2.

38. Finkel. His theory used four "strata" or organizational attributes: (a) doctrinal flexibility, (b) organizational and technological diversity, (c) flexible command and cognitive skills, and (d) mechanisms for the rapid dissemination of lessons learned.

39. Murray, *Military Adaptation in War*, 1.

40. James A. Russell, *Innovation, Transformation, and War, Counterinsurgency Operations in Anbar and Ninewa Provinces, Iraq, 2005–2007* (Stanford: Stanford Security Studies, 2011).

41. Russell, 194.

42. Serena, *A Revolution in Military Adaptation*, 104–19. A more positive assessment of the Army (and Marine Corps) as learning organizations is contained in Janine Davidson, *Lifting the Fog of Peace, How Americans Learned to Fight Modern War* (Ann Arbor: University of Michigan Press, 2010).

43. Farrell's "Introduction" in Farrell, Osinga, and Russell, eds., *Military Adaptation in Afghanistan*, 1–18.

44. Farrell, Osinga, and Russell. See the concluding chapter by Osinga and Russell, 288–307.

45. Anne-Marie Grisogono and Vanja Radenovic, "The Adaptive Stance" (Canberra, Australia: Defence Science and Technology Organization, 2006).

46. Especially Rosen, *Winning the Next War*; Downie, *Learning After Conflict*; and Nagl, *Learning to Eat Soup with a Knife*.

47. Murray, *Military Adaptation in War*, 2.

Chapter 2. On Change

1. Millett, "Patterns of Military Innovation in the Interwar Period," in Murray and Millett, *Military Innovation in the Interwar Period*, 335.

2. Barry R. Posen, *The Sources of Military Doctrine* (Ithaca: Cornell University Press, 1984).

3. Posen, 224.

4. On French and British doctrinal developments based on culture see Kimberly Kier, *Imagining War, British and French Military Doctrine between the Wars* (Princeton: Princeton University Press, 1997), 56–58 and 109–39; and Stephen Rosen, *Winning the Next War*, 10–11. On German innovation see Williamson Murray, "Armored Warfare, the British, French and German Experiences," 6–49, and "Strategic Bombing: The British American and German Experiences," 96–142 in Murray and Millett, *Military Innovation in the Interwar Period*.

5. Deborah Avant, *Political Institutions and Military Change, Lessons from Peripheral Wars* (Ithaca: Cornell University Press, 1994), 8.

6. Avant, 6.

7. Avant, 2.

8. Avant, 47.

9. Daniel A. Levinthal and James G. March, "The Myopia of Learning," *Strategic Management Journal* 14 (1993): 95–112.

10. Rosen, *Winning the Next War*, 5.

11. Rosen, 29, 35.

12. Rosen, 7.

13. Rosen, 251.

14. Rosen, 18–20.

15. Rosen, 180.

16. Graham Allison and Phil Zelikow, *Essence of Decision* (New York: Addison-Wesley Longman, Ltd., 1996); and Morton Halperin, *Bureaucratic Politics and Foreign Policy* (Washington: Brookings Institution, 1974).

17. Harvey M. Sapolsky, *The Polaris System Development: Bureaucratic and Programmatic Success in Government* (Cambridge: Harvard University Press, 1972).

18. Vincent Davis, *The Politics of Innovation: Patterns in Navy Cases* (Denver: University of Denver, 1967); Bradd C. Hayes and Douglas Smith, eds., *The Politics of Naval Innovation* (Newport: Naval War College, Research Report, 4–94, 1994); Owen R. Cote Jr., *The Politics of Innovative Military Doctrine: The U.S. Navy and Fleet Ballistic Missiles* (Boston: Massachusetts Institute of Technology, 1995).

19. Victor Krulak, *First to Fight, An Inside View of the Marine Corps* (Annapolis: Naval Institute Press, 1999).

20. Sapolsky, "On the Theory of Military Innovation," *Breakthroughs* 9, no. 1 (Spring 2000): 35–39.

21. Sapolsky, "Interservice Competition: The Solution, Not the Problem," *Joint Force Quarterly* no. 15 (Spring 1997): 53. Rosen argues that "interservice competition has its creative aspects. Every organization tends to stagnate when it becomes the only game in town or when competition is rigged, from the big three auto makers to IBM, and the Postal Service. Without competitive pressure, the need to respond quickly to changing circumstances or opportunities is reduced." Stephen P. Rosen, "Service Redundancy: Waste or Hidden Capability?" *Joint Force Quarterly* (Summer 1993): 36.

22. Sapolsky, "Interservice Competition," 50.

23. James R. Locher, *Victory on the Potomac: The Goldwater-Nichols Act Unifies the Pentagon* (College Station: Texas A&M University Press, 2002); Christopher Bourne, "Unintended Consequences of the Goldwater-Nichols Act," *Joint Force Quarterly* (Spring 1998): 99–108.

24. This study will refer consistently to Organizational Learning Theory and apply it at all levels of a military service and not merely a tactical (company) or operational level (i.e., division or brigade combat team).

25. R. Cyert and James G. March, *A Behavioural Theory of the Firm* (Englewood Cliffs: Prentice Hall, 1963); Chris Argyris and Don Schon, *Organizational Learning: A Theory of Action Perspective* (New York: Addison-Wesley Longman, Ltd., 1978); R. L. Daft and George Huber, "How Organizations Learn, A Communications Framework," *Research in the Sociology of Organizations* 5 (1987); Barbara Levitt and James G. March, "Organizational Learning," *Annual Review of Sociology*, 14 (1988): 319–40.

26. John S. Richard, *The Learning Army: Approaching the 21st Century as a Learning Organization* (Carlisle: Army War College, 1997); Mike Rigsby, *The Learning Organization, Concept and Application* (Carlisle: Army War College, 1997).

27. Peter Senge, *The Fifth Discipline, The Art and Practice of the Learning Organization* (New York: Currency, 1990), 13.

28. On Australian advances see O'Toole and Talbot, "Fighting for Knowledge," 42–67. For a comparison of British and U.S. Army enhancements see Robert T. Foley, Stuart Griffin, and Helen McCartney, "'Transformation in Contact': Learning the Lessons of Modern War," *International Affairs*, 87, no. 2 (March 2011): 253–70.

29. David A. Garvin, "Building a Learning Organization," *Harvard Business Review,* 71 (July–August 1993), 80.

30. Scott Moreland and Scott Jasper, "Adaptive Organizations Maintaining Competitive Advantage by Exploiting Change" in Derrick Neal et al, eds. *Crosscutting Issues in International Transformation,* (Ft. McNair: Center for Technology and National Security Policy, 2010).

31. Anthony J. Dibella, Edwin C. Nevis and Janet M. Gould, "Understanding Organizational Learning Capability," *Journal of Management Studies* 33, no. 3 (May 1996): 363.

32. Grissom, "The Future of Military Innovation Studies," 920.

33. Russell, *Innovation, Transformation and War*, 35.

34. Argyris, "Double Loop Learning in Organizations," *Harvard Business Review* (September–October 1977): 115–24.

35. Peter M. Senge, "The Leaders New Work: Building Learning Organizations" *Sloan Management Review* (Fall 1990): 7–23.

36. C. Fiol and M. Lyles, "Organizational Learning," *Academy of Management Review* 10 (1985): 803–13.

37. Mary M. Crossan, Henry W. Lane, Roderick E. White, and Lisa Djurfeldt, "Organizational Learning, Dimensions for a Theory," *International Journal of Organizational Analysis* 3, no. 4 (October, 1995): 354.

38. Grissom, footnote 122. Grissom notes that "the characteristics of organizational learning are, as interpreted by Nagl and Downie, limited to information gathering," with a deliberative and centralized decision-making process.

39. Downie, *Learning from Conflict*, 22.

40. Garvin, "Building a Learning Organization," 80.

41. In addition to Serena, examples include Keith B. Bickel, *Mars Learning: The Marine Corps' Development of Small War Doctrine, 1915–1940* (Boulder: Westview, 2001); as well as Les Brownlee and Peter J. Schoomaker, "Serving a Nation at War: A Campaign Quality Army with Joint and Expeditionary Capabilities," *Parameters* (Summer 2004): 5–23.

42. Cited in David Schmidtchen, *The Rise of the Strategic Private: Technology, Control and Change in a Network Enabled Military* (Canberra, Australia: Land Warfare Studies Centre, 2007), 183.

43. Michael Horowitz, *The Diffusion of Military Power, Causes and Consequences for International Politics* (Princeton: Princeton University Press, 2010).

44. Horowitz, 33.

45. W. M. Cohen and D. A. Levinthal, "Absorptive Capacity: A New Perspective on Learning and Innovation," *Administrative Science Quarterly* 35, no. 1 (1990): 128–52.

46. Matthew Alan Tattar, *Innovation and Adaptation in War*, Ph.D. dissertation, Brandeis University, February, 2011.

47. Tattar, 24.

48. Peter Paret, *The Cognitive Challenge of War: Prussia, 1806* (Princeton: Princeton University Press, 2009).

49. Adamsky review, *The Diffusion of Military Power*, 436.

50. Change and adaptation should reflect that it occurs relative to an adversary in a time-competitive environment.

51. These are best exemplified by the peacetime innovation theories found in Posen, *The Sources of Military Doctrine*, and Rosen's *Winning the Next War*.

52. Bottom-up learning has been noted by James A. Russell, *Innovation, Transformation, and War*.

53. Serena notes, "most if not all of the institutional adaptations made during the course of OIF were driven or inspired by adaptations—successful and unsuccessful—made at the tactical unit level in pursuit of mission success. . . . The

decentralized changes the army experienced occurred—by necessity—because the larger institution could not adjust rapidly enough to have a timely effect on suborganization performance and goal realization." *Revolution in Military Adaptation*, 160.

54. Quoted in Serena, *Revolution in Military Adaptation*, 163.

55. Morton Halperin, *Bureaucratic Politics and Foreign Policy* (Washington: Brookings Institution Press, 1976); Graham Allison, *Essence of Decision, Explaining the Cuban Missile Crisis* (Boston: Little, Brown, 1971); James Q. Wilson, *Bureaucracy: What Government Agencies Do and Why They Do It* (New York: Basic Books, 1989).

56. I am indebted to Prof. Theo Farrell for this point. See also James March, "Continuity and Change in Theories of Organizational Action," *Administrative Science Quarterly*, 41, no. 2 (1996): 278–87.

57. March, "Continuity and Change in Theories of Organizational Action," 286.

58. S. Raisch, J. Birkinshaw, G. Probst, and M. Tushman, "Organizational Ambidexterity: Balancing exploitation and exploration for Sustained Performance," *Organization Science*, 20, no. 4 (2009): 685–95.

59. D. A. Levinthal and J. G. March, "A Model of Adaptive Organizational Search," *Journal of Economic Behavior and Organizations* 2, no. 4 (1981): 307–33.

60. Justin Kelly and Mike Brennan, "OODA versus ASDA, Metaphors at War," *Australian Army Journal*, VI, no. 3 (2009): 39–51.

61. Micha Popper and Raanan Lipshitz, "Organizational Learning," *Management Learning*, 31, no. 2 (June 2000): 181–96.

62. Downie, *Learning from Conflict*, 9.

63. Nagl, *Learning to Eat Soup with a Knife*, 8.

64. The notion that an organization conducts multiple loops of the adaptation cycle over time is found in I. Nonaka and H. Takeuchi, *The Knowledge-Creating Company* (New York: Oxford University Press, 1995). See also Thomas Rid, *War and Media Operations* (London: Routledge, 2007).

65. Nonaka and Takeuchi, 192.

66. Nonaka and Takeuchi.

67. On the Boyd Cycle, see Frans P. B. Osinga, *Science, Strategy and War: The Strategic Theory of John Boyd* (London: Routledge, 2005), 80, 229–33, 237–39.

68. John Boyd, "Patterns of Conflict," slide presentation, Dec. 1986, 135.

69. Osinga, *Science, Strategy and War*, 169.

70. Argyris, *On Organizational Learning* (Cambridge: Blackwell, 1993), 123.

71. Argyris, "Double Loop Learning in Organizations," *Harvard Business Review*, 55, no. 1 (1977): 115–25.

72. Andrew Hill and Stephen Gerras, "Systems of Denial: Strategic Resistance to Military Innovation," *Naval War College Review* 69, no. 1 (2016): 1–24.

73. Argyris, *On Organizational Learning*, 25–27.

74. Stuart Griffin, "Military Innovation Studies: Multidisciplinary or Lacking Discipline?" *Journal of Strategic Studies* 40, no. 1–2 (2017): 196–224.

75. Sergio Catignani, "Coping with Knowledge: Organizational Learning in the British Army," *Journal of Strategic Studies* 37, no. 1 (2014): 28–40. Catignani embraces "higher and lower" level learning but defines the former as organizational learning and the equivalent of innovation. His lower-level learning is "the mere correction of errors leading to a change in prescribed practices." The current study defines this as adjustment rather than adaptation. Catignani, 31.

76. As defined in Farrell, Osinga, and Russell, eds, *Military Adaptation in Afghanistan*, 10–18.

77. Edwin C. Nevis, Anthony J. DiBella, and Janet M. Gould, "Understanding Organizations as Learning Systems," *Sloan Management Review* 36, no. 2 (Winter 1995): 61–74; A. Drummond Jr., *Enabling Conditions for Organizational Learning: A Study in International Business Ventures*, (Ph.D. thesis, University of Cambridge, 1997); Steven H. Appelbaum and Walter Reichart, "How to Measure an Organization's Learning Ability: The facilitating factors—part II," *Journal of Workplace Learning* 10, no. 1 (1998): 15–28.

78. Senge, *The Fifth Discipline: The Art and Practice of the Learning Organization* (New York: Currency Doubleday, 1990); Edgar Schein, "Organizational Culture," *American Psychologist* (February 1990): 110; Mary Crossan, H. Lane, R. E. White, and L. Djurfeldt, "Organizational Learning: Dimensions for a Theory," *International Journal of Organizational Analysis,* 3, no. 4 (1995): 337–60; M. Crossan, H. Lane, and R. E. White, "An Organizational Learning Framework: From Intuition to Institution," *Academy of Management Review* 24, no. 3 (1999): 522–37.

79. Rosen, 255. Rosen finds "Many important wartime technical innovations . . . were pursued at the initiative of military officers or with their vigorous support."

80. Posen, *Sources of Doctrine*, 224.

81. Senge, "The Leaders New Work: Building Learning Organizations," *Sloan Management Review* (Fall 1990): 9.

82. Garvin, "Building a Learning Organization," 80.

83. Dusya Vera and Mary Crossan, "Strategic Leadership and Organizational Learning," *Academy of Management Review* 29, no. 2 (2004): 222–40.

84. Paul Kennedy, *Engineers of Victory, The Problem Solvers Who Turned the Tide in the Second World War* (New York: Random House, 2013); Michael D. Doubler, *Busting the Bocage: American Combined Arms Operations in France, 6 June–31 July 1944* (Ft. Leavenworth: U.S. Army Command and General Staff College, 1988), 32–34.

85. Doubler, *Breaking the Bocage*, 42.

86. Russell A. Hart, *Clash of Arms, How the Allies Won in Normandy* (Boulder: Lynne Rienner, 2001), 269, 271, 279.

87. Robert T. Foley, "A Case Study in Horizontal Military Innovation," *Journal of Strategic Studies* 35, no. 6 (December 2012): 799–827.

88. Doubler, *Breaking the Bocage*, 223.

89. Murray, *Military Adaptation*, 311; Finkel, *On Flexibility*, 98–110.

90. Stephen J. Gerras and Leonard Wong, *Changing Minds in the Army: Why It Is So Difficult and What to Do About It* (Carlisle: Strategic Studies Institute, October 2013), 8.

91. Appelbaum and Reichart. "How to Measure an Organization's Learning Ability: The Facilitating Factors," 18. See also Nagl, *Learning to Eat Soup*, 22.

92. See Colin Gray, "Culture: Beliefs, Customs, and Strategic Behavior," *Perspectives on Strategy* (Oxford: Oxford University Press, 2013):79–115.

93. Williamson Murray, "Does Military Culture Matter?" *Orbis* (Winter 1999): 90.

94. Schein, *Organizational Culture and Leadership* (San Francisco: Jossey-Bass, 1985).

95. Schein, "Organizational Culture," *American Psychologist*, (February 1990): 111.

96. Farrell, "Culture and Military Power," 410.

97. Murray, "Does Military Culture Matter?," 134.

98. Schein, "Organizational Culture," 111.

99. Kier, *Imagining War*; Elizabeth Kier, "Culture and Military Doctrine—France between the Wars," *International Security* 19, no. 4 (Spring 1995): 65–93.

100. Farrell and Terriff, *The Sources of Military Change*, 7–8; Theo Farrell, "Figuring Out Fighting Organizations: The New Organizational Analysis in Strategic Studies," *Journal of Strategic Studies* 19, no. 1 (Spring 1996): 122–35; Theo Farrell, "Culture and Military Power," *Review of International Studies* 24, no. 3 (Fall 1998): 407–16.

101. On how military culture shapes the use of force see Isabel V. Hull, *Absolute Destruction. Military Culture and the Practices of War in Imperial Germany* (Ithaca: Cornell University Press, 2004). On American strategic and military culture, see Thomas G. Mahnken, "U.S. Strategic and Organizational Sub-cultures," in Jeannie L. Johnson, Kerry M. Kartchner, and Jeffery A. Larsen, eds., *Strategic Culture and Weapons of Mass Destruction: Culturally Based Insights into Comparative National Security Policymaking* (New York: Palgrave Macmillan, 2009).

102. Anthony J. Dibella, "Perspectives on Changing National Security Institutions," *Joint Force Quarterly*, 69 (2013): 15.

103. How culture and leadership influence change initiatives in U.S. military institutions can be seen in Terry Terriff, "Warriors and Innovators: Military Change and Organizational Culture in the U.S. Marine Corps," *Defense Studies* 6, no. 2 (2006): 215–47.

104. Terriff, 214.

105. Winton, in Winton and Mets, *The Challenge of Change*, xiv.

106. Murray, *Military Adaptation*, 305–28.

107. Hart, *Clash of Arms*, 345.

108. James Corum, "A Comprehensive Approach to Change," in Winton and Mets, *The Challenge of Change*, 54–56.

109. Murray and Millett, *Military Innovation in the Interwar Period*, passim.

110. Builder, *The Masks of War: American Military Styles in Strategy and Analysis* (Baltimore: Johns Hopkins University Press, 1989). Builder overlooked the U.S. Marine Corps, but his framework can be applied, see F. G. Hoffman, "The Marine Mask of War," *Marine Corps Gazette*, December 2011.

111. Brian MacAllister Linn, *The Echo of Battle: The Army's Way of War* (Cambridge: Harvard University Press, 2007). Linn defined the "Guardians" as characterized by an engineering approach to war; "Heroes" as stressing the human dimension: personal

skill, genius, experience, courage, and discipline; and "Managers" as framing war as a large-scale organizational problem.

112. Murray, *Military Adaptation in War*, 15.

113. A major conclusion by Barry Watts and Williamson Murray, in "Military Innovation in Peacetime," from Murray and Millett, *Military Innovation in the Interwar Period*, 410. They conclude "institutional processes for exploring, testing and refining conceptions of future war . . . are literally a *sine qua non* of successful military innovation in peacetime."

114. Foley, Griffin, and McCartney, "Transformation in Contact," 270.

115. R. V. Jones, *The Wizard War: British Scientific Intelligence, 1939–1945* (New York: Coward, McCann & Geoghegan, 1978); Stephen Budiansky, *Blackett's War: The Men Who Defeated the Nazi U-Boats and Brought Science to the Art of Warfare* (New York: Knopf, 2013).

116. Montgomery C. Meigs, *Slide Rules and Submarines* (Ft. McNair: National Defense University Press, 1990).

117. Fleet Admiral Ernest J. King, USN (Ret.), "United States Navy at War: Final Official Report to the Secretary of the Navy," U.S. Naval Institute *Proceedings* (January 1946): 174.

118. Brian McCue, *U-Boats in the Bay of Biscay, An Essay in Operations Analysis* (Ft. McNair: National Defense University Press, 1990), 1.

119. McCue, 6.

120. Gregory Fontenot, "Seeing Red: Creating a Red-Team Capability for the Blue Force," *Military Review* 85, no. 5 (September 2005): 4.

121. Department of Defense, *Report of the Defense Science Board on the Role and Status of DoD Red-Teaming* (Washington: September, 2003).

122. Robert T. Foley, "Dumb Donkeys or Cunning Foxes? Learning in the British and German Armies during the Great War," *International Affairs* 90, no. 2 (2014): 287.

123. Doubler, *Closing with the Enemy*, 299.

124. Tattar, *Innovation and Adaptation in War*, 24. Tattar's organizational capacity to adapt was based on the ability of a leader to form a "dedicated organizational subunit" or "top-level review panel."

125. Raphael D. Marcus, "Military Innovation and Tactical Adaptation in the Israel-Hizbollah Conflict: The Institutionalization of Lessons-Learning in the IDF," *Journal of Strategic Studies* 38, no. 4 (2015): 8–10.

126. See Murray, *Adaptation*, 262–304; Finkel, *On Flexibility*, 150–63.

127. Foley, "A Case Study in Horizontal Military Innovation."

128. Samuel Eliot Morison, *The Battle of the Atlantic: September 1939–May 1943*, vol. 1, *History of the U.S. Naval Operations in World War II* (Annapolis: Naval Institute Press, 2010); Clay Blair, *Hitler's U-Boat War, The Hunted, 1942–1945* (New York: Random House, 2000).

129. Thomas Mahnken, "Asymmetric Warfare at Sea, The Naval Battles of Guadalcanal, 1942–1943," *Naval War College Review* 64, no. 1 (Winter 2011): 95–121; James D. Hornfischer, *Neptune's Inferno: The U.S. Navy at Guadalcanal* (New York: Random House, 2012); Trent

Hone, " "Give Them Hell!' The U.S. Navy's Night Combat Doctrine and the Campaign for Guadalcanal," *War in History* 13, no. 2 (April 2006): 171–99.

130. Doubler, *Closing with the Enemy*, 269.

131. Osinga and Russell, "Conclusion," in *Military Adaptation in Afghanistan*, 306–7.

132. Catignani, "Coping with Knowledge," 30–64; Paddy O'Toole and Steven Talbot, "Fighting for Knowledge: Developing Learning Systems in the Australian Army," *Armed Forces and Society* 37, no. 1 (2011): 42–67.

133. U.S. Army officers created an informal lessons-sharing network which evolved into a quasi-official Army system. See "Company Command Net" at https://www.ausa.org/articles/companycommand-ten-years.

134. Steven Mains and Gil Ariely, "Learning While Fighting: Operational Knowledge Management that Makes a Difference," *Prism* 2, no. 1 (June 2011): 165–76.

135. Foley, Griffin, and McCartney, "Transformation in Contact," 270.

136. Foley, "A Case Study in Horizontal Military Innovation," 799.

Chapter 3. Adapting under the Sea

1. Clay Blair, *Silent Victory: The U.S. Submarine War Against Japan*, vol. I (New York: Lippincott, 1975), 385. USS *Tunny* War Patrol #1 Report, dated February 23, 1943. All war patrol reports cited are from the Historical Naval Ships Association website, at www.hnsa.org/doc/subreports.html.

2. Theodore Roscoe, *United States Submarine Operations in World War II* (Annapolis: U. S. Naval Institute Press, 1949), 257; Charles A. Lockwood, *Sink 'Em All: Submarine Warfare in the Pacific* (New York: Dutton, 1951), 95–96.

3. Trent Hone, *Learning War: The Evolution of Fighting Doctrine in the U.S. Navy, 1898–1945* (Annapolis: Naval Institute Press, 2018), 2–11.

4. The primary material for U.S. strategic planning is at *Records of the Joint Board (1903–1947), Joint Board File No. 325 (War Plans), Serial 19*. Record Group 225.2, National Archives and Records Administration, College Park. Additionally, on the early eras of plans, see Steven T. Ross, *American War Plans 1890–1939* (London: Frank Cass, 2002), 121–83.

5. On the U.S. Navy's planning there is no better reference than Edward S. Miller, *War Plan Orange, The U.S. Strategy to Defeat Japan, 1897–1945* (Annapolis: Naval Institute Press, 1991). In addition see Michael Vlahos, "The Naval War College and the Origins of War-Planning Against Japan," *Naval War College Review* (July–August, 1980): 23–39; Michael K. Doyle, "The U.S. Navy and War Plan Orange, 1933–1940: Making Necessity a Virtue," *Naval War College Review* (May–June 1980): 48–63.

6. Robert O'Connell, *Sacred Vessels, The Cult of the Battleship and the Rise of the U.S. Navy* (Boulder: Westview Press, 1991).

7. On aircraft carriers, see Thomas Hone, Norman Friedman, and Mark Mandeles, *American and British Aircraft Carrier Development, 1919–1941* (Annapolis: Naval Institute Press, 1999). On amphibious capabilities see Allan R. Millett, "Assault from the Sea: The Development of Amphibious Warfare Between the Wars," 70–78, in Williamson Murray and Allan R. Millett, *Military Innovation in the Interwar Period.*

8. Miller, *War Plan Orange,* 151.

9. Henry Gole, *The Road to Rainbow: Army Planning for Global War, 1934–1940* (Annapolis: Naval Institute Press, 2002).

10. Rainbow 1 is reproduced in Steven T. Ross, ed., *U.S. War Plans, 1938–1945* (Boulder: Lynne Rienner, 2002), 17–32.

11. Rainbow 4 is at Ross, *U.S. War Plans, 1938–1945,* 33–54.

12. The revised Rainbow 5 was approved Nov. 19, 1941. Ross, *U.S. War Plans, 1938–1945,* 149.

13. Only in 1939 does Newport react to changes in the strategic environment with Black/Silver (Germany-Italy) games. For details on games see Michael Vlahos, *The Blue Sword,* and Vlahos, "Wargaming, an Enforcer of Strategic Realism: 1919–1942," *Naval War College Review* (March–April, 1986); 7–22.

14. Miller, *War Plan Orange,* 330.

15. Vlahos, *The Blue Sword,* 98.

16. For an overview of all the games: Vlahos, 166-78.

17. Norman Friedman, *Winning a Future War: War Gaming and Victory in the Pacific War* (Washington: Navy History and Museums Division, 2018), 170.

18. Norman Friedman, email correspondence to the author, May 13, 2019.

19. Ian W. Toll, *Pacific Crucible: War at Sea in the Pacific, 1941–1942* (New York: Norton, 2012), xxxiv.

20. Vlahos, "Wargaming, an Enforcer of Strategic Realism," 7.

21. Quoted by George Baer, *One Hundred Years of Sea Power, The U.S. Navy, 1890–1990* (Stanford: Stanford University Press, 1994), 141.

22. Albert A. Nofi, *To Train the Fleet for War: The U.S. Navy Fleet Problems, 1923–1940* (Newport: Naval War College Press, 2010).

23. Nofi, *To Train the Fleet for War,* 271.

24. Rosen, *Winning the Next War,* 75. "Simulating new forms of warfare will always be full of uncertainties, because there is no reality against which to test the simulation. Yet there may be no better way to think through innovative practices in peacetime."

25. Hone, *Learning War,* 122–62.

26. Nofi, *To Train the Fleet for War,* 277.

27. Craig C. Felker, *Testing American Sea Power: U.S. Navy Strategic Exercises, 1923–1940* (College Station: Texas A&M University Press, 2007), 6.

28. I. J. Galantin, *Take Her Deep!: A Submarine against Japan in World War II* (Annapolis: Naval Institute Press, 2007), 18.

29. Wilfred Jay Holmes, *Undersea Victory: The Influence of Submarine Operations on the War in the Pacific* (Garden City, New York: Doubleday, 1966), 47.

30. Felker, *Testing American Sea Power,* 62.

31. Nofi, *To Train the Fleet for War,* 307.

32. Roscoe, *U.S. Submarine Operations,* 57.

33. See J. E. Talbott, "Weapons Development, War Planning and Policy: The U.S. Navy and the Submarine, 1917–1941," *Naval War College Review* (May–June 1984): 53–71;

Ronald H. Spector, *Eagle against the Sun, The American War with Japan* (New York: Free Press, 1985), 54–68, and 478–80.

34. Joel Ira Holwitt, *"Execute Against Japan:" Freedom-of-the-Seas, the U.S. Navy, Fleet Submarines, and the U.S. Decision to Conduct Unrestricted Warfare, 1919–1941* (College Station: Texas A&M University Press, 2009), 479.

35. John T. Kuehn, *Agents of Innovation: The General Board and the Design of the Fleet That Defeated the Japanese Navy* (Annapolis: Naval Institute Press, 2008).

36. Jeffery Juergens, "Impact of the General Board of the Navy on Interwar Submarine Design," Fort Leavenworth, KS, U.S. Army Command and Staff College, unpublished master's thesis. (2009). Accessed at http://cgsc.contentdm.oclc.org/u?/p4013coll2,2474

37. Blair, *Silent Victory*, 47.

38. Blair, 46–47; Anthony Newpower, *Iron Men and Tin Fish: The Race to Build a Better Torpedo during World War II* (Westport: Praeger, 2006), 98–99.

39. Subsequently, the *Gato* Class (SS 212 to 284) was commissioned. The *Gato* had improved engines and batteries that increased their range and patrol duration.

40. Roscoe, *U.S. Submarine Operations*, 7, 187. Norman Friedman, *U.S. Submarines Through 1945 An Illustrated Design History* (Annapolis: Naval Institute Press, 1995), 195–97. The TDC was an early electromechanical computer used to calculate targeting of torpedoes in American subs during World War II.

41. Mick Ryan, "The U.S. Submarine Campaign in the Pacific, 1941–45," *Australian Defence Journal*, no. 90 (March–April 2013), 62–75.

42. Newpower, *Iron Men and Tin Fish*.

43. Flint Whitlock and Ron Smith, *The Depths of Courage: American Submariners at War with Japan, 1941–1945* (New York: Berkley Caliber, 2007), 19.

44. The Mark 14 was the principal antiship torpedo during the war, and more than 13,000 were produced and some 7,000 were actually fired. Newpower, *Iron Men and Tin Fish*, 191.

45. Spector, *Eagle against the Sun*, 484; Blair, *Silent Victory*, 50.

46. Blair, *Silent Victory*, 84; Roscoe, *U.S. Submarine Operations*, 33.

47. Holwitt, *Execute Against Japan*, 120–38.

48. Spector, *Eagle against the Sun*, 985; Nathan Miller, *War at Sea: A Naval History of World War II* (New York: Oxford University Press, 1994), 477–99.

49. Holmes, *Undersea Victory*, 47.

50. Walter Borneman, *The Admirals: Nimitz, Halsey, Leahy, and King—The Five-Star Admirals Who Won the War at Sea* (Boston: Little, Brown, 2012); Thomas B. Buell, *Master of Sea Power: A Biography of Fleet Admiral Ernest J. King* (Boston: Little, Brown, 1980).

51. Holger H. Herwig, "Innovation Ignored: The Submarine Problem Germany, Britain and the United States, 1919–1939," 227–64, in Murray and Millett, eds. *Military Innovation in the Interwar Period*.

52. Blair, *Silent Victory*, 116–18.

53. Newpower, *Iron Men and Tin Fish*, 62; Holmes, *Undersea Victory*, 66.

54. Blair, *Silent Victory*, 118; Newpower, *Iron Men and Tin Fish*, 62–63.

55. *Sargo* War Patrol Report #1, December 22, 1941; Newpower, *Iron Men and Tin Fish*, 65.

56. Blair, *Silent Victory*, 147.

57. Roscoe, *U.S. Submarine Operations*, 52.

58. Similar results were experience by Pete Ferrall in USS *Seadragon*, who fired eight torpedoes for only one hit at short range, and began to suspect the Mark 14 was faulty.
Seadragon War Patrol Report #1, February 13, 1942.

59. *Skipjack* War Patrol Report #2, dated June 25, 1942; Newpower, *Iron Men and Tin Fish*,
71–72.

60. *Skipjack*, 30; Blair, *Silent Victory*, 250–51; Newpower, *Iron Men and Tin Fish*, 65.

61. Roscoe, *U.S. Submarine Operations*, 145; Blair, *Silent Victory*, 251–52.

62. Newpower, *Iron Men and Tin Fish*, 60.

63. Blair, *Silent Victory*, 62.

64. Blair, 175.

65. Newpower, *Iron Men and Tin Fish*, 133.

66. Library of Congress, Lockwood Papers, Box 12, Folder 64, Lockwood letter to Rear
Admiral Edwards at PAC, May 22, 1942, 2–3.

67. Blair, *Silent Victory*, 203.

68. Blair, 185.

69. Blair, 364, 451.

70. Blair, 365.

71. Lockwood Papers, Box 12, Folder 64, Memorandum to Captain Fife, May 24, 1942, 2.

72. Newpower, *Iron Men and Tin Fish*, 102.

73. Lockwood Papers, Box 12, Folder 64, Memo to Admiral Leary, June 4, 1942, 3.

74. Lockwood Papers, Box 12, Folder 63, Letter to Rear Admiral Blandy, July 11, 1942.

75. Roscoe, *U.S. Submarine Operations*, 145–46.

76. Lockwood papers, Box 12, Folder 64, Lockwood letter, May 22, 1942, to Rear Admiral Edwards at Pacific Fleet, Submarines.

77. Roscoe, *U.S. Submarine Operations*, 147.

78. Blair, *Silent Victory*, 277.

79. Lockwood, *Sink 'Em All*, 88–89; Newpower, *Iron Men and Tin Fish*, 134–75.

80. Blair, *Silent Victory*, 183.

81. More than 30 percent were relieved for cause in 1942, "products of an unrealistic
peacetime operations and training system whose insidious effect was not recognized
until the realities of combat disclosed it." Galantin, *Submarine Admiral*, 77; Rosen, *Winning the Next War*, 130–47.

82. Blair, *Silent Victory*, 41; Spector, *Eagle against the Sun*, 484.

83. Lockwood, *Sink 'Em All*, 52.

84. The research team found a total of seven sinkings from thirty-one submerged attacks, out
of total of over three thousand attacks examined. Roscoe, *U.S. Submarine Operations*, 68.

85. Blair, *Silent Victory*, 97.

86. Roscoe, *U.S. Submarine Operations*, 58. This was disconcerting to skippers when tactics
approved of when they departed were irrelevant by the time their patrols were completed. See Holmes, *Undersea Victory*, 93.

87. In fact, *Ryūjō* had been sunk earlier in the Solomon Islands.

88. *Wahoo* War Patrol Report #1, October 18, 1942.

89. *Wahoo* War Patrol Report #2, December 26, 1942.

90. Blair, *Silent Victory*, 335.

91. Eugene B. Fluckey, *Thunder Below!: The USS Barb Revolutionizes Submarine Warfare in World War II* (Urbana: University of Illinois Press, 1992), 153.

92. NARA, RG 38, Box 358, U.S. Navy World War II Command Files, *Submarine Operations of World War II*, vol. 2, 1947, ii–587.

93. Blair, *Silent Victory*, 334–45.

94. Lockwood, *Sink 'Em All*, 27.

95. Blair, *Silent Victory*, 97.

96. NARA, RG 38, Box 358, U.S. Navy World War II Command Files, *Submarine Operations of World War II*, vol. 2, 1947, ii–589.

97. Rosen, *Winning the Next War*, 132, fn3.

98. On the development of aggressive tactics see Richard H. O'Kane, *Wahoo: The Patrols of America's Most Famous World War II Submarine* (New York: Bantam Books, 1989). See also Richard H. O'Kane, *Clear the Bridge!: The War Patrols of the U.S.S. Tang* (Novato, CA.: Presidio Press, 1997).

99. *Wahoo* patrol report #3 February 7, 1943. See page 16 on the tactical adaptation; O'Kane, *Wahoo*, 125–71.

100. But records show that Morton's shot hit the *Harusame* amidships by contact and heavily damaged it. It was beached and later repaired, which strongly suggests the torpedo detonated on contact and not under the keel as a fatal underwater blast.

101. *Wahoo* patrol report #4, April 6, 1943; O'Kane, *Wahoo*, 180–241.

102. Blair, *Silent Victory*, 375.

103. NARA, RG 313, A16 3 (1), Commander, Submarine Force Pacific, Tactical Bulletin No. 2, February 26, 1943. In this bulletin, Lockwood extracted whole sections from *Wahoo*'s patrol report as he felt that it was "considered so outstanding."

104. *Wahoo* War Patrol Report report #5, May 21, 1943; O'Kane, *Wahoo*, 251–71.

105. Lockwood, *Sink 'Em All*, 117; Newpower, *Iron Men and Tin Fish*, 153.

106. Lockwood Papers, Box 13, Folder 66, Ltr Lockwood to Blandy, March 14, 1943.

107. Lockwood Papers, Box 13, Folder 70, Ltr Blandy back to Lockwood, June 19, 1943.

108. Lockwood Papers, Box 13, Folder 70, Lockwood to Blandy, June 9, 1943.

109. Lockwood, *Sink 'Em All*, 103; Newpower, *Iron Men and Tin Fish*, 137.

110. Newpower, *Iron Men and Tin Fish*, 153; Lockwood, *Sink 'Em All*, 114.

111. Holmes, *Undersea Victory*, 237; Blair, *Silent Victory*, 403; Newpower, *Iron Men and Tin Fish*, 158.

112. Lockwood Papers, Box 13, Folder 71, Ltr from Lockwood to Blandy, July 19, 1943.

113. Newpower, *Iron Men and Tin Fish*, 173–75.

114. *Tinosa* War Patrol Report #2, August 4, 1943; Newpower, *Iron Men and Tin Fish*, 171; Holmes, *Undersea Victory*, 240–42; Blair, *Silent Victory*, 406–8.

115. Roscoe, *U.S. Submarine Operations*, 259–60.

116. On *Wahoo*'s sixth patrol, see O'Kane, *Wahoo*, 281–300; Wahoo War Patrol Report #6, August 29, 1943. Morton recommended that activation of influence detonators be left to individual captains.

117. Roscoe, *U.S. Submarine Operations*, 239.

118. Lockwood Papers, Box 13, Folder 72, Lockwood to Edwards, August 27, 1943.

119. Lockwood, *Sink 'Em All*, 112–13; Newpower, *Iron Men and Tin Fish*, 173.

120. Lockwood Papers, Box, 13, Folder 73, Lockwood to Blandy, August 11, 1943.

121. Lockwood Papers, Box 13, Folder 72, Blandy to Lockwood, September 9, 1943.

122. Newpower, *Iron Men and Tin Fish*, 177–80.

123. Holmes, *Undersea Victory*, 247.

124. Newpower, *Iron Men and Tin Fish*, 181.

125. Galantin, *Take Her Deep*, 92.

126. The metal housing mechanism for the firing pin in the contact exploder was too weak, and it impeded the firing pin from making proper contact with the detonator. The engineers at Newport had not properly accounted for the much faster speed of the Mark 14 over the Mark 10 (forty-six versus thirty miles per hour). Newpower, *Iron Men and Tin Fish*, 180.

127. Blair, *Silent Victory*, 439.

128. Newpower, *Iron Men and Tin Fish*, 190.

129. Roscoe, *U.S. Submarine Operations*, 298; Blair, *Silent Victory*, 522.

130. NARA, RG 38, Box 358, U.S. Navy World War II Command Files, Commander, Submarine Force Pacific, Tactical Bulletin 4, July 9, 1943, 33.

131. NARA, RG 38, Box 358, U.S. Navy World War II Command Files, Commander, Submarine Force Pacific, Tactical Bulletin 5, September 4, 1943, 28–29.

132. Roscoe, *U.S. Submarine Operations*, 328–31.

133. USS *Gudgeon*, War Patrol Report, 7th Patrol, April 6, 1943, 49–50.

134. Mike Ostlund, *Find 'Em, Chase 'Em, Sink 'Em: The Mysterious Loss of the WWII Submarine USS Gudgeon* (Guilford, CT.: Lyons, 2012). USS *Gudgeon*, War Patrol: 10th Patrol, December 10, 1943.

135. Roscoe, *U.S. Submarine Operations*, 263.

136. Blair, *Silent Victory*, 482.

137. Steven Trent Smith, *Wolf Pack: The American Submarine Strategy That Helped Defeat Japan* (Hoboken, NJ: John Wiley, 2003), 50. Lockwood noted in a single sentence that he was directed to conduct wolfpack tactics by King. Lockwood, *Sink 'Em All*, 87.

138. Smith, *Wolf Pack*, 51.

139. Smith notes that "Cominch was also aware of just how potent pack tactics could be—all too aware of the huge toll Dönitz's U-boats were taking on Allied Shipping." Smith, *Wolf Pack*, 51.

140. Admiral Galantin's memoirs make the same case, *Take Her Deep!*, 126.

141. Lockwood Papers, Box 12, Folder 63, Letter Lockwood to Admiral H. Leary, July 11, 1942.

142. NARA, RG 313/A16 3 (1), Commander, Submarine Forces Pacific, Tactical Bulletin #1-43, dated January 2, 1943.

143. Charles A. Lockwood and Hans Christian Adamson, *Hellcats of the Sea* (New York: Bantam, 1988), 88.

144. Blair, *Silent Victory*, 360.

145. On U-boat tactics, see Clay Blair, *The Hunters, 1939–1942* (New York: Random House, 1998); Michael Gannon, *Operation Drumbeat* (New York: Harper & Row, 1990), 89–90.

146. Blair, *Silent Victory*, 511–16; Roscoe, *U.S. Submarine Operations*, 240.

147. Lockwood Papers, Box 13/Folder 69, Ltr from Lockwood to Nimitz, May 4, 1943.

148. Galantin, *Take Her Deep!*, 124–29.

149. Galantin, 129.

150. Blair, *Silent Victory*, 479–80.

151. Roscoe, *U.S. Submarine Operations*, 241.

152. NARA, RG 38, Naval Command Files, Box 357, Commander, Submarine Forces Pacific, Tactical Bulletin #6–43, November 22, 1943.

153. Peter Sasgen, *Hellcats: The Epic Story of World War II's Most Daring Submarine Raid* (New York: Caliber, 2010).

154. Holmes, *Undersea Victory*, 459–61.

155. National Archives and Records Administration (NARA), RG 38, Naval Command Files, Box 358, "Operation Barney" in *Submarine Bulletin,* 2 no. 3, September 1945, 10–16.

156. Lockwood and Adamson, *Hellcats of the Sea.*

157. See the list at http://www.valoratsea.com/wolfpacks.htm.

158. Blair, *Silent Victory*, 524.

159. Roscoe, *U.S. Submarine Operations*, 432–33; Blair, *Silent Victory*, 791–93.

160. These boats used the latest in "pro-submarine" technology, including improved sonar systems to avoid Japanese mine fields. On the development of these see Blair, *Silent Victory*, vol. 2, 762–65.

161. Roscoe, *U.S. Submarine Operations*, 491.

162. Roscoe, 4.

163. Lockwood, *Sink 'Em All*, 351.

164. Williamson Murray and Allan R. Millett, *A War to Be Won: Fighting the Second World War* (Cambridge: Belknap/Harvard, 2000), 227.

165. Murray and Millett, 352.

166. In 1944, the submarine service saved 144 downed aviators in the Pacific. In 1945, they plucked another 304 pilots and aircrews from the water.

167. Don Keith, *War Beneath the Waves*, New York: New American Library, 2010, 246.

168. Roscoe, *U.S. Submarine Operations*, 479.

169. Holmes, *Undersea Victory*, 351.

170. Thomas B. Buell, *Master of Sea Power: A Biography of Fleet Admiral Ernest J. King* (Boston: Little, Brown, 1980); Borneman, *The Admirals*, 26–40, 119–26.

171. Buell, 51–55.

172. Buell, 64–83.

173. Borneman, *The Admirals,* 70.

174. Buell, *Master of Sea Power,* 25; Borneman, *The Admirals,* 192.

175. Buell, 31.

176. E. B. Potter, *Nimitz,* (Annapolis: Naval Institute Press, 1976); Borneman, *The Admirals,* 53–65, 79–84.

177. Hone, *Learning War,* 329.

178. Borneman, *The Admirals,* 120.

179. Galantin, *Take Her Deep!,* 29.

180. Galantin.

181. John G. Mansfield, *Cruisers for Breakfast: War Patrols of the U.S.S. Darter and U.S.S. Dash* (Tacoma: Media Center, 1997), 221.

182. Lockwood, *Sink 'Em All,* 33.

183. Roscoe, *U.S. Submarine Operations,* 225.

184. Brayton Harris, *Admiral Nimitz: The Commander of the Pacific Ocean Theater* (New York: Palgrave Macmillan, 2012).

185. Holmes, *Undersea Victory,* 311.

186. Alfred Thayer Mahan, *Mahan on Naval Strategy: Selections from the Writings of Rear Admiral Alfred Thayer Mahan* (Annapolis: Naval Institute Press, 1991).

187. Builder, *Masks of War,* 74–85.

188. Roger W. Barnett, *Navy Strategic Culture: Why the Navy Thinks Differently* (Annapolis: Naval Institute Press, 2009). See also the appendix in Jeannie Johnson, *Assessing the Strategic Impact of Service Culture on Counterinsurgency Operations,* University of Reading, PhD thesis, June 2013.

189. Vlahos, *Blue Sword,* 15.

190. Toll, *Pacific Crucible,* xvi.

191. Vlahos, *Blue Sword,* 67.

192. Holmes, *Undersea Victory,* 34.

193. Stephen L. Moore, *Battle Surface!: Lawson P. "Red" Ramage and the War Patrols of the USS Parche,* (Annapolis: U.S. Naval Institute Press, 2011), 33.

194. Holmes, *Undersea Victory,* 150.

195. James F. Calvert, *Silent Running, My Years on a World War II Attack Submarine* (New York: J. Wiley, 1995), 55.

196. Newpower, *Iron Men and Tin Fish,* 101.

197. Blair, *Silent Victory,* 77; Calvert, *Silent Running,* 55.

198. Friedman, *Winning a Future War,* passim, 31–71.

199. Toll, *Pacific Crucible,* 375.

200. For details, see Lockwood, *Sink 'Em All,* 167–68; Sagsen, *Hellcats,* 171–73.

201. Lockwood, *Sink 'Em All,* 83, 388.

202. Meigs, *Slide Rules and Submarines,* 202.

203. Holmes, *Undersea Victory,* 236.

204. Lockwood and Adamson, *Hellcats,* 357.

205. Meigs, *Slide Rules and Submarines,* 212.

206. Galantin, *Take Her Deep*, 27.

207. NARA, RG 313, Blue 443/2, A16 3 (3), Ltr, Commander SubPac, November 1, 1943.

208. Fluckey, *Thunder Below*, 201.

209. The importance of the patrol reports and endorsements as a source of feedback is reflected in Meigs, 175; and Calvert, 54. Rosen disagrees, *Winning the Next War*, 139.

210. Calvert, *Silent Running*, 55.

211. George Grider and Lydel Sims, *War Fish* (Boston: Little, Brown, 1958), 90.

212. Rosen, *Winning the Next War*, 139.

213. Calvert, *Silent Running*, 54–55; Fluckey, *Thunder Below*, 201. Both authors were new generation submarine captains and claim learning from patrol reports and endorsements.

214. Hone, *Learning War*, 327–28.

215. Holmes, *Undersea Victory*, 368–69.

216. Edward Miller, cited by Baer, *One Hundred Years of Sea Power*, 128.

217. Hone, *Learning War*, 314, citing Wayne Hughes.

218. Rosen, *Winning the Next War*, 22–38.

219. Roscoe, *U.S. Submarine Operations*, 18.

220. Joel Ira Holwitt, "Unrestricted Submarine Victory: The U.S. Submarine Campaign against Japan," in Bruce A. Elleman and S. C. M. Paine, eds., *Commerce Raiding: Historical Case Studies, 1755–2009*, (Newport: Naval War College, October 2013).

221. Jonathan Parshall and Anthony Tulley, *Shattered Sword, The Untold Story of the Battle of Midway* (Dulles: Potomac Books, 2010), 407.

222. R. Evan Ellis, "Organizational Learning Dominance," *Comparative Strategy*, 18, no. 2 (1999): 191–202.

Chapter 4. Airpower

1. Harold R. Winton, "Introduction," in Harold R. Winton and David R. Mets, eds., *The Challenge of Change: Military Institutions and New Realities, 1918–1941* (Lincoln: Nebraska University Press, 2000), xi.

2. Charles E. Heller and William A. Stofft, *America's First Battles, 1776–1965* (Lawrence: University of Kansas Press, 1986).

3. Max Hastings, *The Korean War* (New York: Touchstone Books, 1987); Clay Blair, *The Forgotten War: America in Korea 1950–1953* (New York: Doubleday, 1987); John Toland, *In Mortal Combat: Korea, 1950–1953* (New York: William Morrow, 1991).

4. Phil Haun, *Lectures of the Air Corps Tactical School and American Strategic Bombing in World War II* (Lexington: University Press of Kentucky, 2019) (Hereafter "Lectures of the ACTS").

5. Peter Faber, in Philip Meilinger, ed., *The Paths of Heaven: The Evolution of Airpower Theory* (Maxwell Air Force Base: Air University Press, 1997), 219–23; Robert T. Finney, *History of the Air Corps Tactical School, 1920–1940* (Washington: Air Force History and Museums Program, 1998); Haun, *Lectures of the ACTS*, 19–21, 26–32.

6. Haun, *Lectures of the ACTS*, 29.

7. Williamson Murray and Allan R. Millett, *A War to Be Won: Fighting the Second World War* (Cambridge: Belknap/Harvard, 2000), 331.

8. Cited in David E. Johnson, *Fast Tanks and Heavy Bombers: Innovation in the U.S. Army, 1917–1945* (Ithaca: Cornell University Press, 2003), 174. Eaker would soon be promoted to lieutenant general and command the Eighth Air Force.

9. James Holland, *Big Week: The Biggest Air Battle of World War II* (New York: Atlantic Monthly, 2018), 36–52.

10. Comment provided by historian Williamson Murray, April 28, 2019.

11. Mark Clodfelter, *Beneficial Bombing, The Progressive Foundations of American Airpower, 1917–1945* (Lincoln: University of Nebraska Press, 2010), 148–83; Tami Davis Biddle, *Rhetoric and Reality in Air Warfare: The Evolution of British and American Ideas about Strategic Bombing, 1914–1945* (Princeton: Princeton University Press), 2002, 214–60; and Richard Overy, "The Air War in Europe," 27–52, in John Andreas Olsen, ed., *A History of Air Warfare* (Dulles: Potomac, 2010).

12. Wesley Frank Craven and James Lea Cate, eds., *The Army Air Forces in World War II, Europe, Torch to Point Blank*, vol. 2 (Washington: Office of Air Force History, 1983), 694–969; *The U.S. Army Air Forces in World War II, Europe: ARGUMENT to V-E Day*, vol. 3. (Washington: Office of Air Force History, 1983).

13. Murray and Millett, *A War to Be Won*, 334.

14. Will A. Jacobs, "The Battle for France, 1944," in Benjamin F. Cooling, ed., *Case Studies in the Development of Close Air Support* (Washington: Office of Air Force History, 1990), 237–94; David Spires, *Airpower for Patton's Army: XIX Tactical Air Command in the Second World War* (Washington: Air Force History and Museums Program, 2002), 56–62.

15. Allan R. Millett and Williamson Murray, eds., *Military Effectiveness, The Second World War*, vol. 3 (Cambridge, U.K.: Cambridge University Press, 2010); Richard Overy, *The Bombers and the Bombed: Allied Air War Over Europe 1940–1945* (New York: Viking Penguin, 2013); Richard Overy, *Why the Allies Won* (New York: Norton, 1997), 101–32; Haun, *Lectures of the ACTS*, 204–8, 209–12.

16. Murray and Millet, *A War to Be Won*, 335.

17. The summary report of the USSBS concluded: "Allied airpower was decisive in the war in Western Europe. Hindsight inevitably suggests that it might have been employed differently or better in some respects. Nevertheless, it was decisive. In the air, its victory was complete. . . . Its power and superiority made possible the success of the invasion." United States Strategic Bombing Survey, Summary Report, Washington, July 1, 1946. See also Clodfelter, *Beneficial Bombing*, 183; Overy, *Why the Allies Won*, 131. For a critical assessment see Robert A. Pape, *Bombing to Win: Airpower and Coercion in War* (Ithaca: Cornell University Press, 1996), 137–73.

18. On the U.S. Air Force in Japan see Clodfelter, *Beneficial Bombing*, 184–234; Biddle, *Rhetoric and Reality*, 261–70; and Richard R. Muller, "The Air War in the Pacific," 53–80, in Olsen, *A History of Air Warfare*; Murray and Millett, *A War to Be Won*, 504–8; Haun, *Lectures of the ACTS*, 217–24.

19. Haun, *Lectures of the ACTS*, 217–18.

20. Herman Wolk, *Toward Independence: The Emergence of the U.S. Air Force 1945–1947* (Washington: U.S. Air Force History and Museums, 1996), 7–8.

21. Wesley Frank Craven and James Lea Cate, *The Army Air Forces in World War II*, vol. 5 (Washington: Office of Air Force History, 1983), 612; Murray and Millet, *A War to Be Won*, 506.

22. Murray and Millet, *A War to Be Won*, 508.

23. On the impact of the P-51 see Holland, *Big Week: The Biggest Air Battle of World War II*, 118–37, 209–19.

24. Clodfelter, *Beneficial Bombing*, 233.

25. Robert Farley, "US Air Force Culture, 1947–2017," in Peter R. Mansoor and Williamson Murray, eds., *The Culture of Military Organizations* (New York: Cambridge University Press, 2019), 426–48.

26. David MacIsaac, "Voices from the Central Blue: The Airpower Theorists," in Peter Paret, ed., *Makers of Modern Strategy from Machiavelli to the Nuclear Age* (Princeton: Princeton University Press, 1986); Peter Faber, in Philip Meilinger, ed., *The Paths of Heaven: The Evolution of Airpower Theory* (Maxwell Air Force Base: Air University Press, 1997); Craig F. Morris, *The Origins of American Strategy Bombing Theory*, (Annapolis: Naval Institute Press, 2017), 179–97. World War I Italian Gen. Giulio Douhet believed that airpower was revolutionary and would dominate future wars.

27. William R. Emerson, "Operation Pointbank: A Tale of Bombers and Fighters," in *Harmon Memorial Lectures in Military History* (Washington: Air Force History, 1988), 455.

28. Mike Worden, "Rise of the Fighter Generals: The Problem of USAF Leadership, 1945–1982" (Maxwell Air Force Base: Air University Press, 1998), 1.

29. On the development of the U.S. Air Force during this period see Herman S. Wolk, *The Struggle for Air Force Independence 1943–1947* (Washington: Air Force History and Museums Program, 1997); Herman S. Wolk, *Reflections on Force Independence* (Washington: Air Force History and Museums Program, 2007).

30. In preface in Wolk, *The Struggle for Air Force Independence*, iii.

31. Robert F. Futrell, *Ideas, Concepts, Doctrine: Basic Thinking in the United States Air Force, 1907–1960*, vol. 1 (Maxwell Air Force Base: Air University Press, 1989).

32. Robert Futrell, *The United States Air Force in Korea, 1950–1953* (Washington: Office of Air Force History, 1983), 3–5. (Hereafter cited as simply *Korea*)

33. I. B. Holley Jr., in Cooling, *Case Studies in the Development of Close Air Support*, 535.

34. MacIssac, "Voices of Central Blue," in *Makers of Modern Strategy*, 643.

35. Futrell, *Korea*, 59–60. This adaptation is attributed to two junior officers who combined two kinds of existing fuel tanks into a 265-gallon container that extended the range of the F-80C to 350 miles. These "Misawa" tanks were locally created by Japanese locals at the U.S. base in Misawa, Japan.

36. D. W. Boose, "The Army View of Close Air Support in the Korean War," in Jacob Neufeld and G. M. Watson, Jr., eds., *Coalition Air Warfare in the Korean War, 1950–1953* (Washington: Air Force History and Museums), 2005.

37. Allan Millett, "Korea, 1950–1953," in B. F. Cooling, ed., *Case Studies in the Development of Close Air Support* (Washington: Office of Air Force History, 1990), 358, 361–63. Hereafter cited as "Millett, Korea."

38. Millett. See also Wayne Thompson, "The War in Korea," in Bernard C. Nalty, *Winged Shield, Winged Sword, A History of the U.S. Air Force, 1950–1997*, vol. 2 (Washington: Air Force History and Museums Program, 1997), 9; Michael Lewis, "Lieutenant General Ned Almond, USA: A Ground Commander's Conflicting View with Airmen over CAS Doctrine and Employment" (Maxwell Air Force Base: U.S. Air Force School of Advanced Airpower Studies, 1996).

39. K. F. Kopets, "The Close Air Support Controversy in Korea," in Jacob Neufeld and G. M. Watson, Jr., eds., *Coalition Air Warfare in the Korean War, 1950–1953* (Washington: Air Force History and Museums Program, 2005).

40. Adam R. Grissom, Caitlin Lee, and Karl P. Mueller, *Innovation in the United States Air Force: Evidence from Six Cases* (Santa Monica: RAND, 2014), 21.

41. Lynn Stover, "Marine Close Air Support in Korea, 1950–1953," unpublished Master's thesis, (Maxwell Air Force Base: School of Advanced Airpower Studies, June 2001), 47.

42. Cited in Fred Allison, "Perfecting Close Air Support in Korea," *Naval History* 20, no. 2 (April 2006), accessed at https://www.usni.org/magazines/navalhistory/2006-04/perfecting-close-air-support-korea.

43. Cited in Allison, "Perfecting Close Air Support in Korea."

44. Millett, *Korea*, 348–49.

45. William T. Y'Blood, *Down in the Weeds: Close Air Support in Korea* (Washington: Air Force History and Museums Program, 2002), 2; Millett, *Korea*, 362.

46. Y'Blood, *Down in the Weeds*, 18.

47. Millett, *Korea*, 362; Y'Blood, *Down in the Weeds*, 10.

48. They were also bringing a lot of experience to the game, with 70 percent of their pilots were combat veterans and with an average of 1,000 hours of flying. Millett, *Korea,* 367.

49. Y'Blood, *Down in the Weeds*, 18.

50. Millett, *Korea*, 363; Y'Blood, *Down in the Weeds*, 3, 6, 15.

51. Futrell, *Korea*, 112.

52. Millett, *Korea*, 364; Y'Blood, *Down in the Weeds*, 8–9.

53. Chandler, "Weyland," 42–43.

54. Wayne Thompson, "The War in Korea," 15–16.

55. Y'Blood, *Down in the Weeds*, 12–13, 15.

56. Y'Blood, *Down in the Weeds*, 22.

57. Y'blood, *Down in the Weeds*, 29–30. Operation Killer was the second counteroffensive launched by United Nations forces against the Chinese Communists and the North Korean Army, conducted between February 20 and March 6, 1951.

58. Futrell, *Korea*, 358.

59. Y'Blood, *Down in the Weeds*, 29–30.

60. Y'Blood, *Down in the Weeds*, 41.

61. Y'Blood, *Down in the Weeds*, 1.

62. Millett, *Korea*, 363–64.

63. Y'Blood, *Down in the Weeds*, 47.

64. Boyne, *Wild Blue Yonder*, 73.

65. Millett, *Korea*, 362.

66. Y'Blood, *Down in the Weeds*, 43.

67. Futrell, *Korea*, 98, 101.

68. William T.Y'Blood, *MiG Alley: The Fight for Air Superiority* (Washington: Air Force History and Museums Program, 2000), 2–3.

69. Y'Blood, *MiG Alley*, 20.

70. Futrell, *Korea*, 243–50, "Sabres to the Rescue" See also Doug Dildy and Warren Thompson, *F-86 Sabre vs MiG-15: Korea 1950–53* (New York: Osprey Publishing 2013).

71. Y'Blood, *MiG Alley*, 14; Futrell, *Korea*, 253.

72. Y'Blood, *MiG Alley*, 33.

73. Futrell, *Korea*, 251; Y'Blood, *MiG Alley*, 13–14.

74. In July 1951 the F-86E with leading edge slats entered the war, followed in June 1952 by the F-86F. Y'Blood, *MiG Alley*, 28, 34; Kenneth P. Werrell, "Aces and -86s: The Fight for Air Superiority during the Korean War," in Jacob Neufeld and George M. Watson, eds., *Coalition Air Warfare in the Korean War, 1950–1953* (Washington: U.S. Air Force History and Museums Program), 2005.

75. Thomas Wildenberg, "The A-1C(M) Gunsight: A Case Study in Technological Innovation in the United States Air Force," *Airpower History* 56, no. 2 (Summer 2009): 28–37.

76. Lt. Col. James Jabara, "A Fighter Pilot's Airplane," *Air Force*, August 1960, available at http://www.airforcemag.com/MagazineArchive/Pages/1960/August%20 1960/0860fighter.aspx.

77. Wildenberg, "The A-1C(M) Gunsight," 34.

78. Kenneth P. Werrell, "Aces and -86s," in Jacob Neufeld and George M. Watson, eds., *Coalition Air Warfare*, 56.

79. William T.Y'Blood, ed., *The Three Wars of Lt. Gen. George E. Stratemeyer: His Korean War Diary* (Washington: Air Force History and Museums Program, 1999), 363. (Hereafter "Three Wars of Stratemeyer").

80. Y'Blood, *MiG Alley*, 33.

81. Warren E. Thompson, and David R. McLaren. *MiG Alley: Sabres vs. MiGs Over Korea,* (North Branch, MN: Specialty Press, 2002), 139–155; Futrell, *Korea*, 651.

82. Futrell, *Korea,* 614–16.

83. From the 319th FIS Association website, accessed Feb. 3, 2019 at http://319th.com /korea.htm.

84. Y'Blood, *MiG Alley*, 23.

85. The complete data base is available at https://www.dpaa.mil/portals/85/Documents /KoreaAccounting/korwald_all.pdf.

86. On Russian air operations in the war see Xiaoming Zhang, *Red Wings over the Yalu: China, the Soviet Union, and the Air War in Korea* (College Station: Texas A&M University, 2003); Igor Seidov with Stuart Britton, *Red Devils over the Yalu: A Chronicle of Soviet Aerial Operations in the Korean War, 1950–53* (New York: Helion, 2014).

87. Quote in Conrad Crane, *American Airpower Strategy in Korea 1950–1953* (Lawrence: University Press of Kansas, 2000), 26.

88. Futrell, *Korea,* 91.

89. Cited in Crane, *American Airpower Strategy,* 33; Chandler, *Weyland,* 39.

90. Y'Blood, *Three Wars of Stratemeyer,* 172.

91. Stratemeyer to Vandenberg, in Y'Blood, *Three Wars of Stratemeyer,* 129.

92. Futrell, *Korea,* 195.

93. Y'Blood, *Three Wars of Stratemeyer,* 68.

94. Futrell, *Korea,* 35.

95. Futrell, *Korea,* 125.

96. Futrell, *Korea,* 433–47; Pape, *Bombing to Win,* 149–51.

97. Crane, *American Airpower Strategy,* 80–83; Futrell, *Korea,* 447–53.

98. Futrell, *Korea,* 327–28.

99. Futrell, *Korea,* 413.

100. Gregory A. Carter, "Historical Notes on Aerial Interdiction in Korea," Santa Monica: RAND, September, 1966, 12.

101. Mark Clark, *From the Danube to the Yalu,* 2–3.

102. Pape, *Bombing to Win,* 150; Futrell, *Korea,* 325.

103. Otto P. Weyland, "The Air Campaign in Korea," *Air University Quarterly Review,* 6, no. 4, (Fall 1953): 21.

104. Futrell, *Korea,* 410–13.

105. Futrell, *Korea,* 416–17.

106. Futrell, *Korea,* 320, 322.

107. Y'Blood, *Three Wars of Stratemeyer,* 358.

108. Futrell, *Korea,* 536. In the summer and autumn of 1952, the B-26s of the 3rd Bomber Wing devised "hunter–killer" tactics for nighttime interdiction of transportation targets. These tactics focused on blocking narrow areas (by a Hunter) and strafing runs along major routes (by the Killer partner).

109. Futrell, *Korea,* 456–57.

110. Futrell, *Korea,* 355.

111. *Steadfast and Courageous, the FEAF (Far East Air Forces) Bomber Command and the Air War in Korea, 1950–1953* (Washington: Air Force History and Museums Program, 2000), 41; Futrell, *Korea,* 408–09.

112. Futrell, *Korea,* 136.

113. Futrell, Korea, 164–65.

114. Futrell, *Korea,* 278.

115. Futrell, *Korea,* 135.

116. Futrell, *Korea,* 425.

117. *Steadfast and Courageous*, 38–39, 44–45; On the history of electronic warfare in the Air Force in this era, see Daniel T. Kuehl, "The Radar Eye Blinded: The USAF and Electronic Warfare, 1945–1955," unpublished Ph.D. dissertation, Duke University, 1992.

118. The officers were Col. R. L. Randolph and Lt. Col. B. I. Mayo, USAF. Thomas C. Hone, "Korea," in R. Cargill Hall, ed., *Case Studies in Strategic Bombardment* (Washington: Air Force History and Museum, 1998), 485, 488; Futrell, *Korea*, 478–87; Crane, "Pressure," 114–25.

119. Quoted in Crane, *American Airpower Strategy in Korea*, 116.

120. Crane. *American Airpower Strategy in Korea*, 119.

121. Conrad Crane, "Searching for Lucrative Targets in North Korea," in *Coalition and Air Warfare in the Korean War, 1950–1953*, Jacob Neufeld and George Watson Jr., eds. (Washington: Air Force History and Museums Program, 2005); Staff Study, "The Attack on the Irrigation Dams in North Korea," *Air University Quarterly Review* 4, no. 3 (Winter 1953–54): 40–61.

122. Kenneth Werrell, *Death from the Heavens, A History of Strategic Bombing* (Annapolis: Naval Institute Press, 2009), 298–99; Futrell, *Korea*, 666–70.

123. Futrell, *Korea*, 669.

124. Quoted in Zach Keck, "How American Airpower Destroyed North Korea," *National Interest*, August 12, 2017, at https://nationalinterest.org/blog/the-buzz/how-american-air-power-destroyed-north-korea-21881.

125. The official Soviet Air Force report claims they shot down a total of 564 enemy aircraft in air battles during the period from November 1950 through January 1952. This total includes over two hundred F-86 Sabres. They report their own losses as thirty-four pilots and seventy-one aircraft. "Report from the 64th Fighter Aviation Corps of the Soviet Air Forces in Korea," July, 1953, 21–32. Accessed from the History and Public Policy Program Digital Archive, at http://digitalarchive.wilsoncenter.org/document/114963.

126. Y'Blood, *Three Wars of Stratemeyer*, 101, 105.

127. I thank Col. Jack "Winder" Arnhauld, USAF, for this insight. Interview at the Pentagon, October 15, 2017.

128. Worden, "Rise of the Fighter Generals," 44.

129. Carl Builder, *The Icarus Syndrome: The Role of Airpower Theory in the Evolution and Fate of the U.S. Air Force* (New Brunswick: Transaction, 2003).

130. Herman S. Wolk, "Planning and Organizing the Post-War Air Force, 1943–1947," (Washington: Air Force History, 1984), 41.

131. John W. Huston, *American Airpower Comes of Age—General Henry H. "Hap" Arnold's World War II Diaries*, vol. 2, (Maxwell Air Force Base: Air University Press, 2002), 416.

132. Donald L. Miller, *Masters of the Air: America's Bomber Boys Who Fought the Air War Against Nazi Germany*, 2007; Phillip Meilinger, *Hoyt S. Vandenberg, the Life of a General* (Bloomington: Indiana University Press, 1989); Y'Blood, *Three Wars of Stratemeyer*, 8.

133. David N. Spires, *Patton's Air Force: Forging a Legendary Air-Ground Team* (Washington: Smithsonian Institution Press, 2002).

134. Quote from Michael J. Chandler, "Gen Otto P. Weyland, USAF Close Air Support in the Korean War" (Maxwell Air Force Base: School of Advanced Air and Space Studies), master's thesis, March 2007, 17.

135. Worden, "Fighter Generals," 2.

136. Cited in Crane, *American Airpower Strategy in Korea*, 115.

137. Robert Farley, "US Air Force Culture, 1947–2017," in Mansoor and Murray, *The Culture of Military Organizations*, 431, 437.

138. For assessments of Air Force culture see Brian Laslie, "Born of Insubordination," in Nathan Finney and Tyrell O. Mayfield, eds., *Redefining the Modern Military: The Intersection of Profession and Ethics* (Annapolis: Naval Institute Press, 2018); and Jeffrey W. Donnithorne, *Four Guardians: A Principled Agent View of American Civil-Military Relations* (Baltimore: Johns Hopkins University Press, 2018), 105–27.

139. Builder, *Masks of War*, 32.

140. Builder, *Masks of War*, 23.

141. James M. Smith, *USAF Culture and Cohesion: Building and Air and Space Force for the 21st Century*, INSS Occasional Paper 19 (Colorado Springs: USAF Institute for National Security Studies, June 1998), xi.

142. Builder, *Masks of War*, 23.

143. Smith, *USAF Culture and Cohesion*, 18.

144. Thomas, "The Cultural Identity of the United States Air Force," 10.

145. Builder, *Masks of War*, 21. See also Smith, *USAF Culture and Cohesion*, 13.

146. Builder, *Masks of War*, 22.

147. Lynne E. Vermillion, "Understanding the Air Force Culture," Command and General Staff College, Fort Leavenworth, 1996. "The other services use technology to enhance their traditional warfighting methods at the tactical and operational levels of war; however, the basic Air Force assumption is that technology can be best used for strategic operations. One could think of the Air Force as 'Technology 'R' Us.'" Quote at 29.

148. Donnithorne, *Four Guardians*, 14.

149. Thomas Mahnken, "U.S. Strategic and Organizational Subcultures," in Jeannie L. Johnson, Kerry M. Kartchner, and Jeffrey A. Larsen, eds., *Strategic Culture and Weapons of Mass Destruction: Culturally Based Insights into Comparative National Security Policymaking*, (New York: Palgrave Macmillan, 2009), 78.

150. James Burk, "Military Culture," *Encyclopedia of Violence, Peace, and Conflict*, vol. 2, (San Diego: Academic Press, 1999), 449.

151. Daniel L. Magruder Jr., "The U.S. Air Force and Irregular Warfare: Success as a Hurdle," *Small Wars Journal*, 2009, accessed at http://smallwarsjournal.com/blog/journal/docs-temp/272-magruder.pdf.

152. William C. Thomas, "The Cultural Identity of the United States Air Force," *Air & Space Power Journal Chronicles* (January 30, 2004).

153. Builder, *Masks of War*, 26.

154. Builder, *Masks of War*, 28.

155. Thomas, "The Cultural Identity of the United States Air Force," 7.

156. Donnithorne, *Four Guardians*, 110.

157. Smith, *USAF Culture and Cohesion*, 13. See also Builder, *The Masks of War*, 27.

158. Magruder, Jr., "The U.S. Air Force and Irregular Warfare."

159. Kenneth Beebe, "The Air Force's Missing Doctrine," *Air and Space Power Journal* 20, no. 1 (Spring 2006): 28, 32.

160. James M. Smith, *USAF Culture and Cohesion*, 10.

161. Murray, "Does Military Culture Matter?," 27.

162. 51st Fighter Interceptor Wing study, cited in Futrell, *Korea*, 509.

163. Phillip S. Meilinger, *Bomber: The Formation and Early Years of Strategic Air Command* (Maxwell Air Force Base: Air University Press, 2012), 43–45.

164. Charles W. McArthur, *Operations Analysis in the United States Army Eighth Air Force in World War II* (Providence: American Mathematics Society, 1991). See also Hugh Miser, "Operations Analysis in the Army Air Forces in World War II: Some Reminiscences," *INTERFACES* 23, no. 5 (September–October 1993): 47–49.

165. Millett, "Korea, 1950–1953," 385, 407.

166. Cranc, *American Air Power Strategy in Korea*, 60–61; Glenn O. Barcus, *Evaluation of the United States Air Force in the Korean Campaign* (Barcus Report, Maxwell Air Force Base: Air Force Historical Research Agency 7 vols., Mar. 12, 1951). The Secretary of the Air Force study was conducted by Dr. Robert L. Stearns, president of the University of Colorado (Korean Evaluation Project: Report on Air Operations, January 16, 1951).

167. Millett, "Korea, 1950–1953," in Cooling, *Case Studies in Close Air Support*, 385, 407.

168. Futrell, *Korea*, 632.

169. The term *clobber* was originally British air force slang in World War II, and usually referred to aerial bombing. W. Paddy Harbison, "The Korean Air War," in Jacob Neufeld and George M. Watson Jr., eds., *Coalition Air Warfare in the Korean War* (Washington: U.S. Air Force History and Museums Program, 2005), 50; Richard P. Hallion, ed., *Silver Wings, Golden Valor: The USAF Remembers Korea* (Washington: Air Force History and Museums Program, 2006), 49, 53.

170. Futrell, *Korea*, 470.

171. Kenneth P. Werrell, "Aces and -86s," in Jacob Neufeld and George M. Watson, eds., *Coalition Air Warfare*, 56.

172. From the conclusion of Peter R. Mansoor and Williamson Murray, eds., *The Culture of Military Organizations* (New York: Cambridge University Press, 2019), 449.

173. Tami Davis Biddle, "Airpower and Warfare: A Century of Theory and History" (Carlisle: Strategic Studies Institute, March 2019).

174. I. B. Holley Jr., "A Retrospect on Close Air Support," in Cooling, *Close Air Support*, 542.

Chapter 5. The Army in Vietnam

1. Harold Moore and Joseph Galloway, *We Were Soldiers Once . . . and Young* (New York: Random House, 1992); Charles Heller and William A. Stofft, eds., *America's First Battles, 1776–1965* (Lawrence: University Press of Kansas, 1986), 300.

2. Joe Galloway, "Ia Drang, the Battle That Convinced Ho Chi Minh He Could Win," History.net.com (October 2010), accessed at http://www.historynet.com/ia-drang -where-battlefield-losses-convinced-ho-giap-and-mcnamara-the-u-s-could-never -win.htm.

3. Robert W. Komer, *Bureacracy Does Its Thing* (Santa Monica: RAND, 1972), ix.

4. Ronald Spector, *Advice and Support: The Early Years, 1941–1960, U.S. Army in Vietnam* (Washington: Center of Military History, 1983).

5. Andrew F. Krepinevich, *The Army and Vietnam* (Baltimore: Johns Hopkins University Press, 1986), 29–33.

6. On training and advisory efforts, see *Pentagon Papers*, Washington: Department of Defense, 1969, IV. B. 3, 13–54. Accessed at http://www.nytimes.com/interactive /us/2011_PENTAGON_PAPERS.html?ref=us.

7. Graham A. Cosmas, *MACV: The Joint Command in the Years of Escalation, 1962–1967* (Washington: U.S. Army Center of Military History, 2006).

8. Dale Andradé, "Westmoreland was Right, learning the wrong lessons from the Vietnam War," *Small War and Insurgencies* 19, no. 2 (June 2008): 155.

9. Cosmas, *MACV*, 193.

10. William C. Westmoreland, *A Soldier Reports* (New York: Doubleday, 1976), 104.

11. National Security Action Memorandum 328, dated April 6, 1965. Accessed at http:// www.fas.org/irp/offdocs/nsam-lbj/nsam-328.htm.

12. The decisions regarding the American intervention in Vietnam can be found in *The Pentagon Papers,* IV.B.6.a. For more details see Cosmas, "The Fateful Decisions," 226– 58; Gordon M. Goldstein, *Lessons in Disaster: McGeorge Bundy and the Path to War in Vietnam* (New York: Henry Holt, 2008), 144–85.

13. Westmoreland, *A Soldier Reports*, 180.

14. The strategy development effort is addressed in *The Pentagon Papers*, IV.C.6. See also John M. Carland, "Winning the Vietnam War: Westmoreland's Approach in Two Documents," *The Journal of Military History*, 68 (April 2004): 553–74.

15. MACV Directive 525–4: "Tactics and Techniques for Employment of US Forces in the Republic of Vietnam" (September 17, 1965); Andradé, "Westmoreland was Right," 145–81.

16. Krepinevich, *The Army and Vietnam,* passim.

17. Carland, "Winning the Vietnam War," 569; Andrew J. Birtle, "PROVN, Westmoreland, and the Historians: A Reappraisal," *The Journal of Military History* 72, no. 4 (October 2008).

18. John J. Tolson, *Airmobility: 1961–1971* (Washington: Department of the Army, 1977), vii.

19. James M. Gavin, "Cavalry, and I Don't Mean Horses!," *Armor* 67, no. 3 (May–June, 1958).

20. McNamara, Memo for Mr. Stahr, April 19, 1962, copied in Shelby Stanton, *Anatomy of a Division, The 1st Cav in Vietnam* (New York: Warner, 1987), 15–17.

21. "I shall be disappointed if the . . . re-examination merely produces more of the same, rather than a plan for implementing fresh and perhaps unorthodox concepts which will give us a significant increase in mobility." McNamara, 16–17.

22. U.S. Army Combat Development Command, *The Origins, Deliberations and Recommendations of the U.S. Army Tactical Mobility Requirements Board* (Ft. Leavenworth, 1969).

23. The team was activated in South Vietnam in November, 1962. Army Concept Team, *AirMobile Company in Counterinsurgency Operations* (July 25, 1964).

24. J. D. Coleman, *Pleiku: The Dawn of Helicopter Warfare in Vietnam* (New York: St. Martin's Press, 1988); Kevin J. Dougherty, "The Evolution of Air Assault," *Joint Force Quarterly* (Summer 1999): 51–58; Shelby Stanton, "Lessons Learned or Lost: Air Cavalry and Airmobility," *Military Review* (January 1989): 75–76.

25. Quoted in John M. Carland, "How We Got There: Air Assault and the Emergence of the 1st Cavalry Division (Airmobile), 1950–1965" (Arlington: Land Warfare Institute, No. 42, May 2003): 1.

26. John M. Carland, *Combat Operations: Stemming the Tide, May 1965 to October 1966* (Washington: Center of Military History, 2000), 113–50.

27. Moore and Galloway, *We Were Soldiers Once*, 30.

28. CAAR, 1/7th, Ia Drang Valley Operations, 9 December 1965, 13; Carland, *Stemming the Tide*, 132.

29. Carland, *Stemming the Tide,* 133–45; Moore and Galloway, *We Were Soldiers Once*, 215–91.

30. John Albright, John A. Cash, and Allan W. Sandstrum, *Seven Firefights in Vietnam* (Washington: Government Printing Office, 1970), 7–33; Neil Sheehan, "Battalion of GIs Battered in Trap, Casualties High," *New York Times* (November 19, 1965), 1.

31. CAAR, 1/7 Moore, 13–14.

32. CAAR, 2/7, Silver Bayonet, dated November 24, 1965, 5, accessed at Texas Tech Virtual Vietnam Archive at http://www.vietnam.ttu.edu/virtualarchive/items.php?item=168300010045.

33. CAAR, 1st Cav Airmobile, March 4, 66.

34. Harry W. Kinnard,. "A Victory in the Ia Drang: The Triumph of a Concept," *Army* (September 1967):71–91.

35. Westmoreland, *Report on the War in Vietnam*, 1968, 99; Krepinevich, 169.

36. See George Herring's Ia Drang chapter in Charles Heller and William A. Stofft, eds., *America's First Battles, 1776–1965* (Lawrence: University Press of Kansas, 1986), 300; Krepinevich, *The Army in Vietnam*, 168–69.

37. Moore and Galloway, 339, 345.

38. Carland, *Stemming the Tide*, 168.

39. CAAR, 173rd Brigade, Operation Marauder, January 18, 1966; Thomas Faley, "Operation *Marauder:* Allied Offensive in the Mekong Delta," *Vietnam,* June 12, 2006. Accessed at http://www.historynet.com/operation-marauder-allied-offensive-in-the-mekong-delta.htm.

40. Carland, *Stemming the Tide*, 169–173; CAAR, 173rd Brigade, Operation *Crimp*, February 23, 1966.

41. CAAR, 173rd, Operation Crimp, 17.

42. Commander's Combat Note 91, 173rd Brigade, dated January 22 1966, 6. This note was published by the U.S. Army as ORLL, 1–66 Operation Crimp, March 22, 1966.

43. Carland, *Stemming the Tide*, 173.

44. Carland, *Stemming the Tide*, 201–30; Al Hemingway, "Operation Masher, 1966," *VFW Magazine* (January 2004).

45. 1st Air Cav Division, AAR, "Operation Masher/White Wing," April 28, 1966.

46. MACV, Command History for 1966, January 14, 1967, 4.

47. On this tactic see James Kitfield, *Prodigal Soldiers, How the Generation of Officers Born of Vietnam Revolutionized the American Style of War* (Dulles: Potomac Books, 1997), 70–71; George Wilson, *Mud Soldiers, Life Inside the New American Army* (New York: Scribner's, 1989), 7–40.

48. Carland, *Stemming the Tide*, 306.

49. CAAR, Headquarters, 1st Infantry Division, Operation *Abilene*, n.d., 34.

50. CAAR.

51. DePuy, "Troop A at Ap Tau O," in *DePuy's Selected Papers*, 375–85. Quotation from 384.

52. CAAR, 1st Infantry Division, Operation *Abilene*, 49.

53. Carland, *Stemming the Tide*, 319–24.

54. Maj. Gen. W. E. DePuy, "Minh Thanh Road," July 9, 1966, *The American Traveler* (July 1966). Accessed at http://www.asalives.org/ASAONLINE/uwarriors.htm.

55. Carland, *Stemming the Tide*, 324; CAAR, Operation El Paso II, 1st Inf. Division, 42.

56. CAAR, 1st Infantry Division, Operation El Paso II/III, n.d., 48.

57. Donn A. Starry, *Armored Combat in Vietnam* (New York: Arno, 1980), 66–67.

58. John H. Hay Jr., *Vietnam Studies: Tactical and Material Innovations* (Washington: Department of the Army, 1974), 53–54.

59. Westmoreland, *Report on the War in Vietnam*, 120–22.

60. Headquarters, I Field Force Vietnam, ORLL, dated May 15, 1966, 1 for quote, and Enclosure 1 for kill ratio table.

61. Headquarters, MACV, Lessons Learned No. 55; "The Battle of Annihilation," March 15, 1966.

62. Headquarters I Field Force Vietnam, OR for Quarterly Period Ending October 31, 1966, dated November 30, 1966, 1.

63. COMUSMACV message 07760, May 11, 1966. Cited in Military History Branch Office of the Secretary Joint Staff. *Command History United States Military Assistance Command, Vietnam 1966* (Alexandria: Department of the Army, 1966), 344.

64. Westmoreland, *Report on the War in Vietnam*, 120.

65. *Pentagon Papers*, IV B 6 C, 62.

66. George L. MacGarrigle, *Combat Operations: Taking the Offensive: October 1966 to October 1967* (Washington: Center of Military History, 1998), 35. Hereafter, *Taking the Offensive*. See overview of the campaign, 31–60.

67. Guy S. Meloy, "Operation Attleboro, The Wolfhound's Brave Stand," *Vietnam* (October, 1997): 38–44.

68. DePuy on Attleboro, Oral History, 144–46.

69. Charles K. Nulsen, "Operation Attleboro: The 196th's Light Infantry Brigade Baptism By Fire in the Vietnam War," *Historynet.com*, June 12, 2006; Shelby Stanton, *Anatomy of a Division, The 1st Cav in Vietnam* (New York: Warner, 1987), 105–7.

70. Rod Paschall, "Operation *Attleboro*—From Calamity to Crushing Victory," *HistoryNet .com* (July 20, 2011), accessed at http://www.historynet.com/operation-attleboro -from-calamity-to-crushing-victory.htm.

71. MacGarrigle, *Taking the Offensive*, 56.

72. II Field Force Lessons Learned, for period ending October 31, 1967, 4.

73. CAAR, Operation *Attleboro*, Headquarters 25th Infantry Division, December 11, 1966, 9.

74. MacGarrigle, *Taking the Offensive*, 59.

75. CAAR, 2d Bn, 27th Infantry, The Wolfhounds, Operation *Attleboro*, November 24 1966, 15.

76. Gen. Bernard W. Rogers, *Cedar Falls—Junction City: A Turning Point* (Washington: Department of the Army, 1974), 16.

77. A village made famous by Jonathan Schell, *The Village of Ben Suc* (New York: Knopf, 1967).

78. Rogers, *Cedar Falls—Junction City*, 74.

79. CAAR, Operation Cedar Falls, 173rd Brigade, dated February 23, 1967, 1, 50.

80. Cited in Rogers, *Cedar Falls—Junction City*, 75.

81. CAAR, Operation Cedar Falls, II Field Force, Vietnam, n.d.

82. Cited in Rogers, *Cedar Falls—Junction City*, 79.

83. Rogers, 83, for an overview of the plans see MacGarrigle, *Taking the Offensive*, 115–18.

84. ORLL, II Field Force, for Quarterly Period ending January 31, 1967, dated February 15, 1967, 7, 19–20.

85. MacGarrigle, *Taking the Offensive*, 141–42.

86. Cited in Rogers, *Cedar Falls—Junction City*, 153.

87. Westmoreland, *A Soldier Reports*, 205; drawn from CAAR, II Field Force Vietnam, Operation Cedar Falls, n.d., Incl 2, 110.

88. CAAR, Operation Junction City, 1st Infantry Division. May 8, 1967, 18–19.

89. Rogers, *Cedar Falls—Junction City*, 153.

90. Rogers, 154.

91. Rogers, 156.

92. Willbanks, et al. *Advanced Battle Analysis: Operation Junction City* (Fort Leavenworth: U.S. Army Command and General Staff College, 1983), 37.

93. CAAR-Sam Houston, Headquarters, 4th Infantry Division, May 16, 1967.

94. CAAR-Sam Houston, Headquarters, 4th Infantry Division, 1, 14; MacGarrigle, *Taking the Offensive*, 175.

95. CAAR-Sam Houston, Headquarters, 4th Infantry Division, 4.

96. CAAR-Sam Houston, Headquarters, 4th Infantry Division. The 4th Infantry Division reported 196,000 rounds fired, see ORLL, 4th Infantry, June 15, 1967, 24.

97. CAAR, Sam Houston, Headquarters, 4th Infantry Division, 39.

98. MacGarrigle, *Taking the Offensive*, 177.

99. The National Security Action Memorandum No. 362 is at http://www.lbjlib.utexas .edu/johnson/archives.hom/NSAMs/nsam362.asp.

100. Frank Leith Jones, *Blowtorch: Robert Komer, Vietnam, and American Cold War Strategy* (Annapolis: Naval Institute Press), 2013.

101. Frank L. Jones, "Blowtorch: Robert Komer and the Making of Vietnam Pacification Policy," *Parameters* 35, no. 3 (Autumn 2005): 103–18.

102. Dale Andradé and James H. Willbanks, "CORDS/Phoenix: Counterinsurgency Lessons from Vietnam for the Future," *Military Review* 86, no. 2 (March/April 2006): 9–23.

103. Westmoreland, *Report on the War in Vietnam*, 142; Cosmas, *MACV*, 357–63.

104. Erik Villard, *Combat Operations: Staying the Course*, October 1967 to September 1968 (Washington: Center of Military History, 2017), 10–11.

105. Andradé and Willbanks, 16.

106. Draft MACV Handbook, *Military Support of Revolutionary Development*, Military Assistance Command, Vietnam, 9 May 1967. Cited by 9th Infantry Division in its July 1967 ORLL, 57.

107. Sydney Berry, "Observations of a Brigade Commander," *Military Review* (January 1968): 8.

108. Berry, 17. See also David Richard Palmer, *Summons of the Trumpet, U.S.-Vietnam in Perspective* (Novata: Presidio, 1978), 144.

109. Bruce I. Gudmundsson, *On Artillery* (Westport: Praeger, 1993), 152.

110. *MACV Command History*, 1967, vol. 1 (September 16, 1968), 342–45; Westmoreland, *A Soldier Reports*, 269.

111. Villard, *Combat Operations: Staying the Course*, 9.

112. Villard, *Combat Operations: Staying the Course*, passim.

113. MacGarrigle, *Taking the Offensive*, 347–65.

114. CAAR, 1st Brigade, 1st Infantry Division, December 8, 1967.

115. MacGarrigle, *Taking the Offensive*, 355.

116. David Maraniss, *They Marched into Sunlight: War and Peace Vietnam and American October 1967*, (New York: Simon and Schuster, 2004), 226.

117. On cloverleafs, see Hay, *Tactical and Materiel Innovations*, 42–45.

118. Contemporary Historical Evaluation of Combat Operations, "Ambush at XT 686576," Air Force, Hawaii, December 29, 1967.

119. On the desperate ambush see Maraniss, *They Marched into Sunlight*, 260–83; MacGarrigle, *Taking the Offensive*, 353–61.

120. CAAR, 1st Brigade, 1st Infantry Division, Operation *Shenandoah* II, 20.

121. Hay, *Tactical and Materiel Innovations*, 50–51.

122. ORLL, II Field Force Vietnam, for period ending Oct. 1967, dated January 12, 1968, 30.

123. James E. Shelton, *The Beast Was Out There: The 28th Infantry Black Lions and the Battle of Ong Thanh, Vietnam, October 1967* (Chicago: Cantigny First Division Foundation, 2002).

124. The official history of this period is captured well by Eric Villard, *Combat Operations: Staying the Course, October 1967 to September 1968* (Washington: Center of Army History, 2017), 145–81.

125. CAAR, Operation *Paul Revere* IV, 4th Infantry Division, January 28, 1967.

126. David H. Hackworth with Julie Sherman, *Saving Face, The Odyssey of an American Warrior* (New York: Simon and Schuster, 1989), 570.

127. Maj. Gen. W. R. Peers, Presentation to MACV Commanders Conference, December 3, 1967, 1. Accessed at http://www.virtual.vietnam.ttu.edu/cgi-bin/starfetch. exe?5CaeZmzqgwMHKpueFEBWvl2djSQ1WVeD6zFq0IkvKB9kubBW7rKKZD pDUcrF1sqNYa55NNZejnwO.nqFeL1OBPAslicz5mWrueJuMR7s9T5BNCCA17tAyQ /0010106001.pdf.

128. The fight for Hill 875 is presented in detail in Villard, *Staying the Course*, 170–77.

129. Peers, slides with presentation; John Prados, *Vietnam: The History of an Unwinnable War, 1945–1975* (Lawrence: Kansas University Press, 2009), 226–27.

130. W. C. Westmoreland, transcript, "Progress Report on the War in Vietnam," National Press Club, Washington, November 21, 1967. Accessed at http://www. virtual .vietnam.ttu.edu/cgi-bin/starfetch.exe?4p4WjBcCrYrflmSRaZdZrAcffgMfFLYV .fJnPaO6B.eUsNaaIxpxKhxABYwKquzliaL7AeYFf.7o@370E5N7nR0BtVPysJ1T 5qH7ZEshU.A/2120908021.pdf.

131. Westmoreland, transcript of question and answer period, 3.

132. MACV message to CJCS, 062316Z Dec 67, accessed from LBJ library.

133. MacGarrigle, *Taking the Offensive*, 296, 309, 433.

134. Edward F. Murphy, *Dak To: America's Sky Soldiers in South Vietnam's Central Highlands* (New York: Presidio, 1993); John Prados, "Dak To: One Hell of a Fight," *Veteran Online* (January/February 2012). Accessed at http://vvaveteran.org/32–1/32–1 _dakto67.html.

135. MacGarrigle, *Taking the Offensive*, 327.

136. Maj. Gen. William B. Fulton, *Riverine Operations 1966–1969* (Washington: Department of the Army, 1985).

137. Each RAS had five LCM-6s as command boats, fifty-two LCM-6s as troop carriers, and ten LCM-6 gun boat "Monitors."

138. Fulton, 59. On the early operations of the MRF see MacGarrigle, 393–409; CAAR, Operation River Raider I, 3rd Bn, 47th Infantry, 16 February 16–March 20, 1967.

139. MacGarrigle, *Taking the Offensive*, 408.

140. MacGarrigle, 416–25; ORLL, II Field Force Vietnam, for period ending October 1967, dated January 12, 1968, 24.

141. ORLL, 9th Infantry Division, Period May 1 to July 31, 1967, November 7, 1967, 18; Senior Officer Debriefing Report, Maj Gen. George O'Connor, February 25, 1968, 7.

142. MacGarrigle, *Taking the Offensive*, 430; *MACV Command History*, 1967, vol. 3, 1244. Westmoreland, *A Soldier Reports*, 209.

143. See James H. Willbanks, *The TET Offensive: A Concise History* (New York: Columbia University Press, 2007), 104–9.

144. Eric Hammel, *Fire in the Streets: The Battle for Hue* (Chicago: Contemporary, 1991).

145. *The Pentagon Papers*, IV.C.6.c, 16.

146. MACV Campaign Plan for 1968, dated November 11, 1967, 2.11; MacGarrigle, 443; Westmoreland, *Report on the War*, 136.

147. Westmoreland, *A Soldier Reports*, 321.

148. Ronald Spector, *After Tet: The Bloodiest Year in Vietnam* (New York: Vintage, 1994).

149. Ernest B. Furguson, *Westmoreland: The Inevitable General* (Boston: Little, Brown, 1968).

150. On his military service, see Westmoreland, *A Soldier Reports*, 9–40.

151. Lewis Sorley, *Westmoreland: The General Who Lost Vietnam* (Boston: Houghton, Mifflin, Harcourt, 2011), 12, 18, 25. Westmoreland attended two schools, parachute school and a course in mess management.

152. Quoted in Thomas Ricks, *The Generals: American Military Command from World War II to Today* (New York: Penguin, 2013), 233.

153. Lt. Gen. Phillip Davidson, cited in Ricks, *The Generals*, 235. General Davidson served as Westmoreland's Intelligence Officer at MACV.

154. Stanley Karnow, *Vietnam*, 345; Tom Ricks, *The Generals*, 231–40.

155. Sorley, *Westmoreland*, 52–53.

156. Sorley, 118, quoting Lt. Gen. Walter Ulmer. Gen. John Galvin, later Supreme Allied Commander, Europe in the 1980s, who served with Westmoreland in Vietnam and Washington, once quipped that "Westmoreland had an astonishing lack of interest in a wide range of things." Quoted in Sorely, *Westmoreland*, 264.

157. Ricks, *The Generals*, 233.

158. Henry K. Gole, *General William E. DePuy, Preparing the Army for Modern War* (Lexington: University Press of Kentucky, 2008), 152–53.

159. John R. Galvin, *Fighting the Cold War: A Soldier's Memoir* (Lexington: University of Kentucky, 2015), 128.

160. Romie L. Brownlee and William J. Mullen III, *Changing an Army: An Oral History of General William E. DePuy, USA* (Washington: Center of Military History, 1988), 138.

161. Brownlee and Mullen, 84.

162. Brownlee and Mullen, 140.

163. Sorley, ed., *Press On! Selected Works of General Donn A. Starry* (Leavenworth: Combined Studies Institute Press, 2009), 947–78.

164. Gole, *General William E. DePuy*, fn 15, 32, 314, 316.

165. Gole, 314, see footnote 16.

166. Gole, 153.

167. Ricks, *The Generals*, 246; Gole, *General William E. DePuy*, 151–52.

168. Gole, *General William E. DePuy*, 175.

169. Neil Sheehan, *A Bright and Shining Lie: John Paul Vann and American in Vietnam* (New York: Vintage Books, 1989), 11.

170. Ricks, *The Generals*, 249–51.

171. Gole, *General William E. DePuy*, 153.

172. Gole, 152; Brownlee and Mullen, *Changing an Army*, 151–52, 156.

173. Brownlee and Mullen, *Changing an Army*, 162.

174. DePuy, "Vietnam: What We Might Have Done and Why We Didn't Do It," in Donald L. Gilmore and Carolyn D. Conway, eds., *Selected Papers of General William E. DePuy* (Fort Leavenworth: Combat Studies Institute, 1995), 358.

175. Builder, *The Masks of War*, 186.

176. Russell Weigley, *The American Way of War, A History of U.S. Military Strategy and Policy* (Bloomington: Indiana University Press, 1973), 464–65; Austin Long, "First War Syndrome, Culture, Professionalization and Military Doctrine," Ph.D. dissertation, MIT, February 2011, 74–130, 214–85.

177. Thomas Adams, "Military Doctrine and the Organization Culture of the U.S. Army," Ph.D. dissertation, Syracuse University, 1990.

178. Adams, 6.

179. On West Point's influence see Rick Atkinson, *The Long Gray Line, The American Journey of West Point's Class of 1966* (New York: Henry Holt, 2009).

180. Jorg Muth, *Command Culture: Officer Education in the U.S. Army and the German Armed Forces, 1901–1940* (Denton: University of North Texas, 2011), 194.

181. Brian M. Jenkins, "The Unchangeable War" (Santa Monica: RAND November, 1970.)

182. A German officer's evaluation of the World War II American Army. Found in Muth, *Command Culture*, 210.

183. Brian McAllister Linn, *The Echo of Battle: The Army's War of War* (Cambridge: Harvard University Press, 2007).

184. Linn, 7, 8.

185. Builder, *Mask of War*, 106.

186. Linn, *Echo of Battle*, 185.

187. Kinnard, *War Managers, passem*.

188. Kitfield, *Prodigal Soldiers*, 104.

189. Leonard Wong, "Stifled Innovation?" Carlisle: Army War College, April 2002, 3.

190. Bruce Palmer Jr., "*U.S. Intelligence and Vietnam*," *Special Studies in Intelligence*, 28 (1984): 41, 124–25.

191. Gregory A. Daddis, *No Sure Victory: Measuring U.S. Army Effectiveness and Progress in the Vietnam War* (Oxford: Oxford University Press, 2011), 225.

192. Charles R. Shrader, *History of Operations Research in the United States Army, 1961–1973*, vol. 2 (Washington: Center of Military History, 2008).

193. The CAC work is listed in Operational Report—Lessons Learned Headquarters, U.S. Army Vietnam, for Period Ending October 31, 1967 (February 12, 1968), 44.

194. PROVN stands for Program for the Pacification and Long-Term Development of Vietnam. Krepinevich, 182–83; Sorely, *Westmoreland*, 104–5 and Lewis Sorley, *A Better War, The Unexamined Victories and Final Tragedy of America's Last Years in Vietnam* (New York: Harcourt, Brace, 1999), 19–20. The counter is found at Andrew J. Birtle, "PROVN, Westmoreland and the Historians, A Reappraisal," *The Journal of Military History* 72, no. 1 (October 2008): 1213–47.

195. J. Elmore Swenson, "The Army Concept Team in Vietnam," *United States Army Aviation Digest* (July 1968): 16–18.
196. Mai Elliot, *RAND in Southeast Asia: A History of the Vietnam War Era* (Santa Monica: RAND, 2007).
197. Mai Elliot, viii.
198. Cosmas, *MACV*, 292.
199. Lt. Gen. Julian J. Ewell and Maj. Gen. Ira A. Hunt, Jr., *Sharpening the Combat Edge: The Use of Analysis to Reinforce Military Judgment* (Washington: Department of the Army, 1974).
200. Cosmas, *MACV*, 294.
201. Daddis, *No Sure Victory*, 221.
202. I am indebted to Dr. Thomas X. Hammes for this insight.
203. John E. Mueller, "The Search for the 'Breaking Point' in Vietnam," *International Studies Quarterly* 24, no. 4 (December 1980): 497–519; Gregory A. Daddis, "The Problem of Metrics: Assessing Progress and Effectiveness in the Vietnam War," *War in History* 19, no. 1 (January 2012): 73–98.
204. Galvin, *Fighting the Cold War*, 140. That same major later became a general and served as Supreme Allied Commander, Europe.
205. Daddis, *No Sure Victory*, 234.
206. Cosmas, *MACV*, 295.
207. Dennis Vetock, *Lessons Learned, A History of U.S. Army Lessons Learned* (Carlisle: Army Military History Institute, 1988).
208. S. L. A. Marshall and David H. Hackworth, USA, *Military Operations: Lessons Learned: Vietnam Primer* (Washington: Department of the Army), April 21, 1967.
209. See for example Operational Report—Lessons Learned 9–66, Equipment, December 7, 1966. See also U.S Army, Vietnam, *Battlefield Reports: A Summary of Lessons Learned*, vol. 3, May 1967.
210. Headquarters, U.S. Army Continental Command, *Education and Training Operations Lessons Learned* (October 18, 1965).
211. Senior Officer Debriefing Report, Commander 9th Infantry Division, "Impressions of a Field Force Commander in Vietnam," February 25, 1968–April 5, 1969 (April 15, 1970).
212. Peter Senge, cited in Karen Guttieri, "Unlearning War: US Military Experience with Stability Operations," in M. Leann Brown, Michael Kenney, and Michael Zarkin, eds., *Organizational Learning in the Global Context*, (London: Ashgate, 2006).
213. Andrew J. Birtle, *U.S. Army Counterinsurgency and Contingency Operations Doctrine, 1942–1976* (Washington: Center of Military History, 2006), 419–44.
214. Birtle, 459.
215. *Pentagon Papers*, Book IV, C. 6(a), 127.
216. Komer, *Bureaucracy Does Its Thing*, xi, 7.
217. Jenkins, "The Unchangeable War," 2.
218. Jenkins, 3.

219. Peter Schoomaker, in Foreword to Nagl, *Learning to East Soup with a Knife*, ix.

220. Hay, *Tactical and Material Innovations*, 179.

Chapter 6. From the Halls of Fallujah to the Shores of the Euphrates

1. U.S. Marine Corps, *Marine Corps Operating Concepts* (Quantico: Marine Corps Combat Development Command, June 2010), 24. Accessed at http://www.hqmc.marines.mil/Portals/142/Docs/MOC%20July%2013%20update%202010_Final%5B1%5D.pdf.

2. Robert D. Kaplan, "Five Days in Fallujah," *The Atlantic Monthly* (July–August 2004).

3. Bing West and Raymond Smith, *The March Up: Taking Baghdad with the 1st Marine Division* (New York: Bantam Books, 2003).

4. On the Marines' initial attack Thomas Ricks, *Fiasco: The American Military Adventure in Iraq* (New York: Penguin Press, 2006), 116–48; Michael Gordon and Gen. Bernard Trainor, *Cobra II: The Inside Story of the Invasion and Occupation of Iraq* (New York: Pantheon, 2006), 182–97, 234–59, 411–17.

5. James T. Conway, "Farther and Faster in Iraq," U.S. Naval Institute *Proceedings*, (January 2005).

6. Gen. John Kelly, "Tikrit, South to Babylon," *Marine Corps Gazette* (February 2004).

7. General Mattis' letter is found at Kenneth W. Estes, *U.S. Marine Corps Operations in Iraq, 2003–2006* (Quantico: Marine History Division, 2012), 26–27.

8. Carl E. Mundy III, "Spare the Rod, Save the Nation," *New York Times* (December 30, 2003), A21.

9. Col. Ronald L. Bailey, cited by Janine Davidson, *Lifting the Fog of Peace* (Ann Arbor: University of Michigan Press, 2011), 1.

10. Christopher Conlin, "What Do You Do for an Encore?" *Marine Corps Gazette* (September 2004): 79.

11. Lt. Gen. James N. Mattis, USMC (Ret.) personal interview, Quantico, November 8, 2014.

12. Thomas Connally and Lance McDaniel, "Leaving the Tubes at Home," *Marine Corps Gazette* (October 2005): 31–34.

13. Col. John Toolan, cited in Richard H. Schultz, *The Marines Take Anbar* (Annapolis: Naval Institute Press, 2013), 63.

14. Lieutenant General Conway interview in Timothy McWilliams and Kurtis P. Wheeler, eds., *Al-Anbar Awakening, Vol. I, American Perspectives* (Quantico: Marine University Press, 2009), 43.

15. Michael B. Gordon, "Marines Plan to Use Velvet Glove More than Iron Fist in Iraq," *New York Times*, December 12, 2003; Ricks, *Fiasco*, 317.

16. On the first battle see Bing West, *No True Glory: A Frontline Account of the Battle for Fallujah* (New York: Bantam Books, 2005), 58–73, 112–23; Schultz, *The Marines Take Anbar*, 77–81.

17. Col. John Toolan, powerpoint slide presentation on Fallujah, undated, circa 2007.

18. West, *No True Glory*, 65–93, 112–43.

19. Dexter Filkins and James Glanz, "With Airpower and Armor, Troops Enter Rebel-Held City," *New York Times*, November 8, 2004.

20. Schultz, *The Marines Take Anbar*, 74–84; Estes, *Marine Operations in Iraq*, 33–37, West, *No True Glory*, 172–220; Brendan Miniter, "The Fallujah Brigade," *Wall Street Journal*, June 1, 2004.

21. Carter Malkasian, "Signaling Resolve, Democratization, and the First Battle of Fallujah," *Journal of Strategic Studies* 29, no. 3 (August 2006): 423–52; Rajiv Chandrasekaran, "We Won: Fallujah Rejoices in Withdrawal," *Washington Post*, May 2, 2004.

22. Estes, *Marine Operations in Iraq*, 40; West, *No True Glory*, 74–88, 124–33.

23. Timothy S. McWilliams, with Nicholas Schlosser, *U.S. Marines in Battle: Fallujah, Nov.-Dec 2014* (Quantico: Marine Corps History Division, 2014); Estes, "The Second Al-Fallujah Battle," in *U. S. Marines in Iraq, 2003–2006* (Quantico: Marine Corps History Division, 2011), 49–79.

24. Lt. Gen. John F. Sattler and Lt. Col. Daniel H. Wilson, "Operation Al Fajr: The Battle of Fallujah—Part II," *Marine Corps Gazette* (July 2005); Schultz Jr., *The Marines Take Anbar*, 92–103; Col. Joseph A. L'Etoile interview by John Way, Marine Corps History Division, June 16, 2005, 14.

25. Lt. Gen. John Sattler interview in *Al-Anbar Awakening*, 82.

26. Lt. Gen. John Sattler, Battle of Fallujah Erskine Lecture, Quantico, October 31, 2014. (Author attended this lecture and interviewed the speaker briefly).

27. Lt.Gen. John Sattler, interview by John Way, Marine Corps History Division, April 8, 2005, 10–14.

28. Sattler and Wilson, "Operation Al Fajr," 93.

29. Interview with Lt.Gen. Richard Natonski by Laurence Lessard, Fort Leavenworth, Combat Studies Institute, 2010. Accessed at http://cgsc.contentdm.oclc.org/cdm/singleitem/collection/p4013coll13/id/465/rec/1.

30. Matt Matthews, *Operation Al-Fajr: A Study in Army and Marine Corps Joint Operations* (Fort Leavenworth: Combat Studies Institute, 2006). For additional significant insights about the battle for Fallujah see Gian Gentile et al. *Reimagining the Character of Urban Operations for the U.S. Army* (Santa Monica: RAND, 2017), 67–85.

31. Dexter Filkins, "In Taking Falluja Mosque, Victory by the Inch," *New York Times*, November 10, 2004, A1; Jackie Spinner, "U.S. Forces Battle Into Heart of Fallujah," *Washington Post*, November 10, 2004, 1.

32. Col. Mike Shupp, interview by Matt Matthews, Fort Leavenworth: Combat Studies Institute March 25, 2006, 16. Accessed at https://server16040.contentdm.oclc.org/cdm4/item_viewer.php?CISOROOT=/p4013coll13&CISOPTR=140&CISOBOX=1&REC=1.

33. Jackie Spinner and Karl Vick, "U.S. Forces Meet Fierce Resistance in Fallujah," *Washington Post*, November 13, 2004.

34. This observation is reinforced by a similar finding in Gentile, *Reimagining the Character of Urban Operations*, 92–100.

35. See John R. Ballard, *Fighting for Fallujah: A New Dawn for Iraq* (Westport: Praeger, 2006).

36. West, *No True Glory*, 315–16.

37. Estes, *Marine Corps Operations in Iraq*, 26.

38. Rayburn and Sobchak, *The U.S. Army in the Iraq War*, vol. 2, 344–56.

39. Eric Litaker, "Efforts to Counter the CIED Threat," *Marine Corps Gazette* (January 2005): 29–31.

40. Michael Groen, "Blue Diamond Intelligence during OIF," *Marine Corps Gazette* (February 2004): 22–25.

41. Groen, "Blue Diamond Intelligence," 23.

42. Michael Groen, "The Tactical Fusion Center," *Marine Corps Gazette* (April 2005): 22–25.

43. Groen, "The Tactical Fusion Center," 22.

44. Brig. Gen. Mike Groen, USMC, email interview, October 27, 2014.

45. Krepinevich, *The Army and Vietnam*, 172; Curtis Williamson, "The Marine Corps Combined Action Program: A Proposed Alternative Strategy for Vietnam," master's thesis, Command and Staff College, Quantico, 1999.

46. General Mattis interview in *Al-Anbar Awakening*, 29.

47. Lt. Col. Willard A. Buhl, "Strategic Small Unit Leaders," *Marine Corps Gazette* (January 2006): 54.

48. U.S. Marine Corps, *Doctrinal Publication 3–30.3, Civil Military Operations*, Quantico, 2003.

49. Unattributed Marine officer quotation from Security Cooperation Education and Training Center, Civil Military Operations Conference, briefing slides, Quantico, 2005.

50. Marine Corps Center for Lessons Learned, "Civil Military Operations in OIF II," Quantico, October 2005, 12.

51. Brig. Gen. David Reist, USMC (Ret.), email interview, November 12, 2014.

52. Elaine Grossman, "Mattis, U.S. has barely begun War vs. Jihadis for Global Hearts and Minds," *Inside the Pentagon*, August 25, 2005.

53. FM 3–24, *Counterinsurgency*, December 2006, 5–1 to 5–3.

54. Lt. Col. Joseph A. L'Etoile interview by John Way, Marine Corps History Division, June 16, 2005, 28.

55. U.S. Marine Corps, MCDP 3–42. *Information Operations*, Quantico, September 2003.

56. Major Andy Dietz, RCT-1 information officer, interviewed by John McCool and Matt Matthews, Combat Studies Institute, Fort Leavenworth, 21 February 2006, 2.

57. Tony Perry, "Marine General Gives an Upbeat Report on Iraq," *Los Angeles Times*, March 29, 2005.

58. Shultz, *The Marines Take Anbar*, 104–43.

59. Colonel Steve Davis, RCT-2 commander, interview by David Benhoff, Marine Corps History Division, November 22, 2005, 14.

60. Davis, telephone interview with author, November 10, 2014.

61. Ben Connable, interview in *Al-Anbar Awakening*, 129.

62. Nicholas Schlosser, *The Marines in Battle, Al Qaim* (Quantico: Marine Corps History Division, 2013), 27.

63. Joel D. Rayburn and Frank K. Sobchak, eds., *The U.S. Army in the Iraq War–Vol. 1 Invasion–Insurgency–Civil War, 2003–2006* (Carlisle: Army War College, 2019), 454–56.

64. Julian D. Alford, phone interview with author, November 7, 2014.

65. Alford.

66. Schlosser, *Al-Qaim*, 39.

67. Alford interview, November 7, 2014; Julian D. Alford and Edwin Rueda, "Winning in Iraq," *Marine Corps Gazette* (October 2007): 29–30.

68. Sally Donnelly, "Haditha Murder Charges?" *Time*, December 6, 2008, accessed at https://fliphtml5.com/oevy/byio/basic/.

69. Colonel Davis, phone interview with author, November 4, 2014.

70. Davis, SAW presentation slides, 15 Sept 2006, 22–23; Operations Officer, RCT-2, After Action Review of OIF 04.06, June 1, 2006, 1.

71. 1st. Lt. Zachary J. Iscol, "CAP India," *Marine Corps Gazette* (January 2006): 54–60; Lt. Col. Philip C. Skuta, "Introduction to 2/7 CAP Platoon Actions in Iraq," and 1stLts Jason Goodale and Jon Webre, "The Combined Action Platoon in Iraq," *Marine Corps Gazette* (April 2005): 35–42; Louis J. Palazzo, "To Build a Nation's Army," *Marine Corps Gazette* (December 2005): 35–37.

72. Captain Scott A. Cuomo, "It's Time to Make MTTs the Main Effort," *Marine Corps Gazette*, June 2006; MCLLC, Former and Current Military Advisors Forum, Quantico, December 22, 2005.

73. MCLLC, "Civil Military Operations in OIF II," October 2005; Andrew R. Milburn, "The Future of Marine Civil Affairs," Quantico: School of Advanced Warfighting, April 3, 2006.

74. Michael Walker, "Marine Civil Affairs and the GWOT," *Marine Corps Gazette* (May 2006): 74–78.

75. Anonymous Marine cited in Security Cooperation and Training Center presentation. Marine Corps Lessons Learned Center, Civil Military Operations, OIF II, Quantico, 10 November 2005.

76. Final Report, RCT 2 Public Affairs Officer, Quantico, MCCLL, June 13, 2006.

77. Connable interview in *Al-Anbar Awakening*, 124.

78. Lt. Col. Julian D. Alford interview with Ken Dunn, MCCLL, May 26, 2006.

79. Ben Connable, "All Our Eggs in a Broken Basket," *Military Review* (March–April 2009): 57–64.

80. Barak Salmoni, "Advances in Predeployment Culture Training," *Military Review* (November–December, 2006).

81. Paula Holmes-Eber, *Culture in Conflict, Irregular Warfare, Culture Policy, and the Marine Corps.* (Stanford: Stanford University Press, 2014), 1.

82. Christopher Gideons, Frederick Padilla and Clarke Lethin, "Combat Hunter, The Training Continues," *Marine Corps Gazette* (September 2008): 79–84; Dan Nosowitz, "After $19 Billion Spent Over Six Years, Pentagon Realizes the Best Bomb Detector Is a Dog," *Popular Science*, October 22, 2010.

83. Diana Staneszewski, "What is a Female Engagement Team': An Effective Ad Hoc Organization or Misuse of Manpower?," 97–114, in Jeffrey Meiser, ed., *Shona ba shona* (Washington: College of International Security Affairs, 2014).

84. Headquarters, I Marine Expeditionary Force, Urgent Needs Statement, Camp Fallujah, Iraq, May 6, 2005. The urgent need request is at http://www.usatoday.com/news/military/2007–07–22-mrap-defense_N.htm.

85. DoD IG Report, Marine Corps Implementation of the Urgent Universal Needs Process for Mine Resistant Ambush Protected Vehicles, Washington: Defense Department, March 2008, 8.

86. Estes, *Marine Operations in Iraq*, 105.

87. West, *The Strongest Tribe*, 100.

88. Glen Butler, "Operation Iraqi Freedom," *Marine Corps Gazette*, July 2006, 21–23.

89. Edwin Rueda, "Tribalism in the Al Anbar Province," *Marine Corps Gazette* (October 2006): 11–14.

90. West, *The Strongest Tribe*, 173.

91. For tactical perspectives in Ramadi see Donovan Campbell, *Joker One, A Marine Platoon's Story of Courage, Leadership, and Brotherhood* (New York: Random House, 2009).

92. William M. Jurney interview by Lt. Col. Kurtis Wheeler, Marine Corps History Division, Quantico, February 17, 2007, 3–4.

93. I MEF G-2 Assessment, "State of the Insurgency in Al Anbar," August 17, 2006, included in Thomas E. Ricks, *The Gamble* (New York: Penguin, 2009), 333.

94. Thomas E. Ricks, "Situation Called Dire in West Iraq," *Washington Post*, September 11, 2006, A1.

95. Connable interview, *Al-Anbar Awakening*, 131.

96. Neil Smith and Sean MacFarland, "Anbar Awakens: The Tipping Point," *Military Review* (March–April 2008): 41–52. See also the Army historical summary on Ramada in Rayburn and Sobchak, *The U.S. Army in Iraq*, vol. 1, 601–20.

97. Gordon and Trainor, *Endgame*, 346–47.

98. Austin Long, "The Anbar Awakening," 50, no. 2, *Survival* (April–May 2008), 80.

99. General John Allen, "Anbar Dawn . . . the Defeat of Al Qaeda in the West," lecture transcript, Fletcher School of Law and Diplomacy, March 11, 2009, 28. I am grateful to Dr. Richard Schultz for providing this transcript. Hereafter, Allen, "Anbar Dawn."

100. Rayburn and Sobchak, *The U.S. Army in the Iraq War*, vol. 2, 145–61.

101. Shultz, *The Marines Take Anbar*, 171.

102. They lived next to each other. Alford telephone interview, November 5, 2014. Russell, *Innovation, Transformation and War*, 65–67.

103. Jurney, quoted in *Counterinsurgency Leadership*, 68; see also "Infantry Battalion Urban Operations: 1st Battalion, 6th Marines, Lessons and Observations from Operation Iraqi Freedom, September 2006–May 2007," Quantico: MCCLL, February 2008.

104. Jurney interview by Wheeler, 7, 11. Jurney interview in *Al-Anbar Awakening*, 191.

105. For an incisive assessment of Jurney's tactics see Russell, *Innovation, Transformation and War*, 123–32.

106. Major Daniel R. Zappa interview, 204–05; Colonel Jurney interview, 197–99. Both in *Al-Anbar Awakening*. Also see Russell, *Innovation*, 129.
107. Jurney interview by Chris Wilk, MCCLL, July 13, 2007, 13.
108. West, *The Strongest Tribe*, 267.
109. Major Dan Zappa interview by Chris Wilk, MCCLL, July 11, 2007, 28; R. M. Hancock, "Task Force 1/6 in Ramadi: A Successful Tactical-Level Counterinsurgency Campaign," Quantico, VA: Marine Command and Staff College, April 2008.
110. Personal interview with Colonel John Koenig (Allen's deputy), November 4, 2014.
111. Allen, "Anbar Dawn," 33–34.
112. Daniel Green and William F. Mullen, III, *Fallujah Redux, The Anbar Awakening and the Struggle with Al-Qaeda* (Annapolis: Naval Institute Press), 2014.
113. Green and Mullen, 27.
114. William F. Mullen, III, "Turning Fallujah," *Joint Force Quarterly* (2nd Quarter 57, 2010): 50–55.
115. Major George Benson, interview by Chris Wilk, MCCLL, July 7, 2007, 2.
116. Mullen, "Turning Fallujah," 55.
117. General Allen interview in *Al-Anbar Awakening*, 235.
118. Telephone interview with Colonel Mark Cancian, Marine Assessments Chief in Anbar, November 4, 2014.
119. Quoted in John McCary, "The Anbar Awakening: An Alliance of Incentives," *Washington Quarterly* (January 2009): 43.
120. Allen, Visconage interview, June 27, 2008.
121. Allen, "Anbar Dawn," 25.
122. Allen, "Anbar Dawn," 13.
123. David Furness, "The Art of Battalion Command," 65, in Nicholas Schlosser and James Caiela, eds., *Counterinsurgency Leadership in Afghanistan, Iraq, and Beyond* (Quantico: Marine Corps University Press, 2011).
124. Col. Richard L. Simcock interview by Chris Wilk, MCCLL April 24, 2008, 25–26.
125. Author interview with Dr. Carter Malkasian, November 14, 2014.
126. Brig. Gen. Mark Gurganus interview by Chris Wilk, MCCLL, March 20, 2008, 60–61.
127. Lt. Col. Chris Mayette, Commanding Officer, 5th Battalion, 10th Marines, interview by Colonel Bunn, MCCLL, April 10, 2008.
128. Col. John Koenig, interview by Maj Jennifer Anthis and Douglas Nash, Marine Security Cooperation Education and Training Center, October 17, 2007.
129. Allen interview by Chris Wilks, MCCLL, March 27, 2008, 50–53.
130. Reist, email interview, November 12, 2014.
131. Capt. Scott Cuomo, "It's Time to Make ETT's the Main Effort," *Marine Corps Gazette* (June 2006).
132. Maj. Tom Chalkey, interview by Lawrence Lessard, Fort Leavenworth: Combat Studies Institute, October 22, 2007, 2.
133. Maj. Brian Russell, interview with Marty Deckard, Fort Leavenworth: Combat Studies Institute, July 17, 2008, 4. Accessed at http://cgsc.cdmhost.com/cdm/singleitem/collection/p4013coll13/id/1420/rec/1.

134. Maj. Gen. Rich Zilmer, interview in *Al-Anbar Awakening*, 149.

135. Brig. Gen. Robert Neller, interview in *Al-Anbar Awakening*, 165.

136. Maj. Gen. Walter Gaskin, interview in *Al-Anbar Awakening*, 220.

137. Gen. John Allen, interview by Col. Mike Visconage, Marine Corps History Division, June 27, 2007, 5.

138. Brig. Gen. Mark Gurganus interview by Chris Wilk, MCCLL, March 20, 2008, 59.

139. Allen, "Anbar Dawn," 22.

140. Koenig interview, Anthis and Nash, 3–4.

141. Allen, "Anbar Dawn," 2.

142. Reist, email interview, November 12, 2014.

143. Jonathan Schroden, "What Went Right in Iraq," Arlington: Center for Naval Analyses, 2009, at http://www.cna.org/news/from-cna/2009/what-went-right-in-iraq.

144. Carter Malkasian, "Counterinsurgency in Iraq, May 2003–January 2007," 259 in Daniel Marston and Carter Malkasian, eds., *Counterinsurgency in Modern Warfare* (New York: Osprey, 2008).

145. Mullen, email interview, October 27, 2014.

146. Reist, email interview, November 12, 2014.

147. John Barry, Michael Hastings, and Evan Thomas, "Iraq's Real WMD," *Newsweek*, March 27, 2006.

148. Franz Gayl, *MRAP Ground Combat Advocate Case Study* (Washington: Headquarters, Marine Corps, January 22, 2008), 55.

149. Email from Gayl to author, July 14, 2014. See the chapter on Gayl titled "Betrayal" in Donald Soeken, *Don't Kill the Messenger* (Washington: CreateSpace Independent Publishing, 2014).

150. Jason Sherman, "Marines Rejected Original Request for MRAP in 2005; 'Biden Shocked and Sickened,'" *InsideDefense.com*, May 22, 2007; Tom Vanden Brook, "Corps Refused 2005 Plea for MRAP Vehicles," *USA Today*, May 24, 2007.

151. Gen. James Conway, MRAP Need Statement, Headquarters, U.S. Marine Corps, Washington, March 1, 2007.

152. Conway.

153. "Gates Designates MRAP Pentagon's 'Highest Priority' Acquisition Program," *Inside Defense*, May 8, 2007.

154. Kris Osborn, "Gates Urges Ramping Up MRAP Acquisition," *Army Times*, May 9, 2007; Robert Gates, *Duty, Memoirs of a Secretary at War* (New York: Knopf, 2014), 344.

155. DoD Solicitation M67854-07-R-5082, Mine Resistant Ambush Protected Vehicle II, July 31, 2007, accessed at http://www1.fbo.gov/spg/DON/USMC/M67854/M6785407R5082/listing.html.

156. Col. G. Patrick Garrett, USMC (Ret.), email interview, October 29, 2014.

157. Groen, email interview, October 27, 2014.

158. Mullen, email interview, October 27, 2014.

159. Reist, email interview, November 12, 2014.

160. Franz Gayl, *MRAP Ground Combat Advocate Case Study* (Washington: Headquarters, Marine Corps, January 22, 2008), 53.
161. Andrew Krepinevich and Dakota Wood, *Of IEDs and MRAPs: Force Protection in Complex Irregular Operations* (Washington: Center for Strategic and Budgetary Assessment, 2007); D. R. Stark, "MRAP: A Limited Capability," Quantico: Marine Corps Expeditionary Warfare School, February 19, 2008.
162. U.S. Marine Corps, MCDP 1 *Warfighting* (Quantico, 1997).
163. Furness, *Leadership in Counterinsurgency*, 60–62; U.S. Marine Corps, "RCT-2 and RCT-6 in OIF, A Summary of Lessons and Observations from OIF, January 2007–January 2008," Quantico, VA: Marine Corps Center for Lessons Learned, September 12, 2008.
164. Brig. Gen. Dave Reist, retired, email interview.
165. Brig. Gen. Mike Groen, email interview, October 27, 2014.
166. Groen, author interview.
167. Mullen, author interview.
168. Groen, author interview.
169. Craig Cameron, *American Samurai: Myth, Imagination, and the Conduct of Battle in the First Marine Division 1941–1951* (New York: Cambridge University Press, 1994); Jeannie L. Johnson, *Assessing the Strategic Impact of Service Culture on Counterinsurgency Operations*, Ph.D. thesis, University of Reading, May 2013.
170. Ricks, *Making the Corps*, 19. See also Cameron, *American Samurai:*
171. U.S. Marine Corps, MCDP 3, *Expeditionary Operations*, Quantico, VA: Marine Corps Combat Development Command (1998), 43–44.
172. Victor Krulak, *First to Fight* (Annapolis: Naval Institute Press, 1996), 111.
173. Quoted in Terry Terriff, "Warriors and Innovators: Military Change and Organizational Culture in the U.S. Marine Corps," 66, no. 2, *Defence Studies* (June 2006): 229.
174. John Dickerson, "Marine General at War," *Slate*, April 22, 2010. Accessed at http://www.slate.com/articles/life/risk/2010/04/a_marine_general_at_war.html.
175. Groen interview, concurred with by Mattis and Garrett interviews.
176. Groen email interview.
177. Lt. Gen. Richard Natonski, in response to the author's question at the General Graves B. Erskine Lecture on the tenth anniversary of the battle for Fallujah, held at Quantico, October 29, 2014.
178. Reist, email interview, November 12, 2014.
179. Mark Moyer, *A Question of Command: Counterinsurgency from the Civil War to Iraq* (New Haven: Yale University Press, 2009), 243.
180. William McAllister, interview by Michael Sears, Marine Corps History Division (July 27, 2007), 7.
181. Allen, "Anbar Dawn," 3.
182. David Fitzgerald, *Learning to Forget, US Army Counterinsurgency Doctrine and Practice from Vietnam to Iraq* (Stanford: Stanford University Press, 2013).

183. Positive assessments were offered by Mattis, Groen, and Garrett in interviews; Johnson, *Assessing the Strategic Impact of Service Culture*, 34.

184. Confirming a point made by Terriff, "Warriors and Innovators," 235.

185. On the challenge of assessment in counterinsurgency see Ben Connable, *Embracing the Fog of War, Assessment and Metrics in Counterinsurgency* (Santa Monica: RAND, 2012); Michael P. Noonan, "Iraq and the 'Metrics' System," Foreign Policy Research Institute *E-Notes*, September 2007.

186. Jonathan Schroden, "Why Operation Assessments Fail, It's Not Just the Metrics," *Naval War College Review* 64, no. 4 (Autumn 2011): 89–102.

187. Accessed at http://www.cna.org/sites/default/files/CSD_2014_07.pdf.

188. Iraq Study Bibliography provided by Mr. Mark Geis, Vice President at the Center for Naval Analyses. Personal interview with Carter Malkasian, November 14, 2014.

189. Headquarters Marine Corps, MCO 3504.1 The Marine Corps Lessons Learned Program, and the Marine Corps Center for Lessons Learned (MCCLL) July 31, 2006, 6.

190. Headquarters Marine Corps, MCO 3504.1, 6.

191. William Earl Powers, *Evaluation of the Marine Corps Center for Lessons Learned as a Learning Organization*, doctoral dissertation, Nova Southeastern Florida, 2009.

192. Telephone interview with Col. Mark Cancian, USMCR (Ret.), November 10, 2014.

193. Col. Monte Dunard, "Urban CAS After Action," MCCLL report, July 2006; MCCLL, Information Operations, Lessons and Observations, I MEF Forward, OIF 05–07, Quick Look Report, March 22, 2007.

194. This point was raised by Col. George P. Garrett, USMC (Ret.), in an author interview.

195. Davidson, 192.

196. Author interview with the staff at the Marine Corps Center for Lessons Learned, Quantico, October 11, 2014.

197. William McAllister interview by CWO4 Michael Sears, Marine Corps History Division, July 27, 2007; 6; Allen interview by Visconage, June 27, 2007, 3; Koenig interview with author, November 4, 2014.

198. Col. Dave Garza, panel presentation at the Marine Corps Irregular Warfare II Conference, Quantico, July 12, 2005.

199. Garrett interview, October 29, 2014. Garrett commanded the 6th Marine Regiment from mid-2004 to 2006, and was responsible for coordinating training for all Marine units heading to Iraq. Alford, Jurney, and (briefly) Mullen were battalion commanders in his regiment.

200. Garrett interview.

201. Lt. Gen. James Mattis, personal interview, November 8, 2014; Garrett interview.

202. Garrett interview, November 8, 2014.

203. Garrett interview, October 29, 2014.

204. Scott Cuomo, "3 Tasks, 30 Days," *Marine Corps Gazette*, August 2007, 32.

205. U.S. Marine Corps, *A Tentative Manual for Countering Irregular Threats*, Quantico, VA: Concepts Division, June 6, 2006.

206. Nina Kollars, "Military Innovation's Dialectic: Gun Trucks and Rapid Acquisition," *Security Studies* 23, no. 4, (2014): 787–813.

207. Gen. Joseph F. Dunford, Jr. USMC, Graduation Speech at National Defense University, June 9, 2016, https://www.jcs.mil/Media/Speeches/Article/797847/gen-dunfords -remarks-at-the-national-defense-university-graduation/.

208. Years into the war, Marine battalion commanders in Iraq were carrying reprints of the relic into battle in Anbar. Ed Darack, *The Warriors of Anbar: The Marines Who Crushed Al Qaeda—the Greatest Untold Story of the Iraq War* (Boston: Da Capo, 2019), 115.

209. David Reist, "Innovation in the Battlefield in Iraq," *Middle East Studies Insights* 10, no. 4, Quantico: Marine Corps University (August 2019), 3.

210. Campbell, *Joker One*, 48; Nate Fick, *Counterinsurgency Leadership*, 81.

211. Ucko, *Counterinsurgency Era*, 166.

212. Johnson, *Assessing the Strategic Impact of Service Culture on Counterinsurgency Operations*, 13.

213. Gray, cited in Johnson, 17.

214. Gen. John Allen, (Ret.) comment to author at Pentagon, February 21, 2014.

Chapter 7. Conclusions and Implications

1. Correlli Barnett, *The Swordbearers: Supreme Command in the First World War* (New York: William Morrow and Company, 1964), xvi.

2. Williamson Murray, in Millett and Murray, *Military Effectiveness*, xv.

3. U.S. Joint Chiefs of Staff, *Decade of War*, 20.

4. Grisogono and Radenovic, "The Adaptive Stance."

5. Cohen and Gooch, *Military Misfortunes*, 163, 231–35.

6. On informal learning styles see Dibella, Nevis, and Gould, 374; and Sergio Catignani, "Coping with Knowledge: Organizational Learning in the British Army," *Journal of Strategic Studies* 37, no. 1 (February 2014): 35.

7. See Conrad Crane's chapter, "United States," 59–70, in Thomas Rid and T. Keaney, eds., *Understanding Counterinsurgency: Doctrine, Operations and Challenges* (London: Routledge, 2010).

8. Cohen and Gooch, *Military Misfortunes*, 240.

9. Liam S. Collins, *Military Innovation in War: The Criticality of the Senior Military Leader*, PhD thesis, Princeton University, June 2014.

10. *Marine Corps Operating Concepts*, 3rd ed. (Quantico: Marine Corps Combat Development Command, 2010), 15–26.

11. Gen. Joseph F. Dunford Jr. USMC, Graduation Speech at National Defense University, June 9, 2016, https://www.jcs.mil/Media/Speeches/Article/797847/gen-dunfords -remarks-at-the-national-defense-university-graduation/.

12. Dunford.

13. Theo Farrell, *Norms of War*, 13; Nagl, *Eating Soup with a Knife*, 214; Adamsky, *Culture of Innovation*, 135.

14. Farrell and Terriff, *The Sources of Military Change*, 269–71.

15. Farrell and Terriff, 271.

16. Peter R. Mansoor and Williamson Murray, eds., *The Culture of Military Organizations* (New York: Cambridge University Press, 2019).

17. Futrell, *Korea*, 94–95.

18. Nagl, *Eating Soup with a Knife*, 115.

19. Spector, *After Tet*, 217–19.

20. Tattar, *Innovation and Adaptation in War*.

21. Rosen, *Winning the Next War*, 254.

22. Rosen, 144.

23. On operational assessment in Vietnam, see Ben Connable, *Embracing the Fog of War, Assessment and Metrics in Counterinsurgency* (Santa Monica: RAND, 2012), 95–145.

24. Raphael Marcus, "Military Innovation and Tactical Adaptation in the Israel-Hizbollah Conflict," *Journal of Strategic Studies* 38, no. 4 (2015): 500–528.

25. Peter Mansoor, cited in Serena, *Revolution in Military Adaptation*, 163.

26. For great insights in horizontal learning, see Foley, "A Case Study in Horizontal Military Innovation," 799–827.

27. David Ucko, "Innovation or Inertia: The U.S. Military and the Learning of Counterinsurgency," *Orbis*, 52, no. 2 (Spring 2008: 292). See also Ucko, *Counterinsurgency Era*, 16–17.

28. There are cases from World War I that reflect formal and informal learning, and more horizontal sharing than seen in the Army and Marine Corps cases here. See Robert T. Foley, "Dumb Donkeys or Cunning Foxes? Learning in the British and German Armies during the Great War," *International Affairs* 90, no. 2 (2014): 279–98.

29. Something that other scholars have identified in the British Army. Sergio Catignani, "'Getting COIN' at the Tactical Level in Afghanistan: Reassessing Counterinsurgency Adaptation in the British Army," *Journal of Strategic Studies* 35, no. 4 (2012): 513–39.

30. Robert T. Foley et al., "Transformation in Contact: Learning the Lessons of Modern War," *International Affairs* 82, no. 2 (March 2011): 253–70.

31. Davidson, *Lifting the Fog of Peace*, 22, 192.

32. For "accelerants" of learning, Davidson, 184.

33. Paddy O'Toole and Steven Talbot, "Fighting for Knowledge: Developing Learning Systems in the Australian Army," *Armed Forces and Society* 37, no. 1 (2011): 42–67; Sergio Catignani, "Coping with Knowledge," 38.

34. Rosen, *Winning the Next War*, 242.

35. On the evolutionary character of institutionalizing innovation over time, see Theo Farrell, "Improving in War: Military Adaptation and the British in Helmand Province, Afghanistan, 2006–2009," *Journal of Strategic Studies* 33, no. 4 (August 2010): 569.

36. Farrell and Terriff, *The Sources of Military Change* 6.

37. Rosen, *Winning the Next War*, 255–57.

38. Posen, *Sources of Military Doctrine*, 233–36.

39. Ashton Carter, "Fixing the Pentagon's Greatest Weakness," *Foreign Affairs* (January–February 2014).

40. As shown earlier in Russell, *Innovation, Transformation, and War*, 54–190.

41. Joel Rayburn and Frank Sobchak, *The U.S. Army in the Iraq War*, vols. 1 and 2 (Carlisle: Army War College, 2019), 621.

42. Crane, "United States," in Rid and Keaney, eds., *Understanding Counterinsurgency*.

43. Farrell, in Farrell, Osinga, and Russell, eds., *Military Adaptation in Afghanistan*, 18.

44. Initially suggested by James Russell, *Innovation, Transformation and War*, 52. See also Nina Kollars, "Military Innovation's Dialectic," 787–813.

45. Farrell, "Introduction" to Farrell, Osinga, Russell, *Military Adaptation in Afghanistan*, 8–18. An earlier set of drivers and shapers are explored in Theo Farrell, "The Dynamics of British Adaptation in Afghanistan," *International Affairs* 84, no. 4 (2008): 777–808.

46. H. R. McMaster, *Dereliction of Duty, Lyndon Johnson, Robert McNamara, The Joint Chiefs of Staff and the Lies that Led to Vietnam* (New York: Harper Collins, 1997).

47. Paula Holmes-Eber, *Culture in Conflict: Irregular Warfare, Cultural Policy and the Marine Corps* (Stanford: Stanford University Press, 2014), 194.

48. Farrell, "Introduction," to Farrell, Osinga, and Russell, eds. *Military Adaptation in Afghanistan*, 3, 15–18.

49. I am indebted to Professor Theo Farrell, now at Wollongong University in Australia, for this insight.

50. For the latest research in this area, see Sue Bryant and Andrew Harrison, "Finding Ender: Exploring the Intersections of Creativity, Innovation, and Talent Management in the U.S. Armed Forces," *Strategic Perspectives 31* (Washington: National Defense University Press, 2019).

51. Terry Pierce, *Warfighting and Disruptive Technologies: Disguising Innovation* (New York: Routledge, 2004).

52. Edgar H. Schein, "How Founders and Leaders Embed and Transmit Culture: Socialization from a Leadership Perspective," in *Organizational Culture and Leadership*, 2nd ed. (San Francisco: Jossey-Bass, 1992), 245–70.

53. Grissom, "Future Innovation Studies," 925; Marcus, "Military Innovation and Tactical Adaptation," 7–8.

54. Jonathan Bailey, "Military History and the Pathology of Lessons Learned," 184, in Williamson Murray and Richard Hart Sinnreich, eds., *The Past as Prologue: The Importance of History to the Military Profession* (New York: Cambridge University Press, 2006).

55. Murray, *Military Adaptation in War*, 306–7.

56. Murray, 4, 73.

57. Grissom, "The Future of Military Innovation Studies," 925; Farrell, "The Dynamics of British Adaptation in Afghanistan," 806.

58. Foley, "Dumb Donkeys or Cunning Foxes?" 280.

59. Griffin, "Military Innovation Studies: Multidisciplinary or Lacking Discipline?" passim.

60. Cohen and Gooch, *Military Misfortunes*, 243.

61. Theo Farrell, "Introduction," in Farrell, Osinga, and Russell, *Military Adaptation in Afghanistan*, 3.

Selected Bibliography

Archival Sources

Defense Technical Information Center: Combat After Action Reports, and Operational Reports—Lessons Learned, Vietnam 1965–1968.

Historic Navy Ships Association, Annapolis: Online database, U.S. Submarine War Patrol Reports

Library of Congress, Washington: Vice Adm. Charles A. Lockwood Papers

National Archive and Records Administration, College Park: Joint Planning Board records, Naval Records

Marine Corps History Division, Quantico: Senior Officer Interviews and Oral Histories

Marine Corps Center for Lessons Learned, Quantico: Senior Officer Interviews

National Defense University Special Collections, Washington: Galvin Papers

U.S. Army Heritage and Education Center, Carlisle: Gen. William E. DePuy Papers

U.S. Naval War College, Newport: World War II Planning and Wargame Records

Published Primary Sources and Memoirs

Brownlee, Romie Les, and William J. Mullen. *Changing an Army: An Oral History of General William E. DePuy, USA.* Washington: Center of Military History, 1988.

Calvert, James F. *Silent Running: My Years on a World War II Attack Submarine.* New York: J. Wiley, 1995.

Campbell, Donovan. *Joker One: A Marine Platoon's Story of Courage, Leadership, and Brotherhood.* New York: Random House, 2009.

Fluckey, Eugene B. *Thunder Below!: The USS Barb Revolutionizes Submarine Warfare in World War II.* Urbana: University of Illinois Press, 1992.

Galantin, I. J. *Take Her Deep!: A Submarine against Japan in World War II.* Annapolis: Naval Institute Press, 2007.

Galvin, John R. *Fighting the Cold War: A Soldier's Memoir.* Lexington: University of Kentucky, 2015.

Green, Daniel, and William F. Mullen, *Fallujah Redux: The Anbar Awakening and the Struggle with Al-Qaeda.* Annapolis: Naval Institute Press, 2014.

Grider, George and Lydel Sims, *War Fish.* Boston: Little, Brown, 1958.

Haun, Phil. *Lectures of the Air Corps Tactical School and American Strategic Bombing in World War II*. Lexington: University Press of Kentucky, 2019.

Holmes, Wilfred Jay. *Undersea Victory: The Influence of Submarine Operations on the War in the Pacific*. Garden City: Doubleday, 1966.

Jones, R. V. *The Wizard War: British Scientific Intelligence, 1939–1945*. New York: Coward, McCann & Geoghegan, 1978.

Komer, Robert W. *Bureaucracy Does Its Thing: Institutional Constraints on U.S.-GVN Performance in Vietnam*. Santa Monica: RAND Corporation, 1972.

Lockwood, Charles A., *Sink 'Em All: Submarine Warfare in the Pacific*. New York: Dutton, 1951.

Lockwood, Charles A., and Hans Christian Adamson. *Hellcats of the Sea: Operation Barney and the Mission to the Sea of Japan*. New York: Bantam, 1988.

Mahan, Alfred Thayer. *Mahan on Naval Strategy: Selections from the Writings of Rear Adm. Alfred Thayer Mahan*. Annapolis: Naval Institute Press, 1991.

O'Donnell, Patrick. *We Were One: Shoulder to Shoulder with the Marines Who Took Fallujah*. Harrisburg: Da Capo, 2006.

O'Kane, Richard H. *Clear the Bridge!: The War Patrols of the U.S.S. Tang*. Novato: Presidio Press, 1997.

———. *Wahoo: The Patrols of America's Most Famous World War II Submarine*. New York: Bantam Books, 1989.

Sorley, Lewis, ed., *Press On! Selected Works of General Donn A. Starry*. Vol. II. Fort Leavenworth: Combined Studies Institute Press, 2009.

Swain, Richard M., Donald L. Gilmore, and Carolyn D. Conway, eds., *Selected Papers of General William E. DePuy*. Fort Leavenworth: Combat Studies Institute, 1995.

Westmoreland, William C. *A Soldier Reports*. New York: Doubleday, 1976.

Y'Blood, William T. *The Three Wars of Lt. Gen. George E. Stratemeyer: His Korean War Diary*. Washington: Air Force History and Museums Program, 1999.

Books

Adamsky, Dima. *The Culture of Military Innovation*. Stanford: Stanford University Press, 2012.

Argyris, Chris. *On Organizational Learning*. Cambridge: Blackwell, 1993.

———. *Overcoming Organizational Defenses: Facilitating Organizational Learning*. Needham Heights: Allyn and Bacon, 1990.

Baer, George. *One Hundred Years of Sea Power, The U.S. Navy, 1890–1990*. Stanford: Stanford University Press, 1994.

Bickel, Keith B. *Mars Learning: The Marine Corps' Development of Small War Doctrine, 1915–1940*. Boulder: Westview, 2001.

Biddle, Tami Davis. *Rhetoric and Reality in Air Warfare: The Evolution of British and American Ideas about Strategic Bombing, 1914–1945*. Princeton: Princeton University Press, 2002.

Blair, Clay. *Silent Victory: The U.S. Submarine War Against Japan*. Annapolis: Naval Institute Press, 2001.

Borneman, Walter R. *The Admirals: Nimitz, Halsey, Leahy and King—The Five Star Admirals Who Won the War at Sea.* New York: Little, Brown, and Company, 2012.

Budiansky, Stephen. *Blackett's War: The Men Who Defeated the Nazi U-Boats and Brought Science to the Art of Warfare.* New York: Knopf, 2013.

Buell, Thomas B. *Master of Sea Power: A Biography of Fleet Admiral Ernest J. King.* Boston: Little, Brown, and Co., 1980.

Builder, Carl H. *The Icarus Syndrome: The Role of Air Power Theory in the Evolution and Fate of the U.S. Air Force.* New Brunswick: Transaction, 2003.

———. *The Masks of War: American Military Styles in Strategy and Analysis.* Baltimore: Johns Hopkins University Press, 1989.

Carland, John M. *Combat Operations: Stemming the Tide, May 1965 to October 1966.* Washington: Center of Military History, 2000.

Clodfelter, Mark. *Beneficial Bombing, The Progressive Foundations of American Air Power, 1917–1945.* Lincoln: University of Nebraska Press, 2011.

Cohen, Eliot A., and John Gooch, *Military Misfortunes: The Anatomy of Failure in War.* New York: Free Press, 1996.

Coleman, J. D. *Pleiku: The Dawn of Helicopter Warfare in Vietnam.* New York: St. Martin's Press, 1988.

Connable, Ben. *Embracing the Fog of War: Assessment and Metrics in Counterinsurgency.* Santa Monica: RAND, 2012.

Crane, Conrad. *American Airpower Strategy in Korea, 1950–1953.* Lawrence: University Press of Kansas, 2000.

Daddis, Gregory A. *No Sure Victory: Measuring U.S. Army Effectiveness and Progress in the Vietnam War.* Oxford: Oxford University Press, 2011.

Davidson, Janine. *Lifting the Fog of Peace: How Americans Learned to Fight Modern War.* Ann Arbor: Michigan University Press, 2010.

Donnithorne, Jeffrey W. *Four Guardians: A Principled Agent View of American Civil-Military Relations.* Baltimore: Johns Hopkins University Press, 2018.

Doubler, Michael D. *Closing with the Enemy: How GIs Fought the War in Europe: 1944–1945.* Lawrence: University of Kansas Press, 1994.

Downie, Richard A. *Learning from Conflict: The U.S. Military in Vietnam, El Salvador, and the Drug War.* New York: Praeger, June 1998.

Farrell, Theo, and Terry Terriff. *Sources of Military Change: Culture, Politics, Technology.* London: Lynne Rienner, 2002.

Farrell, Frans, P. B. Osinga, and James A. Russell, eds. *Military Adaptation in Afghanistan.* Stanford: Stanford University Press, 2013.

Felker, Craig C. *Testing American Sea Power: U.S. Navy Strategic Exercises, 1923–1940.* College Station: Texas A&M University Press, 2007.

Finkel, Meir. *On Flexibility, Recovery from Technological and Doctrinal Surprise on the Battlefield.* Stanford: Stanford Security Studies, 2011.

Fitzgerald, David. *Learning to Forget: U.S. Army Counterinsurgency Doctrine and Practice from Vietnam to Iraq.* Stanford: Stanford University Press, 2013.

Friedman, Norman. *U.S. Submarines through 1945: An Illustrated Design History*. Annapolis: Naval Institute Press, 1995.

———. *Winning a Future War: War Gaming and Victory in the Pacific War*. Washington: Naval History and Heritage Command, 2017.

Gannon, Michael. *Operation Drumbeat: The Dramatic True Story of Germany's First U-boat Attacks along the American Coast in World War II*. New York: Harper & Row, 1990.

Goldstein, Gordon M. *Lessons in Disaster: McGeorge Bundy and the Path to War in Vietnam*. New York: Times Books, 2008.

Gole, Henry K. *General William E. DePuy, Preparing the Army for Modern War*. Lexington: University Press of Kentucky, 2008.

Gordon, Michael B., and General Bernard Trainor. *Cobra II: The Inside Story of the Invasion and Occupation of Iraq*. New York: Pantheon, 2006.

Griffith, Paddy. *Battle Tactics on the Western Front 1916–18*. New Haven: Yale University Press, 1994.

Gudmundsson, Bruce I. *Stormtroop Tactics, Innovation in the German Army, 1914–1918*. Westport: Praeger, 1989.

Harris, Brayton. *Admiral Nimitz: The Commander of the Pacific Ocean Theater*. New York: Palgrave Macmillan, 2012.

Hart, Russell A. *Clash of Arms: How the Allies Won in Normandy*. Boulder: Lynne Reinner, 2001.

Heller, Charles E., and William A. Stofft. *America's First Battles, 1776–1965*. Lawrence: University of Kansas Press, 1986.

Holmes-Eber, Paula. *Culture in Conflict: Irregular Warfare, Culture Policy, and the Marine Corps*. Stanford: Stanford University Press, 2014.

Holwitt, Joel Ira. *"Execute Against Japan": Freedom-of-the-Seas, the U.S. Navy, Fleet Submarines, and the U.S. Decision to Conduct Unrestricted Warfare*. College Station: Texas A&M University Press, 2009.

Hone, Thomas, Norman Friedman, and Mark Mandeles, *American and British Aircraft Carrier Development, 1919–1941*. Annapolis: Naval Institute Press, 1999.

Hone, Trent. *Learning War: The Evolution of Fighting Doctrine in the U.S. Navy, 1898–1945*. Annapolis: Naval Institute Press, 2018.

Hornfischer, James D. *Neptune's Inferno: The U.S. Navy at Guadalcanal*. New York: Random House, 2012.

Horowitz, Michael. *The Diffusion of Military Power, Causes and Consequences for International Politics*. Princeton: Princeton University Press, 2010.

Hull, Isabel V. *Absolute Destruction. Military Culture and the Practices of War in Imperial Germany*. Ithaca: Cornell University Press, 2004.

Jensen, Benjamin. *Forging the Sword: Doctrinal Innovation in the U.S. Army*. Stanford: Stanford University Press, 2016.

Johnson, David E. *Fast Tanks and Heavy Bombers: Innovation in the U.S. Army 1917–1945*. Ithaca, New York: Cornell University Press, 1998.

Johnson, Jeannie L., Kerry M. Kartchner, and Jeffery A. Larsen, eds., *Strategic Culture and Weapons of Mass Destruction: Culturally Based Insights into Comparative National Security Policymaking*. New York: Palgrave Macmillan, 2009.

Jones, Frank L. *Blowtorch: Robert Komer, Vietnam, and American Cold War Strategy*. Annapolis: Naval Institute Press, 2013.

Keith, Don. *War Beneath the Waves: A True Story of Courage and Leadership Aboard a World War II Submarine*. New York: New American Library, 2010.

Kier, Elizabeth. *Imagining War: French and British Military Doctrine between the Wars*. Princeton: Princeton University Press, 1997.

Kennedy, Paul. *Engineers of Victory: The Problem Solvers Who Turned the Tide in the Second World War*. New York: Random House, 2013.

Kinnard, Harry W. O. *The War Managers*. Hanover: University Press of New England, 1977.

Kitfield, James. *Prodigal Soldiers: How the Generation of Officers Born of Vietnam Revolutionized the American Style of War*. Dulles: Potomac Books, 1997.

Krepinevich, Andrew J. *The Army in Vietnam*. Baltimore: Johns Hopkins University Press, 1986.

Krulak, Victor H. *First to Fight: An Inside View of the U.S. Marine Corps*. Annapolis: Naval Institute Press, 1996.

Kuehn, John T. *Agents of Innovation: The General Board and the Design of the Fleet That Defeated the Japanese Navy*. Annapolis: Naval Institute Press, 2008.

Linn, Brian MacAllister, *The Echo of Battle: The Army's Way of War*. Cambridge: Harvard University Press, 2007.

MacGarrigle, George L. *Combat Operations: Taking the Offensive: October 1966 to October 1967*. Washington: Center of Military History, 1998.

Mahnken, Thomas. *Uncovering Ways of War: U.S. Intelligence and Foreign Military Innovation, 1918–1941*. Ithaca: Cornell University Press, 2002.

Mansfield, John G. *Cruisers for Breakfast: War Patrols of the U.S.S. Darter and U.S.S. Dash*. Tacoma: Media Center, 1997.

Mansoor Peter R., and Williamson Murray, eds., *The Culture of Military Organizations*. New York: Cambridge University Press, 2019.

Maraniss, David. *They Marched into Sunlight: War and Peace Vietnam and American October 1967*. New York: Simon and Schuster, 2004.

McCue, Brian. *U-Boast in the Bay of Biscay, An Essay in Operations Analysis*. Fort McNair: National Defense University Press, 1990.

McMaster, H. R. *Dereliction of Duty, Lyndon Johnson, Robert McNamara, The Joint Chiefs of Staff and the Lies that Led to Vietnam*. New York: Harper Collins, 1997.

Meigs, Montgomery C. *Slide Rules and Submarines*. Fort McNair: National Defense University Press, 1990.

Meilinger, Phillip S. *Bomber: The Formation and Early Years of Strategic Air Command*. Maxwell: Air University Press, 2012.

Meilinger, Phillip, ed. *The Paths of Heaven: The Evolution of Airpower Theory*. Maxwell Air Force Base: Air University Press, 1997, 219–23.

Miller, Edward S. *War Plan Orange: The U.S. Strategy to Defeat Japan, 1897–1945*. Annapolis: Naval Institute Press, 1991.

Miller, Nathan. *War at Sea: A Naval History of World War II*. New York: Oxford University Press, 1994.

Millett, Allan, and Williamson Murray, eds. *Military Effectiveness, The Second World War.* Vol. 3. New York: Cambridge University Press, 2010.

Moore, Harold, and Joseph Galloway. *We Were Soldiers Once . . . and Young: Ia Drang—The Battle That Changed The War in Vietnam.* New York: Random House, 1992.

Moore, Stephen L. *Battle Surface!: Lawson P. "Red" Ramage and the War Patrols of the USS Parche.* Annapolis: U.S. Naval Institute Press, 2011.

Morison, Samuel Eliot. *The Battle of the Atlantic: September 1939–May 1943.* Vol. 1. Annapolis: Naval Institute Press, 2010.

Morris, Craig F. *The Origins of American Strategy Bombing Theory.* Annapolis: Naval Institute Press, 2017.

Moyer, Mark. *A Question of Command: Counterinsurgency from the Civil War to Iraq.* New Haven: Yale University Press, 2009.

Murphy, Edward F. *Dak To: America's Sky Soldiers in South Vietnam's Central Highlands.* New York: Presidio, 1993.

———. eds., *Military Innovation in the Interwar Era.* New York: Cambridge University Press, 1996.

Murray, Williamson and Allan Millet. *A War to Be Won: Fighting the Second World War.* Cambridge: Belknap/Harvard, 2000.

Murray, Williamson. *Military Adaptation in War: With Fear of Change.* New York: Cambridge University Press, 2011.

Nagl, John. *Learning to Eat Soup with a Knife: Counterinsurgency Lessons from Malaya and Vietnam.* Chicago: University of Chicago Press, 2005.

Newpower, Anthony. *Iron Men and Tin Fish: The Race to Build a Better Torpedo during World War II.* Westport: Praeger, 2006.

Osinga, Frans P. B. *Science, Strategy and War: The Strategic Theory of John Boyd.* London: Routledge, 2005.

Ostland, Mike. *Find 'Em, Chase 'Em, Sink 'Em: The Mysterious Loss of the WWII Submarine USS Gudgeon.* Guilford: Lyons Press, 2012.

Overy, Richard. *The Bombers and the Bombed: Allied Air War Over Europe 1940–1945.* New York: Viking Penguin, 2013.

———. *Why the Allies Won.* New York: Norton, 1997.

Pape, Robert A. *Bombing to Win: Air Power and Coercion in War.* Ithaca, NY: Cornell University Press, 1996.

Posen, Barry R. *The Sources of Military Doctrine: France, Britain, and Germany between the World Wars.* Ithaca, NY: Cornell University Press, 1986.

Potter, E. B. *Nimitz.* Annapolis: Naval Institute Press, 1976.

Rayburn, Joel, and Frank Sobchak, *The U.S. Army in the Iraq War.* Vols. 1 and 2, Carlisle: Army War College, 2019.

Ricks, Thomas E. *Fiasco: The American Military Adventure in Iraq.* New York: Penguin Press, 2006.

———. *Making the Corps.* New York: Scribner, 1997.

Rid, Thomas, and T. Keaney, eds. *Understanding Counterinsurgency: Doctrine, Operations and Challenges.* London: Routledge, 2010.

Roscoe, Theodore. *United States Submarine Operations in World War II.* Annapolis: U.S. Naval Institute, 1949.

Rosen, Stephen Peter. *Winning the Next War: Innovation and the Modern Military.* Ithaca: Cornell University Press, 1991.

Russell, James A. *Innovation, Transformation, and War: Counterinsurgency Operations in Anbar and Ninewa Provinces, Iraq, 2005–2007.* Stanford: Stanford Security Studies, 2011.

Sasgen, Peter. *Hellcats: The Epic Story of World War II's Most Daring Submarine Raid.* New York: Caliber, 2010.

Schein, Edgar H. *Organizational Culture and Leadership.* San Francisco: Jossey-Bass, 1985.

———. *Organizational Culture and Leadership.* 2nd Edition. San Francisco: Jossey-Bass, 1992.

Schultz, Richard H. Jr., *The Marines Take Anbar: The Four-Year Fight against Al Qaeda.* Annapolis: Naval Institute Press, 2013.

Schlosser, Nicholas J, and James M. Caiella, eds. *Counterinsurgency Leadership in Afghanistan, Iraq, and Beyond.* Quantico: Marine Corps University Press, 2011.

Scott, James. *The War Below: The Story of Three Submarines That Battled Japan.* New York: Simon & Schuster, 2013.

Senge, Peter. *The Fifth Discipline: The Art and Practice of the Learning Organization.* New York: Doubleday, 1990.

Serena, Chad C. *A Revolution in Military Adaptation: The U.S. Army in the Iraq War.* Washington: Georgetown University Press, 2011.

Sheehan, Neil. *A Bright and Shining Lie: John Paul Vann and American in Vietnam.* New York: Vintage Books, 1989.

Smith, Steven Trent. *Wolf Pack: The American Submarine Strategy That Helped Defeat Japan.* Hoboken: John Wiley, 2003.

Spector, Ronald H. *After Tet: The Bloodiest Year in Vietnam.* New York: Vintage, 1994.

———. *Eagle Against the Sun, The American War with Japan.* New York: Free Press, 1985.

Sorley, Lewis. *Westmoreland: The General Who Lost Vietnam.* Boston: Houghton, Mifflin, Harcourt, 2011.

Stanton, Shelby. *Anatomy of a Division: The 1st Cav in Vietnam.* New York: Warner, 1987.

Toll, Ian W. *Pacific Crucible: War at Sea in the Pacific, 1941–1942.* New York: Norton, 2012.

Tomes, Robert. *U.S. Defense Strategy from Vietnam to Operation Iraqi Freedom: Military Innovation and the New American Way of War, 1973–2003.* London: Routledge, 2007.

Tuohy, William. *The Bravest Man: The Story of Richard O'Kane and the Amazing Submarine Adventures of the USS Tang.* New York: Presidio Press, 2006.

Ucko, David. *The New Counterinsurgency Era: Transforming the U.S. Military for Modern Wars.* Washington: Georgetown University Press, 2010.

Villard, Eric. *Combat Operations: Staying the Course, October 1967 to September 1968.* Washington: Center of Army History, 2019.

Vlahos, Michael. *The Blue Sword: The Naval War College and the American Mission, 1919–1941.* Newport: Naval War College Press, 1980.

Weigley, Russell. *The American Way of War: A History of U.S Military Strategy and Policy*. Bloomington: Indiana University Press, 1973.

Werrell, Kenneth. *Death from the Heavens, A History of Strategic Bombing*. Annapolis: Naval Institute Press, 2009.

West, Bing, and Raymond Smith. *The March Up: Taking Baghdad with the 1st Marine Division*. New York: Bantam Books, 2003.

Winton, Harold R, and David R. Mets, eds. *The Challenge of Change: Military Institutions and New Realities, 1918–1941*. Lincoln: University of Nebraska Press, 2000.

Worden, Mike. *Rise of the Fighter Generals: The Problem of USAF Leadership, 1945–1982*. Maxwell Air Force Base: Air University Press, 1998.

Dissertations

Adams, Thomas. *Military Doctrine and the Organization Culture of the U.S. Army*. Dissertation, Syracuse University, 1990.

Clark, Joseph R. *Innovation Under Fire: Politics, Learning, and U.S. Army Doctrine*. Dissertation, George Washington University, January 2011.

Drummond, A. Jr. *Enabling Conditions for Organizational Learning: A Study in International Business Ventures*. Ph.D. dissertation, University of Cambridge, 1997.

Hunzeker, Michael A. *Perfecting War: The Organizational Sources of Doctrinal Optimization*. Dissertation, Princeton University, November 2013.

Johnson, Jeannie L. *Assessing the Strategic Impact of Service Culture on Counterinsurgency Operations: Case: United States Marine Corps*. Dissertation, University of Reading, 2013.

Larsen, Kristian. *Substitute for Victory: Performance Measurements in Vietnam, the Gulf War, and Afghanistan*. Dissertation, University of Copenhagen, May 28, 2014.

Long, Austin. *First War Syndrome: Military Culture, Professionalization and Military Doctrine*. Ph.D. dissertation, Massachusetts Institute of Technology, February 2011.

Petraeus, David. *The American Military and the Lessons of Vietnam: A Study of Military Influence and the Use of Force in the Post-Vietnam Era*. Ph.D. dissertation, Princeton University, 1987.

Powers, William. *Marine Corps Center for Lessons Learned as a Learning Organization*, Doctoral dissertation, Nova Southeastern University, Florida, 2009.

Tattar, Matthew Alan. *Innovation and Adaptation in War*. Ph.D. dissertation, Brandeis University, February, 2011.

Articles

Alford, Julian D., and Edwin O. Rueda. "Winning in Iraq." *Marine Corps Gazette* (October 2007).

Andrade, Dale, and James H. Willbanks. "CORDS/Phoenix: Counterinsurgency Lessons from Vietnam for the Future." *Military Review* (March–April 2006): 9–23.

Appelbaum, Steven H., and Walter Reichart. "How to Measure an Organization's Learning Ability: the Facilitating Factors." *Journal of Workplace Learning* 10, no. 1 (1998): 15–28.

Barry, John, Michael Hastings, and Evan Thomas. "Iraq's Real WMD; Deadly Puzzle: IEDs Are Killing U.S. Soldiers at a Scary Clip." *Newsweek* (March 27, 2006).

Berry, Sydney B. "Observations of a Brigade Commander." *Military Review* 48 (January 1968): 31–38.

Birtle, Andrew J. "PROVN, Westmoreland, and the Historians: A Reappraisal." *The Journal of Military History* 72 (October 2008): 1213–47.

Buhl, Willard A. "Strategic Small Unit Leaders." *Marine Corps Gazette* (January 2006).

Carland, John M. "Winning the Vietnam War: Westmoreland's Approach in Two Documents." *Journal of Military History* 68, no. 2 (April 2004): 553–74.

Catignani, Sergio. "Coping with Knowledge: Organizational Learning in the British Army." *Journal of Strategic Studies* 37, no. 1 (2013): 30–64.

———. "'Getting COIN' at the Tactical Level in Afghanistan: Reassessing Counter-Insurgency Adaptation in the British Army." *Journal of Strategic Studies* 35 no. 4 (2012): 513–39.

Cohen, Eliot A. "Change and Transformation in Military Affairs." *Journal of Strategic Studies* 27, no. 3 (2004): 395–407.

Cohen, W. M., and D. A. Levinthal, "Absorptive Capacity: A New Perspective on Learning and Innovation." *Administrative Science Quarterly* 35, no. 1 (1990): 128–52.

Conway, James T. "Farther and Faster in Iraq." U.S. Naval Institute *Proceedings* 131, no. 1, (January 2005).

Crossan, Mary. "An Organizational Learning Framework: From Intuition to Institution," *Academy of Management Review* 24, no. 3 (1999): 522–37.

Crossan, Mary, M. Lane, R. E. White, and L. Djurfeldt. "Organizational Learning: Dimensions for a Theory." *International Journal of Organizational Analysis* 3, no. 4 (1995): 337–60.

Cuomo, Scott A. "Embedded Training Teams." *Marine Corps Gazette* (June 2006): 63–67.

Daddis, Gregory A. "The Problem of Metrics: Assessing Progress and Effectiveness in the Vietnam War." *War in History* 19, no. 1 (January 2012): 73–98.

DePuy, William E. "Minh Thanh Road: 9 July 1966." *The American Traveler*, 1972.

Dibella, Anthony J. "Perspectives on Changing National Security Institutions." *Joint Force Quarterly* no. 69 (2nd Quarter 2013): 13–19.

Dougherty, Kevin J. "The Evolution of Air Assault," *Joint Force Quarterly*, no. 22 (Summer 1999): 51–58.

Doyle, Michael K. "The U.S. Navy and War Plan Orange, 1933–1940: Making Necessity a Virtue." *Naval War College Review* 33 (May–June 1980): 48–63.

Dyson, Tom. "The Military as a Learning Organization: Establishing the Fundamentals of Best-Practice in Lessons Learned." 19/2 *Defense Studies* (2019): 107–29.

Ellis, R. Evan. "Organizational Learning Dominance: The Emerging Key to Success in the New Era of Warfare." *Comparative Strategy* 18, no. 2 (1999): 191–202.

Farrell, Theo. "Culture and Military Power." *Review of International Studies* 24, no. 3, (Fall 1998): 407–16.

———. "Figuring Out Fighting Organizations: The New Organizational Analysis in Strategic Studies." *Journal of Strategic Studies* 19, no. 1 (Spring 1996): 122–35.

———. "Improving in War: Military Adaptation and the British in Helmand, 2006–2009." *Journal of Strategic Studies* 38, no. 4 (2010): 567–94.

————. "The Dynamics of British Military Transformation." *International Affairs* 84, no. 4 (2008): 777–807.

Fastabend, David A., and Robert H. Simpson. "Adapt or Die: The Imperative for a Culture of Innovation in the United States Army." *Army* 54 (February 2004): 14–25.

Foley, Robert T. "A Case Study in Horizontal Military Innovation: The German Army, 1916–1918." *Journal of Strategic Studies* 35, no. 6 (December 2012): 799–827.

————. "Dumb donkeys or cunning foxes? Learning in the British and German armies during the Great War," *International Affairs* 90, no. 2 (2014): 279–98.

Foley, Robert T., Stuart Griffin, and Helen McCartney. "'Transformation in contact': learning the lessons of modern war." *International Affairs* 87, no. 2 (March 2011): 253–70.

Fontenot, Gregory. "Seeing Red: Creating a Red-Team Capability for the Blue Force." *Military Review* 85, no. 5 (September 2005): 4–8.

Galloway, Joe. "Ia Drang—The Battle That Convinced Ho Chi Minh He Could Win" *historynet.com* (October 18, 2010).

Garvin, David A. "Building a Learning Organization," *Harvard Business Review* 71, no. 4 (July–August 1993): 78–91.

Gordon, Michael B. "Marines Plan to Use Velvet Glove More than Iron Fist in Iraq." *New York Times* (December 12, 2003).

Grissom, Adam, "The Future of Military Innovation Studies." *Journal of Strategic Studies*, 29, no. 5 (October 2006): 905–34.

Groen, Michael S. "Blue Diamond Intelligence, Division Level Intelligence Operations during OIF." *Marine Corps Gazette* (February 2004): 22–25.

————. "The Tactical Fusion Center." *Marine Corps Gazette* 89, no. 4 (April 2005): 22–25.

Hoffman, Francis G. "Adapt, Innovate, and Adapt Some More." U.S. Naval Institute *Proceedings* (March 2014).

————. "The Marine Mask of War." *Marine Corps Gazette* (December 2011).

Huber, George. "Organizational Learning, The Contributing Processes and the Literatures" 2, no. 1 *Organizational Science* (1991): 88–115.

Iscol, Zachary J. "CAP India." *Marine Corps Gazette* (January 2006): 54–60.

Jenkins, Brian M. "The Unchangeable War." Santa Monica: RAND, November, 1970.

Jones, Frank L. "Blowtorch: Robert Komer and the Making of Vietnam Pacification Policy." *Parameters* (Autumn 2005): 103–18.

Kaplan, Robert D. "Five Days in Fallujah." *The Atlantic Monthly* (July–August 2004).

Kier, Elizabeth. "Culture and Military Doctrine—France between the Wars." *International Security* 19, no. 4 (Spring 1995): 65–93.

Kinnard, Harry W. "A Victory in the Ia Drang: The Triumph of a Concept." *Army* 17 (September 1967): 71–91.

Kollars, Nina A. "Military Innovation's Dialectic: Gun Trucks and Rapid Acquisition." *Security Studies*, 23, no. 4 (2014): 787–813.

Krepinevich, Andrew J. "Cavalry to Computer: The Pattern of Military Revolutions." *The National Interest* (Fall 1994): 30–42.

Lacey, Jim, and Kevin Woods. "Adapt or Die." U.S. Naval Institute *Proceedings* 133, no. 8, (August 2007): 16–21.

Levinthal, Daniel A., and James G. March. "A Model of Adaptive Organizational Search." *Journal of Economic Behavior and Organizations* 2 (1981): 307–33.

Levinthal and March. "The Myopia of Learning." *Strategic Management Journal* 14 (Winter 1993): 95–112.

Levitt, Barbara, and James G. March. "Organizational Learning" *Annual Review of Sociology*, 14 (1988): 319–40.

Mahnken, Thomas. "Asymmetric Warfare at Sea, The Naval Battles of Guadalcanal, 1942–1943." *Naval War College Review* 64, no. 1 (Winter 2011): 95–121.

Mains, Steven, and Gil Ariely. "Learning While Fighting: Operational Knowledge Management that Makes a Difference." *PRISM* 2, no. 3 (June 2011): 165–76.

Malkasian, Carter. "Signaling Resolve, Democratization, and the First Battle of Fallujah," *Journal of Strategic Studies* 29, no. 3 (August 2006): 423–52.

March, James G. "Continuity and Change in Theories of Organizational Action." *Administrative Science Quarterly* 41, no. 2 (1996): 278–87.

Marcus, Raphael D. "Military Innovation and Tactical Adaptation in the Israel-Hizbollah Conflict." *Journal of Strategic Studies* 38, no. 4 (2014): 500–528.

Matthews, Matt. *Operation Al-Fajr: A Study in Army and Marine Corps Joint Operations.* Fort Leavenworth: Combat Studies Institute, 2006.

McNerney, Michael. "Military Innovation during War: Paradox or Paradigm." *Defense and Security Analysis* 21, no. 2 (2005): 201–12.

Meloy, Guy S. "Operation Attleboro, The Wolfhound's Brave Stand." *Vietnam* 10 (October 1997): 38–44.

Mullen, William F. III, "Turning Fallujah." *Joint Force Quarterly* 57 (2nd Quarter 2010): 50–55.

Mundy, Carl E. III, "Spare the Rod, Save the Nation." *New York Times*, December 30, 2003, 22.

Nevis, Edwin C., Anthony J. DiBella, and Janet M. Gould. "Understanding Organizations as Learning Systems." *Sloan Management Review* 36, no. 2 (January 1995): 61–74.

Nulsen, Charles K. "Operation Attleboro: The 196th's Light Infantry Brigade Baptism by Fire in the Vietnam War." *Historynet.com*, June 12, 2006.

O'Toole, Paddy, and Steven Talbot. "Fighting for Knowledge: Developing Learning Systems in the Australian Army." *Armed Forces and Society* 37, no. 1 (2011): 42–67.

Paschall, Rod. "Operation Attleboro—From Calamity to Crushing Victory." *HistoryNet. com*, July 20, 2011.

Popper, Micha, and Raanan Lipshitz. "Organizational Learning: Mechanisms, Culture, and Feasibility." *Management Learning* 31, no. 2 (June 2000): 181–96.

Prados, John. "Dak To: One Hell of a Fight." *Veteran Online* (January–February 2012).

Raisch, S., J. Birkinshaw, G. Probst, and M. Tushman. "Organizational Ambidexterity: Balancing Exploitation and Exploration for Sustained Performance." *Organization Science* 20, no. 4 (2009): 685–95.

Ryan, Mick. "The U.S. Submarine Campaign in the Pacific, 1941–45." *Australian Defence Journal*, no. 90 (March–April 2013): 62–75.

Sapolsky, Harvey M. "Interservice Competition: The Solution, Not the Problem." *Joint Force Quarterly*. no. 15 (Spring 1997): 50–53.

Sattler, John F., and Daniel H. Wilson. "Operation Al Fajr: The Battle of Fallujah—Part II." *Marine Corps Gazette* (July 2005): 12–24.

Senge, Peter. "The Leader's New Work: Building Learning Organizations." *Sloan Management Review* (Fall 1990): 7–23.

Smith, Neil, and Sean MacFarland. "Anbar Awakens: The Tipping Point." *Military Review* 88, no. 2 (March–April 2008): 41–52.

Stanton, Shelby. "Lessons Learned or Lost: Air Cavalry and Airmobility." *Military Review* 69, no. 2 (January 1989): 75–76.

Talbott, J. E. "Weapons Development, War Planning and Policy: The U.S. Navy and the Submarine, 1917–1941." *Naval War College Review* 37, no. 3 (May–June 1984): 53–71.

Terriff, Terry. "Innovate or Die: Organizational Culture and the Origins of Maneuver Warfare in the U.S. Marine Corps." *Journal of Strategic Studies* 29, no. 3 (June 2006): 475–503.

———. "Warriors and Innovators: Military Change and Organizational Culture in the US Marine Corps." *Defense Studies* 6, no. 2 (2006): 215–47.

Ucko, David. "Innovation or Inertia: The U.S. Military and the Learning of Counterinsurgency." *Orbis* 52, no. 2 (Spring 2008): 290–310.

Vera, Dysya, and Mary Crossan. "Strategic Leadership and Organizational Learning." *Academy of Management Review* 29, no. 2 (2004): 222–40.

Visser, Max. "Learning Under Conditions of Hierarchy and Discipline: The Case of the German Army, 1939–1940." *Learn Inquiry* 2, no. 2 (2008): 127–37.

Vlahos, Michael. "The Naval War College and the Origins of War-Planning against Japan." *Naval War College Review* (July–August 1980): 23–39.

———. "Wargaming, an Enforcer of Strategic Realism: 1919–1942." *Naval War College Review* (March–April 1986): 7–22.

U.S. Government Reports and Studies

Albright, John, John A. Cash, and Allan W. Sandstrum. *Seven Firefights in Vietnam.* Washington: Government Printing Office, 1970.

Birtle, Andrew J. *U.S. Army Counterinsurgency and Contingency Operations Doctrine, 1942–1976.* Washington: Center of Military History, 2006.

Cooling, Benjamin. *Case Studies in the Achievement of Air Superiority.* Washington: Air Force History Program, 1994.

Cooling, Benjamin F. ed. *Case Studies in the Development of Close Air Support.* Washington: Office of Air Force History, 1990.

Cosmas, Graham A. *MACV: The Joint Command in the Years of Escalation, 1962–1967.* Washington: U.S. Army Center of Military History, 2006.

Doubler, Michael D. *Busting the Bocage: American Combined Arms Operations in France, 6 June–31 July 1944.* Fort Leavenworth: U.S. Army Command and General Staff College, 1988.

Estes, Kenneth W. *Into the Fray: U.S. Marines in the Global War on Terror.* Quantico: U.S. Marine Corps History Division, 2011.

————. *U.S. Marine Corps Operations in Iraq, 2003–2006.* Quantico: U.S. Marine Corps History Division, 2009.

Ewell, Julian J., and Ira A. Hunt, Jr. *Sharpening the Combat Edge: The Use of Analysis to Reinforce Military Judgment.* Washington: Department of the Army, 1974.

Fulton, William B. *Riverine Operations 1966–1969.* Washington: Department of the Army, 1985.

Futrell, Robert F. *Ideas, Concepts, Doctrine: Basic Thinking in the United States Air Force, 1907–1960.* Vol. 1, Maxwell Air Force Base: Air University Press, 1989.

———— *The United States Air Force in Korea 1950–1953.* Washington: Office of Air Force History, 1983, 3–5.

Grissom, Adam, Caitlin Lee, and Karl P. Mueller. *Innovation in the United States Air Force Evidence from Six Cases.* Santa Monica: RAND, 2014.

Lorenz, G. O., James H. Willbanks, David H. Petraeus, F. A. Stuart, B. L. Crittenden, D. P. George. *Operation Junction City: Vietnam 1967.* Fort Leavenworth: U.S. Army Command and General Staff College, 1983.

Lupfer, Timothy T. *The Dynamics of Doctrine: The Change in German Tactical Doctrine during the First World War.* Fort Leavenworth: Combat Studies Institute, July 1981.

McWilliams, Timothy S., with Nicholas Schlosser. *U.S. Marines in Battle: Fallujah, November-December 2004.* Quantico: Marine Corps History Division, 2014.

Nalty, Bernard C. *Winged Shield, Winged Sword, A History of the U.S. Air Force, 1950–1997.* Vol. II, Washington: Air Force History and Museums Program, 1997.

Neilsen, Suzanne C. *An Army Transformed: The U.S. Army's Post-Vietnam Recovery and the Dynamics of Change in Military Organizations.* Letort Papers. Carlisle: Army War College, September 2010.

Neufeld, Jacob, and G. M. Watson, Jr., eds., *Coalition Air Warfare in the Korean War, 1950–1953.* Washington: Air Force History and Museums, 2005.

Scholsser, Nicholas J. *Al-Qaim: U.S. Marines in Battle, September 2005–March 2006.* Washington: Marine Corps History Division, 2013.

Shrader, Charles R. *History of Operations Research in the United States Army, 1961–1973.* Vol. 2. Washington: Center of Military History, 2008.

Spector, Ronald H. *Advice and Support: The Early Years, 1941–1960, U.S. Army in Vietnam.* Washington: Center for Military History, 1983.

Starry, Donn A. *Armored Combat in Vietnam.* New York: Arno, 1980.

U.S. Army. Vietnam, *Battlefield Reports: A Summary of Lessons Learned.* Vol. 3, May 1967.

U.S. Army, Military History Branch. *Command History United States Military Assistance Command, Vietnam 1966.* Alexandria: Department of the Army, 1966.

U.S. Army Combat Development Command, *The Origins, Deliberations and Recommendations of the U.S. Army Tactical Mobility Requirements Board.* Fort Leavenworth, 1969.

U.S. Army Concept Team. *AirMobile Company in Counterinsurgency Operations,* Saigon, Vietnam, 25 July 1964.

U.S. Department of Defense. *Defense Science Board Task Force on The Role and Status of DoD Red Teaming.* Washington, 2003.

U.S. Joint Chiefs of Staff (J7). *Decade of War: Enduring Lessons from the Past Decade of Operations.* Suffolk: Joint and Coalition Operational Analysis, June 15, 2012.

U.S. Marine Corps. *Summary Report of USMC Participation in Operation Iraqi Freedom.* Quantico: Combat Assessment Team, January 2004.

U.S. MACV, Headquarters, Lessons Learned no. 55; "The Battle of Annihilation," 15 March 1966.

U.S. MACV Campaign Plan for 1968, Saigon, Vietnam, 11 Nov 1967.

U.S. MACV, *Command History, 1967.* Vol. I, 16 September 1968.

Westmoreland, William, C. *Report on the War in Vietnam.* Saigon, Vietnam: Military Assistance Command, Vietnam, 1968.

Wong, Leonard. *Developing Adaptive Leaders: The Crucible Experience of Operation Iraqi Freedom.* Carlisle: Army Strategic Studies Institute, 2004.

———. *Stifled Innovation?: Developing Tomorrow's Leaders Today.* Carlisle: Army Strategic Studies Institute, April 2002.

Y'Blood, William T. *Down in the Weeds: Close Air Support in Korea.* Washington: Air Force History and Museums Program, 2002.

———. *MiG Alley: The Fight for Air Superiority.* Washington: Air Force History and Museums Program, 2000.

Unpublished Material

Allen, John. "Anbar Dawn . . . the Defeat of Al Qaeda in the West," speaker's notes, lecture delivered at the Fletcher School of Law and Diplomacy, March 11, 2009.

Boyd, John. "Patterns of Conflict," slides, undated (1980s).

Index

adaptation: ability for compared to innovation ability, 4; bottom-up and organic generation of, 12, 18, 34, 43, 272–73, 280–81nn53–54; capacity and mechanisms for, 31–34; complexity of wartime change, 10–12, 17, 102–3, 246–48; concept and definition of, 6–8, 29; continuum of military change, 6–8; external drivers that shape or limit, 12, 18, 19–22, 32, 34, 267–69, 280n52, 322n45; failure to adapt, 34, 246; high adaption capacity, 33–34; importance of and recognition of need for, 2–4, 55, 246–48, 271–73; institutional/internal factor that shape or limit, 4, 12, 13–15, 18–19, 31–34, 43–54, 248, 252–53, 267, 269, 272–73; lessons learned on need for, 2–3; military failures and adaptive failures, 8–9; peacetime innovation and adaptation ability during war, 4; research and studies on, 5–6, 8–12; speed and rates of, 4, 34, 280–81n54; top-down generation of, 12, 18, 19–21, 34, 280n52; understanding through Organizational Learning Theory, 16, 19, 26–31, 54–55

adaptive learning, 30, 262, 272–73

adjustments: concept and definition of, 282n76; continuum of military change, 6–8; failure to adjust, 246; importance of,

2; switching between existing competencies, 7–8; willingness to make rapid, 3–4

Adoption Capacity Theory, 32

Afghanistan: adaptation to warfare in, 3, 12; technologies for war in, 10, 277n32

after-action reports: Army use of, 53, 160, 169–70, 189, 191–92, 193, 250–51, 257; as learning and dissemination mechanism, 49, 51; Marine Corps use of, 211, 258; Navy use of, 96, 97

Air Corps Tactical School (ACTS), 105, 143–44

Air Force, U.S.: adaptations to character of conflict in Korea, 137–41, 151–52, 246–47, 250, 264; air ground operations doctrine of, 114–18, 120; air operations in Europe of, 294n17; culture of, 47–49, 108, 114–18, 120, 141–48, 152, 235, 255–56, 261, 295n26, 300n138, 300n147; dissemination mechanisms of, 150–51, 261, 301n169; doctrine for air operations and bombing, 105–9, 141, 145; European operations during WWII, 105–7, 143; independence of and establishment as separate service, 15, 104, 109, 147–48, 151–52; interservice competition and policy decisions of, 25–26; leadership of, 141–45, 152, 253, 261; learning mechanisms of, 148–50, 257, 261; operational

337

Operations and Rural Development Support (CORDS) program, 174–76, 194, 264, 265, 266, 268; close air support during, 148; Coronado operation, 167, 182; Crimp operation, 161–62, 167; dissemination mechanisms during, 191–95, 261; El Paso II operation, 163–65, 167; external influences on adaptations during, 268; firepower capabilities and mindset for, 15, 264; Francis Marion operation, 167, 179; ground forces request for, 155–56; ground maneuver and supporting fire adaptation during, 175; Ia Drang campaign, 159–60; innovation and adaptation during, 10–11; intelligence system for, 189; Junction City operation, 167, 172–73; leadership during, 160, 184–87, 189, 194–95, 196, 243, 250–51, 253, 261, 308n151, 308n156; learning mechanisms for, 189–91, 194–95, 250–51, 257–58, 261; MacArthur operation, 169, 179–81, 307n128; managers during, 188–89; Marauder operation, 161, 167; Masher/White Wing operation, 162–63, 167; Palm Beach operation, 182; Paul Revere IV operation, 178; Phase I to halt VC offensive, 156, 159–68; Phase II offensive to destroy VC, 156, 167, 168–76; Phase III to restore country to South Vietnamese, 157, 176–83; phased plan for, 154, 156–57; riverine force and operations, 181–82, 193, 196, 264, 307n137; Sam Houston operation, 167, 173–74; search-and-destroy strategy during, 160–65, 175, 176–81, 186–87, 189; Shenandoah II operation, 167, 176–78; sources of military change during, 265–66; systems analysis capabilities during, 189–91, 250–51, 257–58, 309n194; Tet Offensive, 154, 182–83

Wahoo, 73–75, 77–79, 81, 84, 89, 289n87, 289n100, 289n103, 290n116

war: airpower decisive role in, 105–7, 109, 137, 141–48; analysis of military failures, 8–9; as audits of military institutions, 246; complexity of wartime change, 10–12, 17, 102–3; going to war with army you have, 1–2; importance of wartime change, 2–5, 271–73; offensive strikes on trade/commerce, 60, 62; preparation for and response to conflict conditions, 1–5, 9–10, 105, 271–73

weapons: adaptation in response to events, 16; confidence in existing, 1, 16; Razon/Tarzon bombs, 133, 139, 264. See also torpedoes

Westmoreland, William C.: adaptations to character of conflict by, 165–66, 168, 194, 265–66; CORDS program, 174–76, 194; ground forces request from, 155–56, 183; leadership of, 160, 184–85, 187, 189, 196, 243, 253, 308n151, 308n156; opinion about Tet of, 183; Phase I to halt VC offensive, 156, 159, 160, 161, 162; Phase II offensive to destroy VC, 156; Phase III to restore country to South Vietnamese, 157; progress in the war speech by, 180–81, 182; systems analysis use by, 190–91; three-phase plan of, 154, 156–57

Weyland, O. P.: on dissemination of WWII lessons, 113; experience of, 151; FEAF command by, 113; gunsight adaptations role of, 124; leadership of, 143, 144–45; pressure campaign opinion of, 137; Strangle operation opinion of, 131; warfighting tactics for Korea, 127–28, 130, 133

Winning the Next War (Rosen), 9, 22–25

wolfpack/coordinated attack group (CAG) tactics, 84–91, 101–2, 250, 264, 290n137, 290n139

World War II (WWII): air operations in Europe during, 105–7, 143, 294n17; air operations in Pacific theater during, 107–9, 141–43; close air support (CAS) missions during, 113; defensive war of attrition against Japan, 66; German adaptation during, 4, 10, 277n33; leadership role in innovation and adaptation during, 45–46; Navy war planning and War Plan Orange, 57–60, 61, 62–63, 94, 102, 285n5; Pearl Harbor attack, 57; Rainbow war plans for, 59, 286nn10–12; strategic bombing campaigns during, 15; U-boat wolfpack tactics, 84–87, 88, 290n139, 291n145; unrestricted air and submarine warfare order, 66; U.S. innovation and adaptation during, 4, 10. *See also* submarine offensive, Pacific Campaign

About the Author

Dr. Frank Hoffman holds an appointment as a Distinguished Research Fellow at the National Defense University in Washington, DC. He is a retired U.S. Marine Corps infantry officer with service in the 2nd and 3rd Marine Divisions. His forty-two years in the U.S. defense establishment include senior political appointments at the Pentagon, ten years at Headquarters Marine Corps, and service on the Defense Science Board and two Congressional commissions. In addition to his research portfolio in strategy and military innovation, he teaches at the National War College. He is a frequent contributor to various service journals, including *Proceedings* and *Marine Corps Gazette*. Dr. Hoffman graduated from the Wharton Business School at the University of Pennsylvania and holds graduate degrees from George Mason University and the Naval War College. He earned his PhD in war studies from King's College, London.

The Naval Institute Press is the book-publishing arm of the U.S. Naval Institute, a private, nonprofit, membership society for sea service professionals and others who share an interest in naval and maritime affairs. Established in 1873 at the U.S. Naval Academy in Annapolis, Maryland, where its offices remain today, the Naval Institute has members worldwide.

Members of the Naval Institute support the education programs of the society and receive the influential monthly magazine *Proceedings* or the colorful bimonthly magazine *Naval History* and discounts on fine nautical prints and on ship and aircraft photos. They also have access to the transcripts of the Institute's Oral History Program and get discounted admission to any of the Institute-sponsored seminars offered around the country.

The Naval Institute's book-publishing program, begun in 1898 with basic guides to naval practices, has broadened its scope to include books of more general interest. Now the Naval Institute Press publishes about seventy titles each year, ranging from how-to books on boating and navigation to battle histories, biographies, ship and aircraft guides, and novels. Institute members receive significant discounts on the Press' more than eight hundred books in print.

Full-time students are eligible for special half-price membership rates. Life memberships are also available.

For a free catalog describing Naval Institute Press books currently available, and for further information about joining the U.S. Naval Institute, please write to:

Member Services
U.S. Naval Institute
291 Wood Road
Annapolis, MD 21402-5034
Telephone: (800) 233-8764
Fax: (410) 571-1703
Web address: www.usni.org